ISBN 978-1-333-88647-9
PIBN 10726908

1 MONTH OF
FREE
READING

at

www.ForgottenBooks.com

By purchasing this book you are eligible for one month membership to ForgottenBooks.com, giving you unlimited access to our entire collection of over 700,000 titles via our web site and mobile apps.

To claim your free month visit:

www.forgottenbooks.com/free726908

Otterbein Hymnal

FOR USE IN

PUBLIC AND SOCIAL WORSHIP

PREPARED BY

EDMUND S. LORENZ

DAYTON, OHIO
UNITED BRETHREN PUBLISHING HOUSE
1909

THE General Conference of the Church of the United Brethren in Christ, at its session in May, 1889, ordered,—

"That a small hymnal, adapted to general church purposes, be published soon."

ADVISORY COMMITTEE.

MUSICAL.

SAMUEL E. KUMLER,   MRS. A. B. SHAUCK,
CALVIN H. LYON,   JUDGE JOHN A. SHAUCK.

LITERARY.

PROF. J. P. LANDIS, D. D., PH. D

INTRODUCTION.

THE General Conference of 1889 ordered the publication of a hymnal that should be fully adapted to the needs of our church. In compliance with these instructions, the publishing agent, Rev. W. J. Shuey, arranged for its issue. Rev. E. S. Lorenz, well and favorably known throughout the Church, was asked to edit it, and with the assistance of a thoroughly competent committee, has accomplished his task. I have carefully examined it in every part, and cannot see where any improvement can be made. It is pre-eminently a United Brethren Hymn-Book, providing as it does for every phase of our characteristic church life. It combines the solidity and stateliness of the standard hymns of the ages, with the life and sprightliness of the modern gospel songs. The most recent songs are here for the young people, while the older members of the Church will hail with delight the reappearance of old songs dear to the hearts of many of us, because they are precious and good, and because our mothers sang them. Meeting every need of the public service, revival and social meetings, the Sunday-school, and the family, I can most cheerfully recommend this collection of hymns to our people, and trust that it will speedily be permitted to bring its help and blessing into every United Brethren church in our broad land, and beyond the seas, and that it will prove one of the many tender ties that unite our widely scattered members.   J. WEAVER,

Senior Bishop.

DAYTON, OHIO, April 9, 1890

PREFACE.

To be useful, a hymnal must express the peculiar type of Christianity characterizing the denomination it is to serve. The Church of the United Brethren in Christ emphasizes the necessity of Christian experience—experimental religion, the fathers would have phrased it—and recognizes revival effort as the characteristic phase of its church activity; hence, its hymnal must furnish ample expression for its full and varied Christian experience and large facilities for revival work. In attempting to do this, the other phases of church life, which it has in common with other denominations, have not been forgotten or ignored, and it is hoped this collection of hymns and songs will be found as full and symmetrical as the church life it seeks to express.

In order to meet the needs of the many stages of literary and musical culture, hymns and tunes of the highest artistic merit stand side by side with songs whose practical value and spiritual purpose must atone for lack of literary and musical grace.

Doubtless many favorites will be missed from these pages, but the body of popular sacred songs is so large and rich that it was impossible to include everything desirable in so small a volume.

Typographical beauty has often been sacrificed to practical needs. The words are inserted in the music wherever possible. Alternative tunes may be found on the same or opposite pages. A line drawn through a page indicates that the music for the hymn or hymns below it is found on the opposite page.

To the many brethren, whose number makes personal mention impossible, who kindly responded to a call for suggestions and advice, the thanks of the editor are due. While all could not be accepted, they have been very helpful, and have had large influence in giving character to the book. The valuable assistance furnished by the Advisory Committee deserves most kindly and hearty recognition. The owners of the many valuable copyright songs, in connection with which their names severally appear, will accept thanks for the kindness which so greatly enriches these pages.

That this volume will prove an effective instrument in the hands of the workers of the Church of the United Brethren in Christ for the accomplishment of great and lasting good, and bring to many hearts the same comfort and joy which its preparation brought to that of the editor, is his earnest hope and prayer.   E. S. L.

Dayton, Ohio, April 15, 1890.

3

(Otterbein Hymnal.)

TABLE OF CONTENTS.

THE OTTERBEIN HYMNAL.

1 GLORIA PATRI.

With spirit.

W. J. BALTZELL.

Glo-ry be to the Fa-ther, and to the Son, and to the Ho-ly

SOLO.

Ghost, and to the Ho-ly Ghost, As it was in the be-gin-ning, is

FULL CHORUS. *Ritard.*

now, and ev - er shall be, world without end, world without end. Amen.

2 GLORIA PATRI.

GREGORIAN.

Glory be to the Father, and to the Son, and to the Ho - ly Ghost,
As it was in the beginning,
is now, and.......... ev - er shall be, world with-out end. A - MEN.

OLD HUNDRED. L. M.   GUILLUAME FRANC, 1550.

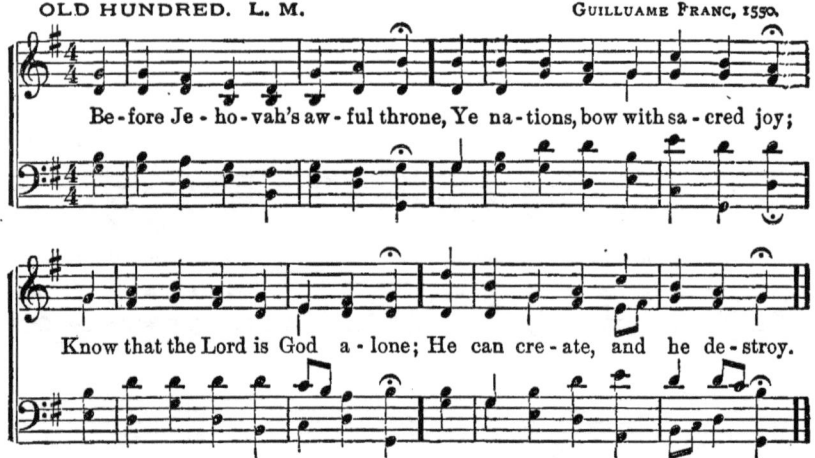

Be-fore Je-ho-vah's aw-ful throne, Ye na-tions, bow with sa-cred joy;

Know that the Lord is God a-lone; He can cre-ate, and he de-stroy.

3   *Psalm 100.*   (1)

BEFORE Jehovah's awful throne,
  Ye nations, bow with sacred joy;
Know that the Lord is God alone;
  He can create, and he destroy.

2 His sovereign power, without our aid,
    Made us of clay, and formed us men;
  And when like wandering sheep we strayed,
    He brought us to his fold again.

3 We are his people, we his care—
    Our souls, and all our mortal frame;
  What lasting honors shall we rear,
    Almighty Maker, to thy name?

4 We'll crowd thy gates with thankful songs,
    High as the heavens our voices raise;
  And earth, with her ten thousand tongues,
    Shall fill thy courts with sounding praise.

5 Wide as the world is thy command;
    Vast as eternity thy love;
  Firm as a rock thy truth shall stand,
    When rolling years shall cease to move.
                              ISAAC WATTS.

4   *All Men Invited to Praise God.*   (3)

FROM all that dwell below the skies,
  Let the Creator's praise arise;
Let the Redeemer's name be sung,
  Through every land, by every tongue.

2 Eternal are thy mercies, Lord;
  Eternal truth attends thy word;
Thy praise shall sound from shore to shore,
  Till suns shall rise and set no more.

3 Your lofty themes, ye mortals, bring;
  In songs of praise divinely sing;
The great salvation loud proclaim,
  And shout for joy the Savior's name.

4 In every land begin the song;
  To every land the strains belong;
In cheerful sounds all voices raise,
  And fill the world with loudest praise.
                              ISAAC WATTS, 1719.

5   *Psalm 103.*   (8)

AWAKE, my soul, awake my tongue,
  My God demands the grateful song;
Let all my inmost powers record
  The wondrous mercy of the Lord.

2 Divinely free his mercy flows,
  Forgives my sins, allays my woes,
And bids approaching death remove,
  And crowns me with indulgent love.

3 His mercy, with unchanging rays,
  Forever shines, while time decays;
And children's children shall record
  The truth and goodness of the Lord.

4 While all his works his praise proclaim,
  And men and angels bless his name,
Oh, let my heart, my life, my tongue
  Attend, and join the blissful song!
                              ANNE STEELE, 1760.

6   *Doxology.*

PRAISE God, from whom all blessings flow;
Praise him, all creatures here below;
Praise him above, ye heavenly host;
Praise Father, Son and Holy Ghost.
                              THOS. KEN.

LORD OF ALL BEING. L. M.   E. S. LORENZ.

Lord of all be-ing! throned a-far, Thy glory flames from sun and star; Center and soul of

ev - 'ry sphere, Yet to each loving heart how near! Yet to each loving heart how near!

7   *Omnipresence.*   (17)

Lord of all being! throned afar,
Thy glory flames from sun and star;
Center and soul of ev'ry sphere,
Yet to each loving heart how near!

2 Sun of our life! thy quick'ning ray
Sheds on our path the glow of day;
Star of our hope! thy softened light
Cheers the long watches of the night.

3 Our midnight is thy smile withdrawn;
Our noontide is thy gracious dawn;
Our rainbow arch thy mercy's sign;
All, save the clouds of sin, are thine.

4 Grant us thy truth to make us free,
And kindling hearts that burn for thee,
Till all thy living altars claim
One holy light, one heavenly flame.
         OLIVER WENDELL HOLMES, 1848.

8   *The Majesty of God.*   (7)

Come, oh, my soul, in sacred lays,
Attempt thy great Creator's praise;
But oh! what tongue can speak his fame?
What mortal verse can reach the theme?

2 Enthroned amidst the radiant spheres,
He glory like a garment wears;
To form a robe of light divine,
Ten thousand suns around him shine.

3 In all our Maker's grand designs,
Omnipotence with wisdom shines;
His works, through all this wondrous frame,
Bear the great impress of his name.

4 Raised on Devotion's lofty wing,
Do thou, my soul! his glories sing;
And let his praise employ thy tongue,
Till listening worlds applaud the song.
         THOMAS BLACKLOCK, 1754.

DUKE STREET. L. M.   J. HATTON, 1790.

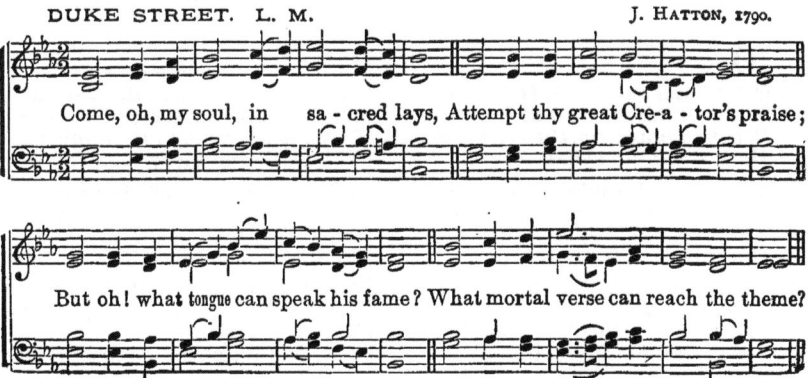

Come, oh, my soul, in   sa - cred lays, Attempt thy great Cre-a - tor's praise;

But oh! what tongue can speak his fame? What mortal verse can reach the theme?

ROCKINGHAM. L. M.   LOWELL MASON. 1832.

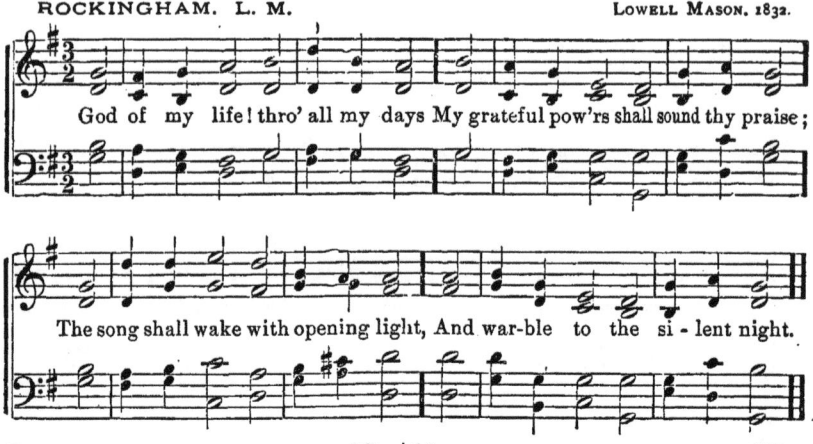

God of my life! thro' all my days My grateful pow'rs shall sound thy praise;

The song shall wake with opening light, And war-ble to the si - lent night.

9   *Life-long Praise.*   (12)

GOD of my life! through all my days
My grateful powers shall sound thy praise;
The song shall wake with opening light,
And warble to the silent night.

2 When anxious cares would break my rest,
And griefs would tear my throbbing breast,
Thy tuneful praises, raised on high,
Shall check the murmur and the sigh.

3 When death o'er nature shall prevail,
And all its powers of language fail,
Joy thro' my swimming eyes shall break,
And mean the thanks I cannot speak.

4 Soon shall I learn th' exalted strains,
Which echo o'er the heavenly plains,
And emulate, with joy unknown,
The glowing seraphs round thy throne.
           PHILIP DODDRIDGE, 1740.

10   *Psalm 106.*   (15)

OH, render thanks to God above,
The fountain of eternal love;
Whose mercy firm, through ages past,
Hath stood, and shall forever last.

2 Who can his mighty deeds express,
Not only vast—but numberless?
What mortal eloquence can raise
His tribute of immortal praise?

3 Extend to me that favor, Lord,
Thou to thy chosen dost afford;
When thou return'st to set them free,
Let thy salvation visit me.
           TATE-BRADY.

11   *God Revealed in Christ.*   (600)

Now to the Lord, a noble song!
Awake, my soul! awake, my tongue,
Hosanna to th' eternal name,
And all his boundless love proclaim.

2 See where it shines in Jesus' face,—
The brightest image of his grace!
God, in the person of his Son,
Has all his mightiest works outdone.

3 Grace!—'t is a sweet, a charming theme;
My thoughts rejoice at Jesus' name:
Ye angels! dwell upon the sound;
Ye heavens! reflect it to the ground.

4 Oh! may I live to reach the place,
Where he unveils his lovely face,
Where all his beauties you behold,
And sing his name to harps of gold.
           ISAAC WATTS, 1707.

12   *Unceasing Praise*   (13)

MY God! my King! thy various praise
Shall fill the remnant of my days;
Thy grace employ my humble tongue,
Till death and glory raise the song.

2 The wings of every hour shall bear
Some thankful tribute to thine ear;
And every setting sun shall see
New works of duty, done for thee.

3 But who can speak thy wondrous deeds?
Thy greatness all our thoughts exceeds;
Vast and unsearchable thy ways—
Vast and immortal be thy praise.
           ISAAC WATTS, 1719.

OTTERBEIN. L. M.   W. A. OGDEN, 1874.

Oh! come, loud an - thems let us sing, Loud thanks to our Almighty King!

For we our voi-ces high should raise, When our salva - tion's Rock we praise.

13   *Psalm* 95.   (4)

OH, come, loud anthems let us sing,
Loud thanks to our Almighty King!
For we our voices high should raise,
When our salvation's Rock we praise.

2 Into his presence let us haste,
To thank him for his favors past;
To him address, in joyful songs,
The praise that to his name belongs.

3 Oh, let us to his courts repair,
And bow with adoration there;
Down on our knees, devoutly, all
Before the Lord, our Maker, fall.
             NAHUM TATE, 1696.

14   *Joining in Praise.*   (75)

SWEET is the work, my God! my King!
To praise thy name, give thanks and sing;
To show thy love by morning light,
And talk of all thy truth at night.

2 Sweet is the day of sacred rest;
No mortal care shall seize my breast;
O may my heart in tune be found,
Like David's harp of solemn sound.

3 My heart shall triumph in the Lord,
And bless his works, and bless his word;
Thy works of grace, how bright they shine!
How deep thy counsels! how divine!
             ISAAC WATTS.

PARK STREET. L. M.   FREDERICK M. A. VENUA, 1810.

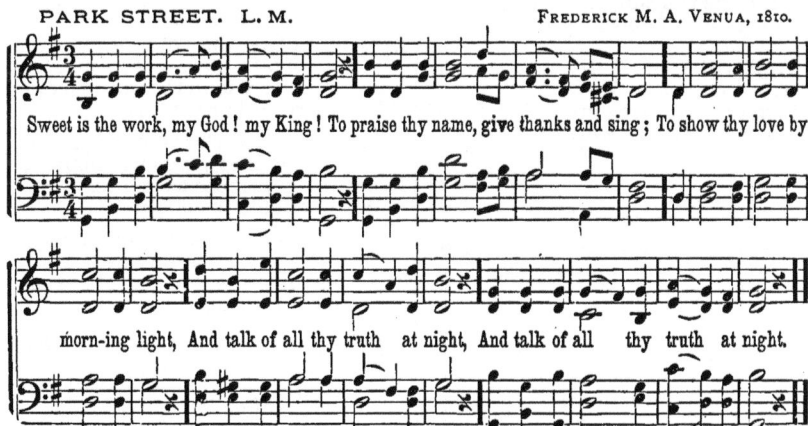

Sweet is the work, my God! my King! To praise thy name, give thanks and sing; To show thy love by

morn-ing light, And talk of all thy truth at night, And talk of all thy truth at night.

HARVEY'S CHANT. C. M.   W. B. BRADBURY.

Animated.

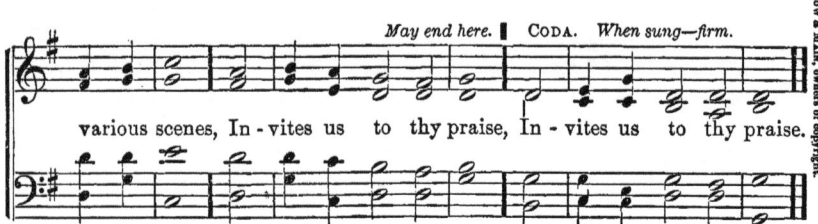

Hail! great Creator, wise and good! To thee our songs we raise; Nature, thro' all her

May end here. CODA. *When sung—firm.*

various scenes, In - vites us to thy praise, In - vites us to thy praise.

15 *The Goodness of God in his Works.* (26)

HAIL! great Creator, wise and good!
  To thee our songs we raise;
Nature, through all her various scenes,
  Invites us to thy praise.

2 At morning, noon, and evening mild,
  Fresh wonders strike our view;
And, while we gaze, our hearts exult
  With transports ever new.

3 Thy glory beams in every star,
  Which gilds the gloom of night;
And decks the smiling face of morn
  With rays of cheerful light.

4 And while, in all thy wondrous ways,
  Thy varied love we see;
Oh, may our hearts, great God, be led
  Through all thy works to thee.
                          ANON., 1795.

16   *Praise at all Times.*   (27)

MY soul shall praise thee, O my God,
  Through all my mortal days,
And in eternity prolong
  Thy vast, thy boundless praise.

2 In every smiling, happy hour,
  Be this my sweet employ;
Thy praise refines my earthly bliss,
  And heightens all my joy.

3 When anxious grief and gloomy care
  Afflict my throbbing breast,
My tongue shall learn to speak thy praise,
  And lull each pain to rest.

4 Nor shall my tongue alone proclaim
  The honors of my God;
My life, with all its active powers,
  Shall spread thy praise abroad.

5 And when these lips shall cease to move,
  When death shall close these eyes,
My soul shall then to nobler heights,
  Of joy and transport rise.
                          O. HEGINBOTHAM.

17   *Psalm 66.*   (24)

LIFT up to God the voice of praise,
  Whose breath our souls inspired;
Loud, and more loud the anthem raise,
  With grateful ardor fired.

2 Lift up to God the voice of praise,
  Whose goodness, passing thought,
Loads every minute as it flies,
  With benefits unsought.

3 Lift up to God the voice of praise,
  From whom salvation flows;
Who sent his Son, our souls to save
  From everlasting woes.

4 Lift up to God the voice of praise,
  For hope's transporting ray,
Which lights, through darkest shades of death,
  To realms of endless day.
                          RALPH WARDLAW, 1803.

18 NICÆA 11s, 12s, & 10s.   JOHN B. DYKES.

1. Ho-ly, ho-ly, ho - ly! Lord God Almight - y! Ear-ly in the
2. Ho-ly, ho-ly, ho - ly! all the saints adore thee, Casting down their
3. Ho-ly, ho-ly, ho - ly! tho' the darkness hide thee, Though the eye of
4. Ho-ly, ho-ly, ho - ly! Lord God Almight - y! All thy works shall

morn-ing our song shall rise to thee; Ho-ly, ho-ly, ho - ly!
gold - en crowns around the glassy sea; Cher-u - bim and sera- phim
sin - ful man thy glo-ry may not see; On - ly thou art ho - ly,
praise thy name, in earth, and sky, and sea; Ho-ly, ho-ly, ho - ly,

mer-ci-ful and might - y! God o - ver all, and blest e - ter - nal-ly.
fall-ing down be-fore thee, Who wast, and art, and evermore shalt be.
there is none be-side thee; Per - fect in pow - er, in love, and purity.
mer-ci-ful and might - y! God o - ver all, and blest e - ter - nal-ly.

REGINALD HEBER—*alt.*

19   *Psalm 95.*   (18)

SING to the Lord Jehovah's name,
   And in his strength rejoice;
When his salvation is our theme,
   Exalted be our voice.

2 With thanks approach his awful sight,
   And psalms of honor sing;
The Lord's a God of boundless might—
   The whole creation's King.

3 Come, and with humble souls adore;
   Come, kneel before his face;
Oh, may the creatures of his power
   Be children of his grace!

4 Now is the time—he bends his ear,
   And waits for your request;
Come, lest he rouse his wrath, and swear,
   "Ye shall not see my rest."

ISAAC WATTS, 1719.

ST. THOMAS. S. M.   WILLIAM TANSUR, 1768.

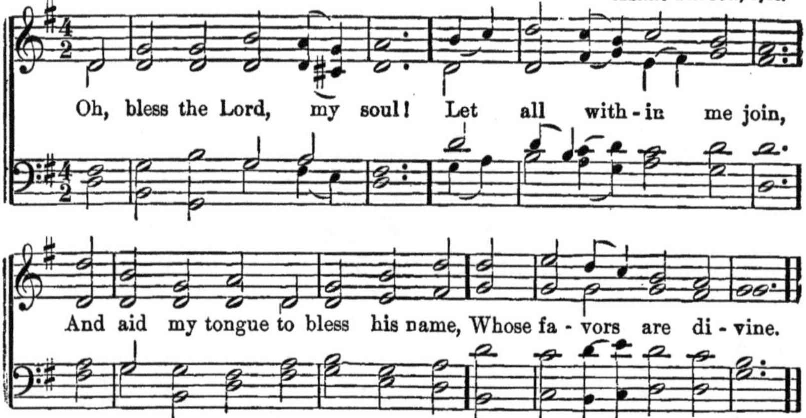

Oh, bless the Lord, my soul! Let all with-in me join,

And aid my tongue to bless his name, Whose fa - vors are di - vine.

20 [FIRST VERSE INSERTED IN MUSIC ABOVE.]
Bless the Lord. (29)

2 Oh, bless the Lord, my soul,
    Nor let his mercies lie
Forgotten in unthankfulness,
    And without praises die.

3 'Tis he forgives thy sins—
    'Tis he relieves thy pain—
'Tis he that heals thy sicknesses,
    And gives thee strength again-

4 He crowns thy life with love,
    When ransomed from the grave;
He who redeemed my soul from hell,
    Hath sovereign power to save.
                        ISAAC WATTS.

21 [FIRST VERSE INSERTED IN MUSIC BELOW.]
Psalm 103. (34)

2 He formed the deeps unknown;
    He gave the seas their bound;
The watery worlds are all his own,
    And all the solid ground.

3 Come, worship at his throne;
    Come, bow before the Lord;
We are his works, and not our own;
    He formed us by his word.

4 To-day attend his voice,
    Nor dare provoke his rod;
Come, like the people of his choice,
    And own your gracious God.
                    ISAAC WATTS, 1719.

SILVER STREET. S. M.   ISAAC SMITH, 1770.

Come, sound his praise a - broad, And hymns of glo - ry sing;

Je - ho - vah is the sov'-reign God, The u - ni - ver - sal King.

GATES OF PRAISE. E. S. LORENZ.

Lift up the Gates of Praise, That we may en-ter in, And o'er salvation's walls proclaim

D. S. *But man a-lone can tell the pow'r*

CHORUS. D. S.

That Christ redeems from sin. The stars may praise the hand, the hand, That decks the sky above, above,

Of Christ's redeeming love.

Copyright, 1880, by E. S. LORENZ.

22 *Gates of Praise.*

1 LIFT up the Gates of Praise,
    That we may enter in,
And o'er salvation's walls proclaim
    That Christ redeems from sin.

2 God's works reveal his might,
    His majesty and grace;
But not the tender Father's love
    That saves a dying race.

3 Then let the voice of praise
    To heavenly courts ascend,
Till with the songs the angels sing
    Our hallelujahs blend.

4 To him that hath redeemed
    Our souls from sin's dark maze;
The Hope and Savior of mankind,
    Be everlasting praise.
                                M. E. SERVOSS.

23 *Exhortation to Praise.* (32)

1 STAND up, and bless the Lord,
    Ye people of his choice !
Stand up, and bless the Lord, your God,
    With heart, and soul, and voice.

2 Though high above all praise,
    Above all blessing high,
Who would not fear his holy name,
    And laud and magnify ?

3 Oh, for the living flame
    From his own altar brought,
To touch our lips, our minds inspire,
    And wing to heaven our thought !

4 God is our strength and song,
    And his salvation ours ;
Then be his love in Christ proclaimed,
    With all our ransomed powers.
                        JAMES MONTGOMERY, 1825.

LEIGHTON. S. M. H. W. GREATOREX, 1849.

Stand up, and bless the Lord, Ye peo - ple of his choice!

Stand up, and bless the Lord, your God, With heart, and soul, and voice.

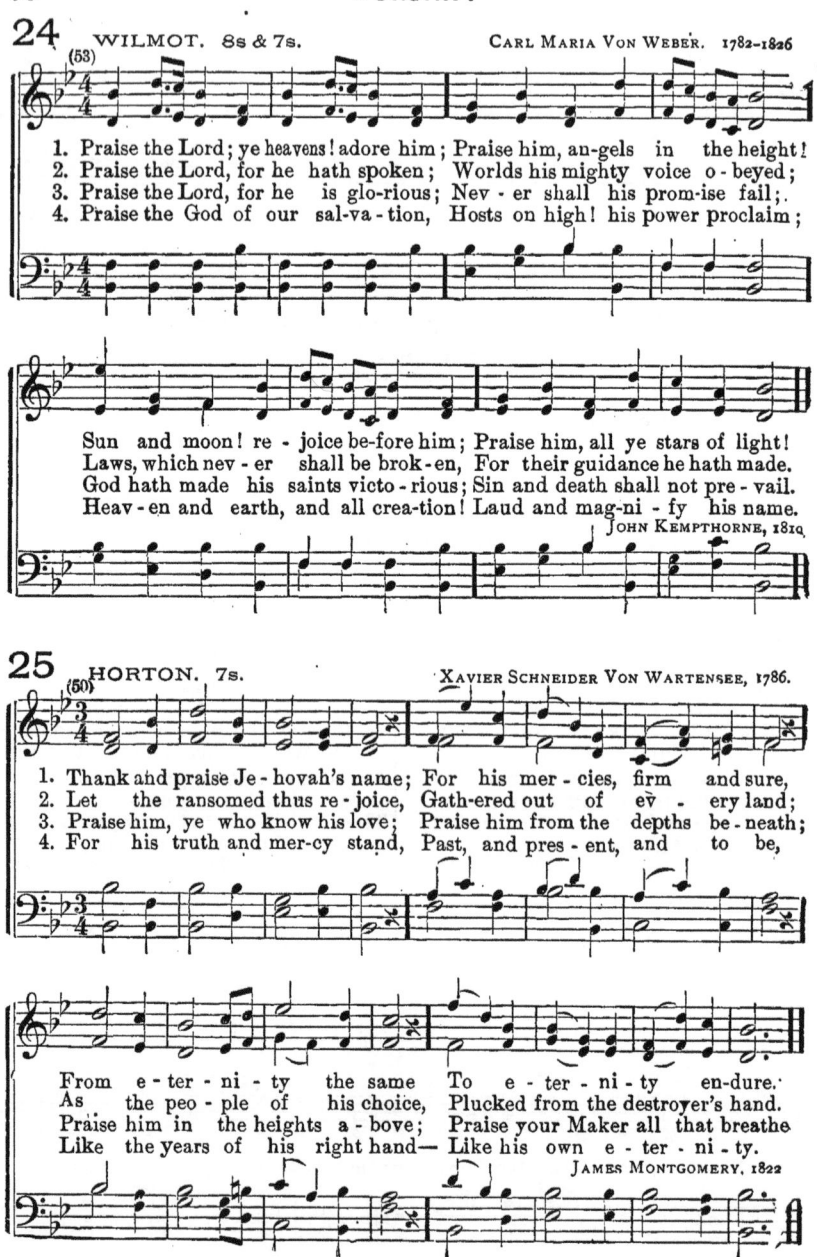

24 (53) WILMOT. 8s & 7s.   CARL MARIA VON WEBER. 1782-1826

1. Praise the Lord; ye heavens! adore him; Praise him, an-gels in the height!
2. Praise the Lord, for he hath spoken; Worlds his mighty voice o-beyed;
3. Praise the Lord, for he is glo-rious; Nev-er shall his prom-ise fail;.
4. Praise the God of our sal-va-tion, Hosts on high! his power proclaim;

Sun and moon! re-joice be-fore him; Praise him, all ye stars of light!
Laws, which nev-er shall be brok-en, For their guidance he hath made.
God hath made his saints victo-rious; Sin and death shall not pre-vail.
Heav-en and earth, and all crea-tion! Laud and mag-ni-fy his name.

JOHN KEMPTHORNE, 1819

25 (50) HORTON. 7s.   XAVIER SCHNEIDER VON WARTENSEE, 1786.

1. Thank and praise Je-hovah's name; For his mer-cies, firm and sure,
2. Let the ransomed thus re-joice, Gath-ered out of ev-ery land;
3. Praise him, ye who know his love; Praise him from the depths be-neath;
4. For his truth and mer-cy stand, Past, and pres-ent, and to be,

From e-ter-ni-ty the same To e-ter-ni-ty en-dure.
As the peo-ple of his choice, Plucked from the destroyer's hand.
Praise him in the heights a-bove; Praise your Maker all that breathe
Like the years of his right hand— Like his own e-ter-ni-ty.

JAMES MONTGOMERY, 1822

26 HALLELUJAH! 8s & 7s.   E. S. LORENZ.

1. Hal - le - lu - jah! song of glad-ness, Song of ev - er - last-ing joy;
2. Hal - le - lu - jah! Church vic-to-rious, Thou mayst lift this joyful strain;
3. Hal - le - lu - jah! let our voic - es Rise to heav'n with full ac - cord;
4. But our earn-est sup - pli - ca-tion, Ho - ly God, we raise to thee;

Hal - le - lu - jah! song the sweet-est That can an - gel hosts em - ploy.
Hal - le - lu - jah! songs of tri-umph Well be - fit the ran-somed train.
Hal - le - lu - jah! ev - 'ry mo-ment Brings us near - er to the Lord.
Bring us to thy bliss-ful pres-ence, Let us all thy glo - ry see.

ANON.

CHORUS.

Praise ye the Lord! sing Hal-le-lu-jah! Praise ye the Lord! sing Hal-le-lu - jah!

Praise ye the Lord! sing Hal - le - lu - jah! Praise ye the Lord!

27 LET US PRAISE HIM TO-DAY. 8s & 7s. W. J. Baltzell.

1. Praise to thee, thou great Cre-a-tor! Praise to thee from ev-'ry tongue;
2. Fa-ther! source of all compassion! Pure, unbounded grace is thine;
3. For ten thou-sand blessings giv-en, For the hope of fut-ure joy,
4. Praise to God, our great Cre-a-tor! Fa-ther, Son, and Ho-ly Ghost;

Join, my soul, with ev-'ry creat-ure, Join the u-ni-ver-sal song.
Hail the Lord of our sal-va-tion! Praise him for his love di-vine.
Sound his praise thro' earth and heaven, Sound Je-ho-vah's praise on high.
Praise him, ev-'ry liv-ing creat-ure, Earth and heav'n's unit-ed host.

J. W. Fawcett, 1767.

CHORUS.

Glo-ry to the Fa-ther and the Son!
Glory to the Fa-ther and the Son! Let us praise him, Let us
Glo-ry to the Spir-it! three in one!
Glory to the Spir-it!

praise him, Let us praise him to-day, And sing his loving kindness on our way.

LYONS. 10s & 11s. F. J. HAYDN.

O wor-ship the King, all-glo-rious a-bove, And grate-ful-ly sing his won-der-ful love; Our Shield and De-fend-er, the An-cient of days, Pa-vil-ioned in splendor and gird-ed with praise.

28 [FIRST VERSE INSERTED IN MUSIC.]
Praise of Divine Love.

2 Thy bountiful care, what tongue can recite?
It breathes in the air, it shines in the light;
It streams from the hills, it descends to the plain,
And sweetly distills in the dew and the rain.

3 Frail children of dust, and feeble as frail,
In thee do we trust, nor find thee to fail;
Thy mercies, how tender! how firm to the end,
Our Maker, Defender, Redeemer, and Friend!

4 Our Father and God, how faithful thy love!
While angels delight to hymn thee above,
The humbler creation, though feeble their lays,
With true adoration shall lisp to thy praise.

SIR ROBERT GRANT, 1839.

29 *Salvation to God.*

YE servants of God, your Master proclaim,
And publish abroad his wonderful name:
The name, all-victorious, of Jesus extol;
His kingdom is glorious, and rules over all.

2 God ruleth on high, almighty to save;
And still he is nigh, his presence we have:
The great congregation his triumph shall sing,
Ascribing salvation to Jesus our King.

3 "Salvation to God, who sits on the throne,"
Let all cry aloud, and honor the Son;
Our Saviour's high praises the angels proclaim,—
Fall down on their faces, and worship the Lamb.

C WESLEY. 1744.

2

30 GERAR. S. M.
(128)

LOWELL MASON.

Moderato.

1. How charming is the place Where my Re-deem-er God Unveils the glories
2. Here, on the mer-cy-seat, With radiant glory crowned, Our joyful eyes be-
3. To him their prayers and cries, Each contrite soul presents; And while he hears their
4. Give me, O Lord, a place Within thy blest abode; Among the children

of his face, Unveils the glories of his face, And sheds his love a-broad!
hold him sit, Our joyful eyes behold him sit, And smile on all a-round.
humble sighs, And while he hears their humble sighs, He grants them all their wants.
of thy grace, Among the children of thy grace, The servants of my God.

S. STENNETT.

31 HENDON. 7s.
(164) *Moderato.*

CÆSAR MALAN, 1830.

1. Lord! we come before thee now; At thy feet we hum-bly bow; Oh, do not our
2. Send some message from thy word, That may joy and peace afford; Let thy Spirit
3. Comfort those who weep and mourn; Let the time of joy re-turn; Those that are cast
4. Grant that those who seek may find Thee, a God sincere and kind; Heal the sick, the

suit dis-dain; Shall we seek thee, Lord, in vain? Shall we seek, thee, Lord, in vain?
now im-part Full sal-va-tion to each heart, Full sal-va-tion to each heart.
down lift up, Strong in faith, in love, and hope, Strong in faith, in love, and hope.
cap-tive free, Let us all re-joice in thee, Let us all re-joice in thee.

WILLIAM HAMMOND, 1745.

SICILY. 8s, 7s & 4s.
SICILIAN MELODY.

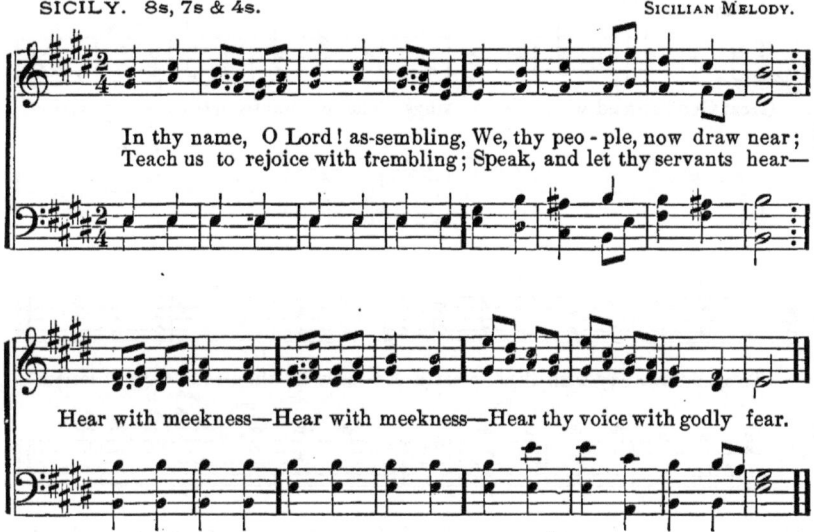

In thy name, O Lord! as-sembling, We, thy peo - ple, now draw near;
Teach us to rejoice with trembling; Speak, and let thy servants hear—

Hear with meekness—Hear with meekness—Hear thy voice with godly fear.

32 *Opening of Service.* (137)

IN thy name, O Lord! assembling,
  We, thy people, now draw near;
Teach us to rejoice with trembling;
  Speak, and let thy servants hear—
    Hear with meekness—
Hear thy word with godly fear.

2 While our days on earth are lengthened,
  May we give them, Lord, to thee;
Cheered by hope, and daily strengthened,
  May we run, nor weary be,
    Till thy glory
Without clouds in heaven we see.

3 There, in worship, purer, sweeter,
  Thee thy people shall adore;
Tasting of enjoyment greater
  Far than thought conceived before;
    Full enjoyment,
Full, unmixed, and evermore.
          THOMAS KELLY, 1809.

Close of Service. (141)

LORD, dismiss us with thy blessing,
  Fill our hearts with joy and peace;
Let us each, thy love possessing,
  Triumph in redeeming grace;
    Oh! refresh us,
Traveling through this wilderness.

2 Thanks we give and adoration,
  For thy gospel's joyful sound;
May the fruits of thy salvation
  In our hearts and lives abound;
    May thy presence
With us, evermore, be found.

3 So, whene'er the signal's given,
  Us from earth to call away,
Borne on angels' wings to heaven,
  Glad the summons to obey,
    We shall surely
Reign with Christ in endless day.
          WALTER SHIRLEY, 1774.

34 *Plea for Parting Blessing.* (139)

GOD of our salvation! hear us;
  Bless, oh, bless us, ere we go;
When we join the world, be near us,
  Lest we cold and careless grow.
    Savior! keep us;
Keep us safe from every foe.

2 As our steps are drawing nearer
  To our everlasting home,
May our view of heaven grow clearer,
  Hope more bright of joys to come;
    And, when dying,
May thy presence cheer the gloom.
          THOMAS KELLY, 1809.

MENDON. L. M.
With ardor.
GERMAN.

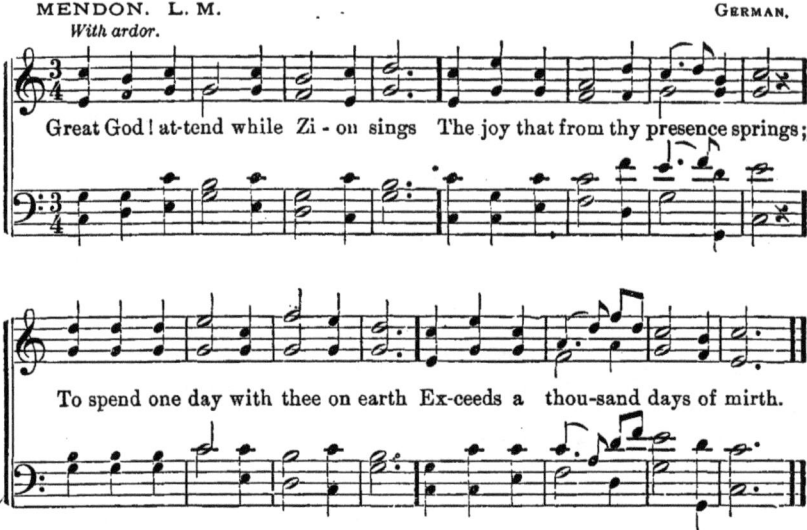

Great God! at-tend while Zi - on sings The joy that from thy presence springs;

To spend one day with thee on earth Ex-ceeds a thou-sand days of mirth.

35   *Psalm 84.*   (119)

GREAT God! attend while Zion sings
The joy that from thy presence springs;
To spend one day with thee on earth
Exceeds a thousand days of mirth.

2 Might I enjoy the meanest place
Within thy house, O God of grace!
Not tents of ease, nor thrones of power,
Should tempt my feet to leave thy door.

3 God is our sun, he makes our day;
God is our shield, he guards our way
From all th' assaults of hell and sin,
From foes without and foes within.

4 All needful grace will God bestow,
And crown that grace with glory too;
He gives us all things, and withholds
No real good from upright souls.

5 O God, our King! whose sovereign sway
The glorious hosts of heaven obey,
And devils at thy presence flee;
Blest is the man that trusts in thee!
ISAAC WATTS, 1719.

36   *The Presence of Christ.*   (124)

How sweet to leave the world awhile,
And seek the presence of our Lord!
Dear Savior! on thy people smile,
And come, according to thy word.

2 From busy scenes we now retreat,
That we may here converse with thee;
Ah! Lord! behold us at thy feet;—
Let this the gate of heaven be.

3 Chief of ten thousand! now appear,
That we by faith may see thy face;
Oh! speak, that we thy voice may hear,
And let thy presence fill this place.
THOMAS KELLY, 1809.

37   *Psalm 84.*   (127)

How pleasant, how divinely fair,
O Lord of hosts, thy dwellings are!
With long desire my spirit faints,
To meet the assemblies of thy saints.

2 My flesh would rest in thine abode;
My panting heart cries out for God;
My God! my King! why should I be
So far from all my joys and thee?

3 Blest are the souls who find a place
Within the temple of thy grace;
There they behold thy gentler rays,
And seek thy face and learn thy praise.

4 Blest are the men whose hearts are set
To find the way to Zion's gate;
God is their strength, and through the road
They lean upon their helper, God.

5 Cheerful they walk with growing strength,
Till all shall meet in heaven at length;
Till all before thy face appear,
And join in nobler worship there.
ISAAC WATTS, 1719.

WARD. L. M.

Arr. by LOWELL MASON, 1830.

Thy presence, gracious God! afford; Pre-pare us to re-ceive thy word;

Now let thy voice engage our ear, And faith be mixed with what we hear.

38 [FIRST STANZA INSERTED IN MUSIC ABOVE.]
Before Sermon. (122)

2 Distracting thoughts and cares remove,
And fix our hearts and hopes above;
With food divine may we be fed,
And satisfied with living bread.

3 To us thy sacred word apply,
With sovereign power and energy;
And may we, in thy faith and fear,
Reduce to practice what we hear.

4 Father, in us thy Son reveal;
Teach us to know and do thy will;
Thy saving power and love display,
And guide us to the realms of day.
JOHN FAWCETT, 1782.

39 [FIRST STANZA INSERTED IN MUSIC BELOW.]
Acts 2: 1. (792)

2 Command thy blessing, Jesus, Lord!
May we thy true disciples be;
Speak to each heart the mighty word—
Say to the weakest, follow me.

3 Command thy blessing in this hour,
Spirit of truth! and fill the place
With wounding and with healing power,
With quickening and confirming grace.

4 Oh, thou, our Maker, Savior, Guide,
One true, eternal God confessed;
Whom thou hast joined none may divide;
None dare to curse whom thou hast blest.
JAMES MONTGOMERY.

MIGDOL. L. M.
Moderato.

DR. L. MASON, 1840.

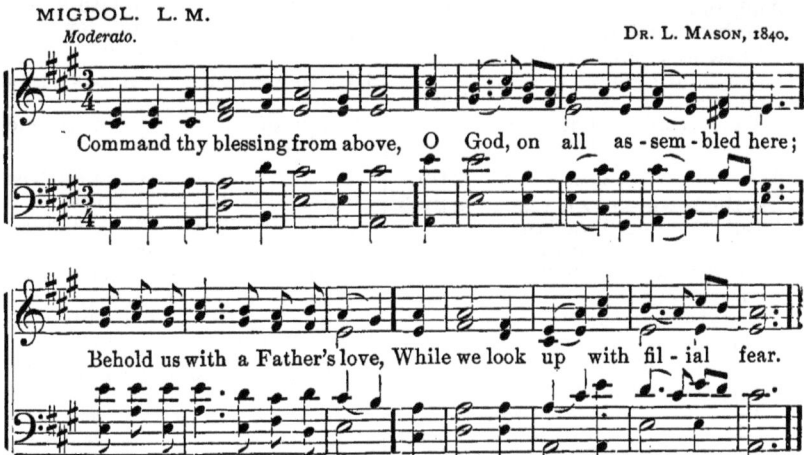

Command thy blessing from above, O God, on all as-sem-bled here;

Behold us with a Father's love, While we look up with fil-ial fear.

MEAR. C. M.   BARNARD'S PSALMS, 1752.

A - gain our earth - ly cares we leave, And in thy courts ap - pear;

A - gain, with joy - ful feet, we come To meet our Sav - ior here.

40   [FIRST VERSE INSERTED IN MUSIC.]
          God's Presence in Sanctuary.   (111)

2 Within those walls let holy peace,
  And love, and concord dwell;
Here give the troubled conscience ease—
  The wounded spirit heal.

3 The feeling heart, the melting eye,
  The humble mind bestow;
And shine upon us from on high,
  To make our graces grow.

4 May we in faith receive thy word,
  In faith present our prayers;
And, in the presence of our Lord,
  Unbosom all our cares.

5 Shew us some token of thy love,
  Our fainting hope to raise;
And pour thy blessing from above,
  That we may render praise.
            JOHN NEWTON, 1779, a.

41   *Dedication.*   (1175)

OH, thou, whose own vast temple stands,
  Built over earth and sea !
Accept the walls that human hands
  Have raised to worship thee.

2 Lord ! from thine inmost glory send,
  Within these walls t' abide,
The peace that dwelleth without end
  Serenely by thy side !

3 May erring minds, that worship here,
  Be taught the better way;
And they who mourn, and they who fear,
  Be strengthened as they pray.

4 May faith grow firm, and love grow warm,
  And pure devotion rise,
While, round these hallowed walls, the storm
  Of earth-born passion dies.
            WILLIAM C. BRYANT, 1835.

42   *Psalm 122.*   (106)

How did my heart rejoice to hear
  My friends devoutly say—
"In Zion let us all appear—
  And keep the solemn day!"

2 I love her gates, I love the road;
  The church, adorned with grace,
Stands like a palace, built for God,
  To show his milder face.

3 Up to her courts, with joys unknown,
  The holy tribes repair;
The Son of David holds his throne,
  And sits in judgment there.

4 He hears our praises and complaints;
  And, while his awful voice
Divides the sinners from the saints,
  We tremble and rejoice.

5 Peace be within this sacred place,
  And joy a constant guest!
With holy gifts and heavenly grace
  By her attendants blest!

6 My soul shall pray for Zion still,
  While life or breath remains;
There my best friends, my kindred, dwell,
  There God, my Savior, reigns.
            ISAAC WATTS, 1719.

43(81) LISBON. S. M.

DANIEL READ, 1785.

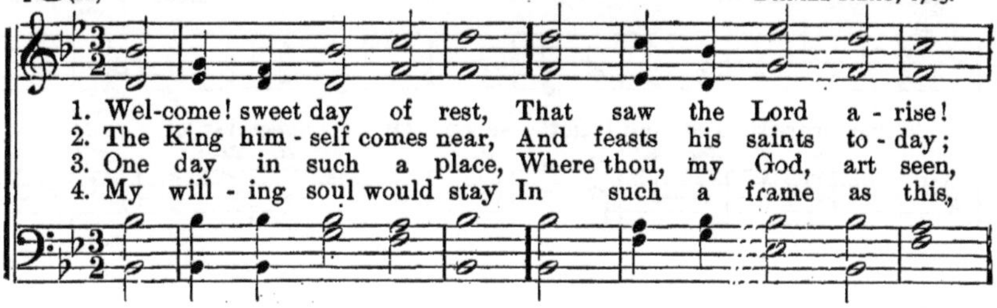

1. Wel-come! sweet day of rest, That saw the Lord a - rise!
2. The King him - self comes near, And feasts his saints to - day;
3. One day in such a place, Where thou, my God, art seen,
4. My will - ing soul would stay In such a frame as this,

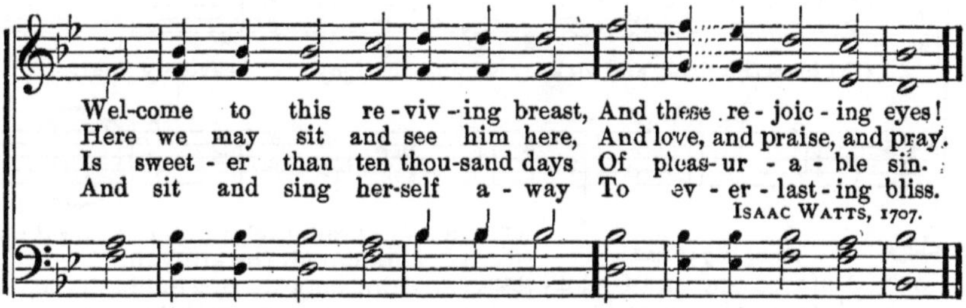

Wel-come to this re - viv - ing breast, And these re - joic - ing eyes!
Here we may sit and see him here, And love, and praise, and pray.
Is sweet - er than ten thou-sand days Of pleas-ur - a - ble sin.
And sit and sing her-self a - way To ev - er - last - ing bliss.

ISAAC WATTS, 1707.

44(98) MENDEBRAS. 7s & 6s. D.

German. Arr. by LOWELL MASON, 1839.

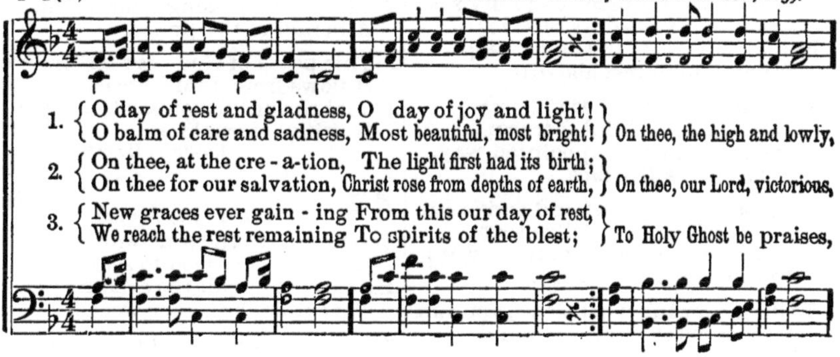

1. { O day of rest and gladness, O day of joy and light! }
   { O balm of care and sadness, Most beautiful, most bright! } On thee, the high and lowly,
2. { On thee, at the cre - a-tion, The light first had its birth; }
   { On thee for our salvation, Christ rose from depths of earth, } On thee, our Lord, victorious,
3. { New graces ever gain - ing From this our day of rest, }
   { We reach the rest remaining To spirits of the blest; } To Holy Ghost be praises,

Before th' eternal throne, Sing Holy! Holy! Holy! To the great Three in One.
The Spirit sent from heaven, And thus on thee, most glorious, A triple light was given.
To Father and to Son; The Church her voice upraises To thee, blest Three in One.

CHRISTOPHER WORDSWORTH, 1858.

AUBURN. C. M.　　　　　HENRY IVISON, 1844.

Come, dear-est Lord, and feed thy sheep, On this sweet day of rest;

Oh! bless this flock, and make this fold En-joy a heaven-ly rest.

45　(　*Sweet Day of Rest.*　(66)

COME, dearest Lord, and feed thy sheep,
　On this sweet day of rest;
Oh, bless this flock, and make this fold
　Enjoy a heavenly rest.

2 Welcome, and precious to my soul
　Are these sweet days of love;
But what a Sabbath shall I keep
　When I shall rest above!

3 I come, I wait, I hear, I pray;
　Thy footsteps, Lord, I trace;
Here, in thine own appointed way,
　I wait to see thy face.

4 These are the sweet and precious days
　On which my Lord I've seen;
And oft, when feasting on his word,
　In raptures I have been.

5 Oh, if my soul, when death appears,
　In this sweet frame be found,
I'll clasp my Savior in mine arms,
　And leave this earthly ground.
　　　　　　JOHN MASON, 1683.

46　　*Sabbath Morn.*　(60)

How sweetly breaks the Sabbath dawn
　Along the eastern skies!
So, when the night of time hath gone,
　Eternity shall rise.

2 How softly spreads the Sabbath light!
　How soon the gloom hath fled!
So o'er the new created sight
　Celestial bliss is spread.

3 What quiet reigns o'er earth and sea,
　Through all the stilly air!
So calm may we this Sabbath be,
　And free from worldly care.

4 Thus let thy peace, O Lord! pervade
　Our bosoms all our days;
And let each passing hour be made
　A herald of thy praise.

5 This peace of God—how full! how sweet
　It flows from Jesus' breast;
It makes our bliss on earth complete.
　It brings eternal rest.
　　　　　　EDWIN F. HATFIELD, 1840.

47　　*The Lord's Day Morning.*　(65)

WHEN the worn spirit wants repose,
　And sighs her God to seek,
How sweet to hail the evening's close
　That ends the weary week!

2 How sweet to hail the early dawn
　That opens on the sight,
When first that soul-reviving morn
　Sheds forth new rays of light!

3 Sweet day! thine hours too soon will cease;
　Yet, while they gently roll,
Breathe, heavenly Spirit, source of peace,
　A Sabbath o'er my soul.

4 When will my pilgrimage be done,
　The world's long week be o'er,
That Sabbath dawn which needs no sun,
　That day which fades no more?
　　　　　　JAMES EDMESTON, 1820.

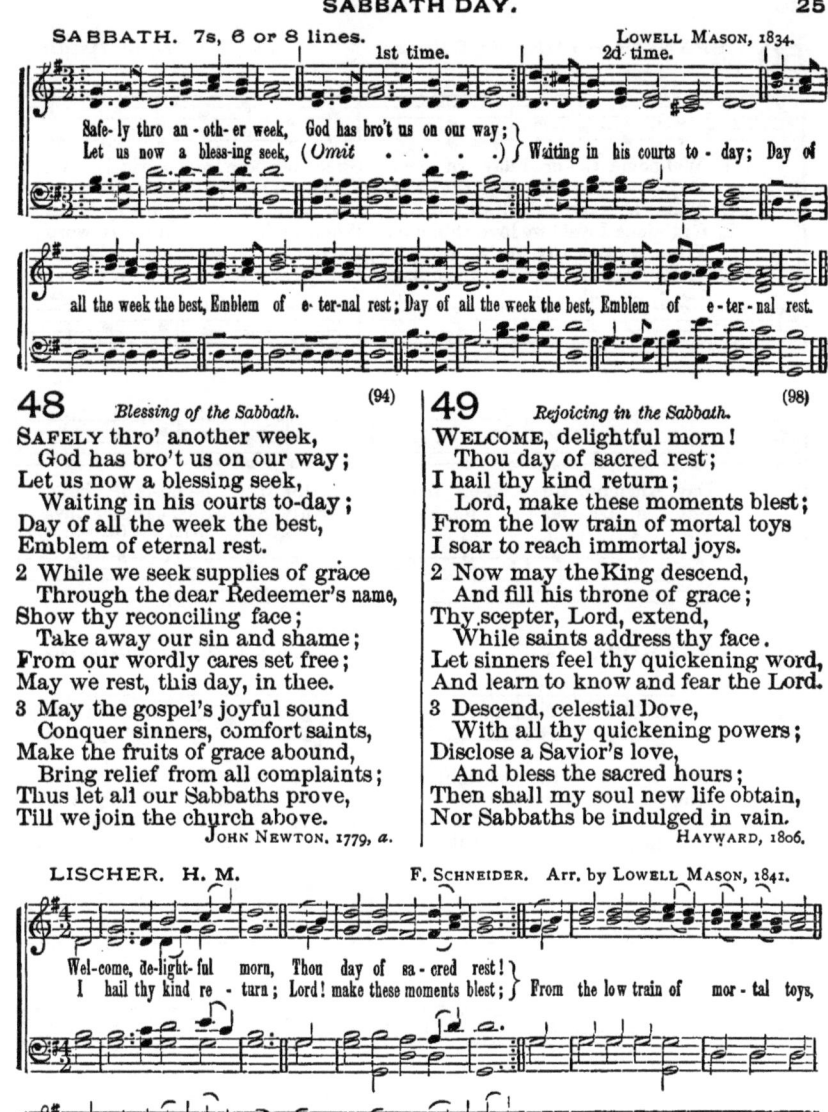

SABBATH. 7s, 6 or 8 lines. LOWELL MASON, 1834.

Safe-ly thro an-oth-er week, God has bro't us on our way;
Let us now a bless-ing seek, (*Omit* . . . .) Waiting in his courts to-day; Day of

all the week the best, Emblem of e-ter-nal rest; Day of all the week the best, Emblem of e-ter-nal rest.

48 *Blessing of the Sabbath.* (94)

SAFELY thro' another week,
  God has bro't us on our way;
Let us now a blessing seek,
  Waiting in his courts to-day;
Day of all the week the best,
Emblem of eternal rest.

2 While we seek supplies of grace
  Through the dear Redeemer's name,
Show thy reconciling face;
  Take away our sin and shame;
From our wordly cares set free;
May we rest, this day, in thee.

3 May the gospel's joyful sound
  Conquer sinners, comfort saints,
Make the fruits of grace abound,
  Bring relief from all complaints;
Thus let all our Sabbaths prove,
Till we join the church above.
  JOHN NEWTON, 1779, *a.*

49 *Rejoicing in the Sabbath.* (98)

WELCOME, delightful morn!
  Thou day of sacred rest;
I hail thy kind return;
  Lord, make these moments blest;
From the low train of mortal toys
I soar to reach immortal joys.

2 Now may the King descend,
  And fill his throne of grace;
Thy scepter, Lord, extend,
  While saints address thy face.
Let sinners feel thy quickening word,
And learn to know and fear the Lord.

3 Descend, celestial Dove,
  With all thy quickening powers;
Disclose a Savior's love,
  And bless the sacred hours;
Then shall my soul new life obtain,
Nor Sabbaths be indulged in vain.
  HAYWARD, 1806.

LISCHER. H. M. F. SCHNEIDER. Arr. by LOWELL MASON, 1841.

Wel-come, de-light-ful morn, Thou day of sa-cred rest!
I hail thy kind re-turn; Lord! make these moments blest; From the low train of mor-tal toys,

I soar to reach im-mor-tal joys, I soar to reach im-mor-tal joys.

I soar to reach im-mor-tal joys.

50 (91) SPANISH HYMN. 7s, 8 lines.　　　　SPANISH MELODY.

Fine.

1. Wel-come, sa - cred day of rest! Sweet re - pose from world-ly care;
Day a - bove all days the best, When our souls for heav'n prepare;

D. C. Thus he vanquished all our foes; Let our lips his glo - ry tell.

2. Gra-cious Lord! we love this day, When we hear thy ho - ly word;
When we sing thy praise, and pray, Earth can no such joys af - ford;

D. C. Rest from sin, and rest from pains, End - less joys and end - less praise.

D. C.

Day, when our Re-deem-er rose, Vic - tor o'er the hosts of hell;
But a bet - ter rest remains, Heav'nly Sab-baths, happier days,

WILLIAM BROWN, 1822.

51 (93) LAST HOPE. 7s.　　　　Arr. from L. M. GOTTSCHALK, 1854.

1. Soft - ly fades the twi-light ray Of the ho - ly Sab-bath day;
2. Night her sol - emn man-tle spreads O'er the earth as day-light fades;
3. Peace is on the world a - broad; 'Tis the ho - ly peace of God—
4. Sav - ior, may our Sabbaths be Days of peace and joy in thee,

Gen - tly as life's set - ting sun, When the Christian's course is run.
All things tell of calm re-pose At the ho - ly Sab-bath's close.
Sym - bol of the peace with-in, When the spir - it rests from sin.
Till in heav'n our souls re-pose, Where the Sabbath ne'er shall close.

SAMUEL F. SMITH, 1843.

52 LOWRY. L. M.   Geo. F. Root.

1. A-wake, my soul, and with the sun Thy dai-ly stage of du - ty run;
2. A-wake, lift up thyself, my heart, And with the an - gels bear thy part,
3. Glo-ry to thee, who safe hast kept, And hast refreshed me when I slept;
4. Lord, I my vows to thee re-new; Scat-ter my sins as morn - ing dew;

Shake off dull sloth, and joyful rise To pay thy morn - ing sac - ri-fice.
Who all night long un-wea-ried sing High praises to th' e - ter - nal king.
Grant, Lord, when I from death shall wake, I may of end - less life partake.
Guard my first springs of thought and will, And with thyself my spir - it fill.
BP. KEN, 1709.

53 VIGIL. S. M.
(1169)   Giovanni Paisello.

1. See how the morn-ing sun Pursues his shin-ing way;
2. Thus would my ris - ing soul Its heavenly Par-ent sing,
3. Se-rene I laid me down, Be-neath his guardian care;
4. My life I would a - new De - vote, O Lord, to thee;

And wide proclaims his Mak-er's praise, With ev'ry bright'ning ray.
And to its great O - rig - i - nal The humble trib - ute bring.
I slept, and I a - woke, and found My kind Pre-serv-er near.
And in thy serv - ice I would spend A long e - ter - ni - ty.
T. SCOTT.

54 EVENING PRAYER. 8s & 7s.

(1171) *Reverently.*   GEORGE C. STEBBINS.

1. Sav-ior, breathe an evening blessing,   E'er repose our spir-its   seal;
2. Though destruction walk around us,   Though the arrows past us   fly;
3. Though the night be dark and dreary,   Darkness can not hide from   thee;
4. Should swift death this night o'ertake us,   And our couch become our   tomb,

Sin and want we come confess-ing,   Thou canst save and thou canst heal.
Angel guards from thee sur-round us,   We are safe if thou art nigh.
Thou art he who, nev-er wear-y,   Watchest where thy peo-ple be.
May the morn in heaven a-wake us,   Clad in bright and deathless bloom.

JAMES EDMESTON, 1820.

55 HURSLEY. L. M.

(1165)   PETER RITTER, 1792. Arr. by W. H. MONK, 1861.

1. Sun of my soul, thou Sav-ior dear,   It is not   night if thou be near;
2. When the soft dews of kind-ly sleep   My wea-ry   eye-lids gen-tly steep,
3. A-bide with me from morn till eve,   For without   thee I can not live;
4. Come near and bless us when we wake,   Ere thro' the world our way we take,

Oh, may no earth-born cloud arise   To hide thee from thy servant's eyes.
Be my last thought, how sweet to rest   For ev-er on   my Sav-ior's breast.
A-bide with me when night is nigh,   For without thee   I dare not die.
Till in the o-cean of thy love   We lose ourselves in heaven a-bove.

REV. J. KEBLE, 1827.

EVENTIDE. 10s.   W. H. MONK, 1861.

1. A-bide with me; fast falls the e-ventide; The darkness deep-ens; Lord, with me abide!

When oth-er help-ers fail, and comforts flee, Help of the helpless, oh, abide with me!

56   *Evening of the Day.*

ABIDE with me: fast falls the eventide;
The darkness deepens; Lord, with me abide!
When other helpers fail, and comforts flee,
Help of the helpless, oh, abide with me!

2 Not a brief glance I beg, a passing word,
But as thou dwell'st with thy disciples, Lord,
Familiar, condescending, patient, free,
Come, not to sojourn, but abide with me.

3 I need thy presence every passing hour:
What but thy grace can foil the tempter's power?
Who like thyself my guide and stay can be?
Thro' cloud and sunshine, oh, abide with me!

4 Swift to its close ebbs out life's little day;
Earth's joys grow dim, its glories pass away:
Change and decay in all around I see;
O thou, who changest not, abide with me!
                                    HENRY FRANCIS LYTE, 1847.

57   *Closing Hymn.*

SAVIOR, again to thy dear name we raise
With one accord our parting hymn of praise;
We rise to bless thee ere our worship cease,
And now, departing, wait thy word of peace.

2 Grant us thy peace upon our homeward way;
With thee began, with thee shall end the day;
Guard thou the lips from sin, the hearts from shame,
That in this house have called upon thy name.

3 Grant us thy peace, Lord, through the coming night;
Turn thou for us its darkness into light;
From harm and danger keep thy children free,
For dark and light are both alike to thee.
                                    JOHN ELLERTON, 1808.

58　SEYMOUR. 7s.　　　　　　　　　C. M. VON WEBER, 1826.

1. Soft - ly now the light of day　Fades up - on my sight a - way;
2. Thou whose all per - vad - ing eye　Naught es - capes with-out, with-in,
3. Soon, for me, the light of day　Shall for ev - er pass. a - way;
4. Thou who, sin-less, yet hast known All　of man's in - firm - i - ty;

Free from care, from la - bor free,　Lord, I would commune with thee.
Par - don each in - firm - i - ty,　O - pen fault, and se - cret sin.
Then, from sin and sor - row free,　Take me, Lord, to dwell with thee.
Then from thine e - ter - nal throne, Je - sus, look with pity - ing eye.

G. W. DOANE, 1824.

59　STOCKWELL. 8s & 7s.　　　　　　　D. E. JONES, 1847.

1. Si - lent - ly　the shades of even - ing　Gather round my low-ly door;
2. O . the lost, the　un - for-got - ten,　Tho' the world be oft for - got!
3. Liv - ing in the　si - lent hours,　Where our spirits on-ly blend—
4. How such ho - ly　memories clus - ter,　Like the stars when storms are past;

Si - lent - ly they bring be-fore me　Fac - es I shall see no more.
O the shroud-ed and the lone - ly!　In our hearts they perish not.
They, unlinked with earth-ly trou-ble;　We, still hoping. for its end.
Pointing up　to that far heav - en　We may hope to gain at last.

C. C. COX.

60 FADING, STILL FADING. P. M., with Refrain. SCOTCH SONG.

1. Fad-ing, still fad-ing, the last beam is shining; Father in heav-en, the
2. Fath-er in heaven, O hear when we call; Hear, for Christ's sake, who

day is de - clining; Safe-ty and innocence flee with the light,
is Sav-ior of all. Feeble and fainting, we trust in thy might;

Temptation and danger walk forth with the night. From the fall of the shade till the
In doubting and darkness thy love be our light; Let us sleep on thy breast while the

REFRAIN.

morning bells chime, Shield us from danger, keep us from crime.
night taper burns, Wake in thine arms when morning returns. Father, have mercy,

2nd verse.

Father, have mercy, Father, have mercy, thro' Jesus Christ our Lord. Amen.
SELINA HUNTINGTON.

61   GOD BE WITH YOU. P. M.   W. G. Tomer.

1. God be with you till we meet again, By his counsels guide, uphold you,
2. God be with you till we meet again, 'Neath his wings securely hide you,
3. God be with you till we meet again, When life's perils thick confound you,
4. God be with you till we meet again, Keep love's banner floating o'er you;

With his sheep secure-ly fold you, God be with you till we meet a-gain.
Dai - ly man-na still pro-vide you, God be with you till we meet a-gain.
Put his arms unfailing round you, God be with you till we meet a-gain.
Smite death's threat'ning wave before you, God be with you till we meet a-gain.

J. E. Rankin, D. D.

CHORUS.

Till we meet, till we meet, Till we meet at Je - sus' feet; Till we meet, . . . till we meet, God be with you till we meet a-gain.

Till we meet, till we meet, till we meet, Till we meet at Je - sus' feet, till we meet; Till we meet, till we meet, till we meet, God be with you till we meet a-gain.

By per. of Rev. J. E. Rankin, D. D., Washington, D. C.

62 WONDERFUL WORDS. P. M. P. P. BLISS.

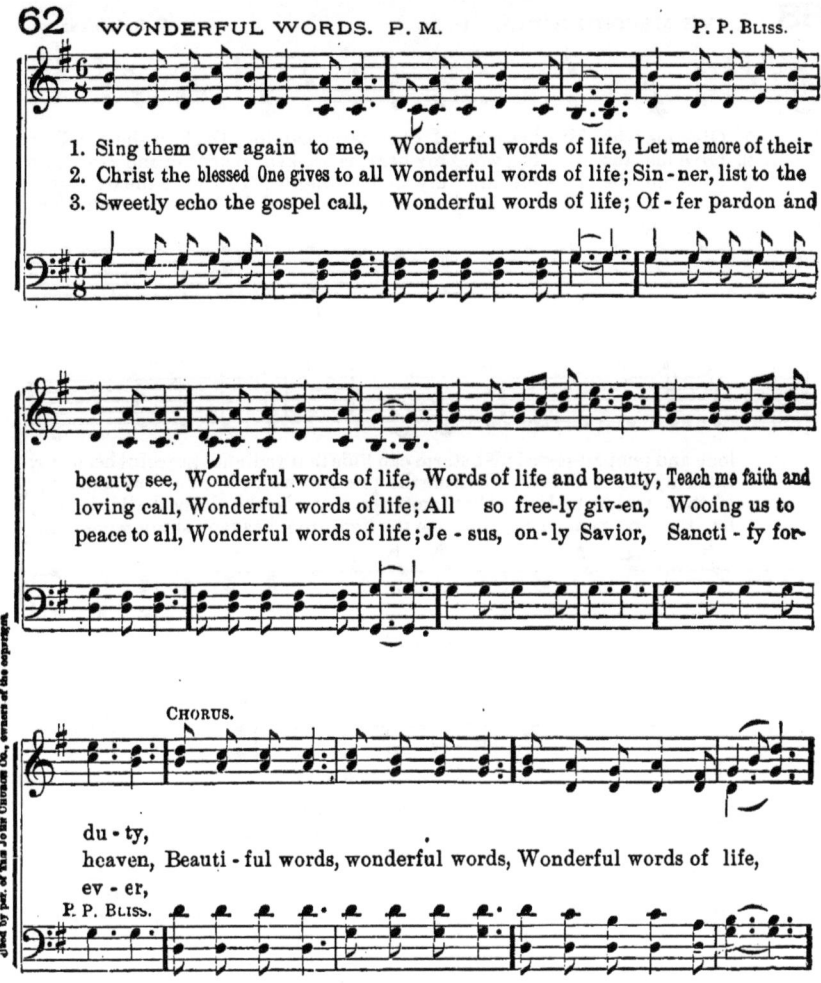

1. Sing them over again to me, Wonderful words of life, Let me more of their
2. Christ the blessed One gives to all Wonderful words of life; Sin-ner, list to the
3. Sweetly echo the gospel call, Wonderful words of life; Of-fer pardon and

beauty see, Wonderful words of life, Words of life and beauty, Teach me faith and
loving call, Wonderful words of life; All so free-ly giv-en, Wooing us to
peace to all, Wonderful words of life; Je-sus, on-ly Savior, Sancti-fy for-

CHORUS.

du - ty,
heaven, Beauti - ful words, wonderful words, Wonderful words of life,
ev - er,

P. P. BLISS.

63   GIVE ME THE BIBLE. P. M.   E. S. LORENZ.

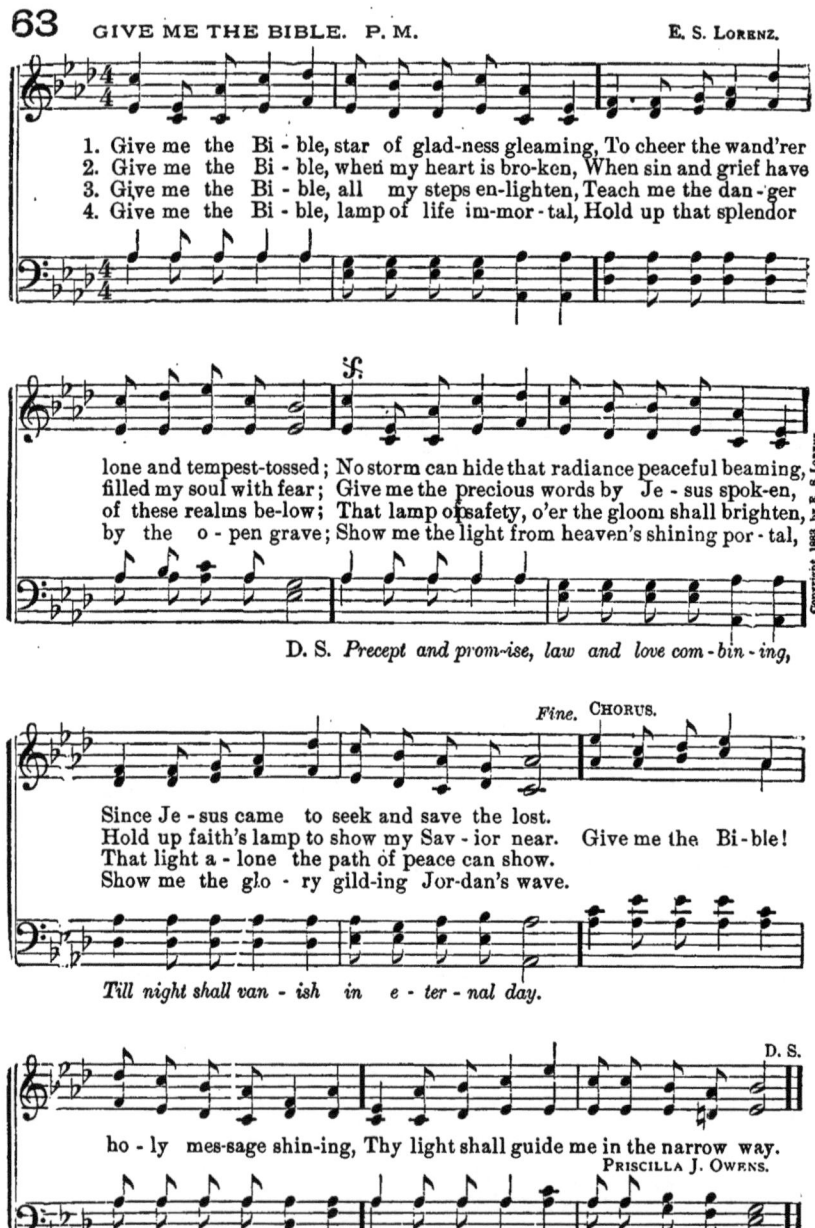

1. Give me the Bi - ble, star of glad-ness gleaming, To cheer the wand'rer
2. Give me the Bi - ble, when my heart is bro-ken, When sin and grief have
3. Give me the Bi - ble, all my steps en-lighten, Teach me the dan - ger
4. Give me the Bi - ble, lamp of life im-mor - tal, Hold up that splendor

lone and tempest-tossed; No storm can hide that radiance peaceful beaming,
filled my soul with fear; Give me the precious words by Je - sus spok-en,
of these realms be-low; That lamp of safety, o'er the gloom shall brighten,
by the o - pen grave; Show me the light from heaven's shining por - tal,

D. S. Precept and prom-ise, law and love com - bin - ing,

Fine. CHORUS.

Since Je - sus came to seek and save the lost.
Hold up faith's lamp to show my Sav - ior near.   Give me the Bi - ble!
That light a - lone the path of peace can show.
Show me the glo - ry gild-ing Jor-dan's wave.

Till night shall van - ish in e - ter - nal day.

D. S.

ho - ly mes-sage shin-ing, Thy light shall guide me in the narrow way.

PRISCILLA J. OWENS.

64 (170) SHIRLAND. S. M.

SAMUEL STANLEY, 1805.

1. Be-hold! the morn-ing sun Be - gins his glo - rious way;
2. But, where the gos - pel comes, It spreads di - vin - er light;
3. How per - fect is thy word! And all thy judg - ments just;
4. My gra - cious God! how plain Are thy di - rec - tions given!

His beams thro' all the na - tions run, And life and light convey.
It calls dead sin - ners from the tombs, And gives the blind their sight
For - ev - er sure thy prom-ise, Lord! And men se - cure-ly trust.
Oh! may I nev - er read in vain, But find the path to heaven

ISAAC WATTS, 1719.

65 DALLAS. 7s.

From MARIA LUIGI CHERUBINI, d. 1846.

1. Ho - ly Bi - ble, book di - vine, Precious treasure, thou art mine;
2. Mine to chide me when I rove; Mine to show a Sav-ior's love;
3. Mine to com-fort in dis - tress, Suf-fering in this wil - der-ness;
4. Mine to tell of joys to come, And the reb - el sin - ner's doom:

Mine to tell me whence I came; Mine to teach me what I am.
Mine thou art to guide and guard; Mine to pun - ish or reward;
Mine to show, by liv - ing faith, Man can triumph o - ver death;
O thou ho - ly book di - vine, Precious treasure, thou art mine.

JOHN BURTON, 1805.

EVAN. (Celtic Melody.) C. M.   Arr., WILLIAM HENRY HAVERGAL, 1846.

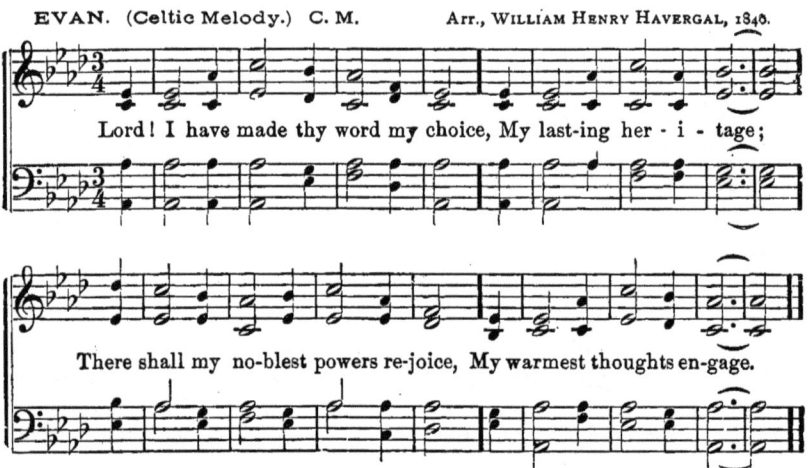

Lord! I have made thy word my choice, My last-ing her - i - tage;

There shall my no-blest powers re-joice, My warmest thoughts en-gage.

66   *Psalm 119.*   (155)

LORD ! I have made thy word my choice,
  My lasting heritage ;
There shall my noblest powers rejoice,
  My warmest thoughts engage.

2 I'll read the histories of thy love,
  And keep thy laws in sight,
While through the promises I rove,
  With ever fresh delight.

3 'Tis a broad land of wealth unknown,
  Where springs of life arise ;
Seeds of immortal bliss are sown,
  And hidden glory lies.

4 The best relief that mourners have—
  It makes our sorrows blest ;
Our fairest hope, beyond the grave,
  And our eternal rest.
          ISAAC WATTS, 1719.

67   *The Latter Day.*   (1018)

LORD ! send thy word, and let it fly,
  Armed with thy Spirit's power ;
Ten thousands shall confess its sway,
  And bless the saving hour.

2 Beneath the influence of its grace,
  The barren wastes shall rise,
With sudden flowers and fruits arrayed,—
  A blooming paradise.

3 Peace, with her olives crowned, shall stretch
  Her wings from shore to shore ;
No trump shall rouse the rage of war,
  Nor murderous cannon roar.

4 Lord ! for these days we wait ;—these days
  Are in thy word foretold :
Fly swifter, sun and stars ! and bring
  This promised age of gold.

5 Amen !—with joy divine, let earth's
  Unnumbered myriads cry ;
Amen !—with joy divine, let heaven's
  Unnumbered choirs reply.
          THOMAS GIBBONS, 1769.

68   *The Incomparable Richness of God's Word.*   (150)

FATHER of mercies, in thy word
  What endless glory shines !
Forever be thy name adored
  For these celestial lines.

2 Here may the wretched sons of want
  Exhaustless riches find—
Riches above what earth can grant,
  And lasting as the mind.

3 Here the fa r tree of knowledge grows,
  And yields a free repast ;
Sublimer sweets than nature knows
  Invite the longing taste.

4 Here the Redeemer's welcome voice
  Spreads heavenly peace around ;
And life and everlasting joys
  Attend the blissful sound.

5 Oh, may these heavenly pages be
  My ever dear delight ;
And still new beauties may I see
  And still increasing light.
          ANNE STEELE, 1760.

DEVIZES. C. M.
ISRAEL TUCKER, 1800.

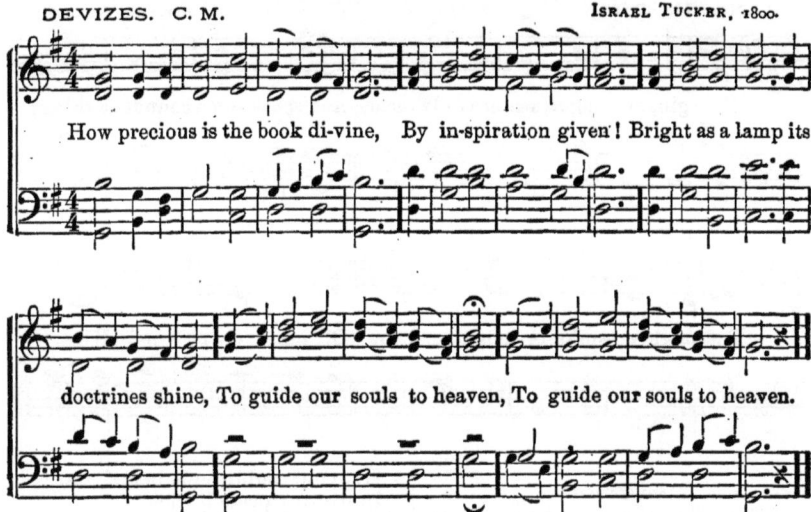

How precious is the book di-vine, By in-spiration given! Bright as a lamp its
doctrines shine, To guide our souls to heaven, To guide our souls to heaven.

69 *The Bible our Light* (149)

How precious is the book divine,
By inspiration given!
Bright as a lamp its doctrines shine,
To guide our souls to heaven.

2 Its light, descending from above,
Our gloomy world to cheer,
Displays a Savior's boundless love,
And brings his glories near.

3 It sweetly cheers our drooping hearts,
In this dark vale of tears;
Life, light, and joy it still imparts,
And quells our rising fears.

4 This lamp, through all the tedious night
Of life, shall guide our way,
Till we behold the clearer light
Of an eternal day.
JOHN FAWCETT, 1782.

70 *Psalm* 119. (156)

How shall the young secure their hearts,
And guard their lives from sin?
Thy word the choicest rules imparts
To keep the conscience clean.

2 'Tis like the sun, a heavenly light,
That guides us all the day;
And, through the dangers of the night,
A lamp to lead our way.

3 Thy precepts make me truly wise;
I hate the sinners' road;
I hate my own vain thoughts that rise,
But love thy law, my God!

4 Thy word is everlasting truth;
How pure is every page!
That holy book shall guide our youth,
And well support our age.
ISAAC WATTS, 1719.

71 *Perfection of the Law and Testimony.* (154)

THY law is perfect, Lord of light;
Thy testimonies sure;
The statutes of thy realm are right,
And thy commandments pure.

2 Let these, O God, my soul convert,
And make thy servant wise;
Let those be gladness to my ears—
The dayspring to mine eyes.

3 By these may I be warned betimes;
Who knows the guile within?
Lord, save me from presumptuous crimes;
Cleanse me from secret sin.

4 So may the words my lips express—
The thoughts that throng my mind—
O Lord, my strength and righteousness,
With thee acceptance find.
C. WESLEY.

MANOAH. C. M.   Arr. from ROSSINI.

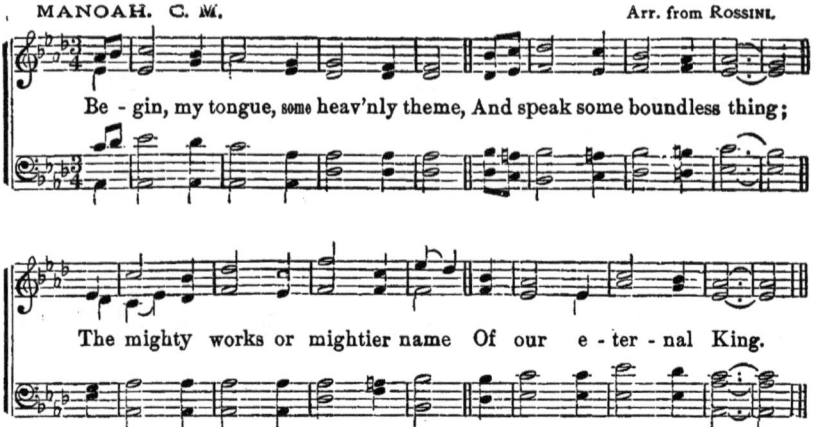

Be - gin, my tongue, some heav'nly theme, And speak some boundless thing;

The mighty works or mightier name Of our e - ter - nal King.

72 *Faithfulness.*

BEGIN, my tongue, some heavenly theme,
  And speak some boundless thing;
The mighty works or mightier name
  Of our eternal King.

2 Tell of his wondrous faithfulness,
  And sound his power abroad;
Sing the sweet promise of his grace,
  And the performing God.

3 His very word of grace is strong,
  As that which built the skies;
The voice that rolls the stars along,
  Speaks all the promises.

4 Oh, might I hear thy heavenly tongue
  But whisper, "Thou art mine!"
Those gentle words should raise my song
  To notes almost divine.
                            ISAAC WATTS.

73   *Power.*

THE Lord, our God, is full of might,
  The winds obey his will;
He speaks,—and, in his heavenly height,
  The rolling sun stands still.

2 Rebel, ye waves, and o'er the land
  With threatening aspect roar;
The Lord uplifts his awful hand,
  And chains you to the shore.

3 Howl, winds of night, your force combine;
  Without his high behest,
Ye shall not, in the mountain pine,
  Disturb the sparrow's nest.

4 His voice sublime is heard afar,
  In distant peals it dies;
He yokes the whirlwind to his car,
  And sweeps the howling skies.

5 Ye nations bend—in reverence bend ·
  Ye monarchs, wait his nod,
And bid the choral song ascend
  To celebrate your God.
                       H. KIRKE WHITE.

74   *Eternity.*

GREAT God! how infinite art thou!
  What worthless worms are we!
Let the whole race of creatures bow,
  And pay their praise to thee.

2 Thy throne eternal ages stood,
  Ere seas or stars were made:
Thou art the ever-living God,
  Were all the nations dead.

3 Eternity, with all its years,
  Stands present in thy view;
To thee there's nothing old appears—
  Great God! there's nothing new.

4 Our lives through various scenes are drawn,
  And vexed with trifling cares;
While thine eternal thought moves on
  Thine undisturbed affairs.

5 Great God! how infinite art thou!
  What worthless worms are we!
Let the whole race of creatures bow
  And pay their praise to thee.
                          ISAAC WATTS

75(394) ITALY. (Italian Hymn.) 6s & 4s.   FELICE GIARDINI, 1760.

1. Come, thou Al-might-y King! Help us thy name to sing, Help us to praise;
2. Come, thou in - car-nate Word! Gird on thy might - y sword; Our pray'r at-tend:
3. Come, ho-ly Com-fort - er! Thy sa-cred wit - ness bear In this glad hour:
4. To the great One in Three, The highest prais - es be, Hence, ev-er-more!

Father, all glorious! O'er all vic-to-ri-ous, Come and reign o-ver us, Ancient of days!
Come, and thy people bless, And give thy word success; Spirit of holiness, On us de-scend.
Thou who almighty art, Now rule in ev'ry heart, And ne'er from us depart, Spir-it of power!
His sov'reign majesty May we in glory see, And to e - ter-ni-ty Love and a-dore.

CHARLES WESLEY, 1757.

76(391) ALL SAINTS. L. M.   WILLIAM KNAPP, 1760.

1. Blest be the Fa - ther and his love, To whose ce - les - tial source we owe
2. Glo - ry to thee, great Son of God! From whose dear, wounded bod - y rolls
3. We give the sa - cred Spir - it praise, Who, in our hearts of sin and woe,
4. Thus, God, the Fa-ther, God, the Son, And God, the Spir - it, we a - dore;

Riv - ers of end-less joy a - bove, And rills of com-fort here be-low.
A pre-cious stream of vi - tal blood—Par - don and life for dy - ing souls.
Makes liv - ing springs of grace a-rise, And in - to boundless glo - ry flow.
That sea of life and love unknown, With-out a bot - tom or a shore.

ISAAC WATTS, 1709.

ELIZABETHTOWN. C. M.   George Kingsley, 1838.

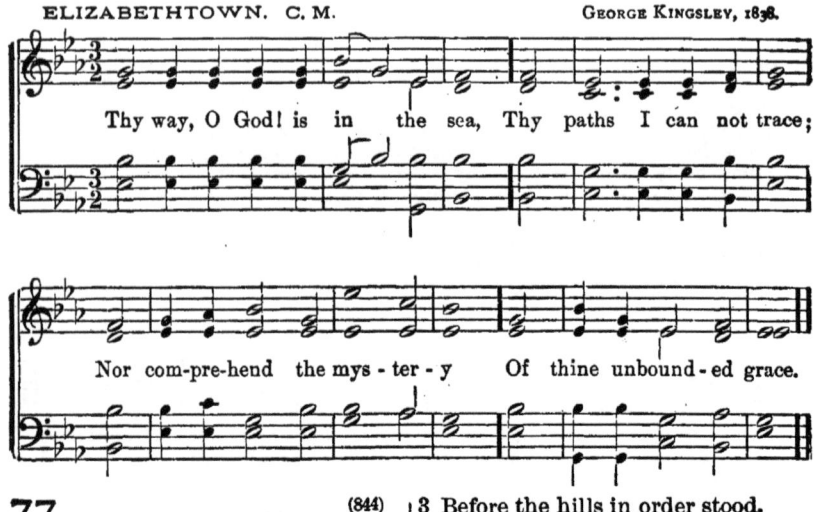

Thy way, O God! is in the sea, Thy paths I can not trace;

Nor com-pre-hend the mys-ter-y Of thine unbound-ed grace.

77   *God Incomprehensible.*   (844)

THY way, O God! is in the sea,
  Thy paths I can not trace;
Nor comprehend the mystery
  Of thine unbounded grace.

2 'Tis but in part I know thy will;
  I bless thee for the sight;
When will thy love the rest reveal,
  In glory's clearer light?

3 Here the dark veils of flesh and sense
  My captive soul surround;
Mysterious deeps of providence
  My wondering thoughts confound.

4 As through a glass, I dimly see
  The wonders of thy love;
How little do I know of thee,
  Or of the joys above!

5 With rapture I shall soon survey
  Thy providence and grace;
And spend an everlasting day
  In wonder, love, and praise.
                    JOHN FAWCETT, 1782.

78   *Eternity of God.*   (1071)

O GOD! our help in ages past,
  Our hope for years to come;
Our shelter from the stormy blast,
  And our eternal home.

2 Under the shadow of thy throne,
  Still may we dwell secure;
Sufficient is thine arm alone,
  And our defense is sure.

3 Before the hills in order stood,
  Or earth received her frame,
From everlasting thou art God,
  To endless years the same.

4 A thousand ages in thy sight
  Are like an evening gone;
Short as the watch that ends the night
  Before the rising sun.

5 The busy tribes of flesh and blood,
  With all their cares and fears,
Are carried downward by the flood,
  And lost in following years.
                    ISAAC WATTS, 1719.

79   *Divine Perfections.*   (182)

I SING th' almighty power of God,
  That made the mountains rise,
That spread the flowing seas abroad,
  And built the lofty skies.

2 I sing the wisdom that ordained
  The sun to rule the day;
The moon shines full at his command,
  And all the stars obey.

3 I sing the goodness of the Lord,
  That filled the earth with food;
He formed the creatures with his word,
  And then pronounced them good.

4 Lord! how thy wonders are displayed
  Where'er I turn mine eye!
If I survey the ground I tread,
  Or gaze upon the sky!
                    ISAAC WATTS.

DUNDEE. (French.) C. M. ANDRO HART's "Psalter," 1615.

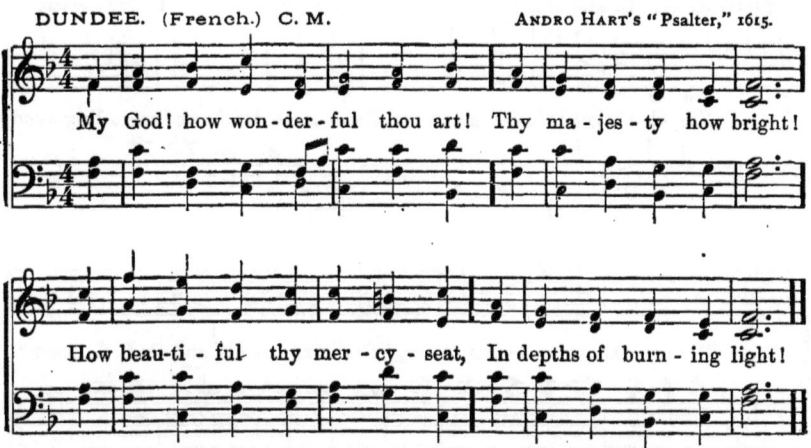

My God! how won-der-ful thou art! Thy ma-jes-ty how bright!

How beau-ti-ful thy mer-cy-seat, In depths of burn-ing light!

80 [FIRST VERSE INSERTED IN MUSIC.]
Our Heavenly Father. (21)

2 How dread are thine eternal years,
  Oh, everlasting Lord!.
By prostrate spirits day and night,
  Incessantly adored.

3 Oh, how I fear thee, living God!
  With deepest, tenderest fears,
And worship thee with trembling hope,
  And penitential tears.

4 Yet I may love thee, too, O Lord!
  Almighty as thou art,
For thou hast stooped to ask of me
  The love of this poor heart.

5 No earthly father loves like thee,
  No mother, half so mild,
Bears and forbears as thou hast done
  With me, thy sinful child.

6 Father of Jesus! love's reward!
  What rapture will it be,
Prostrate before thy throne to lie,
  And gaze and gaze on thee.
      FREDERICK WM. FABER, 1849.

81 *God's Ways not Understood.* (848)
GOD moves in a mysterious way,
  His wonders to perform;
He plants his footsteps in the sea,
  And rides upon the storm.

2 Deep in unfathomable mines
  Of never-failing skill,
He treasures up his bright designs,
  And works his sovereign will.

3 Ye fearful saints! fresh courage take
  The clouds ye so much dread,
Are big with mercy, and shall break
  In blessings on your head.

4 Judge not the Lord by feeble sense,
  But trust him for his grace;
Behind a frowning providence,
  He hides a smiling face.

5 His purposes will ripen fast,
  Unfolding every hour;
The bud may have a bitter taste,
  But sweet will be the flower.

6 Blind unbelief is sure to err,
  And scan his work in vain;
God is his own interpreter,
  And he will make it plain.
      WILLIAM COWPER, 1772.

82 *Majesty.* Ps. 18.
THE Lord descended from above,
  And bowed the heavens most high:
And underneath his feet he cast
  The darkness of the sky.

2 On cherub and on cherubim
  Full royally he rode;
And on the wings of mighty winds
  Came flying all abroad.

3 He sat serene upon the floods,
  Their fury to restrain;
And he, as sovereign Lord and King,
  For evermore shall reign.
      THOMAS STERNHOLD, d. 1549.

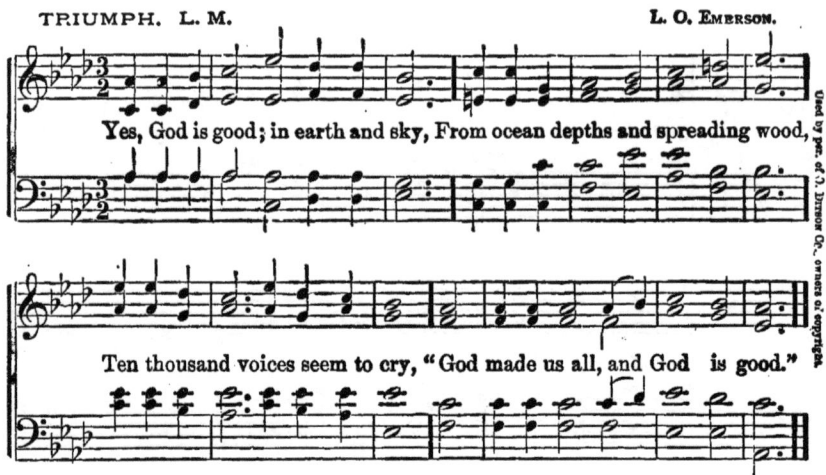

TRIUMPH. L. M.   L. O. EMERSON.

Yes, God is good; in earth and sky, From ocean depths and spreading wood,

Ten thousand voices seem to cry, "God made us all, and God is good."

83 [FIRST VERSE INSERTED IN MUSIC.]
     The Goodness of God.   (176)

2 The sun that keeps his trackless way,
   And downward pours his golden flood,
Night's sparkling hosts all seem to say,
   In accents clear, that God is good.

3 Yes, God is good, all Nature says,
   By God's own hand with speech endued;
And man, in louder notes of praise,
   Should sing for joy that God is good.

4 For all thy gifts, we bless thee, Lord;
   But chiefly for our heavenly food,
Thy pardoning grace, thy quickening word;
   These prompt our song that God is good.
                              JOHN H. GURNEY.

84   *The Eternity of God.*   (173)

ERE mountains reared their forms sublime,
   Or heaven and earth in order stood,
Before the birth of ancient time,
   From everlasting thou art God.

2 A thousand ages in their flight
   With thee are as a fleeting day;
Past, present, future, to thy sight
   At once their various scenes display.

3 But our brief life's a shadowy dream—
   A passing thought, that soon is o'er;
That fades with morning's earliest beam,
   And fills the musing mind no more.

To us, O Lord, the wisdom give,
   Each passing moment so to spend,
That we at length with thee may live
   Where life and bliss shall never end.
                              ISAAC WATTS.

85   *God Seen in Nature.*   (174)

THERE is a God—all nature speaks,
   Through earth, and air, and sea, and skies;
See, from the clouds his glory breaks,
   When earliest beams of morning rise.

2 The rising sun, serenely bright,
   Throughout the world's extended frame,
Inscribes in characters of light
   His mighty Maker's glorious name.

3 Ye curious minds, who roam abroad,
   And trace creation's wonders o'er,
Confess the footsteps of your God—
   Bow down before him and adore.
                              ANNE STEELE.

86   *The Lord God Omnipotent.*   (14)

THE Lord is King; child of the dust!
The Judge of all the earth is just;
Holy and true are all his ways;
Let every creature speak his praise.

2 The Lord is King! lift up thy voice,
Oh, earth! and all ye heavens! rejoice;
From world to world the joy shall ring—
The Lord omnipotent is King.

3 The Lord is King! who then shall dare
Resist his will, distrust his care,
Or murmur at his wise decrees,
Or doubt his royal promises?

4 Oh, when his wisdom can mistake,
His might decay, his love forsake,
Then may his children cease to sing—
The Lord omnipotent is King.
                              JOSIAH CONDER.

FABEN. 8s & 7s. D.   J. H. WILCOX, 1849.

God is love; his mercy brightens All the path in which we rove; Bliss he wakes, and woe he

lightens: God is wisdom, God is love. Chance and change are busy ev - er; Man de-

cays, and ages move; But his mercy waneth nev-er; God is wisdom, God is love.

87 [FIRST STANZA IN MUSIC ABOVE.]
God is Love.

2 E'en the hour the darkest seemeth
  Will His changeless goodness prove;
From the gloom His brightness streameth:
  God is wisdom, God is love.
3 He with earthly cares entwineth
  Hope and comfort from above;
Every-where his glory shineth:
  God is wisdom, God is love.
            Sir John Bowring, 1825.

88 [FIRST STANZA IN MUSIC BELOW.]
The Divine Glory.   (56)

2 Heaven is still with glory ringing,
  Earth takes up the angels' cry—
"Holy, holy, holy!" singing,
  "Lord of hosts! the Lord most high!"
3 Ever thus in God's high praises,
  Brethren! let our tongues unite;
Chief the heart when duty raises
  God-ward at his mystic rite.
            Richard Mant, 1828.

MANNHEIM. 8s & 7s.   From Ludwig von Beethoven, 1800.

Lord! thy glo - ry fills the heav-en; Earth is with its full - ness stored;

Un - to thee be glo - ry giv - en, Ho - ly, ho - ly, ho - ly Lord.

AZMON. C. M.   CARL GOTTHELF GLASER, 1828. Arr. by L. MASON, 1839.

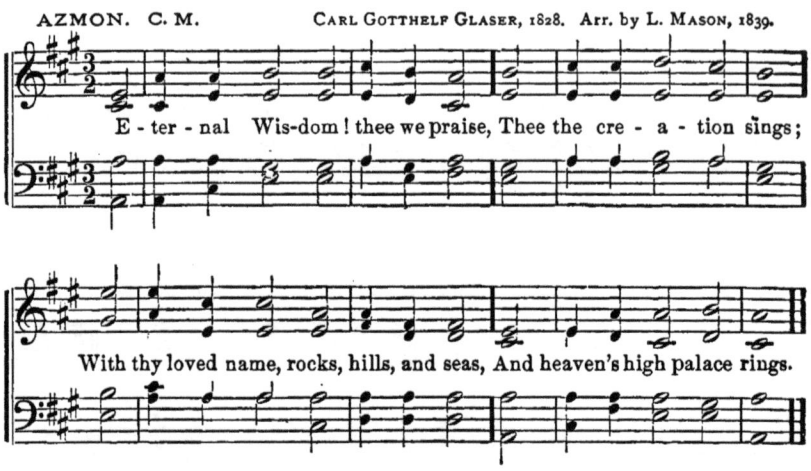

E - ter - nal Wis-dom! thee we praise, Thee the cre - a - tion sings;

With thy loved name, rocks, hills, and seas, And heaven's high palace rings.

89 [FIRST VERSE INSERTED IN MUSIC.]
Creating Wisdom.   (184)

2 Thy hand, how wide it spread the sky!
  How glorious to behold!
Tinged with a blue of heavenly dye,
  And starred with sparkling gold.

3 Infinite strength and equal skill
  Shine through the worlds abroad;
Our souls with vast amazement fill,
  And speak the builder—God.

4 But the sweet beauties of thy grace
  Our softer passions move;
Pity divine, in Jesus' face,
  We see, adore, and love.
                    ISAAC WATTS, 1705.

90   *The Trinity.*   (388)

HAIL! holy, holy, holy Lord,
  Whom One in Three we know;
By all thy heavenly host adored,
  By all thy Church below.

2 One undivided Trinity
  With triumph we proclaim;
The universe is full of thee,
  And speaks thy glorious name.

3 Thee, holy Father, we confess;
  Thee, holy Son, adore;
And thee, the Holy Ghost, we bless,
  And worship evermore.

4 Hail! holy, holy, holy Lord,
  Our heavenly song shall be
Supreme, Essential One, adored
  In co-eternal Three!
                    C. WESLEY, 1767.

91   *God is Love.*   (183)

COME, ye that know and fear the Lord,
  And lift your souls above;
Let every heart and voice accord,
  To sing that—God is love.

2 This precious truth his word declares.
  And all his mercies prove;
Jesus, the Gift of gifts, appears,
  To show that—God is love.

3 Behold his patience lengthened out
  To those who from him rove,
And calls effectual reach their hearts,
  To teach them—God is love.

4 The work begun is carried on
  By power from heaven above;
And every step, from first to last,
  Declares that—God is love.
                    GEORGE BURDER, 1784.

92   *God's Constant Goodness.*   (179)

JEHOVAH God! thy gracious power
  On every hand we see;
Oh, may the blessings of each hour
  Lead all our thoughts to thee.

2 Thy power is in the ocean deeps,
  And reaches to the skies;
Thine eye of mercy never sleeps,
  Thy goodness never dies.

3 In all the varying scenes of time,
  On thee our hopes depend;
In every age, in every clime,
  Our Father and our Friend.
                    JOHN THOMPSON, 1810.

93 GOD IS LOVE. P. M.

E. S. Lorenz.

1. Come, let us all u - nite to sing God is love; Let heav'n and
2. Oh, tell to earth's re - mot -est bound, God is love; In Christ we
3. How hap - py is our por-tion here, God is love; His prom - is-

earth their prais - es bring, God is love; Let ev - 'ry soul from
have re - demp-tion found, God is love; His blood has washed our
es our spir - its cheer, God is love; He is our sun and

sin a - wake, Each in his heart sweet mu-sic make, And sing with us for
sins a - way, His Spir - it turned our night to day, And now we can re-
shield by day, Our help, our hope, our strength and stay; He will be with us

D. S. *Come, let us all u-*

Fine. REFRAIN.

D. S.

Je - sus' sake, For God is love. God is love, God is love.
joice to say That God is love.
all the way; Our God is love. God is love, God is love.

ANON.

nite to sing That God is love.

CAROL. C. M. D.   R. STORRS WILLIS, 1860.

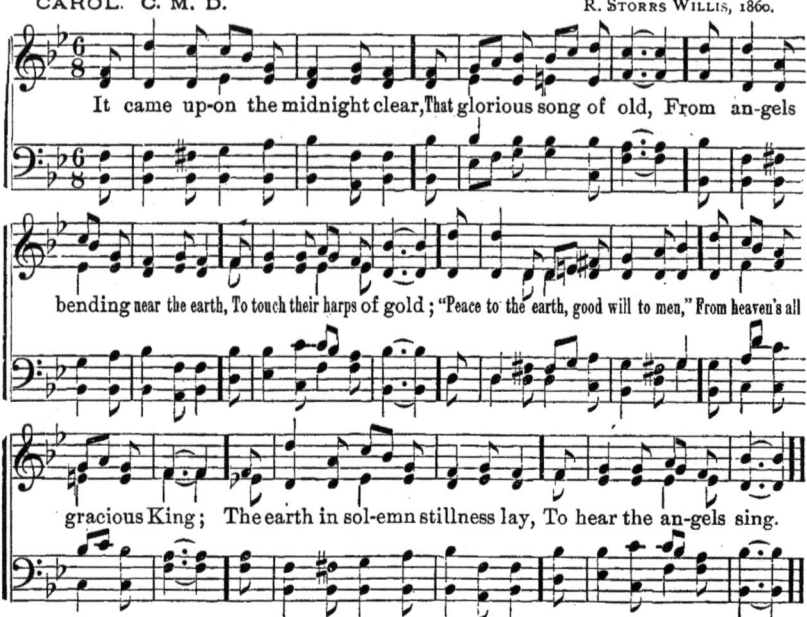

It came up-on the midnight clear, That glorious song of old, From an-gels bending near the earth, To touch their harps of gold; "Peace to the earth, good will to men," From heaven's all gracious King; The earth in sol-emn stillness lay, To hear the an-gels sing.

94   *The Angels' Song.*   (206)

IT came upon the midnight clear,
  That glorious song of old,
From angels bending near the earth,
  To touch their harps of gold;
" Peace to the earth, good-will to men,
  From heaven's all gracious King;"
The earth in solemn stillness lay,
  To hear the angels sing.

2 Still through the cloven skies they come,
  With peaceful wings unfurled;
And still celestial music floats
  O'er all the weary world;
Above its sad and lowly plains
  They bend on heavenly wing,
And ever o'er its Babel sounds,
  The blessed angels sing.

3 O ye, beneath life's crushing load,
  Whose forms are bending low,
Who toil along the climbing way,
  With painful steps and slow;—
Look up! for glad and golden hours
  Come swiftly on the wing;
Oh, rest beside the weary road,
  And hear the angels sing!

4 For lo! the days are hastening on,
  By prophet-bards foretold,
When with the ever-circling years
  Comes round the age of gold!
When peace shall over all the earth
  Its final splendors fling,
And the whole world send back the song
  Which now the angels sing!
                 E. H. SEARS, 1850.

95   *A Light to Lighten the Gentiles.*   (203)

THE race that long in darkness pine
  Have seen a glorious light;
The people dwell in day who dwelt
  In death's surrounding night.
To hail thy rise, thou better Sun,
  The gathering nations come,
With joy, as when the reapers bear
  The harvest treasures home.

2 To us a child of hope is born;
  To us a Son is given;
And him shall all the earth obey,
  And all the hosts of heaven.
His name shall be the Prince of Peace,
  For evermore adored,
The Wonderful, the Counselor,
  The great and mighty Lord.
                 JOHN MORRISON, 1781.

CHRISTMAS. C. M. GEORGE F. HANDEL.

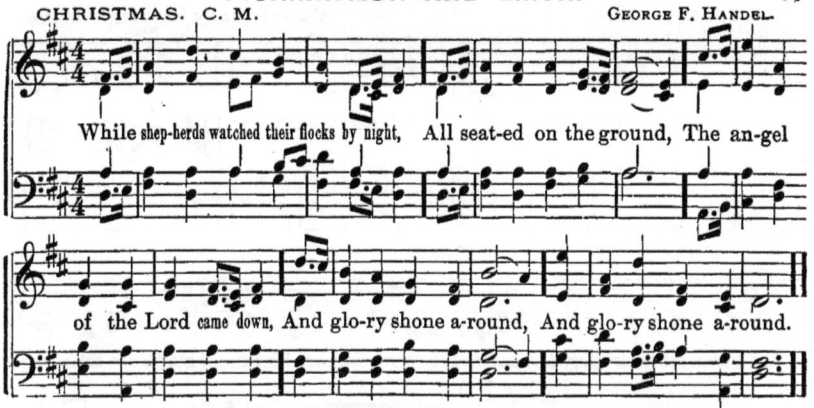

While shep-herds watched their flocks by night, All seat-ed on the ground, The an-gel

of the Lord came down, And glo-ry shone a-round, And glo-ry shone a-round.

96 [FIRST VERSE INSERTED IN MUSIC ABOVE.]
The Angel's Message. (208)

2 "Fear not," said he,—for mighty dread
　Had seized their troubled mind,—
"Glad tidings of great joy I bring
　To you and all mankind.

3 "To you, in David's town, this day,
　Is born of David's line,
The Savior, who is Christ, the Lord;
　And this shall be the sign:

4 "The heavenly babe you there shall find
　To human view displayed,
All meanly wrapped in swathing bands,
　And in a manger laid."

5 Thus spake the seraph; and forthwith
　Appeared a shining throng
Of angels, praising God, and thus
　Addressed their joyful song:

ZERAH. C. M.

6 "All glory be to God on high,
　And to the earth be peace;
Good-will henceforth from heaven to men
　Begin and never cease!"
　　　　　　　　NAHUM TATE, 1696.

97 [FIRST VERSE INSERTED IN MUSIC BELOW.]
The Chorus of Angels. (210)

2 Celestial choirs, from courts above,
　Shed sacred glories there,
And angels, with their sparkling lyres,
　Make music on the air.

3 The answering hills of Palestine
　Send back the glad reply,
And greet, from all their holy heights,
　The day-spring from on high.

4 "Glory to God!" the sounding skies
　Loud with their anthems ring—
"Peace to the earth, good-will to men,
　From heaven's eternal King!"
　　　　　　　　EDMUND H. SEARS, 1835.

LOWELL MASON, 1837.

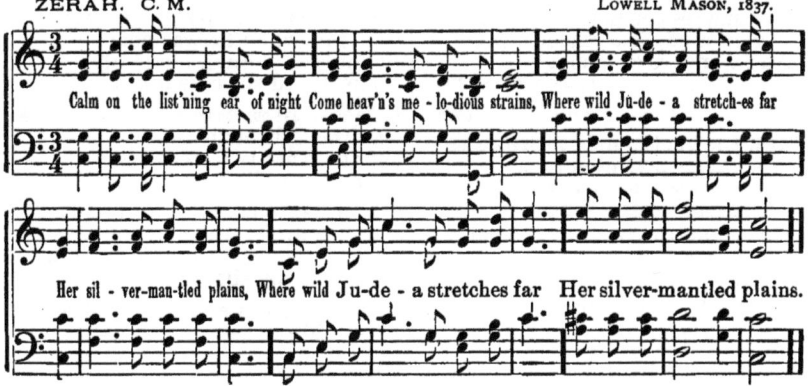

Calm on the list'ning ear of night Come heav'n's me - lo-dious strains, Where wild Ju-de - a stretch-es far

Her sil - ver-man-tled plains, Where wild Ju-de - a stretches far Her silver-mantled plains.

ANTIOCH. C. M.   GEORGE FRED'K HANDEL. Arr. 1839.

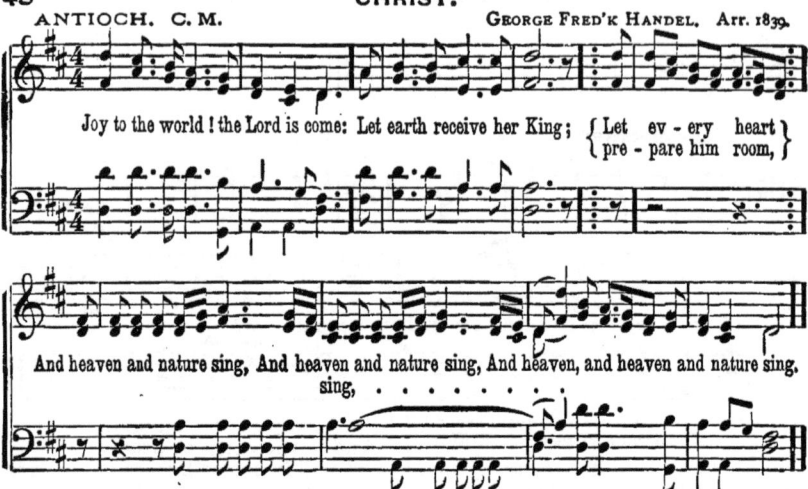

Joy to the world ! the Lord is come: Let earth receive her King; { Let ev-ery heart / pre-pare him room, }

And heaven and nature sing, And heaven and nature sing, And heaven, and heaven and nature sing.
sing, ...

And heaven and nature sing, And heaven and nature sing,

98   *Psalm 98.*   (200)

Joy to the world ! the Lord is come :
  Let earth receive her King ;
Let every heart prepare him room,
  And heaven and nature sing.

2 Joy to the earth ! the Savior reigns :
  Let men their songs employ ;
While fields and floods, rocks, hills, and plains,
  Repeat the sounding joy.

3 No more let sins and sorrows grow,
  Nor thorns infest the ground ;
He comes to make his blessings flow,
  Far as the curse is found.

4 He rules the world with truth and grace,
  And makes the nations prove
The glories of his righteousness,
  And wonders of his love.
              ISAAC WATTS, 1709.

99   *Christ's Mission.*   (202)

HARK the glad sound ! the Savior comes—
  The Savior promised long ;
Let every heart prepare a throne,
  And every voice a song.

2 He comes, the prisoners to release,
  In Satan's bondage held ;
The gates of brass before him burst,
  The iron fetters yield.

3 He comes, the broken heart to bind,
  The bleeding soul to cure ;
And, with the treasures of his grace,
  T' enrich the humble poor.

4 Our glad hosannas, Prince of Peace,
  Thy welcome shall proclaim ;
And heaven's eternal arches ring
  With thy beloved name.
            PHILIP DODDRIDGE, 1735.

100   *Jesus is God.*   (195)

JESUS is God ! the glorious bands
  Of holy angels sing
Songs of adoring praise to him,
  Their Maker and their King.

2 He was true God in Bethlehem's crib,
  On Calvary's cross, true God ;
He who, in heaven, eternal reigned,
  In time, on earth abode.

3 Jesus is God ! there never was
  A time when he was not ;
Boundless, eternal, merciful,
  The Word the Sire begot.

4 Backward our thoughts through ages stretch,
  Onward through endless bliss ;
For there are two eternities,
  And both alike are his.

5 Jesus is God ! oh, could I now,
  But compass land and sea,
To teach and tell this single truth,
  How happy should I be !

6 Oh, had I but an angel's voice,
  I would proclaim so loud,
Jesus, the Good, the Beautiful,
  Is everlasting God.
            FREDERICK WM. FABER, 1862

101 (219) **HERALD ANGELS. 7s D.**
FELIX MENDELSSOHN BARTHOLDY, 1846.

1. Hark! the herald an-gels sing, "Glo-ry to the new-born King! Peace on earth, and
2. See, he lays his glo-ry by, Born that man no more may die; Born to raise the
3. Hail the heaven-born Prince of Peace! Hail the Sun of Right-eous-ness; Light and life to

mer-cy mild, God and sin-ners re-con-ciled." Joyful all ye nations, rise;
sons of earth, Born to give them second birth. Veiled in flesh the Godhead see;
all he brings, Ris'n with healing in his wings. Let us, then, with angels sing,

Join the triumph of the skies! With th' an-gel - ic host proclaim, Christ is born in
Hail th' incarnate De - i-ty. Pleased as man with men to dwell, Je - sus, our Im-
"Glo-ry to the new-born King! Peace on earth, and mer-cy mild, God and sin-ners

Beth - le-hem, With th' an-gel-ic host pro-claim, Christ is born in Beth - le - hem.
man - u - el, Pleased as man with men to dwell, Je - sus, our Im-man-u - el.
re - con-ciled," Peace on earth, and mercy mild, God and sin-ners re - con - ciled.

C. WESLEY, 1739.

102 [TUNE ON OPPOSITE PAGE.] (204)
" Glory to God."

ANGELS rejoiced and sweetly sung
At our Redeemer's birth;
Mortals! awake; let every tongue
Proclaim his matchless worth.

2 Glory to God, who dwells on high,
And sent his only Son
To take a servant's form, and die,
For evils we had done!

3 Good-will to men; ye fallen race!
Arise, and shout for joy;
He comes, with rich abounding grace
To save and not destroy.

4 Lord! send the gracious tidings forth,
And fill the world with light,
That Jew and Gentile, through the earth,
May know thy saving might.
WILLIAM HURN, 1813

103 SALVATION MORNING. 7s & 6s.

E. S. Lorenz.

DUET.

1. What means this glo-rious ra-diance A - cross Ju - de - a's plain?
2. What means this wondrous sto - ry The ho - ly an - gels tell?
3. Why bend these East-ern sa - ges To one ·of low - ly birth?
4. Ye wan-d'rers in earth's darkness, On o - cean deep and land,

These white-winged an - gels sing - ing In such ex - ult-ant strain?
Of one who reigned in heav - en, And now on earth would dwell?
What means this heav'n - ly mes - sage Of love and peace on earth?
Hail! hail! the joy - ful tid - ings, The morn - ing is at hand.

M. E. Servoss.

CHORUS.

The King of glo-ry com-eth, Earth's bro-ken hearts to bind,

And God's sal-va-tion morn-ing Hath dawned for all man-kind.

104   The Forgiving One.   (232)

WHAT grace, O Lord! and beauty shone
  Around thy steps below!
What patient love was seen in all!
  Thy life and death of woe!

2 Thy foes might hate, despise, revile,
  Thy friends unfaithful prove;
Unwearied in forgiveness still,
  Thy heart could only love.

3 Oh, give us hearts to love like thee·
  Like thee, O Lord! to grieve
Far more for others' sins, than all
  The wrongs that we receive.

4 One with thyself, may every eye,
  In us, thy brethren, see
That gentleness and grace that springs
  From union, Lord, with thee.

EDWARD DENNY, 1839.

INVITATION. C. M.   Arr. from W. V. WALLACE, 1856.

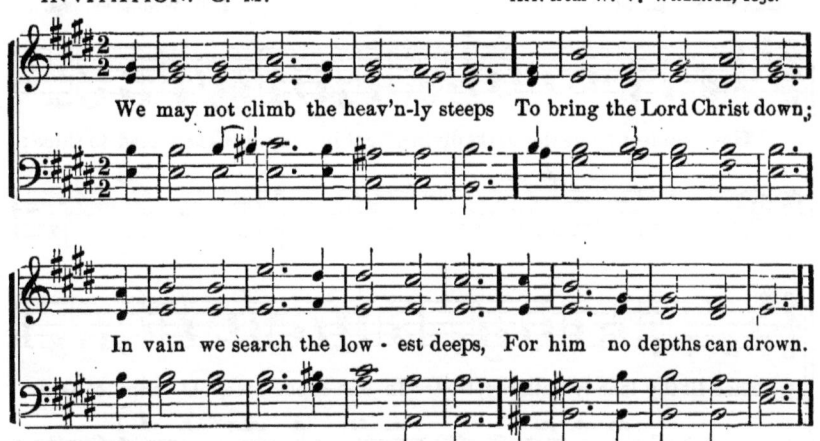

We may not climb the heav'n-ly steeps To bring the Lord Christ down;

In vain we search the low - est deeps, For him no depths can drown.

105   *The True Test.*

WE may not climb the heavenly steeps
  To bring the Lord Christ down;
In vain we search the lowest deeps,
  For him no depths can drown.

2 But warm, sweet, tender, even yet
    A present help is he;
And faith has yet its Olivet,
    And love its Galilee.

3 The healing of the seamless dress
    Is by our beds of pain;
We touch him in life's throng and press,
    And we are whole again.

4 Through him the first fond prayers are said
    Our lips of childhood frame;
The last low whispers of our dead
    Are burdened with his name.

5 O Lord and Master of us all,
    Whate'er our name or sign,
We own thy sway, we hear thy call,
    We test our lives by thine!
                    J. G. WHITTIER.

106   *Childhood of Jesus.*   (228)

IN stature grows the heavenly Child,
    With death before his eyes;
A Lamb unblemished, meek and mild,
    Prepared for sacrifice.

2 The Son of God his glory hides
    With parents mean and poor;
And he who made the heavens abides
    In dwelling-place obscure.

3 Those mighty hands that stay the sky
    No earthly toil refuse;
And he who set the stars on high
    A humble trade pursues.

4 He before whom the angels stand,
    At whose behest they fly,
Now yields himself to man's command,
    And lays his glory by.

5 The Father's name we loudly raise,
    The Son we all adore,
The Holy Ghost, One God, we praise,
    Both now and evermore.
                            ANON.

107   *A Man of Sorrow.*   (229)

A PILGRIM through this lonely world,
    The blessed Savior passed;
A mourner all his life was he,
    A dying Lamb at last.

2 That tender heart which felt for all,
    For us its life-blood gave;
It found on earth no resting-place,
    Save only in the grave.

3 Such was our Lord; and shall we fear
    The cross with all its scorn?
Or love a faithless, evil world
    That wreathed his brow with thorn?

4 No, facing all its frowns or smiles,
    Like him obedient still,
We homeward press, through storm or calm,
    To Zion's blessed hill.
                            H. BONAR.

OLIVET. L. M.   I. B. Woodbury, 1852.

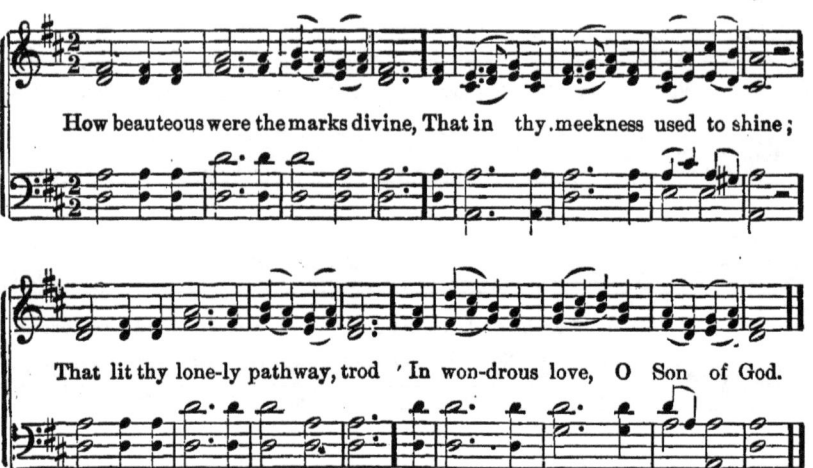

How beauteous were the marks divine, That in thy meekness used to shine;

That lit thy lone-ly pathway, trod 'In won-drous love, O Son of God.

108   *The Meekness of Jesus.*   (242)

How beauteous were the marks divine,
That in thy meekness used to shine;
That lit thy lonely pa hwa , trod
In wondrous love, O Son of God!

2 Oh, who, like thee, so calm, so bright,
Thou God of God, thou Light of Light!
Oh, who, like thee, did ever go
So patient through a world of woe?

3 Oh, who, like thee, so humbly bore
The scorn, the scoffs of men before?
So meek, forgiving, godlike, high,
So glorious in humility?

4 E'en death, which sets the prisoner free,
Was pang, and scoff, and scorn to thee;
Yet love, through all thy torture glowed,
And mercy with thy life-blood flowed.

5 Oh, in thy light, be mine to go,
Illuming all my way of woe!
And give me ever on the road
To trace thy footsteps, Son of God!
      ARTHUR CLEVELAND COXE, 1838.

109   *The Teaching of Jesus.*   (243)

How sweetly flowed the gospel's sound
  From lips of gentleness and grace,
When listening thousands gathered round,
  And joy and reverence filled the place!

2 From heaven he came, of heaven he spoke;
  To heaven he led his followers' way;
Dark clouds of gloomy night he broke,
  Unveiling an immortal day.

3 "Come, wanderers, to my Father's home;
  Come, all ye weary ones, and rest;"
Yes, sacred teacher, we will come,
  Obey thee, love thee, and be blest
      JOHN BOWRING, 1823.

110   *Christ's Example.*   (239)

My dear Redeemer and my Lord,
I read my duty in thy Word;
But in thy life the law appears,
Drawn out in living characters.

2 Such was thy truth, and such thy zeal,
Such deference to thy Father's will,
Such love and meekness so divine,
I would transcribe and make them mine.

3 Cold mountains and the midnight air
Witnessed the fervor of thy prayer;
The desert thy temptations knew;
Thy conflict and thy victory too.

4 Be thou my pattern; make me bear
More of thy gracious image here;
Then God, the Judge, shall own my name
Among the followers of the Lamb.
      ISAAC WATTS. 1709.

OVERBERG. L. M.   J. C. H. RINK, d. 1846.

Be-hold! the blind their sight receive; Be-hold! the dead a-wake and live;

The dumb speak wonders, and the lame Leap, like the hart, and bless his name.

111   *The Miracles of Christ.*   (247)

BEHOLD! the blind their sight receive;
Behold! the dead awake and live;
The dumb speak wonders, and the lame
Leap, like the hart, and bless his name.

2 Thus doth th' eternal Spirit own
And seal the mission of the Son;
The Father vindicates his cause,
While he hangs bleeding on the cross.

3 He dies! the heavens in mourning stood;
He rises, the triumphant God!
Behold the Lord ascending high,
No more to bleed, no more to die.

4 Hence, and forever, from my heart,
I bid my doubts and fears depart;
And to those hands my soul resign,
Which bear credentials so divine.
            ISAAC WATTS, 1709.

112   *Entry into Jerusalem.*   (248)

RIDE on! ride on in majesty!
Hark! all the tribes Hosanna cry;
O Savior meek, pursue thy road
With palms and scattered garments strowed.

2 Ride on! ride on in majesty!
In lowly pomp ride on to die;
O Christ, thy triumphs now begin
O'er captive death and conquered sin.

3 Ride on! ride on in majesty!
The angel armies of the sky
Look down with sad and wondering eyes
To see the approaching sacrifice.

4 Ride on! ride on in majesty!
The last and fiercest strife is nigh;
The Father on his sapphire throne
Awaits his own anointed Son.

5 Ride on! ride on in majesty!
In lowly pomp, ride on to die;
Bow thy meek head to mortal pain,
Then take, O God, thy power and reign.
       HENRY HART MILMAN, 1827.

113   *The Transfiguration.* .   (245)

OH, wondrous type, oh, vision fair,
Of glory that the church shall share,
Which Christ upon the mountain shows,
Where brighter than the sun he glows!

2 From age to age the tale declare,
How with the three disciples there,
Where Moses and Elias meet,
The Lord holds converse high and sweet.

3 The law and prophets there have place,
Two chosen witnesses of grace;
The Father's voice from out the cloud
Proclaimed his only Son aloud.

4 With shining face and bright array,
Christ deigns to manifest to-day,
What glory shall be theirs above
Who joy in God with perfect love!
      Latin. Tr. by J. M. NEALE, 1851.

BAVARIA. 8s & 7s D.   GERMAN.

{ Ev - er would I fain be read-ing, In the an - cient, ho - ly Book,.
Of my Sav - ior's gen - tle pleading, Truth in ev - 'ry word and look.
D. C. How he sought the poor and fear-ful, Called them broth-ers and his own.

How to all the sick and tear - ful Help was ev - er glad - ly shown;

114 [FIRST VERSE IN MUSIC ABOVE.]
Christ our Example. (251)

2 How no contrite soul e'er sought him,
    And was bidden to depart;
How, with gentle words he taught him,
    Took the death from out his heart.
Still I read the ancient story,—
    And my joy is ever new,—
How for us he left his glory,
    How he still is kind and true.

3 How the flock he gently leadeth,
    Whom his Father gave him here;
How his arms he widely spreadeth,
    To his heart to draw us near.
Let me kneel, my Lord! before thee,
    Let my heart in tears o'erflow,
Melted by thy love adore thee,
    Blessed in thee, mid joy or woe.
      Ger., LOUISA HENSEL, 1829.
   Tr., CATHERINE WINKWORTH, 1858.

HEBER. C. M.   GEORGE KINGSLEY, 1838.

Be - hold where, in the Friend of man, Ap-pears each grace di - vine!

The vir - tues all in Je - sus meet, With mild-est ra - diance shine.

115 [FIRST VERSE IN MUSIC ABOVE.]
The Example of Christ. (236)

2 To spread the rays of heavenly light,
    To give the mourner joy,
To preach glad tidings to the poor,
    Was his divine employ.

3 In the last hour of deep distress,
    Before his Father's throne,

With soul resigned, he bowed, and said,
    "Thy will, not mine, be done!"

4 Be Christ our pattern and our guide
    His image may we bear;
Oh, may we tread his sacred steps,
    And his bright glories share.
        WILLIAM ENDFIELD, 1802.

116 WONDERFUL LOVE OF JESUS. P. M.

E. S. Lorenz.

1. In vain in high and ho - ly lays My soul her grateful voice would raise;
2. A joy by day, a peace by night, In storms a calm, in darkness light;
3. My hope for par - don when I call, My trust for lift - ing when I fall;

For who can sing the wor -thy praise Of the won-der-ful love of Je - sus?
In pain a balm, in weakness might, Is the won-der-ful love of Je - sus.
In life, in death, my all in all, Is the won-der-ful love of Je - sus.

E. S. Lorenz.

CHORUS.

Won-der-ful love! won-der-ful love! Won-der-ful love of Je - sus!

Won-der-ful love! won-der-ful love! Won-der-ful love of Je - sus!

OLIVE'S BROW. L. M.   WILLIAM B. BRADBURY, 1853.

'Tis midnight; and on Olive's brow   The star is dimmed that lately shone;

'Tis midnight; in the gar-den, now,   The suffering Savior prays alone.

117 [FIRST VERSE IN MUSIC ABOVE.]
Christ in Gethsemane. (253)

2 'Tis midnight; and, from all removed,
  The Savior wrestles lone with fears;
E'en that disciple whom he loved
  Heeds not his Master's grief and tears.

3 'Tis midnight; and for others' guilt
  The man of sorrows weeps in blood;
Yet he that hath in anguish knelt
  Is not forsaken by his God.

4 'Tis midnight; and from ether plains
  Is borne the song that angels know;
Unheard by mortals are the strains
  That sweetly soothe the Savior's woe.
           W. B. TAPPAN, 1822.

118 [FIRST VERSE IN MUSIC BELOW.] (256)
"Why Hast Thou Forsaken Me?"

2 A horror of great darkness fell
  On thee, thou spotless holy One!
And all the eager hosts of hell
  Conspired to tempt God's only Son.

3 The scourge, the thorns, the deep disgrace,
  These thou could'st bear, nor once repine·
But when Jehovah veiled his face,
  Unutterable pangs were thine.

4 Let the dumb world its silence break;
  Let pealing anthems rend the sky;
Awake, my sluggish soul, awake!
  He died that we might never die.
           JOHN W. CUNNINGHAM, 1820.

WINDHAM. L. M.   DANIEL READ, 1785.

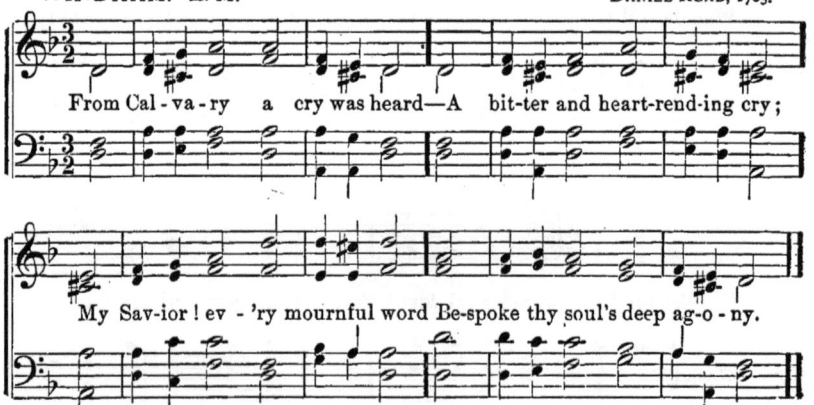

From Cal-va-ry   a   cry was heard—A   bit-ter and heart-rend-ing cry;

My Sav-ior! ev-'ry mournful word Be-spoke thy soul's deep ag-o-ny.

119(261) ZEPHYR. L. M. WILLIAM B. BRADBURY, 1844.

1. When I sur-vey the wondrous cross, On which the Prince of Glo - ry died,
2. For - bid it, Lord, that I should boast, Save in the death of Christ, my God;
3. See, from his head, his hands, his feet, Sor - row and love flow mingled down:
4. Were all the realms of na - ture mine, That were a pres - ent far too small;

My rich-est gain I count but loss, And pour contempt on all my pride.
All the vain things that charm me most, I sac - ri - fice them to his blood.
Did e'er such love and sor - row meet, Or thorns compose so rich a crown?
Love so a - maz - ing, so di-vine, Demands my soul, my life, my all.

ISAAC WATTS, 1707.

120(306) MIRIAM. 7s & 6s. Double. J. P. HOLBROOK.

1. O sacred head, now wounded! With grief and shame weighed down, Now scornfully sur-
2. What thou, my Lord! hast suffered Was all for sinners' gain; Mine, mine was the trans-
3. The joy can ne'er be spo - ken, A-bove all joys be - side, When in thy bod - y

rounded With thorns, thine on - ly crown; O sa-cred head, what glo - ry, What
gres-sion, But thine the dead-ly pain; Lo! here I fall, my Sav-ior! 'Tis
bro - ken, I thus with safe-ty hide; My Lord of life! de - sir - ing Thy

bliss, till now, was thine! Yet tho' despised and gory, I joy to call thee mine.
I deserve thy place; Look on me with thy favor; Vouchsafe to me thy grace.
glo - ry now to see, Beside thy cross ex - pir-ing, I'd breathe my soul to thee.

PAUL GERHARDT, 1659.

AVON. C. M.   HUGH WILSON, 1768.

A - las! and did my Sav - ior bleed? And did my Sovereign die?

Would he de - vote that sa - cred head For such a worm as I?

121 [FIRST VERSE IN MUSIC ABOVE.]
Before the Cross. (281)

2 Was it for crimes that I have done
  He groaned upon the tree?
Amazing pity! grace unknown!
  And love beyond degree!

3 Well might the sun in darkness hide,
  And shut his glories in,
When Christ, the mighty Maker, died
  For man, the creature's sin!

4 Thus might I hide my blushing face,
  While his dear cross appears;
Dissolve my heart in thankfulness,
  And melt mine eyes to tears.

5 But drops of grief can ne'er repay
  The debt of love I owe;
Here, Lord, I give myself away;
  'Tis all that I can do.
                        ISAAC WATTS, 1709.

122 *Jesus Died for Me.*

GREAT God, when I approach thy throne,
  And all thy glory see;
This is my stay, and this alone,
  That Jesus died for me.

2 How can a soul condemned to die,
  Escape the just decree?
Helpless and full of sin am I,
  But Jesus died for me.

3 Burdened with sin's oppressive chain,
  Oh, how can I get free?
No peace can all my efforts gain,
  But Jesus died for me.

4 And, Lord, when I behold thy face,
  This must be all my plea;
Save me by thy almighty grace,
  For Jesus died for me.
                        W. H. BATHURST, d. 1877.

ALAS! AND DID MY SAVIOR BLEED? C. M.   S. J. VAIL.
                              |1st.   Fine.

A - las! and did my Sav - ior bleed? And did my Sovereign die?
Would he de - vote that sa - cred head (Omit) . . . .
D. C. Yes, Je - sus died for all man-kind; Bless God, sal-va - tion's free.

2d. |CHORUS.   D. C. in Chorus.

For such a worm as I?   Je-sus died for you,   and Jesus died for me,
                                for you,   for me,

COWPER. (Fountain.) C. M.   LOWELL MASON, 1830.

O Je-sus! sweet the tears I shed While at thy cross I kneel, Gaze at thy
wounded, fainting head, And all thy sorrows feel, And all thy sorrows feel.

123 *Contrition at the Cross.* (283)

O JESUS! sweet the tears I shed,
  While at thy cross I kneel,
Gaze on thy wounded, fainting head,
  And all thy sorrows feel.

2 My heart dissolves to see thee bleed,
  This heart so hard before;
I hear thee for the guilty plead,
  And grief o'erflows the more.

3 'Twas for the sinful thou didst die,
  And I a sinner stand;
What love speaks from thy dying eye,
  And from each pierced hand!

4 I know this cleansing blood of thine
  Was shed, dear Lord, for me;
For me, for all—oh, grace divine!—
  Who look by faith on thee.
           RAY PALMER, 1867.

124 *Resting Beneath the Cross.* (277)

OPPRESSED with noon-day's scorching heat,
  To yonder cross I flee;
Beneath its shelter take my seat:
  No shade like this for me!

2 Beneath that cross clear waters burst,
  A fountain sparkling free;
And there I quench my desert thirst:
  No spring like this for me!

3 A stranger here, I pitch my tent
  Beneath this spreading tree;
Here shall my pilgrim life be spent:
  No home like this for me!

4 For burdened ones a resting-place
  Beside that cross I see;
Here I cast off my weariness:
  No rest like this for me!
           H. BONAR, 1857.

REMEMBER ME. C. M.   ASA HULL.

A - las! and did my Sav-ior bleed? And did my Sovereign die?
CHO.—Help me, dear Sav - ior, thee to own, And ev - er faith-ful be;
Would he de-vote that sa-cred head For such a worm as I?
And when thou sit - test on thy throne, O Lord, re - mem - ber me.
           ISAAC WATTS.

125 (590) THE CROSS. C. M. with Chorus.   J. H. Stockton.

Slow.

1. The cross,the cross,the blood-stained cross! The hal-low'ed cross I see; Reminding me of
2. The cross,the cross,that heavy cross, My Savior bore for me; It bowed him to the
3. The wounds,the wounds, those pain-ful wounds; Oh, they were made for me! His hands and feet, his
4. The death, the death, the aw-ful death! That Jesus died for me; I heard his groans, his
5. The love,the love,the match-less love, That bled upon the tree! It melts my heart, it

CHORUS. *Slow and soft.*

pre-cious blood   That once was shed for me.
earth with grief   On sad Mount Cal-va-ry.
ho-ly head, All pierced and torn I see.   Oh, the blood, the precious blood, That
pray'r, "Forgive," His bleed-ing side I see.
wins my love, It brings me, Lord, to thee.

J. H. Stockton.

Je-sus shed for me; Up-on the cross, in crimson flood, Just now by faith I see.

Rit.

OWEN. S. M.   J. E. Sweetser, 1849.

Sing rapidly.

Did Christ o'er sin - ners weep,   And shall our cheeks be dry?

Let floods of pen - i - ten-tial grief   Burst forth from ev' - 'ry eye.

By permission.

GORTON. S. M.   LUDWIG VON BEETHOVEN.

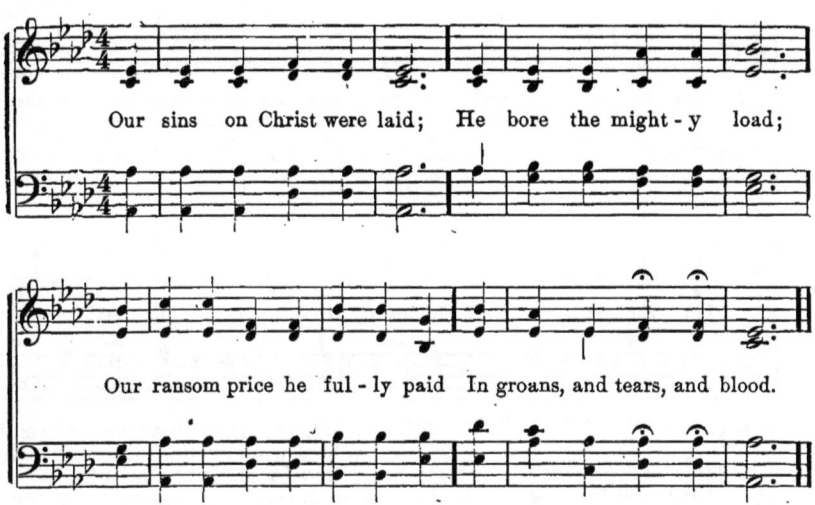

Our sins on Christ were laid; He bore the might-y load;

Our ransom price he ful-ly paid In groans, and tears, and blood.

126 *Our Ransom Paid.* (296)

OUR sins on Christ were laid;
  He bore the mighty load;
Our ransom price he fully paid
  In groans, and tears, and blood.

2 To save a world he dies;
  Sinners, behold the Lamb!
To him lift up your longing eyes;
  Seek mercy in his name.

3 Pardon and peace abound;
  He will your sins forgive;
Salvation in his name is found,—
  He bids the sinner live.

4 Jesus, we look to thee;—
  Where else can sinners go?
Thy boundless love shall set us free
  From wretchedness and woe.
                    J. FAWCETT, 1780.

127 *For Me He died.* (300)

ARE there no wounds for me?
  Hast thou received them all?
How can I, Lord, the anguish see,
  Beneath which thou didst fall?

2 'Tis over now, I know,—
  That suffering life of thine,
Thy precious blood has ceased to flow,
  Thou wear'st thy crown divine;

3 But yet, I weeping see
  The thorns which pierced thy head;
Thou faint'st beneath thy cross for me,
  For me to death thou'rt led!

4 Meekly, with love divine,
  Thy holy head is bent,
And streams of blood, for sins of mine,
  Flow where thy side is rent.

5 Beneath this sacred flood
  I bow my sinful soul;
Dear Savior, let thy precious blood
  Wash me and make me whole.
          MRS. GRACE WEBSTER HINSDALE, 1863

128 *The Savior's Tears.* (298)

DID Christ o'er sinners weep,
  And shall our cheeks be dry?
Let floods of penitential grief
  Burst forth from every eye.

2 The Son of God in tears—
  The wondering angels see!
Be thou astonished, O my soul!
  He shed those tears for thee.

3 He wept—that we might weep—
  Each sin demands a tear;
In heaven alone no sin is found,
  And there's no weeping there.
            BENJAMIN BEDDOME, 1787.

TOPLADY. 7s, 6   Thomas Hastings, 1830.

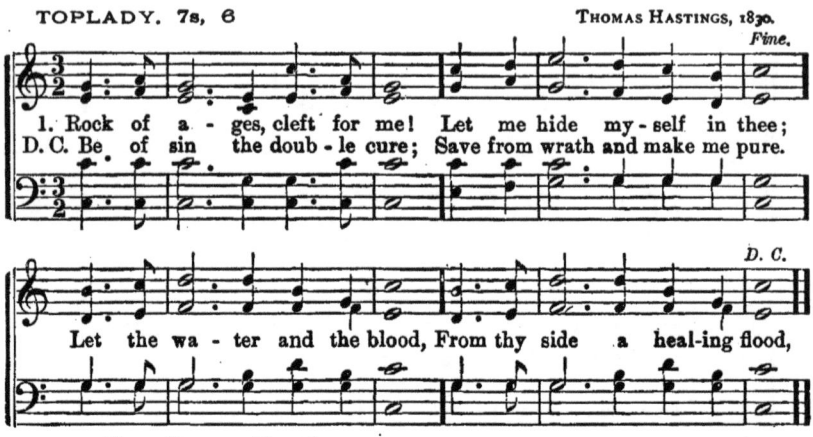

1. Rock of a - ges, cleft for me! Let me hide my - self in thee;
D. C. Be of sin the doub - le cure; Save from wrath and make me pure.

Let the wa - ter and the blood, From thy side a heal-ing flood,

129 [First Verse in Music.] (515)
Rock of Ages.

2 Should my tears forever flow,
Should my zeal no languor know,
All for sin could not atone;
Thou must save, and thou alone;
In my hand no price I bring;
Simply to thy cross I cling.

3 While I draw this fleeting breath,
When mine eyelids close in death,
When I rise to worlds unknown,
See thee on thy judgment throne—
Rock of Ages cleft for me,
Let me hide myself in thee.

          Augustus M. Toplady, 1776.

HOMEWARD. 7s. 8l.   From Franz Abt.

Solo.

Rock of Ages, cleft for me, Let me hide myself in thee; Let the water and the blood, From thy

Chorus.

side a healing flood, Be of sin the double cure—Save from wrath and make me pure. Rock of A-ges,

cleft for me, Let me hide my-self in thee, Let me hide my-self in thee.

SALVATOR MUNDI. 7s. D. E. S. LORENZ.

By thy birth, and by thy tears; By thy human griefs and fears;
By thy conflict in the hour (*Omit*). . . . . . . Of the subtle tempter's power,—Savior, look

with pitying eye; Savior, help me, or I die; Savior, look with pitying eye; Savior, help me, or I die.

130   *The Litany.*   (513)

By thy birth, and by thy tears;
By thy human griefs and fears;
By thy conflict in the hour
Of the subtle tempter's power,—
Savior, look with pitying eye;
Savior, help me, or I die.

2 By the tenderness that wept
O'er the grave where Laz'rus slept;
By the bitter tears that flow'd
Over Salem's lost abode,—
Savior, look with pitying eye;
Savior, help me, or I die.

3 By thy lonely hour of prayer;
By the fearful conflict there;
By thy cross and dying cries;
By thy one great sacrifice,—
Savior, look with pitying eye;
Savior, help me, or I die.

4 By thy triumph o'er the grave;
By thy power the lost to save;
By thy high, majestic throne;
By the empire all thine own,—
Savior, look with pitying eye;
Savior, help me, or I die.

SIR ROBERT GRANT, 1815.

ORON. 7s. 6 lines. I. B. WOODBURY, 1852.

By thy birth, and by thy tears; By thy human griefs and fears;
By thy con-flict in the hour Of the subtle tempter's power,— Savior, look with pitying eye;

Savior, help me, or I die; Savior, help me, Savior, help me, Savior, help me, or I die.

RATHBUN. 8s & 7s.   ITHAMAR CONKEY.

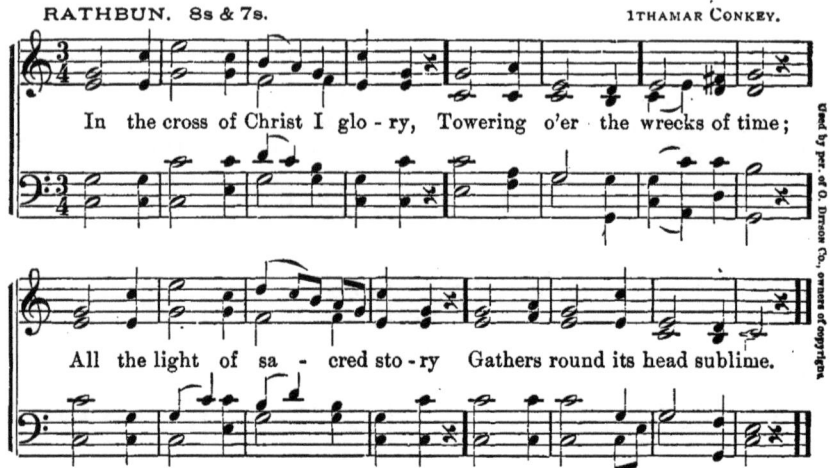

In the cross of Christ I glo-ry, Towering o'er the wrecks of time;

All the light of sa-cred sto-ry Gathers round its head sublime.

131 [FIRST VERSE INSERTED IN MUSIC.]
Glorying in the Cross. (979)

2 When the woes of life o'ertake me,
  Hopes deceive, and fears annoy,
Never shall the cross forsake me;
  Lo! it glows with peace and joy.

3 When the sun of bliss is beaming
  Light and love upon my way,
From the cross the radiance streaming
  Adds more luster to the day.

4 Bane and blessing, pain and pleasure,
  By the cross are sanctified;
Peace is there, that knows no measure,
  Joys that through all time abide.
            SIR JOHN BOWRING, 1825.

132   *Looking to the Cross.* (980)

SWEET the moments, rich in blessing,
  Which before the cross I spend,
Life and health, and peace possessing,
  From the sinner's dying Friend!

2 Here I'll sit, forever viewing
  Mercy's streams in streams of blood:
Precious drops! my soul bedewing,
  Plead, and claim my peace, with God.

3 Truly blessed is this station,
  Low before his cross to lie,
While I see divine compassion
  Floating in his languid eye.

4 Here it is I find my heaven,
  While upon the Lamb I gaze;
Love I much?—I've much forgiven,—
  I'm a miracle of grace.

5 Love and grief my heart dividing,
  With my tears his feet I'll bathe;
Constant still in faith abiding,—
  Life deriving from his death.
      JAMES ALLEN, 1757.
  Altered by WALTER SHIRLEY, 1776.

133   *The Price of Salvation.*

WHEN I view my Savior bleeding,
  For my sins, upon the tree;
Oh, how wondrous!—how exceeding
  Great his love appears to me!

2 Floods of deep distress and anguish,
  To impede his labors, came;
Yet they all could not extinguish
  Love's eternal, burning flame.

3 Now redemption is completed,
  Full salvation is procured;
Death and Satan are defeated,
  By the sufferings he endured.

4 Now the gracious Mediator,
  Risen to the courts of bliss,
Claims for me, a sinful creature,
  Pardon, righteousness, and peace!

5 Sure such infinite affection
  Lays the highest claims to mine;
All my powers, without exception,
  Should in fervent praises join.

6 Jesus, fit me for thy service;
  Form me for thyself alone;
I am thy most costly purchase,—
  Take possession of thine own.
              R. Lee.

134 WHAT HAST THOU DONE FOR ME? P. M.

P. P. Bliss.

Moderato.

1. I gave my life for thee, My precious blood I shed, That thou mightst ransomed be, And
2. My Father's house of light, My glo-ry-circled throne, I left for earthly night, For
3. I suffered much for thee, More than thy tongue can tell, Of bitterest ag-o - ny, To
4. And I have bro't to thee, Down from my home above, Salvation full and free, My

quickened from the dead; I gave, I gave my life for thee, What hast thou given for me?
wand'rings sad and lone; I left, I left it all for thee, Hast thou left aught for me?
res-cue thee from hell; I've borne, I've borne it all for thee, What hast thou borne for me?
pardon and my love; I bring, I bring rich gifts to thee, What hast thou bro't to me?

Frances R. Havergal.

135 COME TO THE CROSS. P. M.

E. S. Lorenz.

Fine.

1. { Come to the cross, where the Sav-ior died, Look to the Lamb that was cru - ci - fied;
{ Turn to the mourn - ful and trag-ic scene, Gaze on the suf - fer-ing Naz-a - rene;
2. { Fall at the feet of the dy - ing One, Trust in the name of the Father's Son;
{ Wash in the fountain of Je-sus' blood, Seek for thy cure in the healing flood;
3. { Fly to the arms of his pard'ning love, Cherish the hope of a crown a - bove;
{ Taste of the sweet-ness of sins for-giv'n, Lean on the promise of rest in heav'n.

Rev. J. H. Martin.

D. C. Come to the cross, where the Sav-ior died, Look to the Lamb that was cru-ci - fied.

CHORUS..

D. C.

Look at the Cru-ci-fied, look and live! Look, for e-ter-nal life he will give.

136   NEAR THE CROSS. P. M.   W. H. DOANE.

1. Jesus, keep me near the cross, There a precious fountain Free to all—a healing stream,
2. Near the cross, a trembling soul, Love and mercy found me; There the bright and morning star
3. Near the cross, O Lamb of God, Bring its scenes before me; Help me walk from day to day,

CHORUS.

Flows from Calvary's mountain.
Shed its beams around me.   In the cross, in the cross, Be my glo-ry ev - er;
With its shadows o'er me.

Till my raptured soul shall find Rest beyond the riv-er.

4 Near the cross I'll watch and wait,
Hoping, trusting ever,
Till I reach the golden strand,
Just beyond the river.
         FANNY J. CROSBY.

137   SAW YE MY SAVIOR? P. M.   AMERICAN SPIRITUAL.

1. Saw ye my Sav-ior, saw ye my Sav-ior, Saw ye my Savior and God? Oh! he
2. He was extend-ed, he was ex - tended, Painfully nailed to the cross; Here he

died on Calva-ry, To atone for you and me, And to purchase our pardon with blood.
bowed his head and died; Thus my Lord was cruci-fied, To a-tone for a world that was lost.

BACA. L. M.
WILLIAM B. BRADBURY.

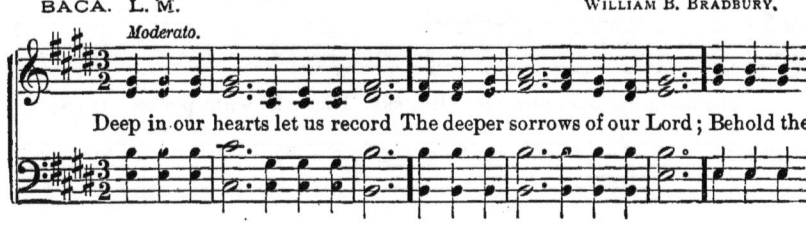

Deep in our hearts let us record The deeper sorrows of our Lord; Behold the

rising billows roll, To overwhelm his holy soul, To overwhelm his holy soul.

138 [FIRST VERSE IN MUSIC.] (264)
Pardon Through the Sufferings of Christ.

2 Yet, gracious God, thy power and love
Have made the curse a blessing prove;
Those dreadful sufferings of thy Son
Atoned for sins that we have done.

3 The pangs of our expiring Lord
The honors of thy law restored;
His sorrows made thy justice known,
And paid for follies not his own.

4 Oh, for his sake our guilt forgive,
And let the mourning sinner live;
The Lord will hear us in his name,
Nor shall our hope be turned to shame.
ISAAC WATTS, 1719.

139 (265)
Peace and Safety at the Cross.

BENEATH thy cross I lay me down,
And mourn to see thy bloody crown;
Love drops in blood from every vein;
Love is the spring of all thy pain.

2 Here, Jesus, will I ever stay,
And spend my longing hours away;

Think on thy bleeding wounds and pain,
And contemplate thy woes again.

3 Oh, unmolested, happy rest!
Where inward fears are all suppressed;
Here I shall love, and live secure,
And patiently my cross endure.
WM. WILLIAMS.

140 (270)
Thanks to Jesus for His Love.

O LOVE! who gav'st thy life for me,
And won an everlasting good
Through thy sore anguish on the tree,
I ever think upon thy blood!

2 O Love! who unto death hast grieved
For this cold heart, unworthy thine,
Whom the cold grave and death received,
I thank thee for that grief divine.

3 I give thee thanks that thou didst die
To win eternal life for me,
To bring salvation from on high:
Oh, draw me up through love to thee!
From the German. Author unknown.

[1ST & 2D VERSES INSERTED IN MUSIC, P. 66.]
Saw Ye My Savior?

3 Hail, mighty Savior! hail, mighty Savior!
Prince, and the Author of peace!
Oh! he burst the bars of death,
And, triumphant from the earth,
He ascended to mansions of bliss.

4 There interceding, there interceding,
Pleading that sinners may live;

Crying, "Father, I have died;
Oh, behold my hands and side!
Oh, forgive them! I pray thee, forgive!"

5 "I will forgive them, I will forgive them
When they repent and believe;
Let them now return to thee,
And be reconciled to me,
And salvation they all shall receive."

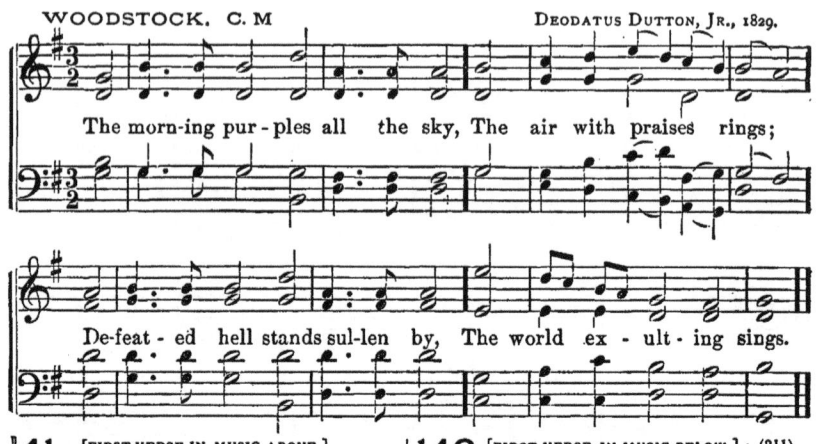

WOODSTOCK. C. M — DEODATUS DUTTON, JR., 1829.

The morn-ing pur - ples all the sky, The air with praises rings;

De-feat - ed hell stands sul-len by, The world ex - ult - ing sings.

141 [FIRST VERSE IN MUSIC ABOVE.]
Christ's Triumph over Death. (309)

2 While he, the King all strong to save,
Rends the dark doors away,
And through the breaches of the grave
Strides forth into the day.

3 Death's captive, in his gloomy prison
Fast fettered he has lain;
But he has mastered death, is risen,
And death wears now the chain.

4 The shining angels cry, "Away
With grief; no spices bring;
Not tears, but songs, this joyful day,
Should greet the rising King!"
DR. A. R. THOMPSON, 1867.

142 [FIRST VERSE IN MUSIC BELOW.] · (311)
Resurrection and Ascension.

2 Death is no more the king of dread,
Since our Immanuel rose;
He took the tyrant's sting away,
And spoiled our hellish foes.

3 See how the conqueror mounts aloft,
And to his Father flies,
With scars of honor in his flesh,
And triumph in his eyes.

4 There our exalted Savior reigns,
And scatters blessings down;
Our Jesus fills the middle seat
Of the celestial throne.
ISAAC WATTS, 1709.

WARWICK. C. M. — SAMUEL STANLEY, 1800.

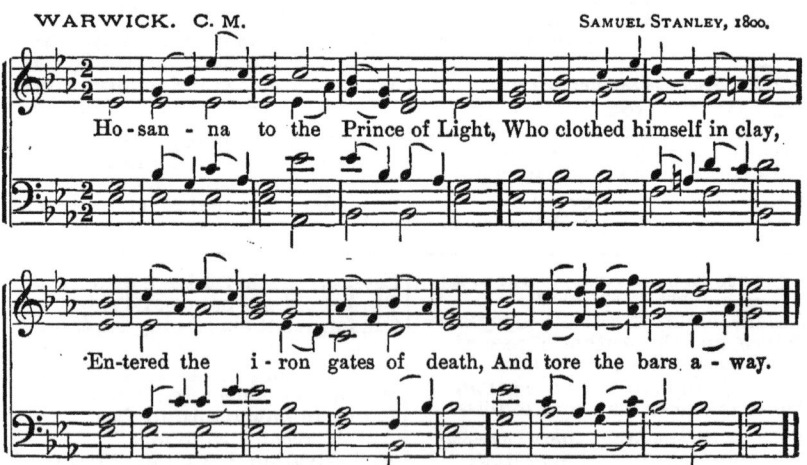

Ho - san - na to the Prince of Light, Who clothed himself in clay,

En-tered the i - ron gates of death, And tore the bars a - way.

NUREMBURG. 7s.　　　　　　　　　　　　　　　　J. R. Ahle, 1664.

Christ, the Lord, is risen to-day, Sons of men and an-gels say:

Raise your joys and triumphs high; Sing, ye heav'ns; thou earth, reply.

143　　*The Lord is Risen.*　(322)

Christ, the Lord, is risen to-day,
Sons of men and angels say:
Raise your joys and triumphs high;
Sing, ye heavens; thou earth, reply.

2 Love's redeeming work is done;
Fought the fight; the battle won:
Lo! our Sun's eclipse is o'er;
Lo! he sets in blood no more.

3 Vain the stone, the watch, the seal—
Christ hath burst the gates of hell;
Death in vain forbids his rise—
Christ hath opened paradise.

4 Lives again our glorious King:
Where, O death, is now thy sting?
Once he died our souls to save:
Where's thy victory, boasting grave?

CHARLES WESLEY, 1739.

EASTER HYMN. 7s.　　　　　　　　　　　　　　J. WORGAN.

Christ, the Lord, is risen to-day; Hal - le-lu - jah! Sons of men and angels

say: Hal - le-lu - jah! Raise your joys and triumphs high: Hal - le-lu-

jah! Sing, ye heav'ns; thou earth, re - ply: Hal - le-lu - jah!

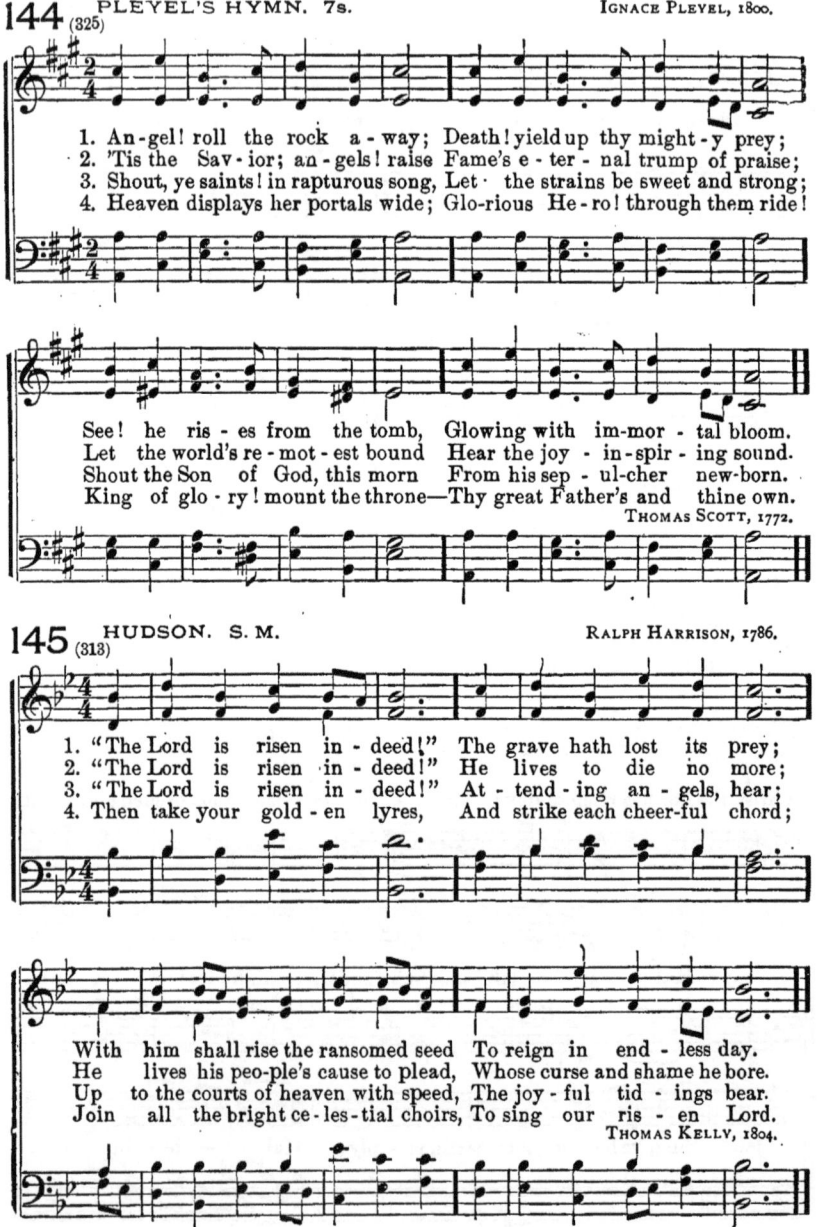

144 (325) PLEYEL'S HYMN. 7s. IGNACE PLEYEL, 1800.

1. An-gel! roll the rock a-way; Death! yield up thy might-y prey;
2. 'Tis the Sav-ior; an-gels! raise Fame's e-ter-nal trump of praise;
3. Shout, ye saints! in rapturous song, Let the strains be sweet and strong;
4. Heaven displays her portals wide; Glo-rious He-ro! through them ride!

See! he ris-es from the tomb, Glowing with im-mor-tal bloom.
Let the world's re-mot-est bound Hear the joy-in-spir-ing sound.
Shout the Son of God, this morn From his sep-ul-cher new-born.
King of glo-ry! mount the throne—Thy great Father's and thine own.

THOMAS SCOTT, 1772.

145 (313) HUDSON. S. M. RALPH HARRISON, 1786.

1. "The Lord is risen in-deed!" The grave hath lost its prey;
2. "The Lord is risen in-deed!" He lives to die no more;
3. "The Lord is risen in-deed!" At-tend-ing an-gels, hear;
4. Then take your gold-en lyres, And strike each cheer-ful chord;

With him shall rise the ransomed seed To reign in end-less day.
He lives his peo-ple's cause to plead, Whose curse and shame he bore.
Up to the courts of heaven with speed, The joy-ful tid-ings bear.
Join all the bright ce-les-tial choirs, To sing our ris-en Lord.

THOMAS KELLY, 1804.

MENDON. L. M.

Arr. LOWELL MASON, 1832.

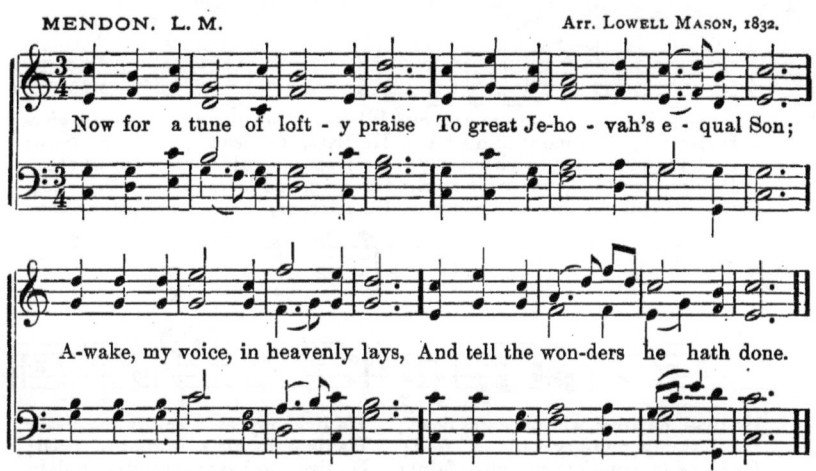

Now for a tune of loft-y praise To great Je-ho-vah's e-qual Son;

A-wake, my voice, in heavenly lays, And tell the won-ders he hath done.

146 [FIRST VERSE IN MUSIC ABOVE.] (318)
Exaltation of Christ.

2 Sing how he left the worlds of light,
And those bright robes he wore above;
How swift and joyful was his flight,
On wings of everlasting love.

3 Among a thousand harps and songs,
Jesus, the God, exalted reigns;
His sacred name fills all their tongues
And echoes through the heavenly plains.
ISAAC WATTS, 1707.

147 *The Lord is Risen Indeed.* (319)

THE morning kindles all the sky;
The heavens resound with anthems high;
The shining angels, as they speed,
Proclaim, "The Lord is risen indeed!"

2 Vainly with rocks his tomb was barred
While Roman guards kept watch and ward;
Majestic from the spoiled tomb,
In pomp of triumph he has come!

3 When the amazed disciples heard,
Their hearts with speechless joy were stirred;

Their Lord's beloved face to see,
Eager they haste to Galilee.

4 His pierced hands to them he shows;
His face with love's own radiance glows;
They with the angel's message speed,
And shout, "The Lord is risen indeed!"
Latin Tr. by MRS. E. CHARLES.

148 *Christ the Unsetting Sun.* (320)

HAIL! morning known among the blest,
Morning of hope, and joy, and love,
Of heavenly peace, and holy rest,
Pledge of the endless rest above.

2 Blest be the Father of our Lord,
Who from the dead hath brought his Son;
Hope to the lost was then restored,
And everlasting glory won.

3 Mercy looked down with smiling eye
When our Immanuel left the dead;
Faith marked his bright ascent on high,
And hope with gladness raised her head.
R. WARDLAW, 1814.

HARMONY GROVE. L. M.

H. K. OLIVER, 1839.

Hail! morning known among the blest, Morning of hope, and joy, and love,
Of heavenly peace, and holy rest, Pledge of the endless rest above.

149   BALTZELL. L. M.   E. S. LORENZ.

1. I know that my Re-deem-er lives! What comfort this sweet sentence gives,
2. He lives, to bless me with his love; He lives, to plead for me a - bove;
3. He lives, to grant me rich sup-ply; He lives, to guide me with his eye;
4. He lives, my kind, wise, heav'n-ly Friend; He lives, and loves me to the end;
5. He lives, all glo - ry to his name! He lives, my Sav - ior still the same—

He lives, he lives, who once was dead; He lives, my ev - er - liv-ing Head.
He lives, my hun-gry soul to feed; He lives, to bless in time of need;
He lives, to com-fort me when faint; He lives, to hear my soul's complaint;
He lives, and while he lives I'll sing: He lives, my Prophet, Priest, and King.
Oh, the sweet joy this sentence gives: I know that my Re-deem-er lives.

SAMUEL MEDLEY, 1789.

150(329)   DORT. 6s & 4s.   DR. L. MASON, 1832.

1. Rise, glorious Conqueror, rise, Into thy native skies, As-sume thy right; And where, in
2. Vic - tor o'er death and hell, Cherubic legions swell The radiant strain; Praises all
3. En - ter, in-car-nate God! No feet but thine have trod The serpent down; Blow the full
4. Li - on of Ju-dah, hail! And let thy name prevail From age to age; Lord of the

many a fold, The clouds are back-ward rolled; Pass thro' those gates of gold, And reign in light.
heav'n inspire; Each angel sweeps his lyre, And claps his wings of fire; Thou Lamb, once slain.
trumpets, blow! Wider your portals throw! Savior, triumphant, go And take thy crown.
rolling years, Claim for thine own the spheres, For thou hast bought with tears Thine her-i - tage.

MATTHEW BRIDGES, 1848.

HARWELL. 8s & 7s. D.   LOWELL MASON.

{ Hark ! ten thousand harps and voices Sound the notes of praise a–bove ;   See, he sits on yonder throne,
{ Je - sus reigns, and heav'n rejoices ; Je - sus reigns, the God of love ;   See, he sits

Je-sus rules the world a-lone, Hal-le - lu-jah, hallelujah, hal-le-lu-jah, A - men.

Jesus rules

151 *Jesus Reigns.* (354)

HARK! ten thousand harps and voices
  Sound the note of praise above;
Jesus reigns, and heaven rejoices;
  Jesus reigns, the God of love:
See, he sits on yonder throne;
Jesus rules the world alone.

2 King of glory! reign forever—
  Thine an everlasting crown;
Nothing, from thy love, shall sever
  Those whom thou hast made thine own;
Happy objects of thy grace,
Destined to behold thy face.

3 Savior! hasten thine appearing;
  Bring, oh, bring the glorious day,
When, the awful summons hearing,
  Heaven and earth shall pass away;—
Then, with golden harps, we'll sing,—
"Glory, glory to our King!"
         THOMAS KELLY, 1806.

152 *The Return to Heaven.* (353)

JESUS comes, his conflict over,—
  Comes to claim his great reward;
Angels round the Victor hover,
  Crowding to behold their Lord;
Haste, ye saints! your tribute bring,
Crown him, everlasting King.

2 Yonder throne for him erected,
  Now becomes the Victor's seat;
Lo, the Man on earth rejected!
  Angels worship at his feet:
Haste, ye saints! your tribute bring,
Crown him, everlasting King.

3 Day and night they cry before him,—
  "Holy, holy, holy Lord!"
All the powers of heaven adore him,
  All obey his sovereign word;
Haste, ye saints! your tribute bring,
Crown him, everlasting King.
         THOMAS KELLY, 1806.

153 *We Live in Him.* (333)

SEE, the Conqueror mounts in triumph
  See the King in royal state,
Riding on the clouds, his chariot,
  To his heavenly palace gate!
Hark! the choirs of angel voices
  Joyful hallelujahs sing,
And the portals high are lifted
  To receive their heavenly King.

2 Who is this that comes in glory,
  With the trump of jubilee?
Lord of battles, God of armies,
  He has gained the victory;
He, who on the cross did suffer,
  He, who from the grave arose,
He has vanquished sin and Satan,
  He by death has spoiled his foes.

3 Thou hast raised our human nature,
  On the clouds to God's right hand;
There we sit in heavenly places,
  There with thee in glory stand;
Jesus reigns, adored by angels;
  Man with God is on the throne;
Mighty Lord! in thine ascension,
  We by faith behold our own.
       CHRISTOPHER WORDSWORTH, 1862.

CORONATION. C. M.

OLIVER HOLDEN, 1793.

All hail the power of Jesus' name, Let angels prostrate fall; Bring forth the roy-al di-a-dem,

And crown him Lord of all, Bring forth the royal diadem, And crown him Lord of all.

[FIRST VERSE IN MUSIC.]

154 *Crown Him Lord of all.* (336)

2 Crown him, ye morning stars of light,
Who fixed this earthly ball;
Now hail the strength of Israel's might,
And crown him Lord of all.

3 Ye chosen seed of Israel's race,
Ye ransomed from the fall,
Hail him who saves you by his grace,
And crown him Lord of all.

4 Sinners, whose love can ne'er forget
The wormwood and the gall;

Go, spread your trophies at his feet,
And crown him Lord of all.

5 Let every kindred, every tribe,
On this terrestrial ball,
To him all majesty ascribe,
And crown him Lord of all.

6 O that with yonder sacred throng
We at his feet may fall!
We'll join the everlasting song,
And crown him Lord of all.
EDWARD PERRONET, *alt.* 1780.

MILES' LANE. C. M.

WM. SHRUBSOLE, 1793.

All hail the pow'r of Jesus' name, Let angels prostrate fall; Bring forth the

roy-al di-a-dem, And crown him, crown him, crown him, crown him Lord of all.

ELIZABETHTOWN. C. M. GEORGE KINGSLEY, 1838.

Come, let us join in songs of praise To our as-cend-ed Priest;

He entered heaven with all our names En-grav-en on his breast.

155 *The Sympathy of Jesus.* (338)

COME, let us join in songs of praise
To our ascended Priest;
He entered heaven with all our names
Engraven on his breast.

2 Below he washed our guilt away,
By his atoning blood;
Now he appears before the throne,
And pleads our cause with God.

3 Clothed with our nature still, he knows
The weakness of our frame,
And how to shield us from the foes
Which he himself o'ercame.

4 Oh! may we ne'er forget his grace,
Nor blush to wear his name;
Still may our hearts hold fast his faith,
Our mouths his praise proclaim.
ANON. 1818.

156 *Perfect Through Suffering.* (337)

THE head, that once was crowned with thorns,
Is crowned with glory now;
A royal diadem adorns
The mighty Victor's brow.

2 The highest place that heaven affords
Is his—is his by right;
"The King of kings, and Lord of lords,"
And heaven's eternal Light.

3 The joy of all who dwell above,
The joy of all below,
To whom he manifests his love,
And grants his name to know.

4 To them the cross, with all its shame,
With all its grace, is given;
Their name—an everlasting name;
Their joy—the joy of heaven.

5 They suffer with their Lord below,
They reign with him above;
Their profit and their joy—to know
The mystery of his love.

6 The cross he bore is life and health—
Though shame and death to him;
His people's hope, his people's wealth,
Their everlasting theme.
THOMAS KELLY, 1820.

157 *Christ's Compassion to the Weak.* (341)

WITH joy we meditate the grace
Of our High Priest above;
His heart is made of tenderness,
His bowels melt with love.

2 Touched with a sympathy within,
He knows our feeble frame;
He knows what sore temptations mean,
For he has felt the same.

3 He, in the days of feeble flesh,
Poured out his cries and tears;
And, in his measure, feels afresh
What every member bears.

4 Then let our humble faith address
His mercy and his power;
We shall obtain delivering grace
In the distressing hour.
ISAAC WATTS, 1709.

158 THE COMING OF THE KINGDOM. P. M.

James McGranahan.

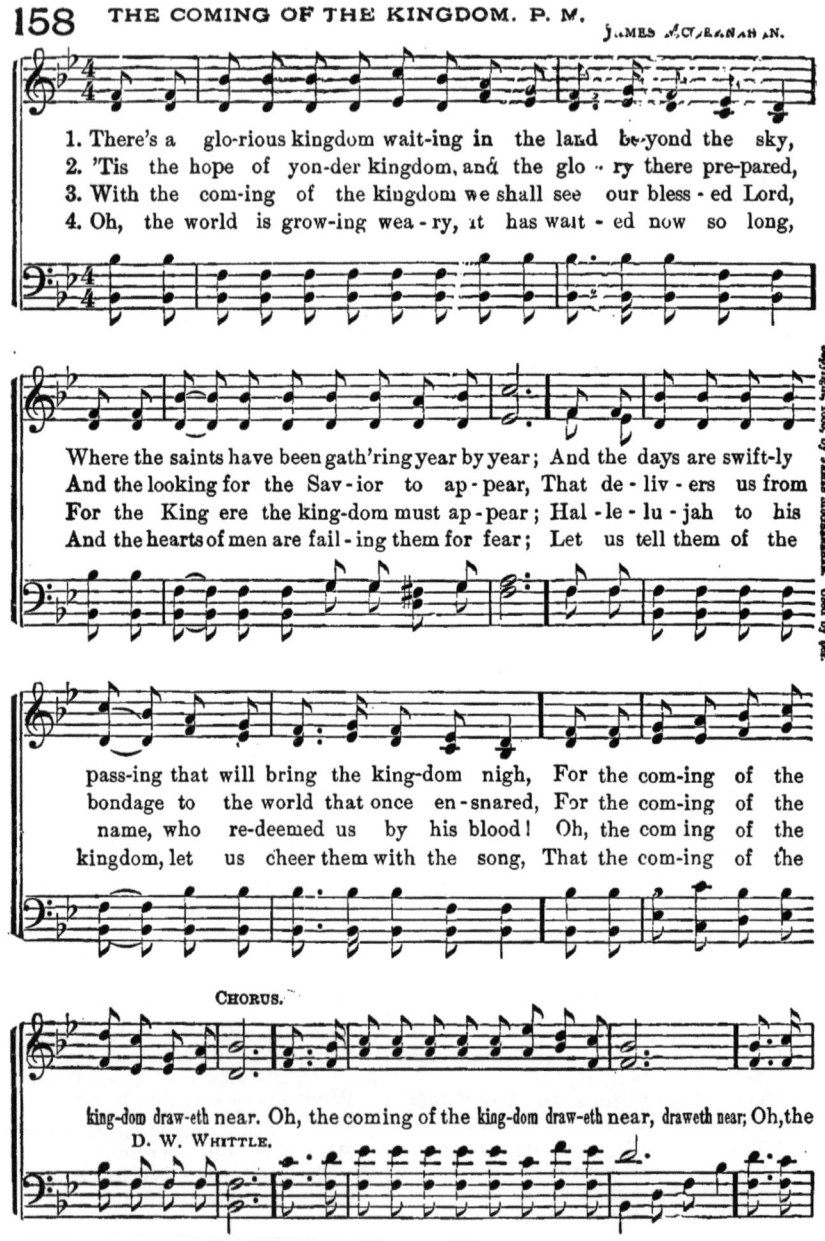

1. There's a glo-rious kingdom wait-ing in the land be-yond the sky,
2. 'Tis the hope of yon-der kingdom, and the glo - ry there pre-pared,
3. With the com-ing of the kingdom we shall see our bless - ed Lord,
4. Oh, the world is grow-ing wea - ry, it has wait - ed now so long,

Where the saints have been gath'ring year by year; And the days are swift-ly
And the looking for the Sav-ior to ap-pear, That de - liv - ers us from
For the King ere the king-dom must ap-pear; Hal - le - lu - jah to his
And the hearts of men are fail - ing them for fear; Let us tell them of the

pass-ing that will bring the king-dom nigh, For the com-ing of the
bondage to the world that once en-snared, For the com-ing of the
name, who re-deemed us by his blood! Oh, the com ing of the
kingdom, let us cheer them with the song, That the com-ing of the

CHORUS.

king-dom draw-eth near. Oh, the coming of the king-dom draw-eth near, draweth near; Oh, the

D. W. Whittle.

THE COMING OF THE KINGDOM. Concluded.

com-ing of the kingdom draweth near, draweth near! Be thou ready, O my soul,

for the trumpet soon may roll, And the King in his glory shall ap-pear.

159(224) LEBANON VALLEY. 8s & 7s.

E. S. LORENZ.

1. Come, thou long - ex-pect-ed Je - sus! Born to set thy peo - ple free!
2. Is-rael's strength and con-so - la - tion, Hope of all the earth thou art;
3. Born, thy peo-ple to de - liv - er; Born a child, and yet a King;
4. By thine own e - ter-nal spir - it Rule in all our hearts a - lone;

From our fears and sins re-lease us, Let us find our rest in thee.
Dear de-sire of ev - 'ry na-tion, Joy of ev - 'ry long-ing heart.
Born to reign in us for ev - er, Now thy gracious kingdom bring.
By thine all - suf - fi - cient mer - it Raise us to thy glorious throne.

CHARLES WESLEY, 1744.

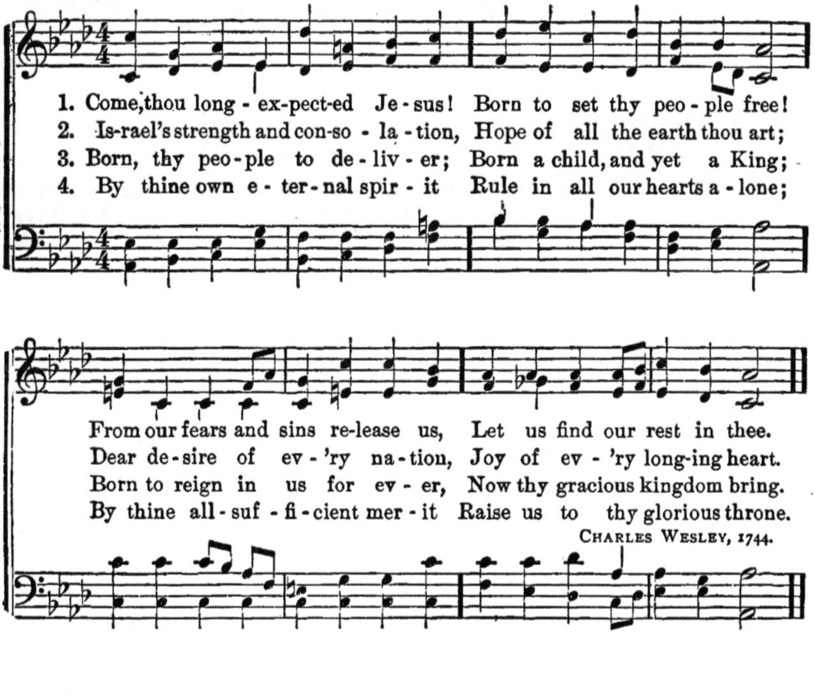

160 THE CROWNING DAY. 7s & 6s.

JAMES McGRANAHAN.

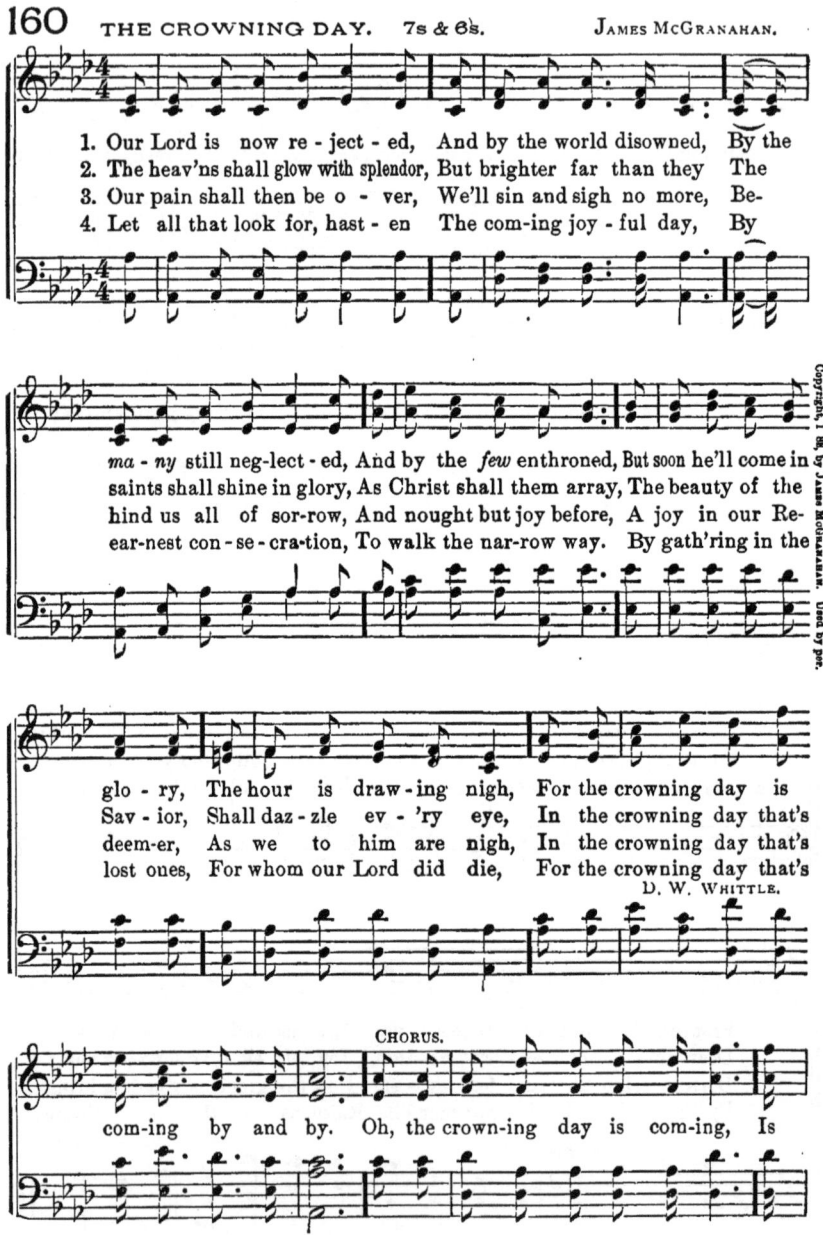

1. Our Lord is now re - ject - ed, And by the world disowned,
2. The heav'ns shall glow with splendor, But brighter far than they
3. Our pain shall then be o - ver, We'll sin and sigh no more,
4. Let all that look for, hast - en The com-ing joy - ful day,

By the ma - ny still neg-lect - ed, And by the *few* enthroned, But soon he'll come in
The saints shall shine in glory, As Christ shall them array, The beauty of the
Be-hind us all of sor-row, And nought but joy before, A joy in our Re-
By ear-nest con - se - cra-tion, To walk the nar-row way. By gath'ring in the

glo - ry, The hour is draw-ing nigh, For the crowning day is
Sav - ior, Shall daz - zle ev - 'ry eye, In the crowning day that's
deem-er, As we to him are nigh, In the crowning day that's
lost ones, For whom our Lord did die, For the crowning day that's

D. W. WHITTLE.

CHORUS.

com-ing by and by. Oh, the crown-ing day is com-ing, Is

THE CROWNING DAY. Concluded.

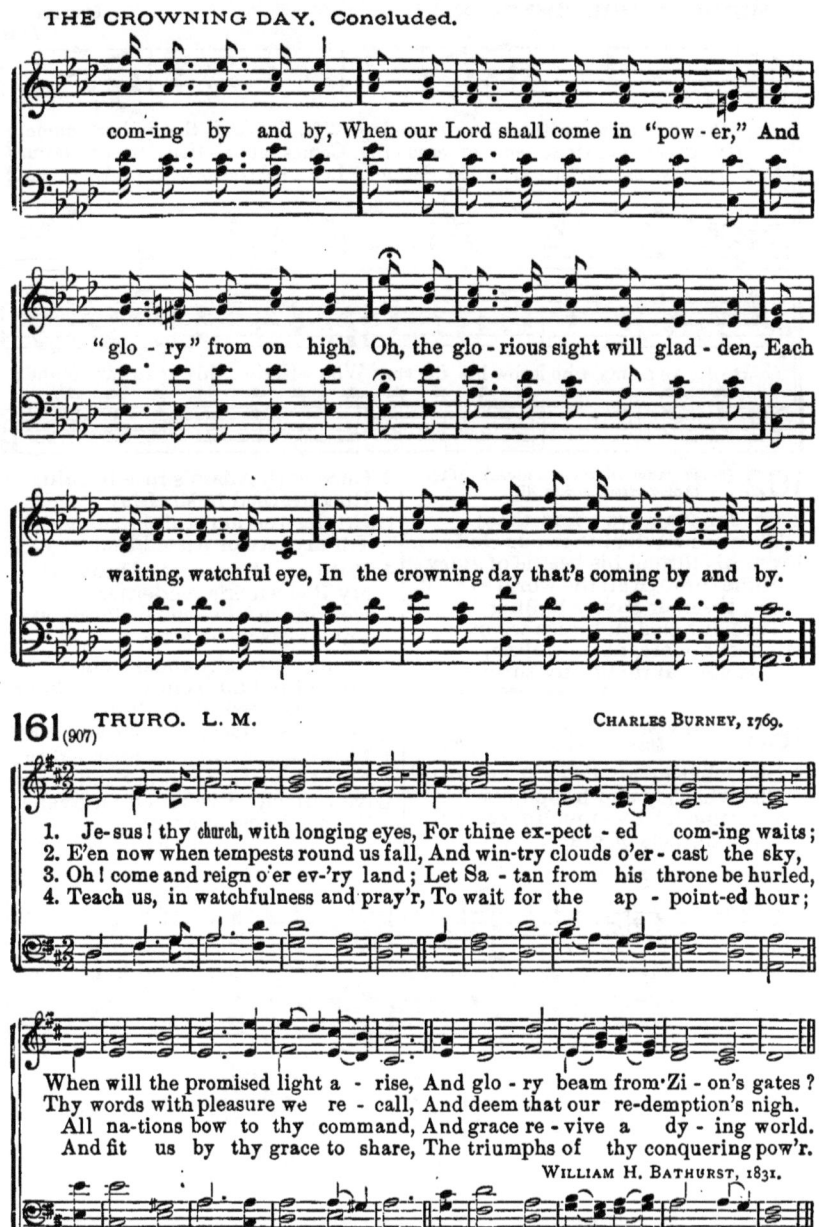

coming by and by, When our Lord shall come in "pow-er," And

"glo-ry" from on high. Oh, the glo-rious sight will glad-den, Each

waiting, watchful eye, In the crowning day that's coming by and by.

161(907) TRURO. L. M.   CHARLES BURNEY, 1769.

1. Je-sus! thy church, with longing eyes, For thine ex-pect-ed coming waits;
2. E'en now when tempests round us fall, And win-try clouds o'er-cast the sky,
3. Oh! come and reign o'er ev-'ry land; Let Sa-tan from his throne be hurled,
4. Teach us, in watchfulness and pray'r, To wait for the ap-point-ed hour;

When will the promised light a-rise, And glo-ry beam from Zi-on's gates?
Thy words with pleasure we re-call, And deem that our re-demption's nigh.
All na-tions bow to thy command, And grace re-vive a dy-ing world.
And fit us by thy grace to share, The triumphs of thy conquering pow'r.

WILLIAM H. BATHURST, 1831.

MIDDLETOWN. 8s & 7s. D.   ENGLISH.

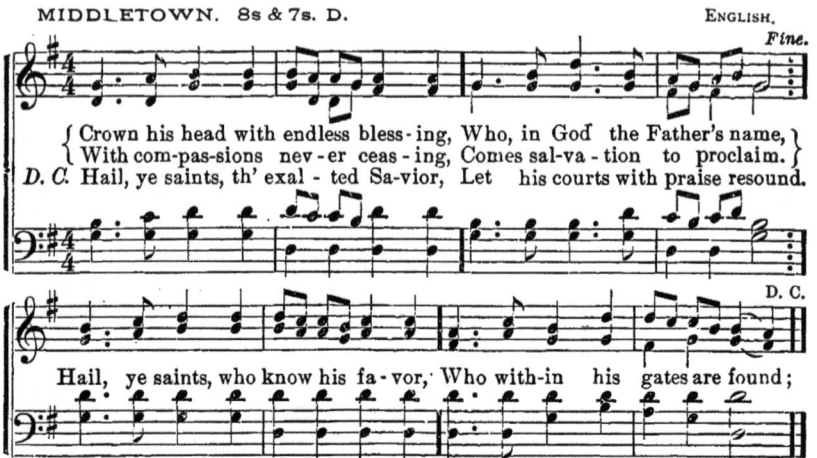

{ Crown his head with endless bless-ing, Who, in God the Father's name, }
{ With com-pas-sions nev-er ceas-ing, Comes sal-va-tion to proclaim. }
D. C. Hail, ye saints, th' exal-ted Sa-vior, Let his courts with praise resound.

Hail, ye saints, who know his fa-vor, Who with-in his gates are found;

162 [FIRST VERSE IN MUSIC ABOVE.] (615)
Crown Him Lord of All.

2 Lo, Jehovah, we adore thee;
  Thee our Savior! thee our God!
From his throne his beams of glory
  Shine through all the world abroad.
Jesus, thee our Savior hailing,
  Thee our God in praise we own;
Highest honors, never failing,
  Rise eternal round thy throne.
             WILLIAM GOODE, 1811.

163 [FIRST VERSE IN MUSIC BELOW.] (616)
Much Forgiven.

2 Oh! what mercy flows from heaven!
  Oh! what joy and happiness!
Love I much? I've much forgiven;
  I'm a miracle of grace.

3 Once with Adam's race in ruin,
  Unconcerned in sin I lay;
Swift destruction still pursuing,
  Till my Savior passed that way.

4 Witness, all ye host of heaven!
  My Redeemer's tenderness;
Love I much? I've much forgiven;
  I'm a miracle of grace.

5 Shout, ye bright angelic choir!
  Praise the Lamb enthroned above;
Whilst, astonished, I admire
  God's free grace, and boundless love.

6 That blest moment, I received him,
  Filled my soul with joy and peace:
Love I much? I've much forgiven;
  I'm a miracle of grace.
            JOHN WINGROVE, 1806.

ABT. 8s & 7s.   Arranged from ABT.

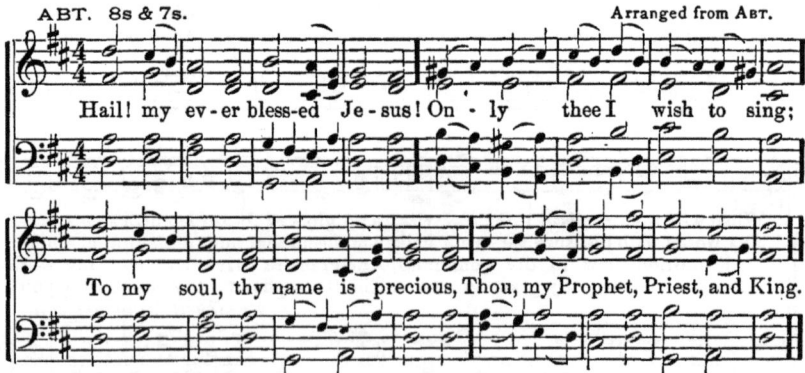

Hail! my ev-er bless-ed Je-sus! On-ly thee I wish to sing;

To my soul, thy name is precious, Thou, my Prophet, Priest, and King.

OLIVET. 6s & 4s.   LOWELL MASON, 1831.

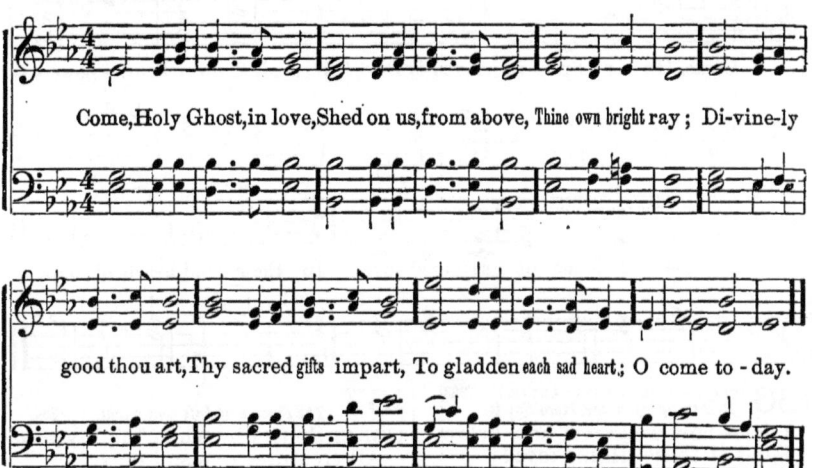

Come, Holy Ghost, in love, Shed on us, from above, Thine own bright ray ; Di-vine-ly

good thou art, Thy sacred gifts impart, To gladden each sad heart.; O come to-day.

164   *Veni, Sancte, Spiritus!*   (386)

COME, Holy Ghost! in love,
Shed on us, from above,
  Thine own bright ray:
Divinely good thou art;
Thy sacred gifts impart,
To gladden each sad heart;
  Oh! come to-day!

2 Come, tenderest Friend, and best,
Our most delightful Guest!
  With soothing power;
Rest, which the weary know;
Shade, 'mid the noontide glow;
Peace, when deep griefs o'erflow;
  Cheer us, this hour!

3 Come, Light serene, and still
Our inmost bosoms fill;
  Dwell in each breast;
We know no dawn but thine;
Send forth thy beams divine,
On our dark souls to shine,
  And make us blest.

4 Exalt our low desires;
Extinguish passion's fires;
  Heal every wound;
Our stubborn spirits bend;
Our icy coldness end;
Our devious steps attend,
  While heavenward bound.
        Lat., ROBERT II. of France, 996.
        Tr., RAY PALMER, 1858.

165   *The Spirit of Truth.*   (387)

THOU! whose almighty word
Chaos and darkness heard,
  And took their flight,
Hear us, we humbly pray,
And, where the gospel's day
Sheds not its glorious ray,
  "Let there be light!"

2 Thou! who didst come to bring,
On thy redeeming wing,
  Healing and sight,
Health to the sick in mind,
Sight to the inly blind;—
Oh! now to all mankind,
  "Let there be light!"

3 Spirit of truth and love,
Life-giving holy Dove!
  Speed forth thy flight:
Move o'er the water's face,
Bearing the lamp of grace,
And, in earth's darkest place,
  "Let there be light!"
        JOHN MARRIOTT. 1813.

BALERMA. C. M.   Adapted by R. Simpson.

Come, Ho - ly Spir - it, heaven-ly Dove! With all thy quickening powers,—

Kin-dle a flame of sa - cred love, In these cold hearts of ours.

166 [FIRST VERSE IN MUSIC ABOVE.] (363)
Breathing after the Holy Spirit.

2 Look—how we grovel here below,
  Fond of these trifling toys!
Our souls, how heavily they go,
  To reach eternal joys.

3 In vain we tune our formal songs,
  In vain we strive to rise;
Hosannas languish on our tongues,
  And our devotion dies.

4 Dear Lord! and shall we ever live,
  At this poor dying rate?
Our love so faint, so cold to thee,
  And thine to us so great?

5 Come, Holy Spirit, heavenly Dove!
  With all thy quickening powers;
Come, shed abroad a Savior's love,
  And that shall kindle ours.
            ISAAC WATTS, 1707.

167 *The Source of Life and Light.* (364)

GREAT Spirit! by whose mighty powe
  All creatures live and move,
On us thy benediction shower;
  Inspire our souls with love.

2 Hail, Source of light! arise and shine;
  Darkness and doubt dispel;
Give peace and joy, for we are thine;
  In us forever dwell.

3 From death to life our spirits raise;
  Complete redemption bring;
New tongues impart, to speak the praise
  Of Christ, our God and King.

4 Thine inward witness bear, unknown
  To all the world beside;
Exalting, then, we feel, and own
  Our Jesus glorified.
            THOMAS HAWEIS, 1792.

STEPHENS. C. M.   W. JONES, 1780.

Great Spir - it! by whose might-y pow'r All crea-tures live and move,

On us thy ben - e - dic - tion show'r; In-spire our souls with love.

ARLINGTON. C. M.   THOMAS A. ARNE, 1762.

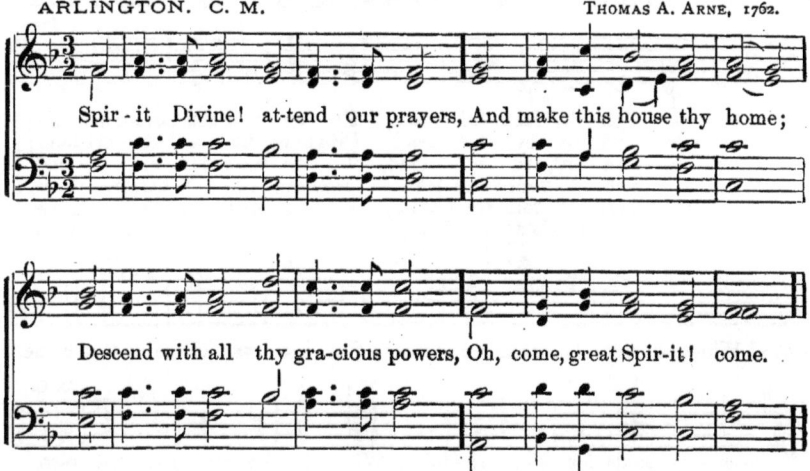

Spir-it Divine! at-tend our prayers, And make this house thy home;

Descend with all thy gra-cious powers, Oh, come, great Spir-it! come.

168 *The Descent of the Spirit.* (369)
SPIRIT Divine! attend our prayers,
 And make this house thy home;
Descend with all thy gracious powers,
 Oh, come, great Spirit! come.

2 Come as the light; to us reveal
 Our emptiness and woe;
And lead us in those paths of life
 Where all the righteous go.

3 Come as the fire; and purge our hearts,
 Like sacrificial flame;
Let our whole soul an offering be
 To our Redeemer's name.

4 Come as the dove; and spread thy wings,
 The wings of peaceful love;
And let thy church on earth become
 Blessed as the church above.

5 Come as the wind; with rushing sound,
 And pentecostal grace;
That all, of woman born, may see
 The glory of thy face.
                    ANDREW REED, 1841.

169 *Assurance.*
WHY should the children of a King
 Go mourning all their days?
Great Comforter, descend, and bring
 Some tokens of thy grace.

2 Dost thou not dwell in all the saints,
 And seal the heirs of heaven?
When wilt thou banish my complaints,
 And show my sins forgiven?

3 Assure my conscience of her part
 In the Redeemer's blood;
And bear thy witness with my heart,
 That I am born of God.

4 Thou art the earnest of his love,
 The pledge of joys to come;
And thy soft wings, celestial Dove,
 Will safe convey me home.
                    ISAAC WATTS, 1709.

170 *The Spirit's Work.* (366)
ETERNAL Spirit! by whose power
 Are burst the bands of death,
On our cold hearts thy blessing shower,
 And stir them with thy breath.

2 'Tis thine to point the heavenly way,
 Each rising fear control,
And, with a warm, enlivening ray,
 To melt the icy soul.

3 'Tis thine to cheer us when distressed,
 To raise us when we fall;
To calm the doubting, troubled breast,
 And aid when sinners call.

4 'Tis thine to bring God's sacred word,
 And write it on our heart;
There its reviving truths record,
 And there its peace impart.

5 Almighty Spirit! visit thus
 Our hearts, and guide our ways;
Pour down thy quickening grace on us,
 And tune our lips to praise.
                    WM. HILEY BATHURST, 1830.

171 HOLY SPIRIT, FAITHFUL GUIDE. 7s. D.　　MARCUS MORRIS WELLS.

Fine.

1. Ho - ly Spir - it, faith-ful guide, Ev - er near the Christian's side; }
　Gen - tly lead us by the hand, Pil-grims in a des - ert land; }
2. Ev - er pres - ent, tru - est friend, Ev - er near thine aid to lend, }
　Leave us not to doubt and fear, Grop-ing on in darkness drear, }
3. When our days of toil shall cease, Wait-ing still for sweet re-lease, }
　Noth-ing left but heav'n and pray'r, Wond'ring if our names were there; }

D. C. Whis-per soft - ly, wand'rer come! Fol - low me, I'll guide thee home.

D. C.

Wea - ry souls for e'er re - joice, While they hear that sweet-est voice
When the storms are rag - ing sore, Hearts grow faint, and hopes give o'er,
Wad - ing deep the dis - mal flood, Plead-ing nought but Je - sus' blood,

M. M. WELLS.

172 (383)　PLEYEL. 7s.　　　　　IGNACE PLEYEL, cir. 1800.

1. Gra-cious Spir - it, love di - vine, Let thy light with-in me shine;
2. Speak thy pard'ning grace to me, Set the burdened sin - ner free:
3. Life and peace to me im - part, Seal sal - va - tion on my heart;
4. Let me nev - er from thee stray, Keep me in the nar - row way;

All my guilt - y fears re-move, Fill me full of heav'n and love.
Lead me to the Lamb of God, Wash me in his pre-cious blood.
Breathe thyself in - to my breast, Earn-est of im-mor - tal rest.
Fill my soul with joy di - vine, Keep me, Lord, for - ev - er thine.

JOHN STOCKER, 1776.

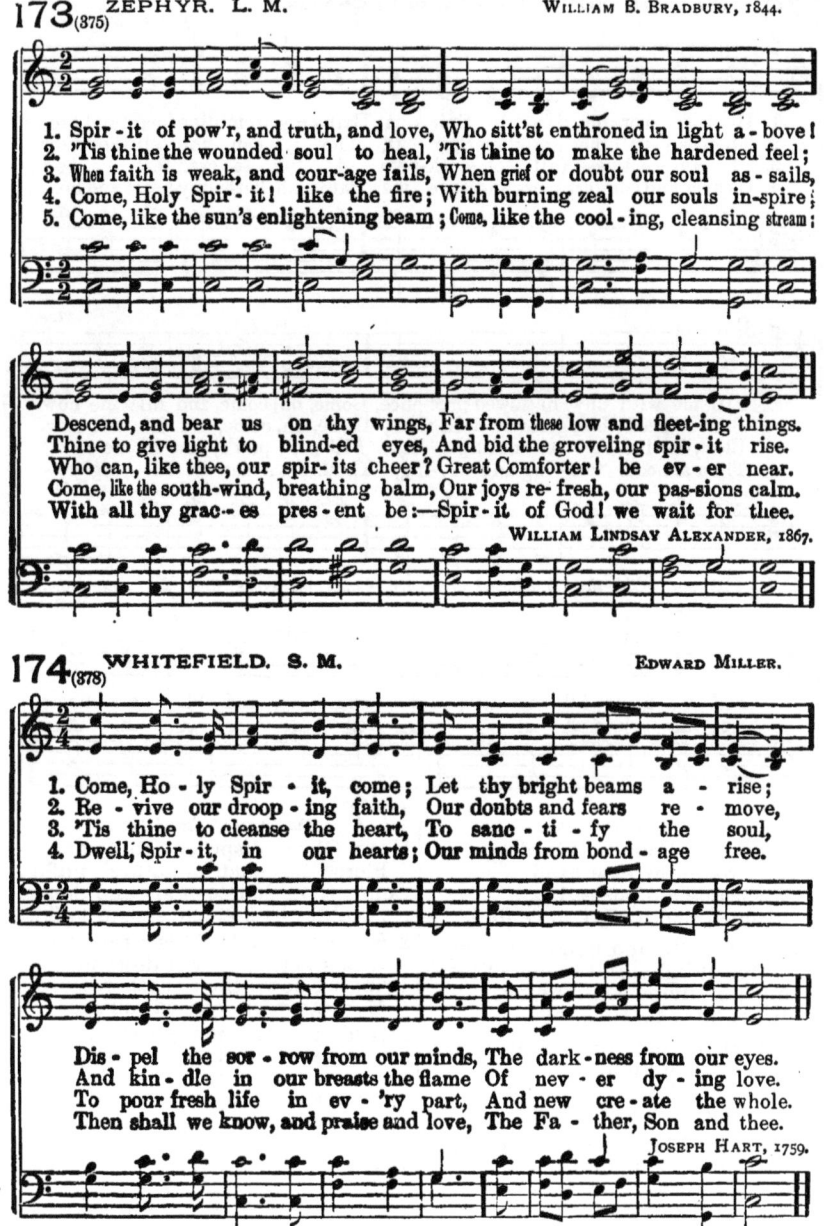

173(375) ZEPHYR. L. M. WILLIAM B. BRADBURY, 1844.

1. Spir-it of pow'r, and truth, and love, Who sitt'st enthroned in light a-bove!
2. 'Tis thine the wounded soul to heal, 'Tis thine to make the hardened feel;
3. When faith is weak, and cour-age fails, When grief or doubt our soul as-sails,
4. Come, Holy Spir-it! like the fire; With burning zeal our souls in-spire;
5. Come, like the sun's enlightening beam; Come, like the cool-ing, cleansing stream;

Descend, and bear us on thy wings, Far from these low and fleet-ing things.
Thine to give light to blind-ed eyes, And bid the groveling spir-it rise.
Who can, like thee, our spir-its cheer? Great Comforter! be ev-er near.
Come, like the south-wind, breathing balm, Our joys re-fresh, our pas-sions calm.
With all thy grac-es pres-ent be:—Spir-it of God! we wait for thee.

WILLIAM LINDSAY ALEXANDER, 1867.

174(378) WHITEFIELD. S. M. EDWARD MILLER.

1. Come, Ho-ly Spir-it, come; Let thy bright beams a-rise;
2. Re-vive our droop-ing faith, Our doubts and fears re-move,
3. 'Tis thine to cleanse the heart, To sanc-ti-fy the soul,
4. Dwell, Spir-it, in our hearts; Our minds from bond-age free.

Dis-pel the sor-row from our minds, The dark-ness from our eyes.
And kin-dle in our breasts the flame Of nev-er dy-ing love.
To pour fresh life in ev-'ry part, And new cre-ate the whole.
Then shall we know, and praise and love, The Fa-ther, Son and thee.

JOSEPH HART, 1759.

175 FILL ME NOW. 8s & 7s, with Chorus.

JNO. R. SWENEY.

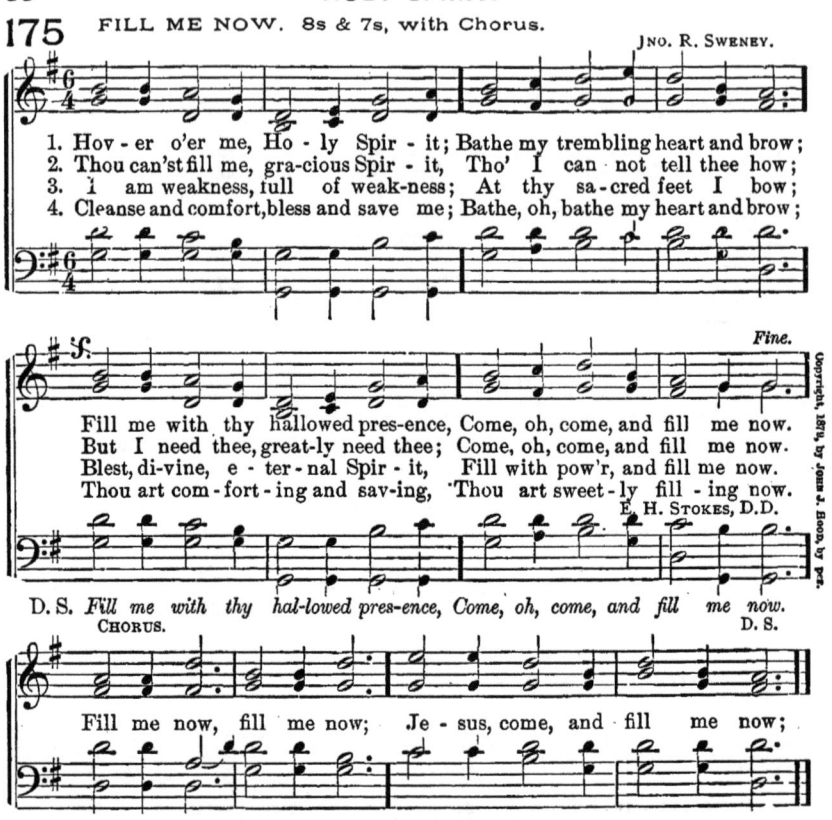

1. Hov - er o'er me, Ho - ly Spir - it; Bathe my trembling heart and brow;
2. Thou can'st fill me, gra-cious Spir - it, Tho' I can not tell thee how;
3. I am weakness, full of weak-ness; At thy sa - cred feet I bow;
4. Cleanse and comfort, bless and save me; Bathe, oh, bathe my heart and brow;

Fine.

Fill me with thy hallowed pres-ence, Come, oh, come, and fill me now.
But I need thee, great-ly need thee; Come, oh, come, and fill me now.
Blest, di-vine, e - ter - nal Spir - it, Fill with pow'r, and fill me now.
Thou art com - fort - ing and sav-ing, Thou art sweet-ly fill - ing now.

E. H. STOKES, D.D.

D. S. *Fill me with thy hal-lowed pres-ence, Come, oh, come, and fill me now.*

CHORUS.

D. S.

Fill me now, fill me now; Je - sus, come, and fill me now;

176 *Guide and Comforter.*

HOLY Spirit, Fount of blessing,
  Ever watchful, ever kind,
Thy celestial aid possessing,
  Prisoned souls deliverance find.

2 Seal of truth, and Bond of union,
  Source of light, and Flame of love,
Symbol of divine communion,
  In the olive-bearing dove;

3 Heavenly Guide from paths of error,
  Comforter of minds distressed,
When the billows fill with terror,
  Pointing to an ark of rest;

4 Promised Pledge, eternal Spirit,
  Greater than all gifts below,
May our hearts thy grace inherit;
  May our lips thy glories show!
         THOMAS J. JUDKIN.

177 *The Source of Consolation.*

HOLY Ghost, dispel our sadness;
  Pierce the clouds of nature's night;
Come, thou Source of joy and gladness,
  Breathe thy life, and spread thy light.

2 From the height which knows no measure,
  As a gracious shower descend,
Bringing down the richest treasure
  Man can wish, or God can send.

3 Author of the new creation,
  Come with unction and with power;
Make our hearts thy habitation;
  On our souls thy graces shower.

4 Hear, O hear our supplication,
  Blessed Spirit, God of peace!
Rest upon this congregation,
  With the fullness of thy grace.
        PAUL GERHARDT, 1653.
Tr. by J. C. JACOBI, 1725. Alt.

KENTUCKY. S. M. AARON CHAPIN, 1822.

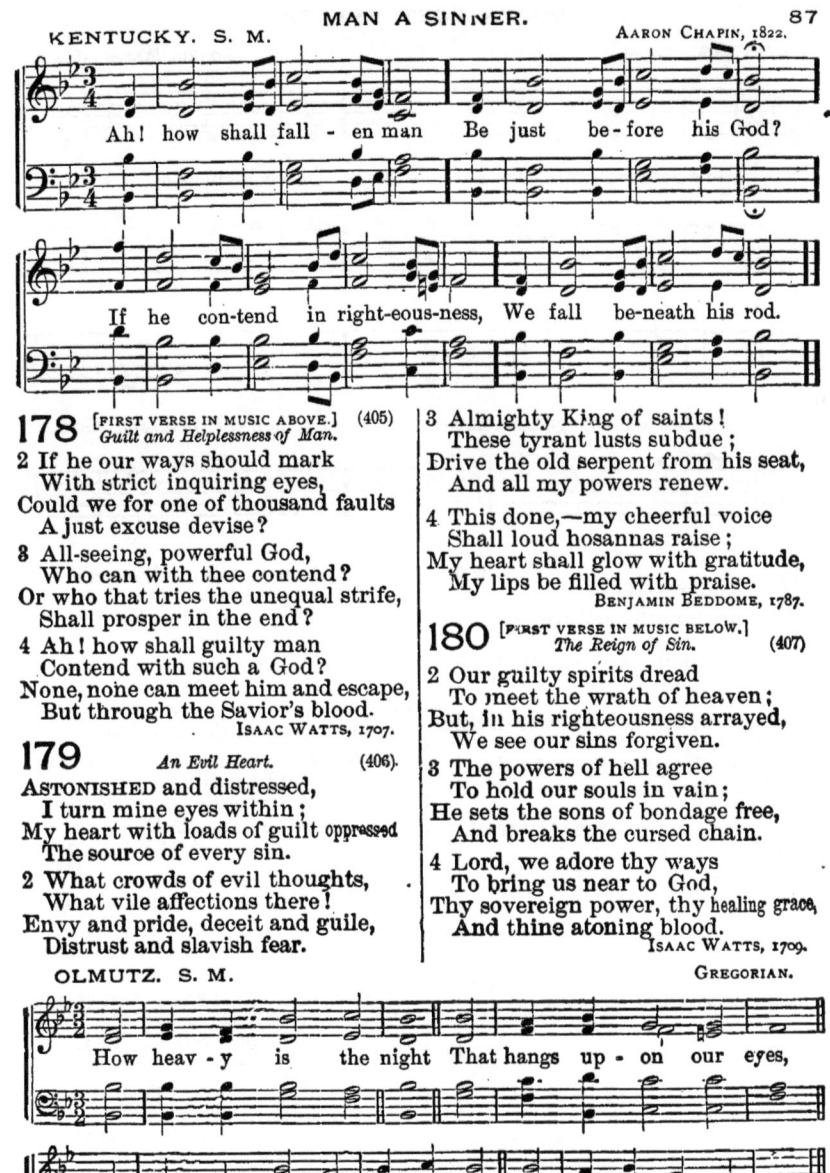

Ah! how shall fall - en man Be just be - fore his God?

If he con-tend in right-eous-ness, We fall be-neath his rod.

178 [FIRST VERSE IN MUSIC ABOVE.] (405)
Guilt and Helplessness of Man.

2 If he our ways should mark
  With strict inquiring eyes,
Could we for one of thousand faults
  A just excuse devise?

3 All-seeing, powerful God,
  Who can with thee contend?
Or who that tries the unequal strife,
  Shall prosper in the end?

4 Ah! how shall guilty man
  Contend with such a God?
None, none can meet him and escape,
  But through the Savior's blood.
                    ISAAC WATTS, 1707.

179 *An Evil Heart.* (406).

ASTONISHED and distressed,
  I turn mine eyes within;
My heart with loads of guilt oppressed
The source of every sin.

2 What crowds of evil thoughts,
  What vile affections there!
Envy and pride, deceit and guile,
  Distrust and slavish fear.

3 Almighty King of saints!
  These tyrant lusts subdue;
Drive the old serpent from his seat,
  And all my powers renew.

4 This done,—my cheerful voice
  Shall loud hosannas raise;
My heart shall glow with gratitude,
  My lips be filled with praise.
                    BENJAMIN BEDDOME, 1787.

180 [FIRST VERSE IN MUSIC BELOW.]
The Reign of Sin. (407)

2 Our guilty spirits dread
  To meet the wrath of heaven;
But, in his righteousness arrayed,
  We see our sins forgiven.

3 The powers of hell agree
  To hold our souls in vain;
He sets the sons of bondage free,
  And breaks the cursed chain.

4 Lord, we adore thy ways
  To bring us near to God,
Thy sovereign power, thy healing grace,
  And thine atoning blood.
                    ISAAC WATTS, 1709.

OLMUTZ. S. M. GREGORIAN.

How heav - y is the night That hangs up - on our eyes,

Till Christ with his re - viv-ing light O - ver our souls a - rise.

DOWNS. C. M.

LOWELL MASON 1830.

How help-less guilt - y nat- ure lies, Un - con-scious of its load!

The heart,unchanged,can nev - er rise To hap -pi - ness and God.

181   *The Need of Regeneration*   (396)

How helpless guilty nature lies,
  Unconscious of its load !
The heart, unchanged, can never rise
  To happiness and God.

2 Can aught, beneath a power divine,
  The stubborn will subdue?
'Tis thine, almighty Spirit ! thine,
  To form the heart anew.

3 'Tis thine, the passions to recall,
  And upward bid them rise;
To make the scales of error fall,
  From reason's darkened eyes.

4 Oh ! change these wretched hearts of ours,
  And give them life divine;
Then shall our passions and our powers,
  Almighty Lord ! be thine.
          ANNE STEELE, 1760.

182 *Pardon and Sanctification in Christ.*   (397)

How sad our state by nature is !
  Our sin—how deep it stains !
And Satan binds our captive minds,
  Fast in his slavish chains.

2 But there's a voice of sovereign grace,
  Sounds from the sacred word ;—
"Ho ! ye despairing sinners ! come
  And trust a faithful Lord."

3 My soul obeys the gracious call
  And runs to this relief;
I would believe thy promise, Lord !
  Oh ! help my unbelief.

4 To the blest fountain of thy blood,
  Incarnate God ! I fly;
Here let me wash my spotted soul,
  From crimes of deepest dye.

5 A guilty, weak, and helpless worm,
  On thy kind arms I fall;
Be thou my strength and righteousness,
  My Jesus, and my all.
          ISAAC WATTS, 1707.

183 *Man's Need of the New Birth.*   (400)

SINNERS, this solemn truth regard,
  Hear, all ye sons of men;
For Christ, the Savior, hath declared,
  " Ye must be born again."

2 Whate'er might be your birth or blood,
  The sinner's boast is vain;
Thus saith the glorious Son of God,
  " Ye must be born again."

3 That which is born of flesh is flesh
  And flesh it will remain :
Then marvel not that Jesus saith,
  " Ye must be born again."

4 Spirit of life, thy grace impart,
  And breathe on sinners slain :
Bear witness, Lord, in ev'ry heart,
  That we are born again.
          JOHN FAWCETT

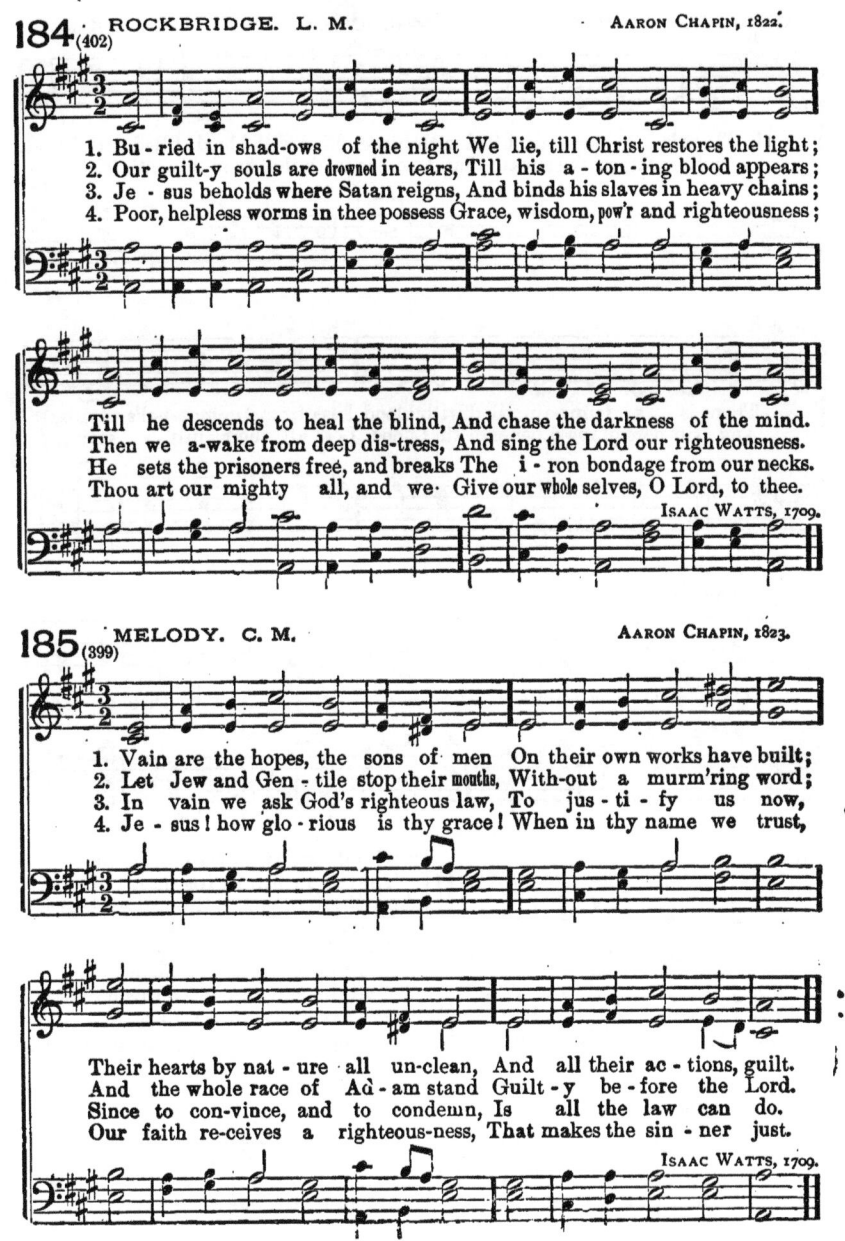

184 (402) ROCKBRIDGE. L. M.
AARON CHAPIN, 1822.

1. Bu - ried in shad-ows of the night We lie, till Christ restores the light;
2. Our guilt-y souls are drowned in tears, Till his a - ton-ing blood appears;
3. Je - sus beholds where Satan reigns, And binds his slaves in heavy chains;
4. Poor, helpless worms in thee possess Grace, wisdom, pow'r and righteousness;

Till he descends to heal the blind, And chase the darkness of the mind.
Then we a-wake from deep dis-tress, And sing the Lord our righteousness.
He sets the prisoners free, and breaks The i - ron bondage from our necks.
Thou art our mighty all, and we Give our whole selves, O Lord, to thee.

ISAAC WATTS, 1709.

185 (399) MELODY. C. M.
AARON CHAPIN, 1823.

1. Vain are the hopes, the sons of men On their own works have built;
2. Let Jew and Gen - tile stop their mouths, With-out a murm'ring word;
3. In vain we ask God's righteous law, To jus - ti - fy us now,
4. Je - sus! how glo - rious is thy grace! When in thy name we trust,

Their hearts by nat - ure all un-clean, And all their ac - tions, guilt.
And the whole race of Ad - am stand Guilt - y be - fore the Lord.
Since to con-vince, and to condemn, Is all the law can do.
Our faith re-ceives a righteous-ness, That makes the sin - ner just.

ISAAC WATTS, 1709.

GLORIOUS FOUNTAIN. C. M. With Chorus.   T. C. O'KANE.

1. There is a fountain filled with blood, filled with blood, filled with blood,
And sinners plung'd beneath that flood, beneath that flood, beneath that flood,

There is a fount-ain filled with blood, Drawn from Im-man-uel's veins,
And sin-ners plung'd beneath that flood, Lose all their guilt-y stains.

By permission.

CHORUS.

Oh, glo-ri-ous fountain! Here will I stay, And in thee ev-er

Wash my sins a-way.

2 The dying thief ‖: rejoiced to see,:‖
That fountain in his day,
And there may I, ‖: though vile as he,:‖
Wash all my sins away.

3 Thou dying Lamb, ‖: thy precious blood,:‖
Shall never lose its power,
Till all the ransomed ‖: church of God,:‖
Are saved to sin no more.

4 E'er since by faith ‖: I saw the stream :‖
Thy flowing wounds supply,
Redeeming love ‖: has been my theme,:‖
And shall be till I die.

186   *Glorious Fountain.*   (407)

THERE is a fountain ‖: filled with blood,:‖
Drawn from Immanuel's veins,
And sinners plunged ‖: beneath that flood,:‖
Lose all their guilty stains.

5 And when this feeble, ‖: faltering tongue :‖
Lies silent in the grave,
Then, in a nobler, ‖: sweeter song,:‖
I'll sing thy power to save.

WILLIAM COWPER, 1779.

SILOAM. C. M.　　　　I. B. Woodbury, 1850.

When wound-ed sore, the strick - en soul Lies bleed-ing and un-bound:

One hand a - lone, a pierc - ed hand, Can heal the sin - ner's wound.

187 [FIRST VERSE IN MUSIC ABOVE.]
The All-Sufficient Grace. (488)

2 When sorrow swells the laden breast,
　And tears of anguish flow,
One heart alone, a broken heart,
　Can feel the sinner's woe.

3 'Tis Jesus' blood, that washes white,
　His hand, that brings relief;
His heart, that's touched with all our joys,
　And feeleth for our grief.

4 Lift up thy bleeding hand, O Lord!
　Unseal that cleansing tide;
We have no shelter from our sin,
　But in thy wounded side.

　　　　Mrs. Cecil F. Alexander, 1858.

188　　　*Salvation.*

Salvation! oh, the joyful sound!
　What pleasure to our ears;
A sovereign balm for every wound,
　A cordial for our fears.

2 Salvation! let the echo fly
　The spacious earth around,
While all the armies of the sky
　Conspire to raise the sound.

3 Salvation! O Thou bleeding Lamb!
　To Thee the praise belongs:
Salvation shall inspire our hearts,
　And dwell upon our tongues.

　　　　Isaac Watts.

CLEANSING FOUNTAIN. C. M.　　　Western Melody.

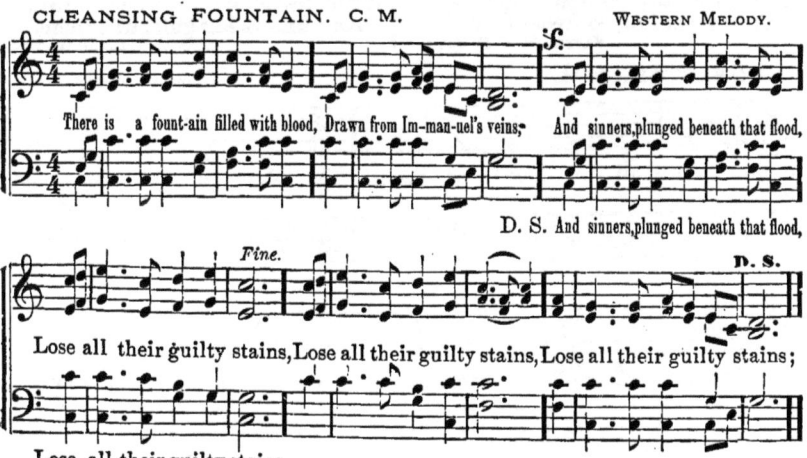

There is a fount-ain filled with blood, Drawn from Im-man-uel's veins; And sinners, plunged beneath that flood,

D. S. And sinners, plunged beneath that flood,

Fine.　　　　D. S.

Lose all their guilty stains, Lose all their guilty stains, Lose all their guilty stains;

Lose all their guilty stains.

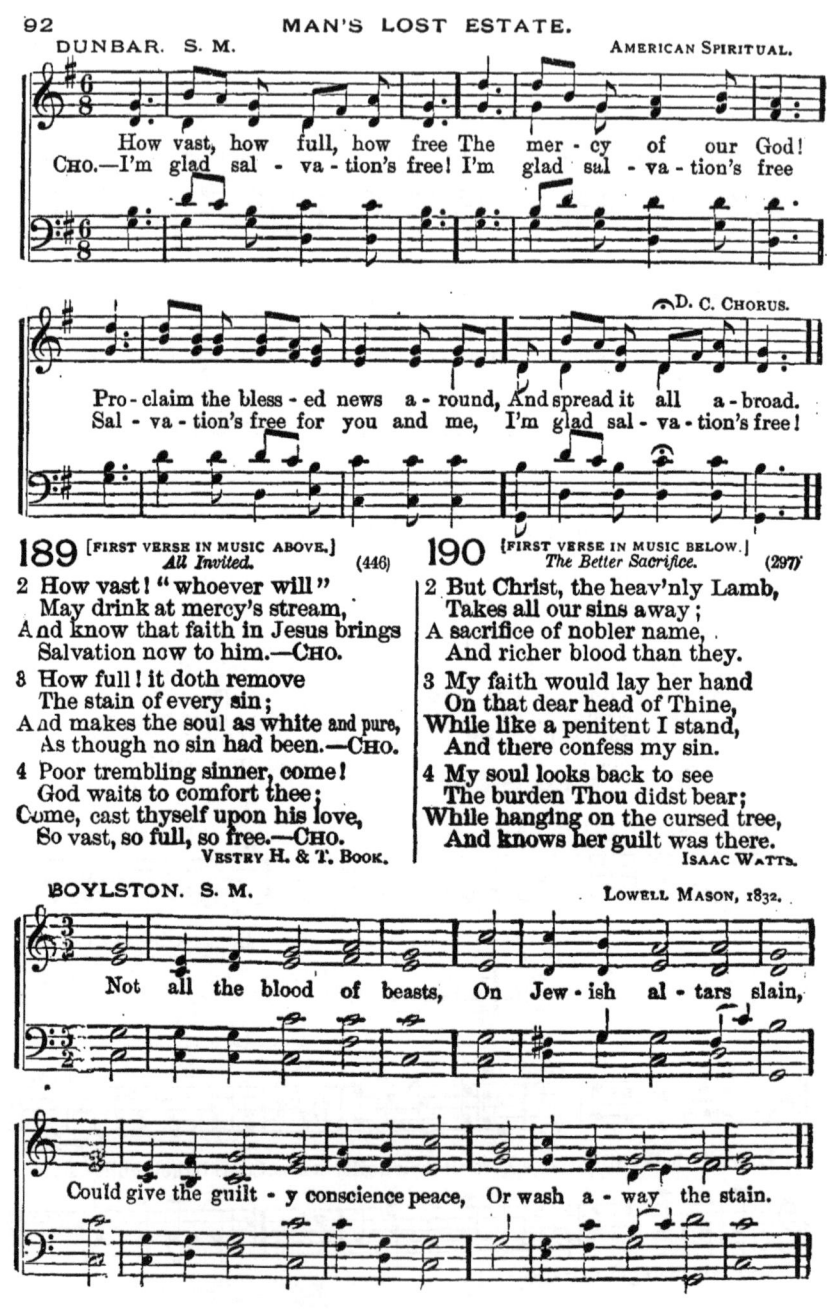

DUNBAR. S. M. AMERICAN SPIRITUAL.

How vast, how full, how free The mer - cy of our God!
CHO.—I'm glad sal - va - tion's free! I'm glad sal - va - tion's free

ᴅ. C. Chorus.

Pro - claim the bless - ed news a - round, And spread it all a - broad.
Sal - va - tion's free for you and me, I'm glad sal - va - tion's free!

189 [FIRST VERSE IN MUSIC ABOVE.]
All Invited. (446)

2 How vast! "whoever will"
　May drink at mercy's stream,
And know that faith in Jesus brings
　Salvation now to him.—CHO.

3 How full! it doth remove
　The stain of every sin;
And makes the soul as white and pure,
　As though no sin had been.—CHO.

4 Poor trembling sinner, come!
　God waits to comfort thee;
Come, cast thyself upon his love,
　So vast, so full, so free.—CHO.
　　　　　　　VESTRY H. & T. BOOK.

190 [FIRST VERSE IN MUSIC BELOW.]
The Better Sacrifice. (297)

2 But Christ, the heav'nly Lamb,
　Takes all our sins away;
A sacrifice of nobler name,
　And richer blood than they.

3 My faith would lay her hand
　On that dear head of Thine,
While like a penitent I stand,
　And there confess my sin.

4 My soul looks back to see
　The burden Thou didst bear;
While hanging on the cursed tree,
　And knows her guilt was there.
　　　　　　　ISAAC WATTS.

BOYLSTON. S. M. LOWELL MASON, 1832.

Not all the blood of beasts, On Jew - ish al - tars slain,

Could give the guilt - y conscience peace, Or wash a - way the stain.

191 JESUS SAVES. P. M. Wm. J. Kirkpatrick.

1. We have heard the joy-ful sound, Je-sus saves, Je-sus saves! Spread the tid-ings
2. Waft it on the roll-ing tide, Je-sus saves, Je-sus saves! Tell to sin - ners
3. Sing a - bove the bat-tle strife, Je-sus saves, Je-sus saves! By his death and
4. Give the winds a might-y voice, Je-sus saves, Je-sus saves! Let the na - tions

all around, Jesus saves, Jesus saves! Bear the news to ev- 'ry land, Climb the
far and wide, Jesus saves, Jesus saves! Sing, ye isl - ands of the sea, Ech - o
endless life, Jesus saves, Jesus saves! Sing it soft - ly thro' the gloom, When the
now rejoice, Jesus saves, Jesus saves! Shout sal-va - tion full and free, High - est

steeps and cross the waves; On-ward! 'tis our Lord's com - mand; Jesus saves, Jesus saves!
back, ye o - cean caves; Earth shall keep her ju-bi-lee; Jesus saves, Jesus saves!
heart for-mer-cy craves; Sing in triumph o'er the tomb, Jesus saves, Jesus saves!
hills and deepest caves; This our song of vic - to - ry, Jesus saves, Jesus saves!

Priscilla J. Owens.

From "Royal Fountain," by per. John J. Hood.

---

192 *Ark of Salvation.*

Like Noah's weary dove
    That soared the earth around,
But not a resting-place above
    The cheerless waters found.

2 Oh, cease, my wandering soul,
    On restless wing to roam;
All the wide world, to either pole,.
    Has not for thee a home.

3 Behold the ark of God,
    Behold the open door;
Hasten to gain that dear abode,
    And rove, my soul, no more.

4 There safe thou shalt abide,
    There sweet shall be thy rest,
And every longing satisfied,
    With full salvation blessed.
        Wm. A. Muhlenberg

193   CHRIST RECEIVETH SINFUL MEN.   7s.   JAMES McGRANAHAN.

1. Sin - ners Je - sus will re-ceive; Sound this word of grace to all
2. Come, and he will give you rest; Trust him, for his word is plain;
3. Now my heart condemns me not, Pure be - fore the law I stand;
4. Christ re - ceiv - eth sin - ful men, E - ven me with all my sin;

Who the heav'nly path-way leave, All who lin - ger, all who fall.
He will take the sin - ful - est; Christ re - ceiv - eth sin - ful men.
He who cleansed me from all spot, Sat - is - fied its last de-mand.
Purged from ev - 'ry spot and stain, Heav'n with him I en - ter in.

REFRAIN.

Sing it o'er   and o'er a - gain: Christ re-
Sing it o'er a-gain,   Sing it o'er again:

ceiv - eth sin-ful men,   Make the mes - - sage
ceiveth sinful men, Christ re-ceiveth sinful men;   Make the message plain,

CHRIST RECEIVETH SINFUL MEN. Concluded.

clear and plain: . . Christ re - céiv - eth sin - ful men.
Make the message plain:

Arr. from NEUMASTER, 1671.

194 (507) DEPTH OF MERCY. 7s.

W. H. ROBERTS.

Moderato legato.

1. Depth of mercy! can there be Mer-cy still reserved for me? Can my God his
2. I have long withstood his grace, Long provoked him to his face; Would not hearken
3. There for me the Savior stands; Shows his wounds and spreads his hands; God is love; I
4. Now incline me to re-pent; Let me now my fall lament; Now my foul re-

CHORUS. *Faster.*

wrath for-bear? Me, the chief of sinners, spare?
to. his calls; Grieved him by a thousand falls. God is love; I know, I feel;
know, I feel; Je-sus weeps, and loves me still.
volt de-plore; Weep, believe, and sin no more.

Smoothly. *Repeat pp.*

Je-sus weeps, and loves me still; Je - sus weeps, he weeps, and loves me still.

CHARLES WESLEY, 1740.

LENOX. H. M.   J. EDSON, 1782.

Blow ye the trump-et, blow! The glad-ly sol-emn sound; Let all the na-tions know, To earth's re-mot-est bound, The year of ju-bi-lee is come, The year of ju-bi-lee is come, Re-turn, ye ransomed sin-ners, home.

195 [FIRST VERSE INSERTED IN MUSIC.]
The Jubilee Proclaimed.   (461)

2 Jesus, our great High Priest,
    Hath full atonement made;
Ye weary spirits! rest,
    Ye mournful souls! be glad;
The year of jubilee is come;
Return, ye ransomed sinners! home.

3 Extol the Lamb of God,—
    The all-atoning Lamb;
Redemption in his blood,
    Throughout the world, proclaim;
The year of jubilee is come;
Return, ye ransomed sinners! home.

4 Ye, who have sold for naught
    Your heritage above!
Shall have it back unbought,
    The gift of Jesus' love;
The year of jubilee is come;
Return, ye ransomed sinners! home.
       CHARLES WESLEY, 1755.

196   *The Sacrifice.*

ARISE, my soul, arise,
    Shake off thy guilty fears;
The bleeding sacrifice
    In my behalf appears;
Before the throne my Surety stands,
My name is written on His hands.

2 He ever lives above,
    For me to intercede;
His all-redeeming love,
    His precious blood to plead;
His blood atoned for all our race,
And sprinkles now the throne of grace.

3 Five bleeding wounds He bears,
    Received on Calvary;
They pour effectual prayers,
    They strongly speak for me;
Forgive him, O forgive, they cry,
Nor let that ransomed sinner die.

4 The Father hears Him pray,
    His dear Anointed One;
He can not turn away
    The presence of His Son;
His spirit answers to the blood,
And tells me I am born of God.

5 My God is reconciled,
    His pard'ning voice I hear,
He owns me for his child,
    I can no longer fear;
With confidence I now draw nigh,
And Father, Abba, Father, cry.

ALL TO CHRIST I OWE. 6s. JOHN T. GRAPE.

I hear the Sav-ior say, Thy strength in-deed is small;

Child of weak-ness, watch and pray, Find in Me thine all in all

CHORUS.

Je - sus paid it all, All to him I owe;

Sin had left a crim-son stain, He washed it white as snow.

197 [FIRST VERSE INSERTED IN MUSIC.]
Jesus Paid it All.

2 Lord, now indeed I find
  Thy power, and Thine alone,
Can change the leper's spots,
  And melt the heart of stone. —CHO.

3 For nothing good have I
  Whereby Thy grace to claim—
I'll wash my garment white
  In the blood of Calvary's Lamb.—CHO.

4 When from my dying bed
  My ransomed soul shall rise,
Then "Jesus paid it all"
  Shall rend the vaulted skies.—CHO.

5 And when before the throne
  I stand in Him complete,
I'll lay my trophies down,
  All down at Jesus' feet.—CHO.
          MRS. ELVINA M. HALL.

198 *Rev. 22 : 17.* (279)

COME to the blood-stained tree;
  The Victim bleeding lies;
God sets the sinner free,
  Since Christ, a ransom, dies.

2 The Spirit will apply
  His blood to cleanse thy stain;
Oh, burdened soul, draw nigh,
  For none can come in vain!

3 Dark though thy guilt appear,
  And deep its crimson stain,
There's boundless mercy here,
  Oh, do not still disdain.

4 Look not within for peace,
  Within, there's nought to cheer:
Look up, and find release
  From sin, and self, and fear.

7

199   WHAT A WONDERFUL SAVIOR. P. M.

Elisha A. Hoffman.

1. Christ has for sin a - tone-ment made, What a won - der - ful Sav - ior!
2. I praise him for the cleans-ing blood, What a won - der - ful Sav - ior!
3. He cleansed my heart from all its sin, What a won - der - ful Sav - ior!
4. He walks be - side me in the way, What a won - der - ful Sav - ior!
5. He gives me o - ver - com-ing power, What a won - der - ful Sav - ior!
6. To him I've giv - en all my heart, What a won - der - ful Sav - ior!

We are redeem'd, the price is paid, What a won - der - ful Sav - ior!
That rec - on - ciled my soul to God, What a won - der - ful Sav - ior!
And now he reigns and rules there-in, What a won - der - ful Sav - ior!
And keeps me faith-ful day by day, What a won - der - ful Sav - ior!
And tri-umph in each con-flict hour, What a won - der - ful Sav - ior!
The world shall nev-er share a part, What a won - der - ful Sav - ior!

E. A. Hoffman.

CHORUS.

What a won - der - ful Sav - ior is Je - sus, my Je - sus!

What a won - der - ful Sav - ior is Je - sus, my Lord!

200 WONDERFUL GRACE. P. M.

I. BALTZELL.

1. 'Tis grace, 'tis grace, 'tis won - der - ful grace, This great sal-
2. 'Tis grace, 'tis grace, 'tis won - der - ful grace, Which saves the
3. 'Tis grace, 'tis grace, 'tis won - der - ful grace; . Its streams are

va - tion brings; The soul, de - liv - ered of its load, In
soul from sin; The power of ris - ing e - vil days, And
full and free; Are flow - ing now for all the race, They

'Tis grace, ... 'tis grace, ...

CHORUS.

sweet - est rapt - ure sings.
reigns su - preme with - in. 'Tis wonderful grace, 'tis wonderful grace,
e - ven flow to me.

REV. W. H. BURRELL.

grace, ... 'Tis grace, ...

Won - der - ful, won - der - ful, won - der - ful grace, 'Tis won - der - ful grace,

'tis won - der - ful grace, Flow - ing still free - ly for me.

201 SEEKING FOR ME. P. M.

EMERSON E. HASTY.

1. Je-sus, my Sav-ior, to Beth - le - hem came, Born in a man - ger to
2. Je-sus, my Sav-ior, on Cal - va - ry's tree Paid the great debt, and my
3. Je-sus, my Sav-ior, the same as of old, While I did wan - der a-
4. Je-sus, my Sav-ior, shall come from on high; Sweet is the prom-ise as

sor-row and shame; Oh, it was won-der-ful, blest be his name, Seek-ing for
soul he set free; Oh, it was won-der-ful, how could it be? Dy - ing for
far from the fold, Gen-tly and long he hath plead with my soul, Call - ing for
wea - ry years fly; Oh, I shall see him de-scend-ing the sky, Com - ing for

for me, ...   for me, ...

me, for me, Seeking for me, seek-ing for me, Seeking for me, seeking for me,
me, for me, Dy-ing for me, dy - ing for me, Dy-ing for me, dy - ing for me,
me, for me, Call-ing for me, call-ing for me, Calling for me, call- ing for me,
me, for me, Com-ing for me, com-ing for me, Coming for me, com-ing for me,

Oh, it was won-der - ful, blest be his name, Seek-ing for me, for me.
Oh, it was won-der - ful, how could it be? Dy - ing for me, for me.
Gently and long he hath plead with my soul, Call-ing for me, for me.
Oh, I shall see him de-scend-ing the sky, Com-ing for me, for me.

E. E. HASTY.

THE STRANGER AT THE DOOR. L. M.   T. C. O'KANE.

1. Be-hold a stran-ger at the door, He gent - ly knocks, has knocked be-fore;

Has wait-ed long, is wait-ing still; You treat no oth - er friend so ill.

CHORUS.

Oh, let the dear Savior come in, come in, He'll cleanse the heart from sin, from sin;

Oh, keep him no more out at the door, But let the dear Savior come in, come in.

202 [FIRST VERSE INSERTED IN MUSIC.]
At the Door. (429)

2 Oh, lovely attitude—he stands
With melting heart and loaded hands;
Oh, matchless kindness—and he shows
This matchless kindness to his foes.

3 But will he prove a friend indeed?
He will—the very friend you need;
The Friend of sinners? Yes, 'tis he,
With garments dyed on Calvary.

4 Rise, touched with gratitude divine,
Turn out his enemy and thine;
That soul-destroying monster, sin,
And let the heavenly Stranger in.

5 Admit him, ere his anger burn—
His feet, departed, ne'er return;
Admit him, or the hour's at hand
You'll at his door rejected stand.
JOSEPH GRIGG, 1765.

203 *Why not be Saved To-night?* (430)

OH, do not let the word depart,
And close thine eyes against the light;
Poor sinner, harden not thy heart;
Thou would'st be saved, why not to-night?

2 To-morrow's sun may never rise
To bless thy long-deluded sight;
This is the time, oh, then be wise!
Thou would'st be saved, why not to-night?

3 Our God in pity lingers still;
And wilt thou thus his love requite?
Renounce at length thy stubborn will;
Thou would'st be saved, why not to-night?

4 The world has nothing left to give,
It has no new, no pure delight;
Oh, try the life which Christians live;
Thou would'st be saved, why not to-night?

SPANISH HYMN. 7s. D.   Spanish Melody.

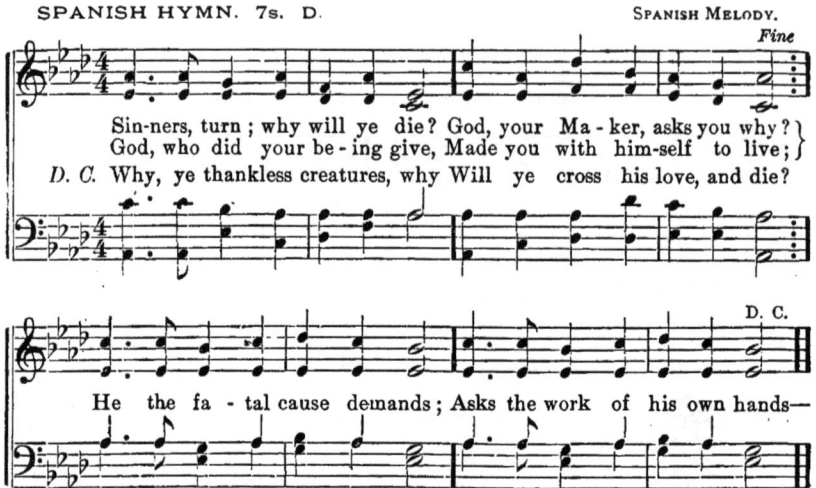

Sin-ners, turn ; why will ye die? God, your Ma - ker, asks you why ?
God, who did your be - ing give, Made you with him-self to live ;

D. C. Why, ye thankless creatures, why Will ye cross his love, and die?

He the fa - tal cause demands ; Asks the work of his own hands—

204   *Sinners, Turn !*

SINNERS, turn ; why will ye die ?
God, your Maker, asks you why ?
God, who did your being give,
Made you with himself to live ;
He the fatal cause demands ;
Asks the work of his own hands,—
Why, ye thankless creatures, why
Will ye cross his love, and die ?

2 Sinners, turn ; why will ye die ?
God, your Savior, asks you why?
He, who did your souls retrieve,
Died himself, that ye might live.
Will ye let him die in vain ?
Crucify your Lord again?
Why, ye ransomed sinners, why
Will ye slight his grace and die?

3 Sinners, turn ; why will ye die ?
God, the Spirit, asks you why?
He who all your lives hath strove,
Urged you to embrace his love.
Will ye not his grace receive ?
Will ye still refuse to live ?
O ye dying sinners, why,
Why will ye forever die ?
              REV. C. WESLEY, 1745.

205   *Delay.*   (454)

HASTEN, sinner ! to be wise,
   Stay not for the morrow's sun :
Wisdom, if thou still despise,
   Harder is she to be won.

2 Hasten, mercy to implore,
   Stay not for the morrow's sun,
Lest thy season should be o'er,
   Ere this evening's stage be run.

3 Hasten, sinner ! to return,
   Stay not for the morrow's sun,
Lest thy lamp should fail to burn,
   Ere salvation's work is done.

4 Hasten, sinner ! to be blessed,
   Stay not for the morrow's sun,
Lest perdition thee arrest,
   Ere the morrow is begun.
              THOMAS SCOTT, 1773.

206   *The Voice of Jesus.*   (451)

COME, says Jesus' sacred voice,
Come, and make my paths your choice ;
I will guide you to your home ;
Weary pilgrim ! hither come.

2 Thou, who, houseless, sole, forlorn
Long hast borne the proud world's scorn,
Long hast roamed this barren waste
Weary pilgrim ! hither haste.

3 Ye, who, tossed on beds of pain,
Seek for ease, but seek in vain !
Ye, by fiercer anguish torn,
In remorse for guilt who mourn !—

4 Hither come, for here is found
Balm that flows for every wound,
Peace that ever shall endure,
Rest eternal, sacred, sure.
         MRS. ANNA L. BARBAULD, 1812

207 WHY DO YOU WAIT? P. M.   GEO. F. ROOT.

1. Why do you wait, dear brother, Oh, why do you tar-ry so long? Your
2. What do you hope, dear brother, To gain by a further de-lay? There's
3. Do you not feel, dear brother, His Spir-it now striving with-in? Oh,
4. Why do you wait, dear brother, The harvest is pass-ing a-way, Your

Sav-ior is wait-ing to give you A place in his sanc-ti-fied throng,
no one to save you but Je-sus, There's no oth-er way but his way.
why not ac-cept his sal-va-tion, And throw off thy bur-den of sin.
Sav-ior is long-ing to bless you, There's danger and death in de-lay.

GEO. F. ROOT.

CHORUS.

Why not? why not? Why not come to him now? Why not? Why not? Why not come to him now?

(TUNE ON OPPOSITE PAGE, OMITTING REPEAT.)

208   *Come and Welcome.*   (455)

FROM the cross uplifted high,
'Where the Savior deigns to die,
'What melodious sounds we hear,
Bursting on the ravished ear!—
"Love's redeeming work is done—
Come and welcome, sinner, come!

2 "Sprinkled now with blood the throne—
Why beneath thy burdens groan?
On my pierced body laid,
Justice owns the ransom paid—
Bow the knee, and kiss the Son—
Come and welcome, sinner, come!

3 "Spread for thee, the festal board—
See with richest bounty stored;
To thy Father's bosom pressed,
Thou shalt be a child confessed,
Never from his house to roam;
Come and welcome, **sinner**, come!

4 "Soon the days of life shall end—
Lo, I come—your Savior, Friend!
Safe your spirit to convey
To the realms of endless day,
Up to my eternal home—
Come and welcome, sinner, come!"

T. HAWEIS, 1791.

AZMON. C. M.   CARL GOTTHELF, 1828. Arr. by MASON, 1839.

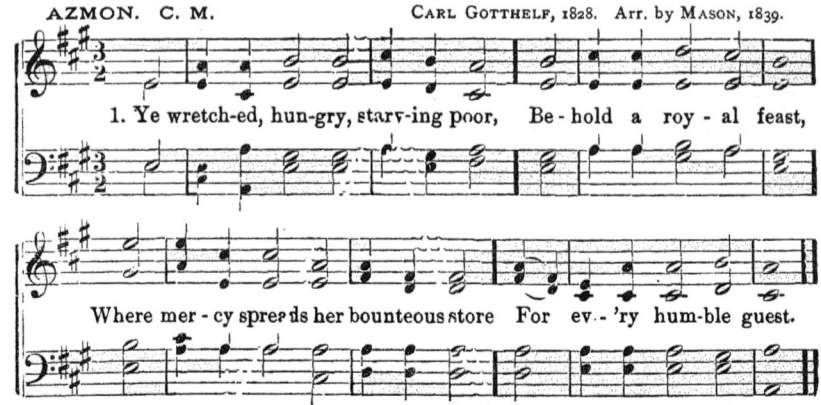

1. Ye wretch-ed, hun-gry, starv-ing poor, Be-hold a roy-al feast,

Where mer-cy spreads her bounteous store For ev-'ry hum-ble guest.

209   *The Gospel Feast.*   (417)

YE wretched, hungry, starving poor!
  Behold a royal feast,
Where mercy spreads her bounteous store,
  For every humble guest.

2 See, Jesus stands, with open arms;
  He calls,—he bids you come;
Guilt holds you back, and fear alarms;
  But, see! there yet is room.

3 Room, in the Savior's bleeding heart;
  There love and pity meet;
Nor will he bid the soul depart,
  That trembles at his feet.

4 Oh! come, and with his children taste
  The blessings of his love:
While hope attends the sweet repast
  Of nobler joys above.

5 There, with united heart and voice,
  Before th' eternal throne,
Ten thousand thousand souls rejoice,
  In ecstasies unknown.

6 And yet ten thousand thousand more
  Are welcome still to come;
Ye longing souls! the grace adore,
  Approach, there yet is room.
                 ANNE STEELE, 1760.

210   *Gen. 6: 3.*   (245)

THERE is a line, by us unseen,
  That crosses every path,
The hidden boundary between
  God's patience and his wrath.

2 To pass that limit is to die,
  To die as if by stealth,
It does not quench the beaming eye,
  Nor pale the glow of health.

3 Oh! where is this mysterious bourne
  By which our path is crossed;
Beyond which God himself hath sworn
  That he who goes is lost?

4 How far may we go on to sin?
  How long will God forbear?
Where does hope end, and where begin
  The confines of despair?

5 An answer from the skies is sent,—
  "Ye that from God depart,
While it is called to-day, repent,
  And harden not your heart."
          JOSEPH ADDISON ALEXANDER.

211   *The Last Resolve.*   (416)

COME, humble sinner! in whose breast
  A thousand thoughts revolve:
Come, with your guilt and fear oppressed,
  And make this last resolve:—

2 "I'll go to Jesus, though my sin
  Like mountains round me close;
I know his courts, I'll enter in
  Whatever may oppose.

3 "Prostrate I'll lie before his throne,
  And there my guilt confess;
I'll tell him I'm a wretch undone,
  Without his sovereign grace.

4 "Perhaps he will admit my plea,
  Perhaps will hear my prayer;
But, if I perish, I will pray,
  And perish only there.

5 "I can but perish if I go,
  I am resolved to try;
For, if I stay away, I know
  I must forever die."
           EDMUND JONES, 1772.

SESSIONS. L. M.   L. O. EMERSON, 1842.

Say, sinner, hath a voice with-in Oft whispered to thy secret soul,

Urged thee to leave the ways of sin, And yield thy heart to God's control?

212 [FIRST VERSE IN MUSIC ABOVE.] (427)
My Spirit Shall not Always Strive.

2 Sinner! it was a heavenly voice,—
  It was the Spirit's gracious call;
It bade thee make the better choice,
  And haste to seek in Christ thine all.

3 Spurn not the call to life and light;
  Regard in time the warning kind;
That call thou may'st not always slight
  And yet the gate of mercy find.

4 God's Spirit will not always strive
  With hardened self-destroying men;
Ye, who persist his love to grieve,
  May never hear his voice again.

5 Sinner! perhaps this very day
  Thy last accepted time may be:
Oh! should'st thou grieve him now away
  Then hope may never beam on thee.
          MRS. ANN B. HYDE, 1825.

213 [FIRST VERSE IN MUSIC BELOW.]
Just as Thou Art.   (426)

2 Thy sins I bore on Calvary's tree;
  The stripes, thy due, were laid on me,
That peace and pardon might be free;—
  Oh, wretched sinner! come,—now come.

3 Burdened with guilt, would'st thou be blessed?
  Trust not the world; it gives no rest;
I bring relief to hearts oppressed;—
  Oh, weary sinner! come,—now come.

4 Come, hither bring thy boding fears,
  Thy aching heart, thy bursting tears;
'Tis mercy's voice salutes thine ears;—
  Oh, trembling sinner! come,—now come.

5 "The Spirit and the Bride say, Come!"
  Rejoicing saints re-echo, "Come!"
Who faints, who thirsts, who will, may come;
  Thy Savior bids thee come,—now come.
          RUSSELL S. COOK, 1850, a.

JUST AS THOU ART. L. M.   W. H. LANTHURN, 1874.

Just as thou art—with-out one trace Of love, or joy, or inward grace,—

Or meekness for the heav'nly place,—Oh, guilty sinner! come,—now come.

214   JESUS IS CALLING. P. M.   GEO. C. STEBBINS.

1. Je-sus is tender-ly calling thee home—Calling to-day, calling to-day;
2. Je-sus is calling the wea-ry to rest—Call-ing to-day, calling to-day;
3. Je-sus is waiting, oh, come to him now—Waiting to-day, waiting to-day;
4. Je-sus is pleading, oh, list to his voice—Hear him to-day, hear him to-day;

Why from the sunshine of love wilt thou roam, Farther and farther a-way?
Bring him thy bur-den and thou shalt be blest; He will not turn thee a-way.
Come with thy sins, at his feet low-ly bow; Come, and no long-er de-lay;
They who be-lieve on his name shall rejoice; Quickly a-rise and a-way.

FANNY J. CROSBY.

REFRAIN.

Call - ing to - day, . . Call - ing to - day, . .

Call-ing, call-ing to-day, to-day; Call-ing, call-ing to-day, to-day;

Je - - sus is call - ing, Is ten-der-ly calling to-day.

Je-sus is ten-der-ly calling to-day.

GOSHEN. 11s.　　　　　　　　　　　GERMAN.

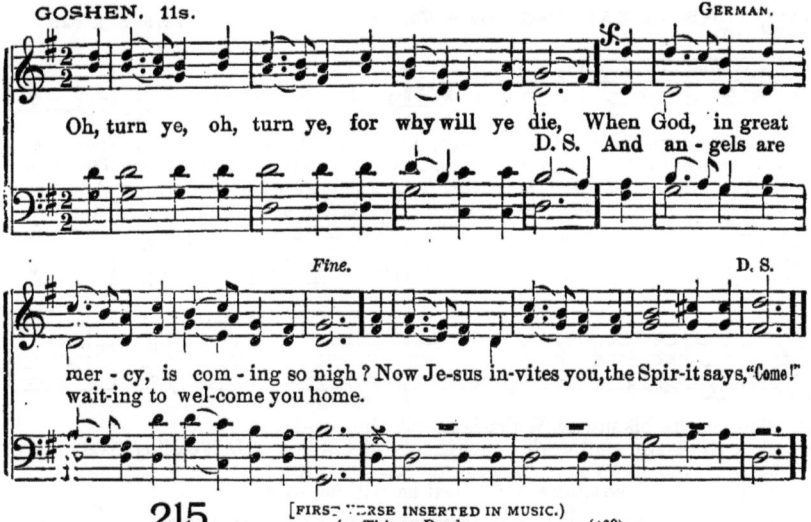

Oh, turn ye, oh, turn ye, for why will ye die, When God, in great

D. S. And an - gels are

Fine.　　　　　　　　　　　　　　D. S.

mer - cy, is com - ing so nigh? Now Je-sus in-vites you, the Spir-it says, "Come!"
wait-ing to wel-come you home.

215　[FIRST VERSE INSERTED IN MUSIC.]
　　　All Things Ready.　　　(469)

2 How vain the delusion, that while you delay,
Your hearts may grow better by staying away!
Come wretched, come starving, come just as you be
While streams of salvation are flowing so free.

3 And now Christ is ready your souls to receive;
Oh! how can you question, if you will believe?
If sin is your burden, why will you not come?
'Tis you he bids welcome; he bids you come home.

4 Why will you be starving, and feeding on air?
There's mercy in Jesus, enough and to spare;
If still you are doubting, make trial and see,
And prove that his mercy is boundless and free.
　　　　　　　　　　　JOSIAH HOPKINS, 1830.

216　　　*Danger of Delay.*　　　(470)

DELAY not, delay not; oh, sinner! draw near,
　The waters of life are now flowing for thee;
No price is demanded, the Savior is here,
　Redemption is purchased, salvation is free.

2 Delay not, delay not; why longer abuse
　The love and compassion of Jesus, thy God?
A fountain is opened,—how canst thou refuse
　To wash, and be cleansed in his pardoning blood?

3 Delay not, delay not, oh sinner! to come,
　For mercy still lingers and calls thee to-day;
Her voice is not heard in the vale of the tomb,—
　Her message, unheeded, will soon pass away.

4 Delay not, delay not; the Spirit of grace,
　Long grieved and resisted, may take its sad flight;
And leave thee in darkness to finish thy race,—
　To sink in the vale of eternity's night.
　　　　　　　　　　　THOMAS HASTINGS, 1831.

217 (477) HE IS CALLING. 8s & 7s.

Arr. by S. J. Vail

1. There's a wideness in God's mer-cy, Like the wideness of the sea; There's a
2. There's no place where earth-ly sorrows Are more felt than up in heaven; There's no
3. For the love of God is broader Than the measure of man's mind, And the
4. But we make his love too nar-row, By false lim-its of our own; And we

REFRAIN.

kindness in his justice, Which is more than lib - er - ty.
place where earthly failings Have such kindly judg-ment given. He is calling, "Come to me;"
heart of the E-ter-nal Is most won-der-ful-ly kind.
mag- ni - fy his strictness With a zeal he will not own.

Lord, I'll gladly haste to thee.

5 Pining souls, come nearer Jesus;
   Come, but come not doubting thus;
   Come with faith that trusts more freely
   His great tenderness for us.

6 If our love were but more simple,
   We should take him at his word;
   And our lives would be all sunshine
   In the sweetness of our Lord.
                    FRED'K FABER, ab

218 (478) COME TO JESUS.

Come to Je-sus, come to Je-sus, Come to Je-sus just now, Just now come to

Jesus, Come to Jesus just now.

2 He will save you.
3 Oh, believe him.
4 He is able.
5 He is willing.
6 He'll receive you.
7 Call upon him.
8 He will hear you.
9 Look unto him.

10 He'll forgive you.
11 Flee to Jesus.
12 He will cleanse you.
13 He will clothe you.
14 Jesus loves you.
15 Don't reject him.
16 Only trust him.
17 Hallelujah. Amen.

219 WHO'LL BE THE NEXT? P. M. Rev. Robert Lowry.

1. Who'll be the next to fol - low Je - sus? Who'll be the next the cross to bear?
2. Who'll be the next to fol - low Je - sus—Fol - low his wea - ry, bleeding feet?
3. Who'll be the next to fol - low Je - sus? Who'll be the next to praise his name?
4. Who'll be the next to fol - low Je - sus, Down thro' the Jordan's rolling tide?

Some one is read - y, some one is wait-ing; Who'll be the next a crown to wear?
Who'll be the next to lay ev - 'ry bur - den Down at the Father's mercy-seat?
Who'll swell the chorus of free redemption—Sing, hallelujah! praise the Lamb?
Who'll be the next to join with the ransomed, Sing-ing up-on the oth-er side?

Annie S. Hawks.

REFRAIN.

Who'll be the next? Who'll be the next? Who'll be the next to fol-low Je-sus?

Who'll be the next to fol - low Je - sus now? Fol - low Je - sus now?

220   LET HIM IN. P. M.   E. O. EXCELL.

1. There's a stranger at the door,   Let   him in,
2. O-pen now to him your heart,   Let   him in,
3. Hear you now his lov-ing voice,   Let   him in,
4. Now ad-mit the heavenly Guest,   Let   him in,

Let the Savior in,   let the Savior in.

He has been there oft before,   Let   him in;
If you wait he will de-part,   Let   him in;
Now, oh, now make him your choice,   Let   him in;
He will make for you a feast,   Let   him in;

Let the Savior in,   let the Savior in.

Let him in ere he is gone, Let him in, the Ho - ly One, Je-sus
Let him in, he is your Friend, He your soul will sure de-fend, He will
He is standing at the door, Joy to you he will re-store, And his
He will speak your sins for-giv'n, And when earth ties all are riven, He will

Christ, the Fath - er's Son,   Let   him in.
keep you to the end,   Let   him in.
name you will a - dore,   Let   him in.
take you home to heaven,   Let   him in.

Let the Savior in,   let the Savior in.

REV. J. B. ATCHISON.

221(475) ALMOST PERSUADED. P. M.

P. P. Bliss.

1. "Al - most per-suad - ed" now to be - lieve; "Al - most per-suad - ed"
2. "Al - most per-suad - ed," come, come to - day; "Al - most per-suad - ed,"
3. "Al - most per-suad - ed," harv - est is past! "Al - most per-suad - ed,"

Christ to re - ceive; Seems now some soul to say, "Go, Spir - it,
turn not a - way; Je - sus in - vites you here, An - gels are
doom comes at last! "Al - most" can not a - vail; "Al - most" is

go thy way; Some more con - ven - ient day On thee I'll call."
ling'ring near, Pray'rs rise from hearts so dear; Oh, wan-d'rer, come!
but to fail! Sad, sad that bit - ter wail,—"Al - most," BUT LOST!

P. P. Bliss.

222(476) TO-DAY. 6s & 4s.

L. Mason.

1. To-day the Savior calls! Ye wand'rers, come; Oh, ye benighted souls, Why longer roam?
2. To-day the Savior calls! Oh, hear him now; Within these sacred walls To Je-sus bow.
3. To-day the Savior calls! For refuge fly! The storm of justice falls, And death is nigh.
4. The Spirit calls to-day; Yield to his power; Oh, grieve him not away, 'Tis mercy's hour.

GREENVILLE. 8s, 7s & 4s.　　　　　　JEAN JACQUES ROUSSEAU.

Come, ye sinners, poor and needy, Weak and wounded, sick and sore; { Jesus ready stands to save you, }
D. C. He is a-ble, he is a-ble, He is willing, doubt no more. { Full of pity, love and (*Omit*) } pow'r;

223 [FIRST VERSE IN MUSIC ABOVE.]
Invitation Hymn. (463)

2 Now, ye needy, come and welcome;
　God's free bounty glorify;
True belief and true repentance,
　Every grace that brings you nigh,
　　Without money,
Come to Jesus Christ and buy.

3 Let not conscience make you linger,
　Nor of fitness fondly dream;
All the fitness he requireth
　Is to feel your need of him:
　　This he gives you;
'Tis the Spirit's glimmering beam.

4 Come, ye weary, heavy-laden,
　Bruised and mangled by the fall;
If you tarry till you're better,
　You will never come at all;
　　Not the righteous,—
Sinners Jesus came to call.
　　　　　　JOSEPH HART, 1759.

224　　*The Voice of Mercy.*　(466)

LISTEN, sinner! mercy hails you;
　With her sweetest voice she calls;
Bids you hasten to the Savior,
　Ere the hand of justice falls:
　　Listen, sinner!
'Tis the voice of mercy calls.

2 See! the storm of vengeance gathering
　O'er the path you dare to tread!
Hark! the awful thunders rolling
　Loud and louder o'er your head!
　　Flee, oh, sinner!
Lest the lightnings strike you dead.

3 Haste, ah! hasten to the Savior;
　Sue his mercy while you may;
Soon the day of grace is over;
　Soon your life will pass away;
　　Hasten, sinner!
You must perish, if you stay.
　　　　　　ANDREW REED, 1817.

COME, YE SINNERS. 8s & 7s.　　　　JEREMIAH INGALLS, 1830.

Come, ye sin-ners, poor and needy, Weak and wounded, sick and sore; }
Je-sus read-y stands to save you, Full of pit-y, love and pow'r; }
D. C. Glo-ry, hon-or and sal-va-tion, Christ, the Lord, is come to reign.

CHORUS.

Turn to the Lord, and seek sal-vation, Sound the praise of his dear name:

225 (458) RHINEHART. 7s & 6s.

SPIRITUAL. Arr. by I. BALTZELL.

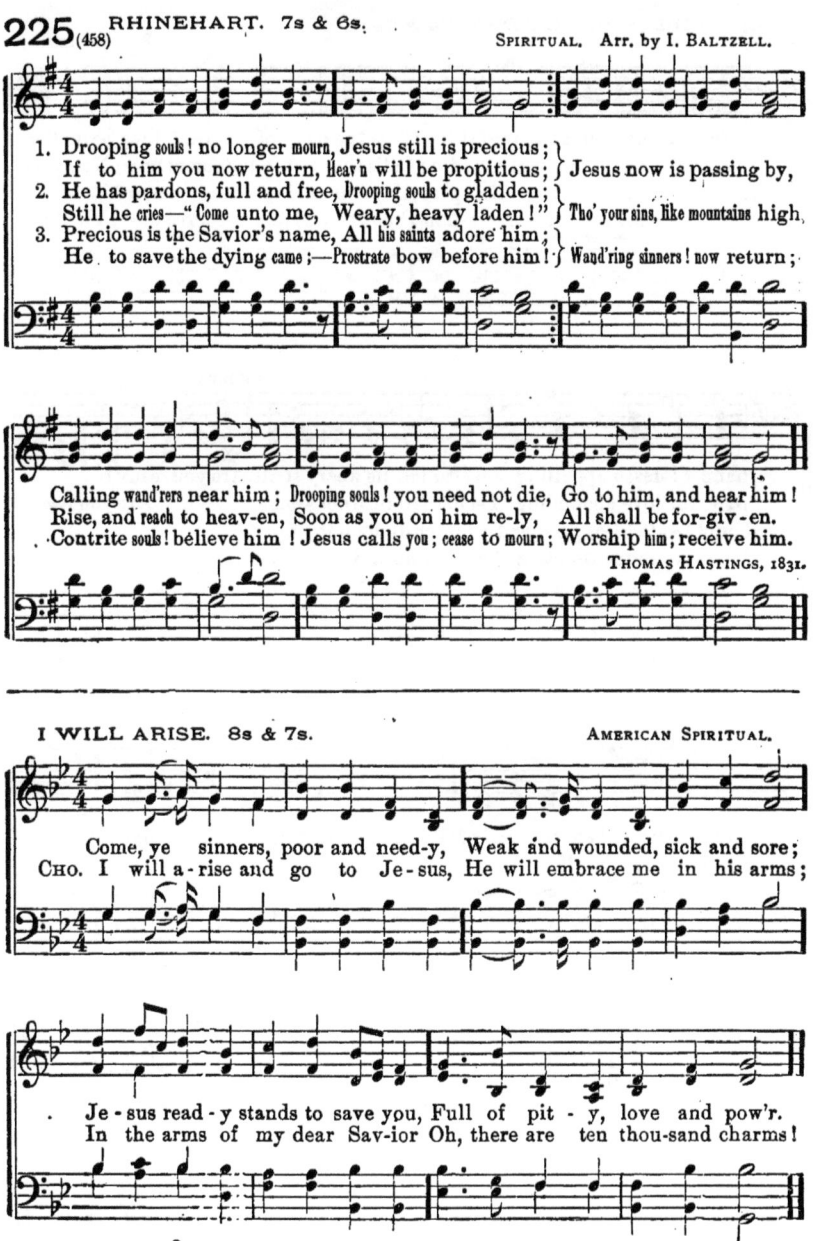

1. Drooping souls! no longer mourn, Jesus still is precious;
   If to him you now return, Heav'n will be propitious; } Jesus now is passing by,
2. He has pardons, full and free, Drooping souls to gladden;
   Still he cries—"Come unto me, Weary, heavy laden!" } Tho' your sins, like mountains high,
3. Precious is the Savior's name, All his saints adore him;
   He to save the dying came;—Prostrate bow before him! } Wand'ring sinners! now return;

Calling wand'rers near him; Drooping souls! you need not die, Go to him, and hear him!
Rise, and reach to heav-en, Soon as you on him re-ly, All shall be for-giv-en.
Contrite souls! believe him ! Jesus calls you; cease to mourn; Worship him; receive him.

THOMAS HASTINGS, 1831.

I WILL ARISE. 8s & 7s.

AMERICAN SPIRITUAL.

Come, ye sinners, poor and need-y, Weak and wounded, sick and sore;
Cho. I will a-rise and go to Je-sus, He will embrace me in his arms;

Je-sus read-y stands to save you, Full of pit-y, love and pow'r.
In the arms of my dear Sav-ior Oh, there are ten thou-sand charms!

8

226   ARE YOU READY?   8s & 7s.

E. S. LORENZ.

1. Soon the evening shadows falling Close the day of mor-tal life; Soon the
2. Soon the awful trumpet sounding Calls thee to the judgment throne; Now pre-
3. Oh, how fa-tal 'tis to lin-ger! Art thou read-y—read-y now? Read-y
4. Priceless love and free sal-va-tion Free-ly still are of-fered thee; Yield no

CHORUS.

hand of death appalling Draws thee from its weary strife. Are you ready?
pare, for love abounding Yet has left thee not a-lone.   Are you ready?
should Death's i-cy fin-ger Lay its chill upon thy brow.
long-er to temp-ta-tion, But from sin and sorrow flee.

J. W. SLAUGHENHAUPT.

are you ready? are you ready? 'Tis the Spir-it call-ing, why de-lay? Are you

ready?   Are you ready?   Do not lin-ger longer, come to-day.
are you ready?   Are you ready?

227 WINDHAM. L. M.   DANIEL READ, 1785.

1. Broad is the road that leads to death, And thousands walk to - geth-er there;
2. "De - ny thy - self and take thy cross," Is the Re-deem-er's great command;
3. The fear - ful soul that tires and faints, And walks the ways of God no more,
4. Lord, let not all my hopes be vain; Create my heart en - tire - ly new—

But wis-dom shows a nar - row path, With here and there a trav - el - er.
Nat-ure must count her gold but dross, If she would gain this heavenly land.
Is but esteemed al-most a saint, And makes his own de-struc-tion sure.
Which hypocrites could ne'er at - tain, Which false a - pos - tates nev - er knew.

ISAAC WATTS.

228 (504) GORTON. S. M.   LUDWIG VON BEETHOVEN.

1. Oh, where shall rest be found— Rest for the wea - ry soul?
2. The world can nev - er give The bliss for which we sigh:
3. Be - yond this vale of tears There is a life a - bove,
4. There is a death, whose pang Out - lasts the fleet - ing breath;
5. Lord God of truth and grace, Teach us that death to shun.

'Twere vain the o - cean depths to sound, Or pierce to eith - er pole.
'Tis not the whole of life to live, Nor all of death to die.
Un-meas-ured by the flight of years; And all that life is love.
Oh, what e - ter - nal hor - rors hang A-round the sec - ond death!
Lest we be ban-ished from thy face, And ev - er-more un - done.

JAMES MONTGOMERY, 1819.

229 NO ROOM IN HEAVEN. P. M. I. BALTZELL.

1. How sad it would be, if when thou didst call, All hopeless and un-for-
2. How sad it would be, the har-vest all past, The bright summer days all
3. Oh, haste thee, and fly, while mercy is near, Remember the love that he

giv-en, The an-gel that stands at the beau-ti-ful gate, Should
o-ver; To know that the reap-ers had gath-ered the grain, And
gave you; The love that has sought thee is seek-ing thee still, And

REFRAIN.

answer, No room in heav-en.
left thee alone for-ev-er. Sad, sad, sad would it be! No room in
Je-sus now waits to save you.

W. O. CUSHING.

heav-en for thee! No room, no room, No room in heav-en for

Slow and soft.

thee! No room, no room, No room in heav-en for thee!

230 WHEN THE KING COMES IN. P. M. E. S. Lorenz.

1. Called to the feast by the King are we, Sitting, perhaps, where his
2. Crowns on the head where the thorns have been, Glo-ri-fied he who once
3. Like lightning's flash will that in-stant show Things hidden long from both
4. Joy-ful his eye shall on each one rest Who is in white wedding

peo-ple be, How will it fare, friend, with thee and me,
died for men, Splen-did the vis-ion be-fore us then,
friend and foe, Just what we are will each neigh-bor know,
gar-ments dressed, Ah well for us if we stand the test,

Refrain.

When the King comes in. When the King comes in, brother, When the King comes

in! How will it fare with thee and me When the King comes in?

5 Endless the separation then,
  Bitter the cry of deluded men,
A wful that moment beyond all ken,
  When the King comes in.

6 Lord, grant us all, we implore thee, grace,
  So to await thee each in his place,
  That we may fear not to see thy face
  When thou comest in.

J. E. Landor.

231 WHEN THE DOOR IS SHUT. P. M.   E. S. Lorenz.

1. The door of sal-va-tion is o-pen wide, And Je-sus in-vites you to come;
2. The feast of the gos-pel a-waits its guests, The day and the hour are at hand;
3. Dear friends, if you ev-er should stand with-out, And plead for admittance in vain,

While mer-cy and par-don a-wait with-in, Oh, en-ter while yet there is room.
Ye hun-gry and perishing souls, draw near; Oh, why do you doubtingly stand?
You'd think of the Savior's entreating voice, And long for this mo-ment a-gain.

M. E. Servoss.

REFRAIN. *Soft and Slow.*

When the door once is shut, To en-treat will be vain; 'Twill nev-er, no, nev-er Be o-pened a-gain.

JUSTINA. L. M.   E. S. Lorenz.

Show pit-y, Lord, O Lord, for-give, Let a re-pent-ing reb-el live;

Are not thy mercies large and free? May not a sin-ner trust in thee?

HEBRON. L. M.   LOWELL MASON, 1830.

Oh, that my load of sin were gone; Oh, that I could at last sub-mit

At Je-sus' feet to lay it down— To lay my soul at Je-sus' feet.

232 [FIRST VERSE IN MUSIC.] (495)
My Yoke is Easy, my Burden Light.

2 Rest for my soul I long to find;
Savior of all, if mine thou art,
Give me the meek and lowly mind,
And stamp thine image on my heart.

3 Break off the yoke of inbred sin,
And fully set my spirit free;
I can not rest till pure within—
Till I am wholly lost in thee.

4 Fain would I learn of thee, my God;
Thy light and easy burden prove;
The cross all stained with hallowed blood,
The labor of thy dying love.

5 I would, but thou must give the power;
My heart from every sin release;
Bring near, bring near the joyful hour,
And fill me with thy perfect peace.
CHARLES WESLEY, 1742.

233 *Pardon Penitently Implored.* (493)

Show pity, Lord, O Lord, forgive;
Let a repenting rebel live;
Are not thy mercies large and free?
May not a sinner trust in thee?

2 My crimes, though great, can not surpass
The power and glory of thy grace;
Great God, thy nature hath no bound,
So let thy pard'ning love be found.

3 Oh, wash my soul from every sin,
And make my guilty conscience clean;
Here, on my heart, the burden ʼⁱⁿᵍ
And past offenses pain mine ey

4 My lips with shame my sins confess,
Against thy law, against thy grace;
Lord, should thy judgment grow severe,
I am condemned, but thou art clear.

5 Yet save a trembling sinner, Lord,
Whose hope, still hovering round thy word,
Would light on some sweet promise there,
Some sure support against despair.
CHARLES WESLEY, 1742.

234 *Deprecating the Withdrawal of the Spirit.* (494)

STAY, thou insulted Spirit, stay,
Though I have done thee such despite,
Nor cast the sinner quite away,
Nor take thine everlasting flight.

2 Though I have steeled my stubborn heart,
And still shook off my guilty fears;
And vexed and urged thee to depart,
For many long rebellious years;

3 Though I have most unfaithful been,
Of all whoe'er thy grace received!
Ten thousand times thy goodness seen;
Ten thousand times thy goodness grieved;

4 This only woe I deprecate;
This only plague I pray remove;
Nor leave me in my lost estate;
Nor curse me with this want of love.

5 Now, Lord, my weary soul release,
Upraise me with thy gracious hand,
And guide into thy perfect peace,
And bring me to the promised land.
CHARLES WESLEY, 1740.

235(489) WOODWORTH. L. M.

WILLIAM B. BRADBURY.

1. Just as I am, without one plea, But that thy blood was shed for me,
2. Just as I am, and wait-ing not To rid my soul of one dark blot,
3. Just as I am, tho' tossed a-bout With many a conflict, many a doubt,
4. Just as I am—poor, wretched, blind; Sight, riches, healing of the mind,
5. Just as I am—thou wilt receive, Wilt welcome, pardon, cleanse, relieve;
6. Just as I am—thy love unknown Hath broken ev-ery barrier down;

And that thou bidd'st me come to thee, O Lamb of God, I come! I come!
To thee whose blood can cleanse each spot, O Lamb of God, I come! I come.
Fight-ings within, and fears without, O Lamb of God, I come! I come!
Yea, all I need, in thee to find, O Lamb of God, I come! I come!
Be-cause thy promise I be-lieve, O Lamb of God, I come! I come!
Now, to be thine, yea, thine a-lone, O Lamb of God, I come! I come!

CHARLOTTE ELLIOTT, 1836.

236(506) BADEA. S. M.

GERMAN MELODY.

1. And can I yet de-lay My lit-tle all to give?
2. Nay, but I yield, I yield, I can hold out no more:
3. Tho' late, I all for-sake, My friends, my all re-sign;
4. Come and pos-sess me whole, Nor hence a-gain re-move;

To tear my soul from earth a-way, For Je-sus to re-ceive?
I sink, by dy-ing love compelled, And own thee con-quer-or.
Gracious Re-deem-er, take, oh, take, And seal me ev-er thine.
Set-tle and fix my wav'-ring soul With all thy weight of love.

CHARLES WESLEY, 1740.

237 I AM LISTENING. 8s & 7s. W. S. MARSHALL.

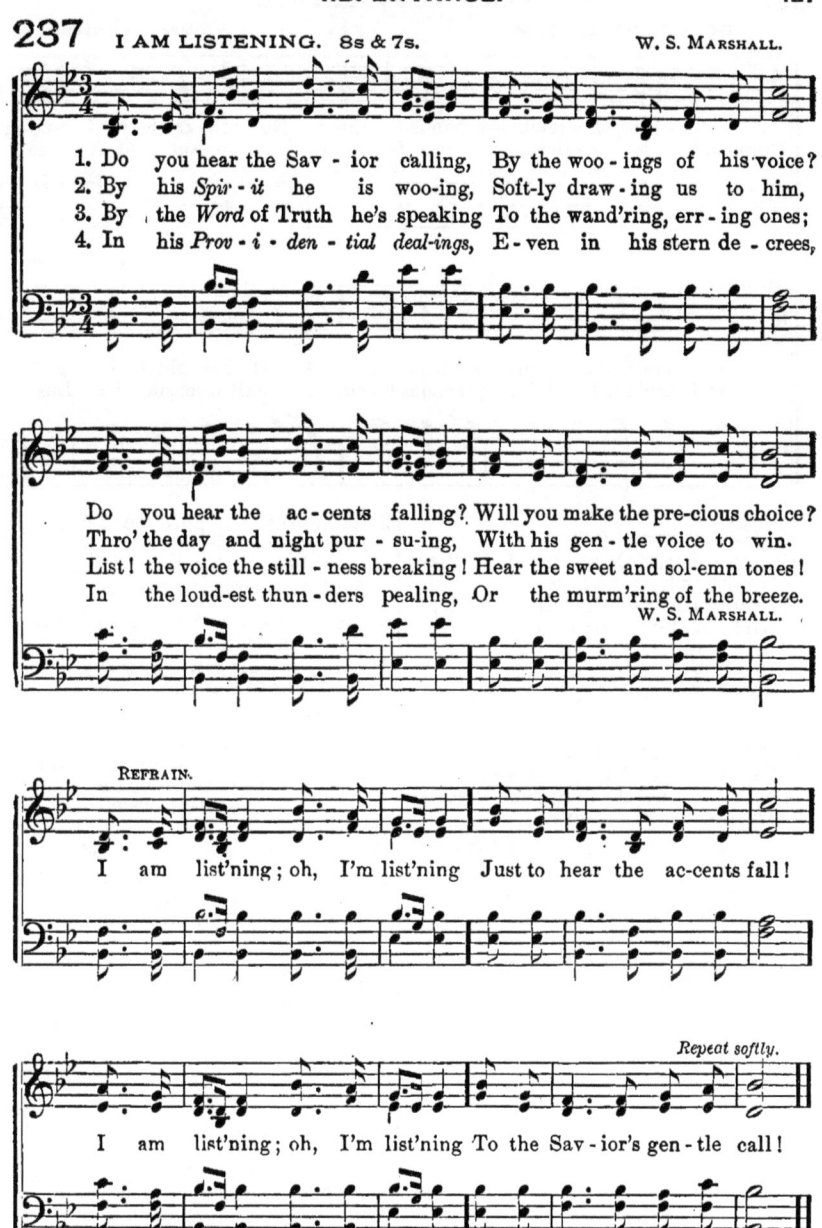

1. Do   you hear the Sav - ior calling, By the woo-ings of his voice?
2. By   his *Spir - it* he   is woo-ing, Soft-ly draw-ing us   to him,
3. By   the *Word* of Truth he's speaking To the wand'ring, err-ing ones;
4. In   his *Prov - i - den - tial deal-ings,* E - ven in   his stern de - crees,

Do   you hear the ac-cents falling? Will you make the pre-cious choice?
Thro' the day and night pur - su-ing, With his gen-tle voice to win.
List! the voice the still-ness breaking! Hear the sweet and sol-emn tones!
In   the loud-est thun-ders pealing, Or   the murm'ring of the breeze.

W. S. MARSHALL.

REFRAIN.

I   am   list'ning; oh, I'm list'ning Just to hear the   ac-cents fall!

Repeat softly.

I   am   list'ning; oh, I'm list'ning To the Sav-ior's gen-tle call!

I DO BELIEVE. C. M.   AMERICAN SPIRITUAL.

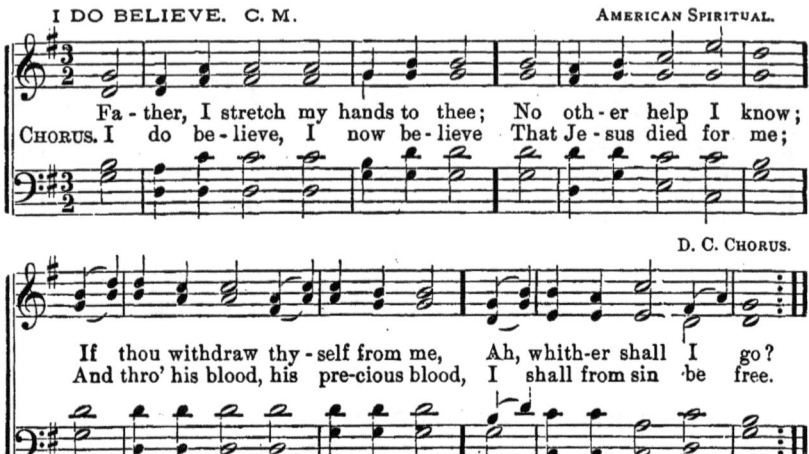

Fa - ther, I stretch my hands to thee; No oth - er help I know;
CHORUS. I do be - lieve, I now be - lieve That Je - sus died for me;

D. C. CHORUS.

If thou withdraw thy - self from me, Ah, whith-er shall I go?
And thro' his blood, his pre-cious blood, I shall from sin be free.

238 *Unwearied Earnestness.* (491)

FATHER, I stretch my hands to thee;
No other help I know:
If thou withdraw thyself from me,
Ah! whither shall I go?

2 What did thine only Son endure,
Before I drew my breath?
What pain, what labor, to secure
My soul from endless death!

3 O Jesus, could I this believe,
I now should feel thy power;
And all my wants thou would'st relieve,
In this accepted hour.

4 Author of faith! to thee I lift
My weary, longing eyes:
Oh, let me now receive that gift—
My soul without it dies.

5 Surely thou canst not let me die;
Oh, speak, and I shall live,
And here I will unwearied lie,
Till thou thy Spirit give.

6 How would my fainting soul rejoice,
Could I but see thy face;
Now let me hear thy quick'ning voice,
And taste thy pard'ning grace.
                              CHARLES WESLEY

239 *The Friend of Sinners.* (485)

JESUS! thou art the sinner's Friend;
As such I look to thee;
Now, in the fullness of thy love
O Lord, remember me.

2 Remember thy pure word of grace,—
Remember Calvary;
Remember all thy dying groans,
And, then, remember me.

3 Thou wondrous Advocate with God'
I yield myself to thee;
While thou art sitting on thy throne,
Dear Lord! remember me.

4 Lord! I am guilty—I am vile,
But thy salvation's free;
Then, in thine all abounding grace,
Dear Lord! remember me.
                    RICHARD BURNHAM, 1783, a.

240 *Approaching the Mercy-Seat.* (482)

APPROACH, my soul, the mercy-seat,
Where Jesus answers prayer;
There humbly fall before his feet,
For none can perish there.

2 Thy promise is my only plea,
With this I venture nigh;
Thou call'st the burdened souls to thee,
And such, O Lord, am I.

3 Bowed down beneath a load of sin,
By Satan sorely pressed;
By wars without and fears within,
I come to thee for rest.

4 Oh, wondrous love! to bleed and die,
To bear the cross and shame;
That guilty sinners, such as I,
Might plead thy gracious name.
                         JOHN NEWTON, 1779.

241 TAKE ME AS I AM. P. M.

Rev. J. H. Stockton.

1. Je - sus, my Lord, to thee I cry; Un-less thou help me, I must die; Oh,
2. Helpless I am, and full of guilt, But yet for me thy blood was spilt, And
3. I thirst, I long to know thy love, Thy full sal-va-tion I would prove; But

Fine. REFRAIN

bring thy free sal-va-tion nigh, And take me as I am. Take me as I
thou canst make me as thou wilt, But take me as I am.
since to thee I can not move, Oh, take me as I am. Take me, take me

bring thy free sal - va - tion nigh, And take me as I am.

D.S.

am, Take me as I am; Oh,
as I am, Take me, take me as I am;

4 If thou hast work for me to do,
  Inspire my will, my heart renew,
  And work both in and by me, too,
  But take me as I am.

5 And when at last the work is done,
  The battle o'er, the victory won,
  Still, still my cry shall be alone,
  Oh, take me as I am.
      Eliza H. Hamilton.

BROWN. C. M.

William B. Bradbury, 1840.

Ap-proach, my soul, the mer - cy - seat, Where Je - sus an-swers prayer;

There hum - bly fall be - fore his feet, For none can per - ish there.

242   FIX YOUR EYES UPON JESUS. P. M.   James McGranahan.

1. Would you lose your load of sin? Fix your eyes upon Je-sus; Would you know God's
2. Would you calmly walk the wave? Fix your eyes upon Je-sus; Would you know his
3. Would you have your cares grow light? Fix your eyes upon Je-sus; Would you songs have
4. Griev-ing, would you comfort know? Fix your eyes upon Je-sus; Hum-ble be when
'5. Would you strength in weakness have? Fix your eyes upon Je-sus; See a light be-

CHORUS.

peace with-in? Fix your eyes up-on   Je - sus;
pow'r to save? Fix your eyes up-on   Je - sus; Jesus who on the cross did die,
in   the night? Fix your eyes up-on   Je - sus;
bless-ings flow? Fix your eyes up-on   Je - sus;
yond the grave? Fix your eyes up-on   Je - sus;

D. W. Whittle.

Jesus who *lives* and *reigns* on high, He alone can justify; Fix your eyes upon Je-sus.

---

243   *Rom.* 5 : 2.   (664)

I stand; but not as once I did,
  Beneath my load of guilt;
The blessed Jesus bore it all—
  For me his blood was spilt.

2 I stand; but not on Calvary's Mount,
  With arms around the cross;
I have been there, and left behind
  Earth's pleasures, joys, and dross.

3 I stand e'en now where he appears,
  In union with my Lord;
In him I'm saved, oh, wondrous thought,
  I read it in his word.

4 Oh, bless the Lord! in him alone—
  In him we are complete;
We live by faith! but soon in sight
  Our coming Christ we'll greet.
          Unknown.

244 (492) AT THE CROSS. C. M. With Chorus.

R. E. HUDSON.

1. Oh, wond-rous, deep, unbounded love, My Sav-ior can it be That thou hast borne the
2. I kneel, repent-ing, at thy feet, I give my-self to thee; I plead thy mer-its,
3. Oh, let me plunge beneath the tide, For sin-ners flowing free, Then rise, renewed by
4. And when I reach thy place a-bove, My sweetest notes will be, Redemption through a

CHORUS.

crown of thorns, And suffered death for me. At the cross, at the cross, where I
thine a - lone, For thou hast died for me.
grace di - vine, And shout salva - tion free.
Sav - ior's name, Who bled and died for me.

FANNY CROSBY, 1873.

first saw the light, And the burden of my heart rolled away— It was rolled a-way,

there by faith I received my sight, And now I am happy all the day.

245 SAVED BY FAITH. P. M.

I. BALTZELL.

1. I have found redemption in the Savior's blood, I am saved by faith in his
2. Oh, how sweet the sto-ry of his wondrous grace, I am saved by faith in his
3. I will sing of Je-sus while the days go by, I am saved by faith in his
4. I will keep on sing-ing as I march a-long, I am saved by faith in his

blood, in his blood; I am sweet-ly trust-ing in the word of God, I am
blood, in his blood; I will trust in Je-sus while I run my race, I am
blood, in his blood; I will trust his promise, on his strength re-ly, I am
blood, in his blood; In my home in glo-ry this shall be my song, I am

CHORUS.

saved by faith in his blood. I am saved, . . yes, sweetly saved,

I. BALTZELL.   I am saved, sweetly saved, I am saved, sweetly saved,

1st time.   2d time.

I am saved by faith in the blood he shed for me, I am saved by faith in his blood, in his blood.

246 ONLY TRUST HIM. C. M.

Rev. J. H. Stockton.

1. Come, ev - 'ry soul by sin oppressed, There's mer-cy with the Lord;
2. For Je - sus shed his pre - cious blood Rich bless-ings to be - stow;
3. Yes, Je - sus is the Truth, the Way, That leads you in - to rest;
4. Come, then, and join this ho - ly band, And on to glo - ry go,

And he will sure - ly give you rest By trust - ing in his word.
Plunge now in - to the crim - son flood That wash - es white as snow.
Be - lieve in him with - out de - lay, And you are ful - ly blest.
To dwell in that ce - les - tial land, Where joys im-mor - tal flow.

J. H. Stockton.

CHORUS.

On - ly trust him, on - ly trust him, On - ly trust him now;

He will save you, he will save you, He will save you now.

247   IS MY NAME WRITTEN THERE? P. M.

FRANK M. DAVIS.

1. Lord, I care not for rich-es, Nei-ther sil-ver nor gold; I would
2. Lord, my sins, they are ma-ny, Like the sands of the sea, But thy
3. Oh, that beau-ti-ful cit-y, With its mansions of light, With its

make sure of heav-en, I would en-ter the fold. In the book of thy
blood, oh, my Sav-ior, Is suf-fi-cient for me! For thy prom-ise is
glo-ri-fied be-ings, In pure gar-ments of white; Where no e-vil thing

kingdom, With its pa-ges so fair, Tell me, Je-sus, my Sav-ior, Is my
writ-ten, In bright letters that glow, "Tho' your sins be as scar-let, I will
com-eth To de-spoil what is fair; Where the an-gels are watching, Yes, my

D. S. *In the book of thy king-dom, Is my*

Fine. CHORUS.   D. S.

name written there? Is my name written there? On the page white and fair?
make them like snow." Yes, my name's, etc.
name's written there, Yes, my name's, etc.

MRS. MARY A. KIDDER.

name writ-ten there?

248 CONVERT. P. M.

Spiritual. Arr. by E. S. L.

1. Oh, how hap-py are they Who their Sav-ior o-bey, And have
2. That sweet comfort was mine, When the fa-vor di-vine I first
3. 'Twas a heav-en be-low My Re-deem-er to know, And the

laid up their treas-ures a-bove; Tongue can not ex-press
found in the blood of the Lamb; When my heart it be-lieved,
an-gels could do noth-ing more Than to fall at his feet,

The sweet com-fort and peace Of a soul in its ear-li-est love.
What a joy I re-ceived, What a heav-en in Je-sus' rame.
And the sto-ry re-peat, And the Lov-er of sin-ners a-lore.

4 Jesus, all the day long,
　Was my joy and my song;
O that all his salvation might see!
　He hath loved me, I cried,
　He hath suffered and died
To redeem such a rebel as me.

5 On the wings of his love
　I was carried above
All sin and temptation and pain
　And I could not believe
　That I ever should grieve—
That I ever should suffer again.

6 I then rode on the sky,
　Freely justified I,
Nor did envy Elijah his seat;

My soul mounted higher,
In a chariot of fire,
And the moon it was under my feet.

7 O the rapturous height
　Of that holy delight
Which I felt in the life-giving blood,
　Of my Savior possessed,
　I was perfectly blest,
As if filled with the fullness of God.

8 Never more will I stray
　From my Savior away,
But I'll follow the Lamb till I die;
　I will take up my cross,
　And count all things but loss,
Till I meet with my Lord in the sky
　　　　　　　CHARLES WESLEY.

9

HALLOWED SPOT. P. M.   AMERICAN SPIRITUAL. Arr. by E. S. LORENZ.

There is a spot to me more dear 'Than na-tive vale or mountain;
A spot to which af-fection's tear Springs grateful from its fountain;
D. C. But where I first my Sav-ior found, And felt my sins for-giv-en.

'Tis not where kindred souls abound—Tho' that is al-most heav-en—

249 [FIRST VERSE IN MUSIC ABOVE.] (249)

2 Hard was my toil to reach the shore,
  Long tossed upon the ocean,
Above me was the thunder's roar,
  Beneath, the wave's commotion.
Darkly the pall of night was thrown
Around me, faint with terror;
In that dark hour how did my groans
  Ascend for years of error.

3 Sinking and panting as for breath,
  I knew not help was nigh me,
And cried, O save me, Lord, from death—
  Immortal Jesus, hear me.

Then, quick as thought, I felt him mine—
  My Savior stood before me;
I saw his brightness round me shine,
  And shouted glory, glory.

4 O sacred hour, O hallowed spot!
  Where love divine first found me;
Wherever falls my distant lot,
  My heart shall linger round thee:
And as from earth I rise, to soar
  Up to my home in heaven,
Down will I cast my eyes once more,
  Where I was first forgiven.
                    WILLIAM HUNTER, D. D.

250   BOYLSTON. S. M.   LOWELL MASON, 1832.

1. How sol-emn are the words, And yet to faith how plain, Which
2. "Ye must be born a-gain!" For so hath God de-creed; No
3. "Ye must be born a-gain!" And life in Christ must have; In
4. "Ye must be born a-gain!" Or nev-er en-ter heav'n; 'Tis

Je-sus ut-tered while on earth—"Ye must be born a-gain!"
ref-or-ma-tion will suf-fice—'Tis life poor sin-ners need.
vain the soul may elsewhere go—'Tis he a-lone can save.
on-ly blood-washed ones are there—The ran-somed and for-giv'n.
                    ANON.

251 IT IS WELL WITH MY SOUL. P. M.

P. P. BLISS.

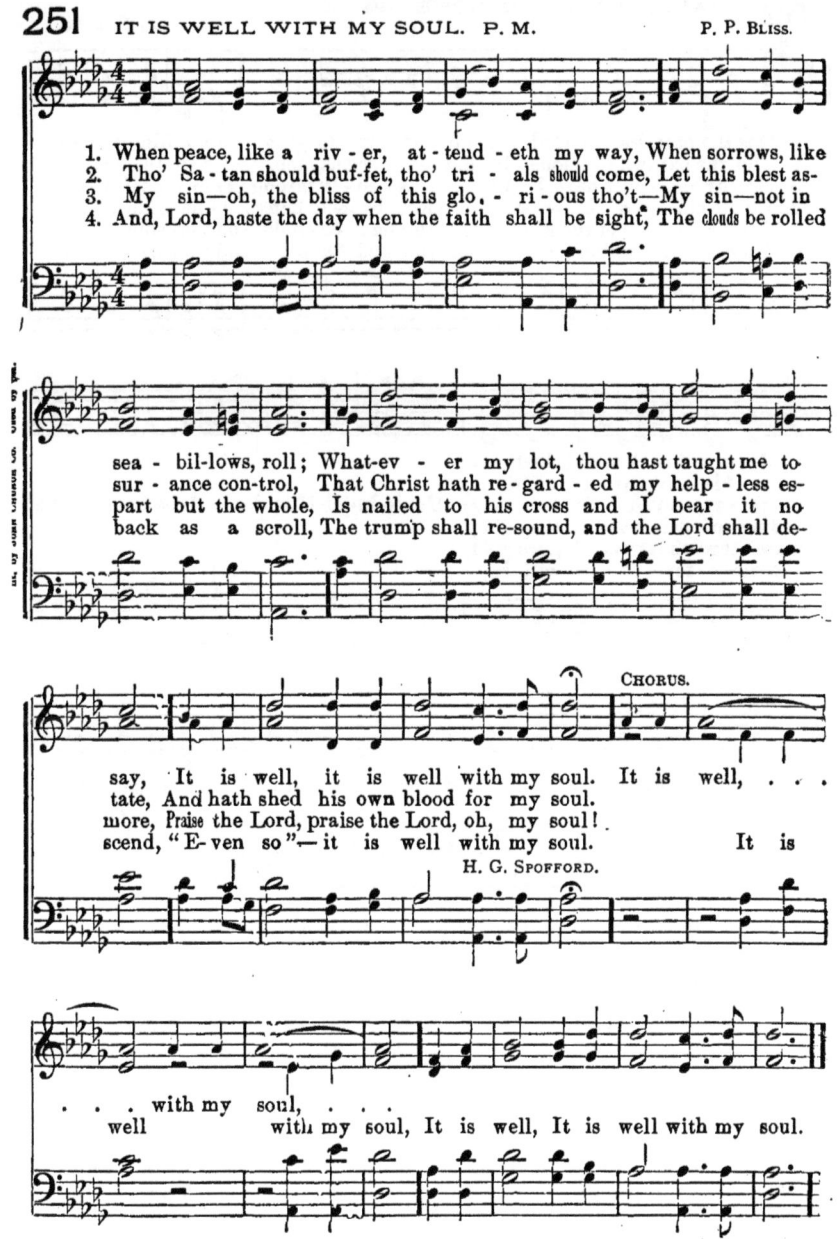

1. When peace, like a riv-er, at-tend-eth my way, When sorrows, like
2. Tho' Sa-tan should buf-fet, tho' tri - als should come, Let this blest as-
3. My sin—oh, the bliss of this glo. - ri-ous tho't—My sin—not in
4. And, Lord, haste the day when the faith shall be sight, The clouds be rolled

sea - bil-lows, roll; What-ev - er my lot, thou hast taught me to-
sur - ance con-trol, That Christ hath re - gard - ed my help - less es-
part but the whole, Is nailed to his cross and I bear it no
back as a scroll, The trump shall re-sound, and the Lord shall de-

CHORUS.

say, It is well, it is well with my soul. It is well, . . .
tate, And hath shed his own blood for my soul.
more, Praise the Lord, praise the Lord, oh, my soul!
scend, "E- ven so"— it is well with my soul. It is

H. G. SPOFFORD.

. . . with my soul, . . .
well with my soul, It is well, It is well with my soul.

252 HALLELUJAH! 'TIS DONE. 12s.

P. P. Bliss.

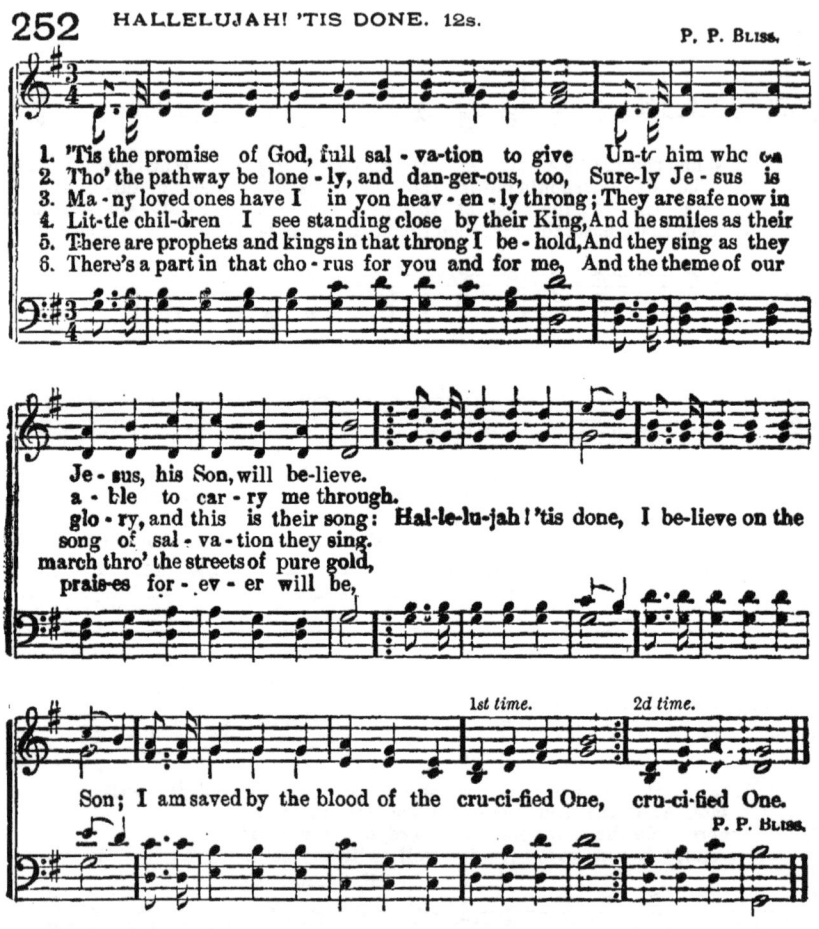

1. 'Tis the promise of God, full sal - va-tion to give Un-to him whc ca
2. Tho' the pathway be lone - ly, and dan-ger-ous, too, Sure-ly Je - sus is
3. Ma - ny loved ones have I in yon heav - en - ly throng; They are safe now in
4. Lit-tle chil-dren I see standing close by their King, And he smiles as their
5. There are prophets and kings in that throng I be - hold, And they sing as they
6. There's a part in that cho - rus for you and for me, And the theme of our

Je - sus, his Son, will be-lieve.
a - ble to car - ry me through.
glo - ry, and this is their song: Hal-le-lu-jah! 'tis done, I be-lieve on the
song of sal - va-tion they sing.
march thro' the streets of pure gold,
prais-es for - ev - er will be,

1st time. *2d time.*

Son; I am saved by the blood of the cru-ci-fied One, cru-ci-fied One.

P. P. Bliss.

---

253 *From Darkness to Light.* (522)

LORD! I know thy grace is nigh me,
  Thee thyself I can not see;
Jesus, Master! pass not by me;
  Son of David! pity me.

2 While I sit in weary blindness,
  Longing for the blessed light,
Many taste thy loving kindness;
  "Lord! I would receive my sight."

3 I would see thee and adore thee,
  And thy word the power can give;

Hear the sightless soul implore thee;
  Let me see thy face and live.

4 Ah! what touch is this that thrills me?
  What this burst of strange delight?
Lo! the rapturous vision fills me!
  This is Jesus! this is sight!

5 Room, ye saints that throng behind him!
  Let me follow in the way;
I will teach the blind to find him
  Who can turn their night to day.

H. D. GANSE.

BARTIMEUS. 8s & 7s. DANIEL READ, 1804.

"Mer-cy, oh, thou Son of Da-vid!" Thus blind Bar-ti-me-us prayed;

"Oth-ers by thy word are sav-ed, Now to me af-ford thine aid."

254 [FIRST VERSE IN MUSIC ABOVE.]
The Blind Man Healed. (521)

2 Many for his crying chid him,—
  But he called the louder still;
Till the gracious Savior bade him,—
  "Come, and ask me what you will."

3 Money was not what he wanted,
  Though by begging used to live;
But he asked, and Jesus granted,
  Alms which none but he could give:

4 "Lord! remove this grievous blindness,
  Let mine eyes behold the day!"

Straight he saw, and, won by kindness,
Followed Jesus in the way.

5 Oh! methinks I hear him praising,
  Publishing to all around,
"Friends! is not my case amazing?
  What a Savior I have found!

6 "Oh! that all the blind but knew him,
  And would be advised by me!
Surely would they hasten to him,
  He would cause them all to see."
  JOHN NEWTON, 1779.

255 SITTING AT THE FEET OF JESUS. P. M.

E. S. LORENZ.
Fine.

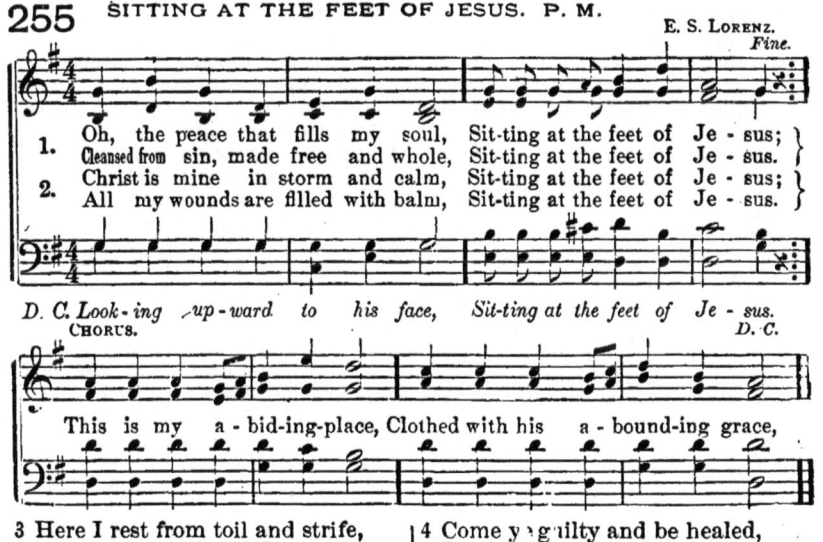

1. Oh, the peace that fills my soul, Sit-ting at the feet of Je-sus;
   Cleansed from sin, made free and whole, Sit-ting at the feet of Je-sus.
2. Christ is mine in storm and calm, Sit-ting at the feet of Je-sus;
   All my wounds are filled with balm, Sit-ting at the feet of Je-sus.

D. C. Look-ing up-ward to his face, Sit-ting at the feet of Je-sus.
CHORUS.
D. C.

This is my a-bid-ing-place, Clothed with his a-bound-ing grace,

3 Here I rest from toil and strife,
  Sitting at the feet of Jesus;
Safe beneath the Tree of Life,
  Sitting at the feet of Jesus.

4 Come ye guilty and be healed,
  Sitting at the feet of Jesus;
Freely is God's love revealed,
  Sitting at the feet of Jesus.
  PRISCILLA J. OWENS.

ORTONVILLE. C. M.   THOMAS HASTINGS, 1837.

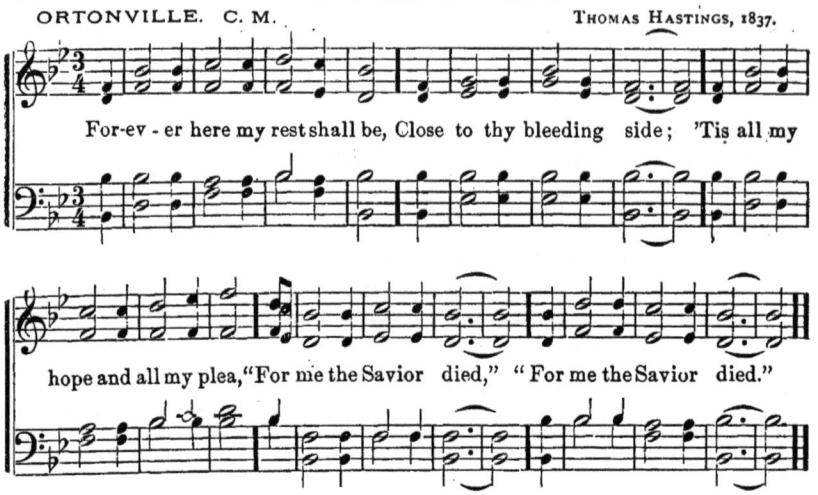

For-ev - er here my rest shall be, Close to thy bleeding side; 'Tis all my

hope and all my plea, "For me the Savior died," "For me the Savior died."

256 [FIRST VERSE INSERTED IN MUSIC.]
Prayer for Entire Purification. (649)

2 My dying Savior and my God,
  Fountain for guilt and sin,
Sprinkle me ever with thy blood,
  And cleanse and keep me clean.

3 Wash me and make me thus thine own,
  Wash me, and mine thou art!
Wash me, but not my feet alone,
  My hands, my head, my heart!

4 Th' atonement of thy blood apply,
  Till faith to sight improve,
Till hope in full fruition die,
  And all my soul be love.
                CHARLES WESLEY, 1740.

257   *The Believer's Rest.*   (654)

LORD, I believe a rest remains
  To all thy people known;
A rest where pure enjoyment reigns,
  And thou art loved alone.

2 A rest where all our soul's desire
  Is fixed on things above;
Where fear, and sin, and grief expire,
  Cast out by perfect love.

3 Oh, that I now the rest might know,
  Believe and enter in:
Now, Savior, now the power bestow,
  And let me cease from sin.

4 Remove this hardness from my heart;
  This unbelief remove:
To me the rest of faith impart—
  The Sabbath of thy love.
                CHARLES WESLEY.

258   *Longing for Christ.*   (648)

OH! could I find from day to day,
  A nearness to my God;
Then should my hours glide sweet away,
  And live upon thy word.

2 Lord! I desire with thee to live,
  Anew from day to day,
In joys the world can never give,
  Nor ever take away.

3 O Jesus! come and rule my heart,
  And I'll be wholly thine;
And never, never more depart;
  For thou art wholly mine.

4 Thus, till my last expiring breath,
  Thy goodness I'll adore;
And, when my flesh dissolves in death,
  My soul shall love thee more.
                BENJAMIN CLEVELAND, 1790.

259   *Self-Dedication.*   (662)

WELCOME, O Savior! to my heart;
  Possess thine humble throne;
Bid every rival hence depart,
  And claim me for thine own.

2 The world and Satan I forsake,—
  To thee I all resign;
My longing heart, O Jesus! take,
  And make it all divine.

3 Oh! may I never turn aside,
  Nor from thy bosom flee;
Let nothing here my heart divide—
  I give it all to thee.
                HUGH BOURNE, 1825.

RHINE. 'C. M.   GERMAN MELODY.

My God, I know, I feel thee mine, And will not quit my claim Till all I
have is lost in thine, And all renewed I am, And all renewed I am.

260 *Prayer for Entire Sanctification.* (652)

My God, I know, I feel thee mine,
 And will not quit my claim
Till all I have is lost in thine,
 And all renewed I am.

2 I hold thee with a trembling hand,
 And will not let thee go,
Till steadfastly by faith I stand
 And all thy goodness know.

3 Jesus, thine all-victorious love
 Shed in my heart abroad:
Then shall my feet no longer rove,
 Rooted and fixed in God.

4 Refining fire, go through my heart,
 Illuminate my soul;
Scatter thy life through every part,
 And sanctify the whole.
                    CHARLES WESLEY.

261 *Self-Consecration.* (646)

My God! accept my heart this day,
 And make it always thine,
That I from thee no more may stray,
 No more from thee decline.

2 Before the cross of him who died,
 Behold I prostrate fall;
Let every sin be crucified;
 Let Christ be All in All.

3 May the dear blood, once shed for me,
 My blest atonement prove,
That I, from first to last, may be
 The purchase of thy love.

4 Let every thought, and work, and word,
 To thee be ever given;
Then life shall be thy service, Lord!
 And death the gate of heaven.
                    MATTHEW BRIDGES, 1848.

BEMERTON. C. M.   H. W. GREATOREX, 1849.

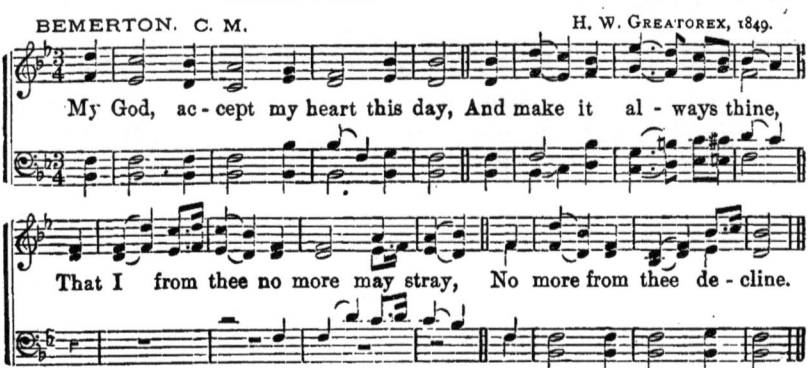

My God, ac-cept my heart this day, And make it al-ways thine,
That I from thee no more may stray, No more from thee de-cline.

UXBRIDGE. L. M.   LOWELL MASON, 1830.

My gracious Lord, I own thy right To ev-'ry serv-ice I can pay,

And call it my su-preme de-light To hear thy dic-tates and o - bey.

262   *Living to Christ Alone.*   (815)

My gracious Lord! I own thy right
  To every service I can pay,
And call it my supreme delight,
  To hear thy dictates and obey.

2 What is my being, but for thee,
  Its sure support, its noblest end ?
Thine ever-smiling face to see,
  And serve the cause ol such a Friend.

3 I would not breathe for worldly joy,
  Or to increase my worldly good ;
Nor future days or powers employ,
  To spread a sounding name abroad.

4 'Tis to my Savior I would live,
  To him, who for my ransom died ;
Nor could all worldly honor give
  Such bliss as crowns me at his side.
          PHILIP DODDRIDGE, 1740.

263   *God Wills our Holiness.*   (679)

HE wills that I should holy be ;
  That holiness I long to feel ;
That full divine conformity
  To all my Savior's righteous will.

2 See, Lord, the travail of thy soul
  Accomplished in the change of mine;
And plunge me, every whit made whole,
  In all the depths of love divine.

3 On thee, O God, my soul is stayed,
  And waits to prove thine utmost will;
The promise by thy mercy made,
  Thou canst, thou wilt in me fulfill.

4 No more I stagger at thy power,
  Or doubt thy truth, which can not move;
Hasten the long-expected hour,
  And bless me with thy perfect love.
          CHARLES WESLEY.

GRATITUDE. L. M.   A. BOST.

He wills that I should ho - ly be; That ho - li - ness I long to feel;

That full di - vine con-form - i - ty To all my Sav-ior's righteous will.

DUANE STREET. L. M. D.   REV. GEORGE COLES.

Je - sus, my all, to heav'n is gone, He whom I fixed my hopes up-on;

His track I see, and I'll pur-sue The nar-row way till him I view.

The way the ho - ly prophets went, The road that leads from banishment;

The King's highway of ho - li - ness; I'll go, for all his paths are peace.

264 [FIRST VERSE INSERTED IN MUSIC.]
The Way to God.

2 This is the way I long have sought,
And mourned because I found it not;
My grief a burden long has been,
Because I was not saved from sin.
The more I strove against its power,
I felt its weight and guilt the more;
Till late I heard my Savior say,
"Come hither, soul, I am the way."

3 Lo! glad I come; and thou, blest Lamb,
Shalt take me to thee, as I am;
Nothing but sin have I to give;
Nothing but love shall I receive.
Then will I tell to sinners round,
What a dear Savior I have found:
I'll point to thy redeeming blood,
And say, "Behold the way to God."
JOHN CENNICK, 1743.

265   *Bought with a Price.*

LORD, I am thine, entirely thine,
Purchased and saved by blood divine,
With full consent thine I would be,
And own thy sovereign right in me.

2 Grant one poor sinner more a place
Among the children of thy grace:
A wretched sinner, lost to God,
But ransomed by Immanuel's blood.

3 Thine would I live, thine would I die,
Be thine through all eternity;
The vow is past beyond repeal;
And now I set the solemn seal.

4 Here at that cross where flows the blood
That bought my guilty soul for God,
Thee, my new Master now I call,
And consecrate to thee my all.
REV. SAMUEL DAVIES, 1769. *Ab.*

ELLESDIE. 8s & 7s. D.   W. A. MOZART.

Je-sus, I my cross have taken. All to leave and follow thee ; Naked, poor, despised, forsaken,
D. S.   Yet how rich is my con-di - tion,

Fine.

Thou, from hence, my all shalt be ! Per-ish, every fond ambition, All I've sought, or hoped, or known,
God and heaven are still my own!
D. C.

266 [FIRST VERSE IN MUSIC ABOVE.]
Leaving All to Follow Christ.   (704)

2 Let the world despise and leave me—
 They have left my Savior too;
Human hearts and looks deceive me—
 Thou art not, like them, untrue.
And while thou shalt smile upon me,
 God of wisdom, love, and might,
Foes may hate and friends disown me,
 Show thy face and all is bright.

5 Go, then, earthly fame and treasure;
 Come, disaster, scorn, and pain !
In thy service pain is pleasure,
 With thy favor, loss is gain.

I have called thee, Abba, Father,
 I have set my heart on thee ;
Storms may howl, and clouds may gather—
 All must work for good to thee.

4 Haste thee on from grace to glory,
 Armed by faith, and winged by prayer;
Heaven's eternal day's before thee,
 God's own hand shall guide thee there.
Soon shall close thy earthly mission,
 Soon shall pass thy pilgrim days;
Hope shall change to glad fruition,
 Faith to sight, and prayer to praise.
HENRY FRANCIS LYTE, 1829.

GEINSHEIM. 8s & 7s. D.   VOLKSLIED. Arr. by E. S. LORENZ.
Fine.

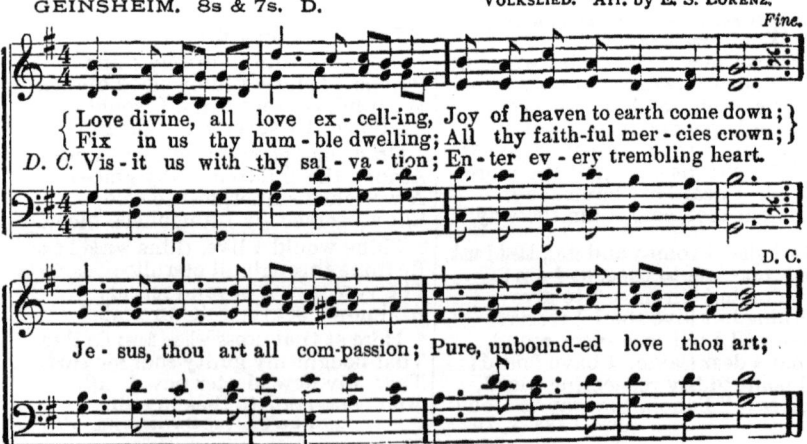

{ Love divine, all love ex - cell-ing, Joy of heaven to earth come down ; }
{ Fix in us thy hum - ble dwelling; All thy faith-ful mer - cies crown; }
D. C. Vis - it us with thy sal - va - tion; En - ter ev - ery trembling heart.

D. C.

Je - sus, thou art all com-passion; Pure, unbound-ed love thou art;

AUTUMN. 8s & 7s. Double. SPANISH MELODY.

Love di-vine, all love ex-celling, Joy of heaven, to earth come down; Fix in us thy humble

dwelling; All thy faith-ful mercies crown; Je-sus, thou art all com-pas-sion; Pure, un-

bound - ed love thou art; Vis - it us with thy salvation; Enter every trembling heart.

267 *Desiring Sanctification.* (701)

LOVE divine, all love excelling,
Joy of heaven, to earth come down;
Fix in us thy humble dwelling;
All thy faithful mercies crown;
Jesus, thou art all compassion;
Pure, unbounded love thou art;
Visit us with thy salvation;
Enter every trembling heart.

2 Breathe, oh, breathe thy Holy Spirit
Into every troubled breast,
Let us all thy grace inherit;
Let us find thy promised rest:
Take away the love of sinning;
Take our load of guilt away;
End the work of thy beginning;
· Bring us to eternal day.

3 Carry on thy new creation;
Pure and holy may we be;
Let us see our whole salvation
Perfectly secured by thee:
Change from glory into glory,
Till in heaven we take our place,
Till, we cast our crowns before thee,
Lost in wonder, love, and praise.
CHARLES WESLEY. 1747.

268 *Union with Jesus.* (700)

IN thy service will I ever,
Jesus, my Redeemer, stay;
Nothing me from thee shall sever,
Gladly would I go thy way.
Yes, Lord Jesus, I am ever
Thine in sorrow and in joy;
Death the union shall not sever,
Nor eternity destroy.

2 Let thy light on me be shining
When the day is almost gone,
When the evening is declining,
And the night is drawing on:
Bless me, oh, my Savior! laying
Thy hands on my weary head;
"Here thy day is ended," saying,
"Yonder live the faithful dead."

3 Stay beside me, when the stillness
And the icy touch of death
Fill my trembling soul with chillness,
Like the morning's frosty breath;
As my failing eyes grow dimmer,
Let my spirit grow more bright,
As I see the first faint glimmer
Of the everlasting light.
P. SPITTA. 1833.

EVEN ME. 8s & 7s. WILLIAM B. BRADBURY, 1862.

Lord, I hear of show'rs of bless-ing Thou art scatt'ring broad and free: }
Show'rs, the thirst-y land re-fresh-ing— Let their fullness fall on me, }

REFRAIN.

E - ven me, e - ven me, Let their full-ness fall on me.

269 *Pass Me Not.* (523)

LORD! I hear of showers of blessing,
  Thou art scattering, broad and free;
Showers, the thirsty land refreshing;
  Let their fullness fall on me.

2 Pass me not, oh, gracious Father!
  Sinful, though my heart may be;
Thou might'st curse me, but the rather
  Let thy mercy fall on me.

3 Pass me not, oh, tender Savior!
  Let me love and cling to thee;
I am longing for thy favor;
  When thou comest, call for me.

4 Pass me not, oh, mighty Spirit!
  Thou canst make the blind to see;
Witnesser of Jesus' merit,
  Speak the word of power to me.

5 Have I long in sin been sleeping,
  Long been slighting, grieving thee?
Has the world my heart been keeping?
  Oh! forgive and rescue me.

6 Love of God, so pure and changeless,—
  Blood of God, so rich and free,—
Grace of God, so strong and boundless,—
  Magnify them all in me.
    ELIZABETH CODNER, 1860.

270 *Self-Consecration.* (524)

TAKE me, oh, my Father! take me,
  Take me, save me, through thy Son;
That which thou would'st have me, make me,
  Let thy will in me be done.

2 Long from thee my footsteps straying,
  Thorny proved the way I trod;
Weary come I now, and praying—
  Take me to thy love, my God!

3 Fruitless years with grief recalling,
  Humbly I confess my sin;
At thy feet, O Father! falling,
  To thy household take me in.

4 Freely now to thee I proffer
  This relenting heart of mine;
Freely, life and soul I offer—
  Gift unworthy love like thine.

5 Once the world's Redeemer dying,
  Bore our sins upon the tree;
On that sacrifice relying,
  Now I look in hope to thee;

6 Father! take me; all forgiving,
  Fold me to thy loving breast;
In thy hope forever living,
  I must be forever blest!
    RAY PALMER. 1865.

271 *Restore my Peace.* (637)

O JESUS! full of grace,
  To thee I make my moan:
Let me again behold thy face—
  Call home thy banished one.

2 Again my pardon seal,
  Again my soul restore,

And freely my backslidings heal,
  And bid me sin no more.

3 Thine utmost mercy show;
  Say to my drooping soul—
In peace and full assurance go;
  Thy faith hath made thee whole.
    CHARLES WESLEY, 1756.

272 I CAN NOT DO WITHOUT THEE. 7s & 6s.

E. S. Lorenz.

CHORUS.

1. I can not do without thee, O Sav-ior of the lost! ⎞
Whose pre-cious blood re-deemed me At such tremendous cost. ⎠

2. I can not do without thee, I can not stand a-lone; ⎫ I can not, would not,
I have no strength or good-ness, No wis-dom of my own. ⎭

D. C. *I have no strength or goodness, No wis-dom of my own.*

Dare not, could not, Will not do without thee.

3 I can not do without thee,
I do not know the way;
Thou knowest, and thou leadest,
And wilt not let me stray.

4 I can not do without thee,
For years are fleeting fast,
And soon, in solemn loneliness,
The river must be passed.

FRANCES R. HAVERGAL, Alt.

273 (635) FERGUSON. S. M.

GEORGE KINGSLEY, 1843.

1. Mine eyes and my de-sire Are ev-er to the Lord;
2. Lord, turn thee to my soul; Bring thy sal-va-tion near;
3. When shall the sov-'reign grace Of my for-giv-ing God
4. Oh, keep my soul from death, Nor put my hope to shame;

I love to plead his prom-is-es, And rest up-on his word.
When will thy hand re-lease my feet From sin's de-struc-tive snare?
Re-store me from those dangerous ways My wand'ring feet have trod?
For I have placed my on-ly trust In my Re-deem-er's name.

ISAAC WATTS, 1719.

274 (694) TRUSTING. 7s.

W. G. FISCHER.

1. I am com-ing to the cross; I am poor, and weak, and blind;
2. Long my heart has sighed for thee; Long has e-vil reigned with-in;
3. Here I give my all to thee—Friends,and time,and earth-ly store;
4. In the prom-is-es I trust; Now I feel the blood ap-plied;
5. Je-sus comes! he fills my soul! Per-fect-ed in love I am!

CHORUS. I am trust-ing, Lord, in thee, Blest Lamb of Cal-va-ry;

I am count-ing all but dross; I shall thy sal-va-tion find.
Je-sus sweet-ly speaks to me— I will cleanse you from all sin.
Soul and bod-y thine to be— Whol-ly thine—for-ev-er-more.
I am pros-trate in the dust; I with Christ am cru-ci-fied.
I am ev-'ry whit made whole; Glo-ry! glo-ry to the Lamb!

WM. McDONALD.

Hum-bly at thy cross I bow; Save me, Je-sus,save me now.

275 I'LL LIVE FOR HIM. P. M.

C. R. DUNBAR.

1. My life, my love I give to thee,Thou Lamb of God, who died for me;
2. I now be-lieve thou dost receive, For thou hast died that I might live;
3. Oh, thou who died on Cal-va-ry, To save my soul and make me free,

CHO.—I'll live for him who died for me, How hap-py, then, my life shall be!

D. C.

Oh, may I ev-er faith-ful be, My Sav-ior and my God.
And now henceforth I'll trust in thee, My Sav-ior and my God.
I con-se-crate my life to thee, My Sav-ior and my God.

I'll live for him who died for me, My Sav-ior and my God.

276 TAKE MY HEART, DEAR JESUS. P. M.

I. BALTZELL.

1. Take my heart, dear Jesus, Make it all thine own, all thine own,
2. Take my heart, dear Jesus, Make it pure and clean, pure and clean,
3. Take my heart, dear Jesus, Make it white as snow, white as snow,

all thine own: Let thy Ho - ly Spir - it Break this heart of stone,
pure and clean: Let thy blood, still flowing, Wash a - way my sin,
white as snow; May the cleansing fountain, May thy pre-cious flow,

CHORUS.

And make me all thine own. Take my heart, . . and let it
And make me pure and clean.
Still keep me white as snow.   Take my heart, and let it

I. BALTZELL.

be   Ev - 'ry mo - . . - ment more like thee;
be, and let it be,   Ev - 'ry mo-ment, ev - 'ry moment more like thee;

At thy feet I bow; Take my heart just now, And make me all thine own.

277 ENTIRE CONSECRATION. 7s.   Wm. J. Kirkpatrick.

1. Take my life, and let it be   Con - se - crat - ed, Lord, to thee;
2. Take my feet, and let them be   Swift and beau - ti - ful for thee;
3. Take my lips, and let them be   Filled with mes - sa - ges for thee·
4. Take my moments and my days,   Let them flow in end - less praise;

Take my hands and let them move   At the im-pulse of   thy love.
Take my voice, and let me sing   Al - ways, on - ly for my King.
Take my sil - ver and my gold—   Not a mite would I with-hold.
Take my in - tellect, and use   Ev - 'ry pow'r as thou shalt choose.

CHORUS.

{ Wash me in the Savior's precious blood, the precious blood, }
{ Cleanse me in its pu - ri - fy-ing flood, the healing flood, } Lord, I give to

thee my life and all, to be Thine, henceforth e - ter - nal - ly.

5. Take my will, and make it thine;
It shall be no longer mine;
Take my heart,—it is thine own,—
It shall be thy royal throne.

6 Take my love,—my Lord, I pour
At thy feet its treasure-store!
Take myself, and I will be
Ever, only, all for thee!

Frances Ridley Havergal.

278 DRAW ME TO THEE. 8s & 6s.   E. S. LORENZ.

1. Lord, weak and im-po-tent I stand, As fet-tered by an un-seen hand;
2. In vain I struggle to be free; I would, but can not, fly to thee;
3. Oh, bring me near-er, near-er still, That thine own peace my soul may fill,
4. Here, Lord, I would for - ev - er bide, And nev - er wander from thy side;

Break thou the strong and sub - tle band, And draw me close to thee.
Ope thou the pris - on door for me, And draw me close to thee.
And I may rest in thy sweet will; Lord, draw me close to thee.
Be - neath thy wing do thou me hide, And draw me close to thee.

M. A. W. COOK.

D. S. *Beneath thy wing do thou me hide, And draw me close to thee.*

CHORUS.

Draw me close to thee, Savior, Draw me close to thee;
close to thee, Savior, close to thee;

279   *Clinging to Christ.*   (668)

O HOLY Savior! Friend unseen,
Since on thine arm thou bid'st me lean,
Help me, throughout life's changing scene,
 By faith to cling to thee!
CHO.—Help me cling to thee, Savior,
 Help me cling to thee!
Help me, throughout life's changing scene,
 By faith to cling to thee!

2 Without a murmur I dismiss
My former dreams of earthly bliss;
My joy, my recompense be this,
 Each hour to cling to thee!

3 Though faith and hope are often tried,
I ask not, need not, aught beside;
So safe, so calm, so satisfied,
 The soul that clings to thee!
 CHARLOTTE ELLIOT

10

280 DRAW ME NEARER. P. M.

W. H. Doane.

1. I am thine, O Lord, I have heard thy voice, And it told thy love to me;
2. Con-se-crate me now to thy service, Lord, By the pow'r of grace divine;
3. O the pure delight of a sin-gle hour That before thy throne I spend,
4. There are depths of love that I can not know Till I cross the nar-row sea,

But I long to rise in the arms of faith, And be clos-er drawn to thee.
Let my soul look up with a steadfast hope, And my will be lost in thine.
When I kneel in pray'r, and with thee, my God, I commune as friend with friend.
There are heights of joy that I may not reach Till I rest in peace with thee.

FANNY J. CROSBY.

REFRAIN.

Draw me near - er, nearer, blessed Lord, To the cross where thou hast died;
near-er, nearer,

Draw me near-er, near-er, nearer, blessed Lord, To thy precious, bleeding side.

281 WHITER THAN SNOW. 11s. WM. G. FISHER, 1872.

1. Lord Je-sus, I long to be per-fect-ly whole; I want thee for-
2. Lord Je-sus, look down from thy throne in the skies, And help me to
3. Lord Je-sus, for this I most hum-bly en-treat; I wait, blessed
4. Lord Je-sus, thou seest I pa-tient-ly wait; Come now, and with-

ev - er, to live in my soul; Break down ev-'ry i - dol, cast
make a complete sac - ri - fice; I give up my-self, and what-
Lord, at thy cru - ci - fied feet, By faith for my cleansing, I
in me a new heart cre - ate; To those who have sought thee, thou

out ev - 'ry foe; Now wash me, and I shall be whit - er than snow.
ev - er I know—Now wash me, and I shall be whit - er than snow.
see thy blood flow—Now wash me, and I shall be whit - er than snow.
nev - er said'st no—Now wash me, and I shall be whit - er than snow.

JAMES NICHOLSON.

CHORUS.

Whit - er than snow, yes, whit - er than snow;

Now wash me, and I shall be whit - er than snow.

282 ARE YOU WASHED IN THE BLOOD? P. M.

Rev. E. A. Hoffman.

1. Have you been to Je-sus for the cleansing pow'r? Are you washed in the
2. Are you walk-ing dai-ly by the Sav-ior's side? Are you washed in the
3. When the Bride-groom com-eth will your robes be white, Pure and white in the
4. Lay a-side the garments that are stained with sin, And be washed in the

blood of the Lamb? Are you ful-ly trust-ing in his grace this hour?
blood of the Lamb? Do you rest each mo-ment in the Cru-ci-fied?
blood of the Lamb? Will your soul be read-y for the man-sions bright?
blood of the Lamb; There's a fount-ain flow-ing for the soul un-clean,

CHORUS.

Are you washed in the blood of the Lamb? Are you washed in the
Are you washed in the blood of the Lamb?
And be washed in the blood of the Lamb?
Oh, be washed in the blood of the Lamb. Are you washed

E. A. Hoffman.

blood, In the soul-cleans-ing blood of the Lamb? Are your garments
in the blood, of the Lamb?

ARE YOU WASHED IN THE BLOOD? Concluded.

spotless, are they white as snow? Are you washed in the blood of the Lamb?

283 THE CLEANSING WAVE. C. M.

MRS. JOS. F. KNAPP.

1. Oh, now I see the crimson wave, The fount-ain deep and wide;
2. I rise to walk in heaven's own light, A - bove the world and sin,
3. A - maz- ing grace! 'tis heaven be - low To feel the blood ap - plied;

Je - sus, my Lord, might - y to save, Points to his wound - ed side.
With heart made pure, and garments white, And Christ enthroned with-in.
And Je - sus, on - ly Je - sus know, My Je - sus cru . ci . fied.

MRS. PHŒBE PALMER.

CHORUS.

The cleansing stream I see! I see! I plunge, and oh, it cleans-eth me;

Oh, praise the Lord! it cleanseth me, It cleans-eth me, yes, cleanseth me.

284 BEULAH LAND. L. M. JNO. R. SWENEY.

1. I've reach'd the land of corn and wine, And all its riches freely mine; Here shines undimm'd
2. The Savior comes and walks with me, And sweet communion here have we; He gent-ly leads
3. A sweet perfume upon the breeze, Is borne from ever vernal trees, And flow'rs that
4. The zephyrs seem to float to me, Sweet sounds of heaven's melody, As angels, with

CHORUS.

one blissful day, For all my night has pass'd away.
me with his hand, For this is heaven's border land. O Beu-lah land, sweet Beulah land,
never fading grow Where streams of life forever flow.
the white-robed throng, Join in the sweet redemption song.

EDGAR PAGE STITES.

As on thy highest mount I stand, I look away across the sea, Where mansions are pre-

pared for me. And view the shining glory shore, My heav'n, my home forevermore.

Used by permission.

285 THE LAND OF BEULAH. 8s & 7s. D   AMERICAN MELODY.

1. I am dwell-ing on the mountain, Where the gold-en sun-light gleams
2. I can see far down the mountain, Where I wandered wea-ry years,
3. I am drink-ing at the fount-ain, Where I ev-er would a-bide;
4. Tell me not of heav.-y cross-es, Nor the bur-dens hard to bear,
5. Oh, the Cross has wondrous glo-ry! Oft I've proved this to be true;

O'er a land whose wondrous beauty Far ex-ceeds my fond-est dreams;
Oft-en hin-dered in my-jour-ney By the ghosts of doubts and fears;
For I've tast-ed life's pure riv-er, And my soul is sat-is-fied;
For I've found this great sal-va-tion Makes each burden light ap-pear;
When I'm in the way so nar-row I can see a pathway thro';

Where the air is pure e-the-real, La-den with the breath of flow'rs,
Bro-ken vows and dis-ap-point-ments, Thickly sprinkled all the way,
There's no thirsting for life's pleasures, Nor a-dorn-ing, rich and gay.
And I love to fol-low Je-sus, Glad-ly count-ing all but dross,
And how sweet-ly Je-sus whis-pers: Take the cross, thou need'st not fear,

CHO. Is not this the land of Beu-lah, Bless-ed, bless-ed land of light?

D. S. CHORUS.

They are bloom-ing by the fountain, 'Neath the am-a-ranthine bow'rs.
But the Spir-it led un-err-ing, To the land I hold to-day.
For I've found a rich-er treas-ure, One that fad-eth not a-way.
Worldly hon-ors all for-sak-ing For the glo-ry of the cross.
For I've tried this way be-fore thee, And the glo-ry lin-gers near.

REV. WM. HUNTER.

Where the flow-ers bloom for-ev-er, And the sun is al-ways bright.

ORTONVILLE. C. M.   THOMAS HASTINGS, 1837.

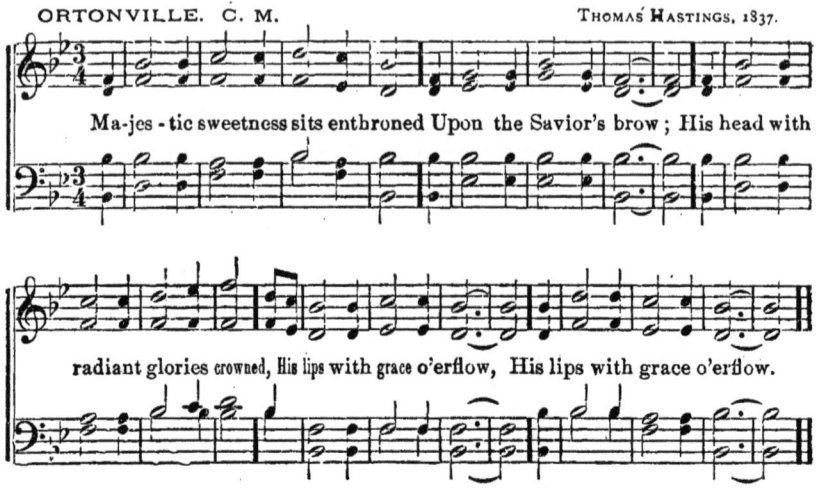

Ma-jes-tic sweetness sits enthroned Upon the Savior's brow; His head with

radiant glories crowned, His lips with grace o'erflow, His lips with grace o'erflow.

286   *Christ Incomparable*   (590)

MAJESTIC sweetness sits enthroned
  Upon the Savior's brow;
His head with radiant glories crowned,
  His lips with grace o'erflow.

2 No mortal can with him compare
  Among the sons of men;
Fairer is he, than all the fair
  Who fill the heavenly train.

3 He saw me plunged in deep distress,
  And flew to my relief;
For me he bore the shameful cross,
  And carried all my grief.

4 To heaven, the place of his abode,
  He brings my weary feet;
Shows me the glories of my God,
  And makes my joys complete.
                SAMUEL STENNETT, 1787.

287   *Christ Jesus, All in All.*   (591)

I'VE found the pearl of greatest price!
  My heart doth sing for joy;
And sing I must, for Christ is mine!
  Christ shall my song employ.

2 Christ is my Prophet, Priest, and King;
  My Prophet full of light,
My great High Priest before the throne,
  My King of heavenly might.

3 Christ is my peace; he died for me,
  For me he gave his blood;
And, as my wondrous Sacrifice,
  Offered himself to God.

4 Christ Jesus is my All in All,—
  My Comfort, and my Love;
My Life below, and he shall be
  My Joy and Crown above.
                JOHN MASON, 1683, a.

288   *Invitation to Praise the Redeemer.*   (588)

OH, for a thousand tongues, to sing
  My great Redeemer's praise,
The glories of my God and King,
  The triumphs of his grace.

2 My gracious Master, and my God,
  Assist me to proclaim—
To spread, through all the earth abroad,
  The honors of thy name.

3 Jesus! the name that charms our fears,
  That bids our sorrows cease;
'Tis music in the sinner's ears,
  'Tis life, and health, and peace.

4 He breaks the power of canceled sin,
  He sets the pris'ner free;
His blood can make the foulest clean—
  His blood availed for me.

5 He speaks—and, list'ning to his voice,
  New life the dead receive;
The mournful, broken hearts rejoice,
  The humble poor believe.

6 Hear him, ye deaf; his praise, ye dumb,
  Your loosened tongues employ;
Ye blind, behold your Savior come;
  And leap, ye lame, for joy.
                CHARLES WESLEY, 1740.

HENRY. C. M.
SYLVANUS B. POND, 1835.

Come, let us all u - nite to praise The Savior of man-kind;

Our thank-ful hearts in sol - emn lays Be with our voic - es joined.

89 *Praise to Christ.* (596)

OME, let us all unite to praise
The Savior of mankind;
ur thankful hearts in solemn lays
Be with our voices joined.

O Lord! we can not silent be;
By love we are constrained
To offer our best thanks to thee,
Our Savior, and our Friend.

Let every tongue thy goodness show,
And spread abroad thy fame;
Let every heart with praise o'erflow,
And bless thy sacred name.

Worship and honor, thanks and love,
Be to our Jesus given,
By men below, by hosts above,
By all in earth and heaven.
MARTIN MADAN (?) 1760.

290 *The Incarnation.* (205)

AWAKE, awake, the sacred song,
To our incarnate Lord;
Let every heart and every tongue
Adore th' eternal Word.

2 That awful Word, that sovereign Power,
By whom the worlds were made;
Oh, happy morn—illustrious hour—
Was once in flesh arrayed.

3 To dwell with misery here below,
The Savior left the skies,
And sunk to wretchedness and woe,
That worthless man might rise.

4 Adoring angels tuned their songs,
To hail the joyful day;
With rapture, then, let human tongues
Their grateful worship pay.
ANNE STEELE, 1760.

CAMBRIDGE. C. M.
JOHN RANDALL, 1790.

Awake, awake, the sa-cred song To our in-carnate Lord; Let ev'ry heart and

ev'ry tongue Adore th' eternal Word, Adore th' eternal Word, Adore th' eternal Word.

ST. AGNES. C. M.　　　　　　　　JOHN B. DYKES, 1858.

Je - sus, the ver - y tho't of thee With sweetness fills my breast;

But sweet-er far thy face to see, And in thy pres-ence rest.

291　　*Jesus our Joy.*　　(548)

JESUS, the very tho't of thee
　With sweetness fills my breast;
But sweeter far thy face to see,
　And in thy presence rest.

2 Nor voice can sing, nor heart can frame,
　Nor can the mem'ry find
A sweeter sound than thy blest name,
　O Savior of mankind!

3 Oh, hope of ev'ry contrite heart!
　Oh, joy of all the meek!
To those who fall, how kind thou art!
　How good to those who seek.

4 And those who find thee, find a bliss
　Nor tongue nor pen can show;
The love of Jesus, what it is
　None but his loved ones know.

5 Jesus! our only joy be thou,
　As thou our prize wilt be;
Jesus! be thou our glory now,
　And through eternity.
　　　　BERNARD OF CLAIRVAUX, 1140.
　　　　　　Tr. E. CASWALL, 1848.

292　　*All-Absorbing Love.*　　(551)

O JESUS, Jesus, dearest Lord!
　Forgive me, if I say,
For very love, thy sacred name
　A thousand times a day.

2 I love thee so, I know not how
　My transports to control;
Thy love is like a burning fire
　Within my very soul.

3 Oh! wonderful! that thou should'st
　So vile a heart as mine
Love thee with such a love as this,
　And make so free with thine!

4 O Light in darkness, Joy in grief!
　O Heaven begun on earth!
Jesus my Love, my Treasure! who
　Can tell what thou art worth?

5 O Jesus, Jesus, sweetest Lord!
　What art thou not to me?
Each hour brings joys before unknow
　Each day new liberty.
　　　　FREDERICK WM. FABER, 1848.

293　　*Supreme Love to Christ.*　　(545)

Do not I love thee, oh, my Lord?
　Behold my heart, and see;
And turn each worthless idol out,
　That dares to rival thee.

2 Do not I love thee, from my soul
　Then let me nothing love;
Dead be my heart to every joy,
　Which thou dost not approve.

3 Is not thy name melodious still,
　To mine attentive ear?
Doth not each pulse with pleasure thril
　My Savior's voice to hear?

4 Thou know'st I love thee, dearest Lord
　But, oh! I long to soar
Far from the sphere of mortal joys,
　And learn to love thee more.
　　　　PHILIP DODDRIDGE, 174•

HOW I LOVE JESUS. C. M.   AMERICAN SPIRITUAL.

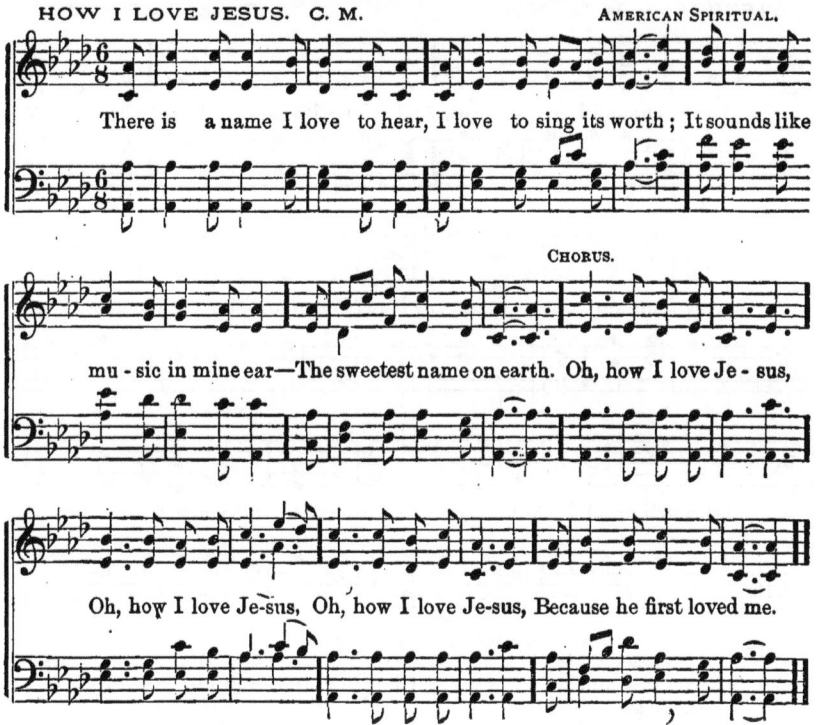

There is a name I love to hear, I love to sing its worth; It sounds like

CHORUS.

mu - sic in mine ear—The sweetest name on earth. Oh, how I love Je - sus,

Oh, how I love Je-sus, Oh, how I love Je-sus, Because he first loved me.

294 *The Dearest Name.* (537)

THERE is a name I love to hear,
    I love to sing its worth;
It sounds like music in mine ear,
    The sweetest name on earth.

2 It tells me of a Savior's love,
    Who died to set me free;
It tells me of his precious blood,
    The sinner's perfect plea.

3 It tells me what my Father hath
    In store for every day,
And, though I tread a darksome path,
    Yields sunshine all the way.

4 It tells of One, whose loving heart
    Can feel my deepest woe,
Who in each sorrow bears a part,
    That none can bear below.
                    FREDERICK WHITFIELD, 1859.

295 *The Precious Name.* (538)

How sweet the name of Jesus sounds
    In a believer's ear;

It soothes his sorrow, heals his wounds,
    And drives away his fear.

2 It makes the wounded spirit whole,
    And calms the troubled breast;
'Tis manna to the hungry soul,
    And to the weary, rest.

3 Dear Name, the rock on which I build,
    My shield and hiding-place;
My never-failing treasure, filled
    With boundless stores of grace.

4 Jesus, my Shepherd, Savior, Friend,
    My Prophet, Priest, and King,
My Lord, my Life, my Way, my End,
    Accept the praise I bring.

5 I would thy boundless love proclaim
    With every fleeting breath,
So shall the music of thy name
    Refresh my soul in death.
                    JOHN NEWTON, 1779.

WEBB. 7s & 6s, D. GEORGE JAMES WEBB, 1837.

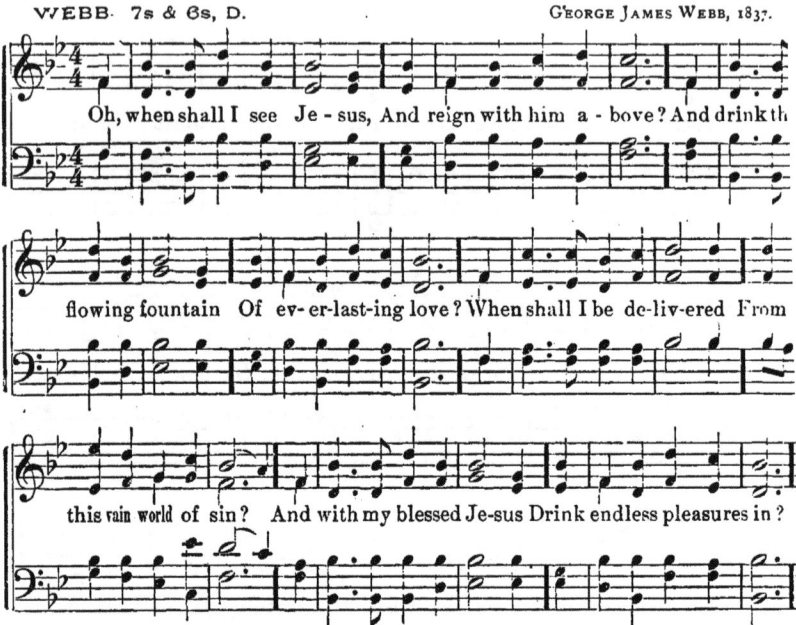

Oh, when shall I see Je-sus, And reign with him a-bove? And drink th'

flowing fountain Of ev-er-last-ing love? When shall I be de-liv-ered From

this vain world of sin? And with my blessed Je-sus Drink endless pleasures in?

296 [FIRST VERSE INSERTED IN MUSIC.]
The Joyful Prospect.

2 But now I am a soldier,
  My Captain's gone before;
He's given me my orders,
  And tells me not to fear;
And if I hold out faithful,
  A crown of life he'll give,
And all his valiant soldiers
  Eternal life shall have.

3 Through grace I am determined
  To conquer, though I die,
And then away to Jesus
  On wings of love I'll fly!
Farewell to sin and sorrow,
  I bid them all adieu;
And you, my friends, prove faithful,
  And on your way pursue.

4 Oh! do not be discouraged,
  For Jesus is your friend;
And if you lack for knowledge,
  He'll not forget to lend:
Neither will he upbraid you,
  Though often you request;
He'll give you grace to conquer,
  And take you home to rest.
                                    ANON.

297 *Praise to the Savior.* (622)

To thee, my God and Savior!
  My heart exulting sings,
Rejoicing in thy favor,
  Almighty King of kings!
I'll celebrate thy glory,
  With all thy saints above,
And tell the joyful story
  Of thy redeeming love.

2 Soon as the morn, with roses,
  Bedecks the dewy east,
And when the sun reposes
  Upon the ocean's breast;
My voice, in supplication,
  Well-pleased thou shalt hear:
Oh! grant me thy salvation,
  And to my soul draw near.

3 By thee, through life supported,
  I pass the dangerous road,
With heavenly hosts escorted,
  Up to their bright abode;
There, cast my crown before thee,—
  Now, all my conflicts o'er,—
And day and night adore thee:—
  What can an angel more?
                        THOMAS HAWEIS, 1792.

298 (612) HEAVENLY KING. 7s. D.   AMERICAN MELODY.
Fine.

Chil - dren of the heaven-ly King; As we jour - ney let us sing;
Sing our Sav-ior's wor - thy praise, Glo-rious in his works and ways.
D. C. They are hap - py now, and we Soon their hap - pi - ness shall see.

D. C.

We are trav - 'ling home to God, In the way our fa-thers trod;

2 Fear not, brethren, joyful stand
On the borders of our land;
Jesus Christ, our Father's Son,
Bids us undismayed go on.

Lord! obediently we'll go,
Gladly leaving all below:
Only thou our leader be,
And we still will follow thee.
JOHN CENNICK, 1742.

299 (575) ATONING LAMB. 7s.   L. O. EMERSON.

1. Earth has noth-ing sweet or fair, Love-ly forms or beauties rare,
2. When the morning paints the skies, When the golden sun-beams rise,

But be - fore my eyes they bring Christ, of beau - ty Source and Spring.
Then my Sav-ior's form I find Bright-ly im - aged on my mind.

3 When the day-beams pierce the night,
Oft I think on Jesus' light,—
Think,—how bright that light will be,
Shining through eternity.

4 When, as moonlight softly steals,
Heaven its thousand eyes reveals,
Then I think;—who made their light
Is a thousand times more bright.

5 When I see, in spring-tide gay,
Fields their varied tints display,
Wakes the thrilling thought in me,—
What must their Creator be?

6 Lord of all that's fair to see!
Come, reveal thyself to me;
Let me, 'mid thy radiant light,
See thine unveiled glories bright.
Ger. JOHANN SCHEFFLER, 1657.
Tr. FRANCES ELIZABETH COX, 1841.

LUTHER. S. M.   T. Hastings, 1835.

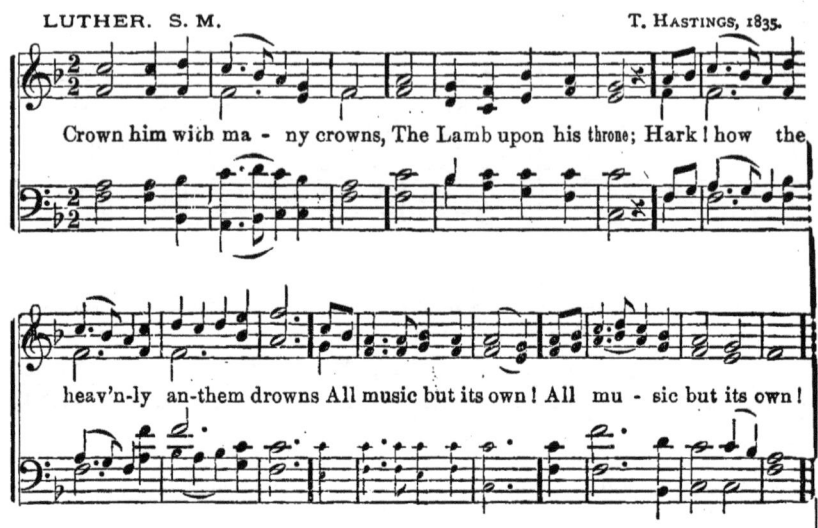

Crown him with ma - ny crowns, The Lamb upon his throne; Hark! how the

heav'n-ly an-them drowns All music but its own! All mu - sic but its own!

300 *The Song of the Seraphs.*   (349)

Crown him with many crowns,
  The Lamb upon his throne;
Hark! how the heavenly anthem drowns
  All music but its own!

2 Awake, my soul! and sing
  Of him who died for thee;
And hail him as thy matchless King,
  Through all eternity.

3 Crown him, the Lord of love!
  Behold his hands and side,
Rich wounds, yet visible above
  In beauty glorified:

4 Crown him, the Lord of peace!
  Whose power a scepter sways,
From pole to pole, that wars may cease,
  Absorbed in prayer and praise:

5 Crown him, the Lord of years!
  The Potentate of time;
Creator of the rolling spheres,
  Ineffably sublime!
                MATTHEW BRIDGES, 1852.

301 *The Song of Moses and the Lamb.*   (350)

Awake, and sing the song
  Of Moses and the Lamb;
Wake, every heart, and every tongue!
  To praise the Savior's name.

2 Sing of his dying love;
  Sing of his rising power;

Sing how he intercedes above
  For those whose sins he bore.

3 Sing on your heavenly way,
  Ye ransomed sinners! sing;
Sing on, rejoicing, every day,
  In Christ, th' eternal King.

4 Soon shall ye hear him say,
  "Ye blessed children! come;"
Soon will he call you hence away,
  And take his wanderers home.
              WILLIAM HAMMOND, 1745.
        Altered by MARTIN MADAN, 1760.

302   *Living to God.*   (562)

Bless'd be thy love, dear Lord!
  That taught us this sweet way,
Only to love thee for thyself,
  And for that love obey.

2 Oh, thou, our soul's chief Hope!
  We to thy mercy fly;
Where'er we are, thou canst protect,
  Whate'er we need, supply.

3 Whether we sleep or wake,
  To thee we both resign;
By night we see, as well as day,
  If thy light on us shine.

4 Whether we live or die,
  Both we submit to thee;
In death we live, as well as life,
  If thine in death we be.
                JOHN AUSTIN, 1668.

03 (623)   ARIEL. C. P. M.

LOWELL MASON, 1836.

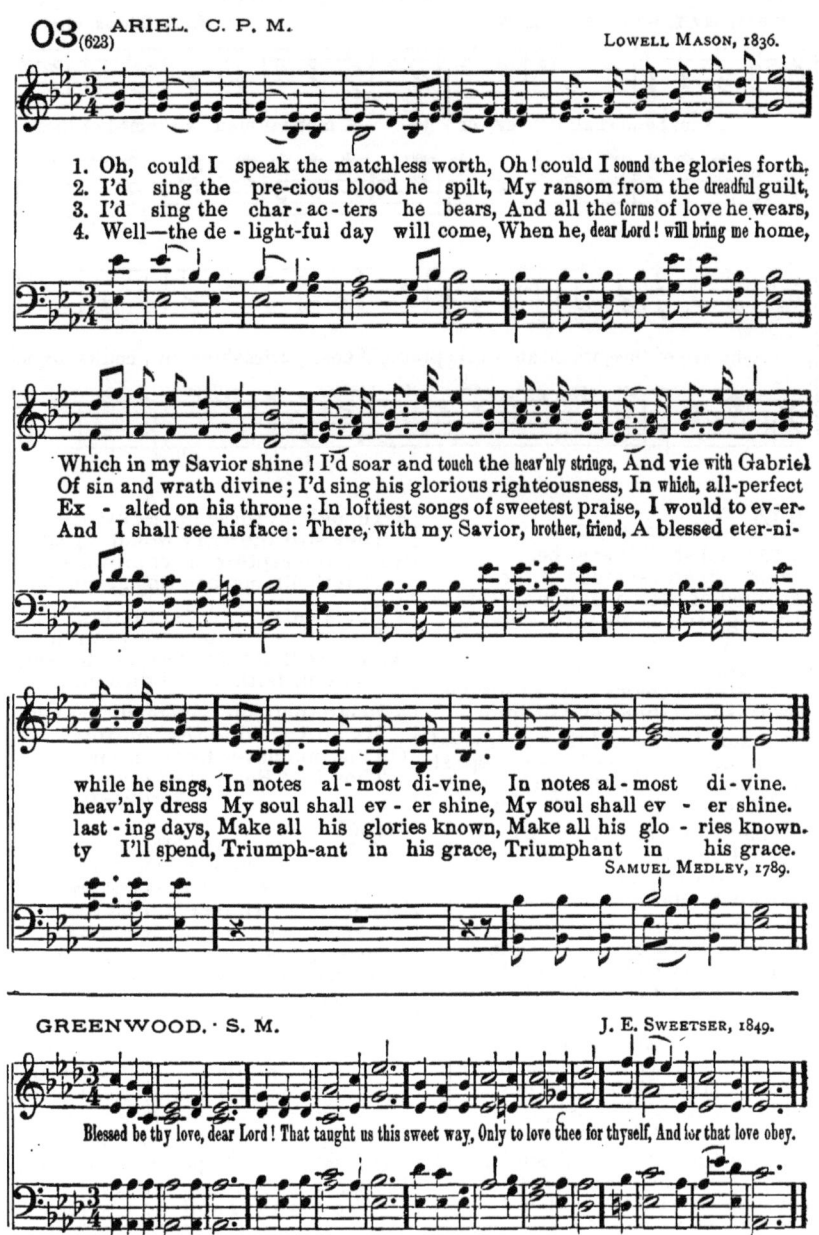

1. Oh, could I speak the matchless worth, Oh! could I sound the glories forth,
2. I'd sing the pre-cious blood he spilt, My ransom from the dreadful guilt,
3. I'd sing the char-ac-ters he bears, And all the forms of love he wears,
4. Well—the de-light-ful day will come, When he, dear Lord! will bring me home,

Which in my Savior shine! I'd soar and touch the heav'nly strings, And vie with Gabriel
Of sin and wrath divine; I'd sing his glorious righteousness, In which, all-perfect
Ex - alted on his throne; In loftiest songs of sweetest praise, I would to ev-er-
And I shall see his face: There, with my Savior, brother, friend, A blessed eter-ni-

while he sings, In notes al-most di-vine, In notes al-most di-vine.
heav'nly dress My soul shall ev - er shine, My soul shall ev - er shine.
last-ing days, Make all his glories known, Make all his glo - ries known.
ty I'll spend, Triumph-ant in his grace, Triumphant in his grace.

SAMUEL MEDLEY, 1789.

GREENWOOD. · S. M.   J. E. SWEETSER, 1849.

Blessed be thy love, dear Lord! That taught us this sweet way, Only to love thee for thyself, And for that love obey.

FEDERAL STREET. L. M.　　　　　　　　H. K. Oliver, 1832.

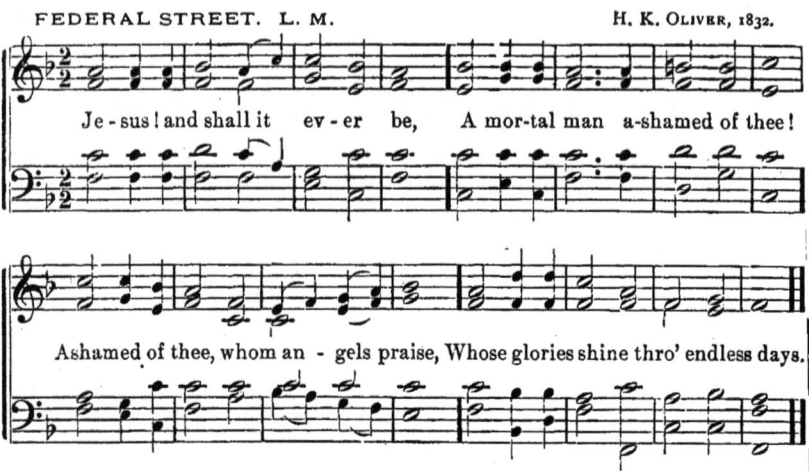

Je-sus! and shall it ev-er be, A mor-tal man a-shamed of thee!

Ashamed of thee, whom an - gels praise, Whose glories shine thro' endless days.

304　　*Ashamed of Me.*

Jesus! and shall it ever be,
A mortal man ashamed of thee!
Ashamed of thee, whom angels praise,
Whose glories shine thro' endless days.

2 Ashamed of Jesus! sooner far
Let evening blush to own a star;
He sheds the beams of light divine
O'er this benighted soul of mine.

3 Ashamed of Jesus! that dear Friend
On whom my hopes of heaven depend!
No; when I blush, be this my shame,
That I no more revere his name.

4 Ashamed of Jesus! yes, I may,
When I've no guilt to wash away;
No tear to wipe, no good to crave,
No fears to quell, no soul to save.

5 Till then—nor is my boasting vain—
Till then, I boast a Savior slain!
And, oh, may this my glory be
That Christ is not ashamed of me!
　　　　Joseph Grigg, 1765.　*Ab. and alt.*

305　　*All-Engrossing Love.*　　(509)

Jesus! my heart within me burns,
To tell thee all its conscious love;
And from earth's low delight it turns,
To taste a joy like that above.

2 When thou to me dost condescend,
In love divine, thou blessed One,
The moments that with thee I spend,
Seem e'en as Heaven itself begun.

3 Though oft these lips my love have told,
They still the story would repeat;
To me the rapture ne'er grows old,
That thrills me, bending at thy feet.

4 I breathe my words into thine ear;
I seem to fix mine eyes on thine;
And, sure that thou dost wait to hear,
I dare in faith to call thee mine.

5 Reign thou sole Sovereign of my heart;
My all I yield to thy control;
Oh! let me never from thee part,
Thou best Beloved of my soul!
　　　　Ray Palmer, 1869.

306　　*The Song of Songs.*　　(603)

Come, let us sing the song of songs,
With hearts and voices swell the strain;
The homage which to Christ belongs;—
"Worthy the Lamb, for he was slain!"

2 Slain to redeem us by his blood,
To cleanse from every sinful stain,
And make us kings and priests to God:
"Worthy the Lamb, for he was slain!"

3 To him who suffered on the tree,
Our souls, at his soul's price, to gain,
Blessing, and praise, and glory be!—
"Worthy the Lamb, for he was slain!"

4 Come, Holy Spirit! from on high,
Our faith, our hope, our love sustain,
Living to sing, and dying cry,—
"Worthy the Lamb, for he was slain!"
　　　　James Montgomery, 1853.

NEW HAVEN. 6s & 4s.   Thos. Hastings, 1833.

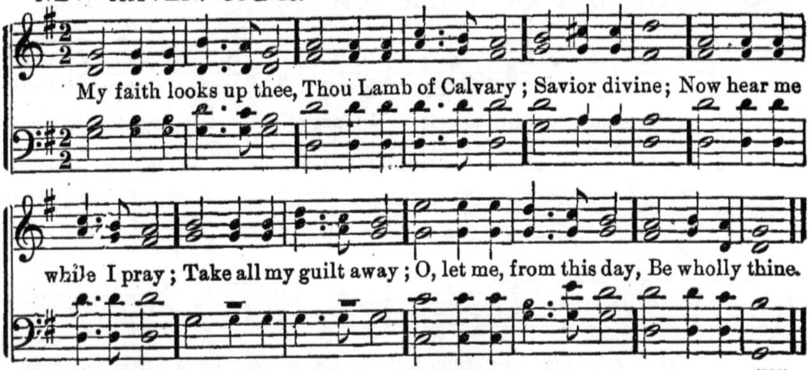

My faith looks up thee, Thou Lamb of Calvary ; Savior divine; Now hear me

while I pray ; Take all my guilt away ; O, let me, from this day, Be wholly thine.

307 [FIRST VERSE INSERTED IN MUSIC.]   (587)
Looking to Jesus.

? May thy rich grace impart
Strength to my fainting heart;
   My zeal inspire;
As thou hast died for me,
Oh! may my love to thee
Pure, warm, and changeless be,
   A living fire!

3 While life's dark maze I tread,
And griefs around me spread,
   Be thou my Guide;
Bid darkness turn to day,
Wipe sorrow's tears away,
Nor let me ever stray
   From thee aside.

4 When ends life's transient dream,
When death's cold, sullen stream
   Shall o'er me roll,
Blest Savior! then, in love,
Fear and distrust remove;
Oh! bear me safe above,
   A ransomed soul!
          RAY PALMER, 1830.

308   (586)
Jesus, my Lord.

JESUS, thy name I love,
All other names above,
   Jesus, my Lord!
Oh, thou art all to me!
Nothing to please I see,
Nothing apart from thee,
   Jesus, my Lord!

2 When unto thee I flee,
Thou wilt my refuge be,
   Jesus, my Lord!'
What need I now to fear?
What earthly grief or care,
Since thou art ever near,
   Jesus, my Lord!

3 Soon thou wilt come again!
I shall be happy then,
   Jesus, my Lord!
Then thine own face I'll see,
Then I shall like thee be,
Then evermore with thee,
   Jesus, my Lord!
          J. G. DECK, 1837.

OLIVET. 6s & 4s.   Lowell Mason, 1831.

My faith looks up to thee, Thou Lamb of Cal-va-ry, Sav-ior di-vine; Now hear me

while I pray, Take all my guilt away ; Oh, let me from this day Be wholly thine.

11

309   EVERY DAY AND HOUR. P. M.   W. H. DOANE.

Slowly.

1. Savior, more than life to me,   I am clinging, clinging close to thee;
2. Thro' this changing world below, Lead me gently, gently as I go;
3. Let me love thee more and more, Till this fleeting, fleeting life is o'er;

Let thy precious blood applied, Keep me ev-er, ev-er near thy side.
Trusting thee, I can not stray, I can never, never lose my way.
Till my soul is lost in love, In a brighter, brighter world above.

FANNY J. CROSBY.

REFRAIN.

Ev-ery day,   ev-ery hour,   Let me feel thy cleansing power;
Ev-ery day and hour ev-ery day and hour,

May thy ten-der love to me Bind me clos-er, clos-er, Lord to thee.

310   *Love to Christ Desired.*   (584)

MORE love to thee, O Christ,
    More love to thee !
Hear thou the prayer I make
    On bended knee :
This is my earnest plea—
More love, O Christ, to thee !
    More love to thee !

2 Once earthly joy I craved—
    Sought peace and rest ;
Now thee alone I seek :

Give what is best.
This all my prayer shall be—
More love, O Christ, to thee ;
    More love to thee!

3 Then shall my latest breath
    Whisper thy praise ;
This be the parting cry
    My heart shall raise—
This still its prayer shall be,
More love, O Christ, to thee !
    More love to thee !

MRS. E. P. PRENTISS, 1869.

BETHANY. 6s & 4s. LOWELL MASON, 1859.

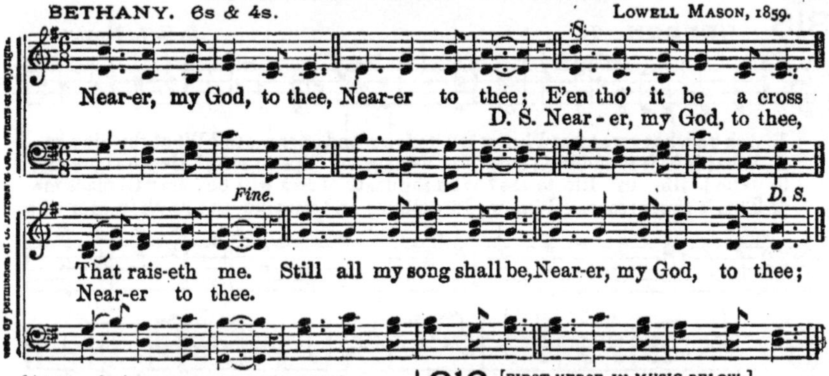

Near-er, my God, to thee, Near-er to thee; E'en tho' it be a cross
D. S. Near-er, my God, to thee,

Fine. D. S.

That rais-eth me. Still all my song shall be, Near-er, my God, to thee;
Near-er to thee.

311 [FIRST VERSE IN MUSIC ABOVE.]
Nearer to God. (709)

2 Though like the wanderer,
The sun gone down,
Darkness be over me,
My rest a stone,
Yet, in my dreams, I'd be
Nearer, my God! to thee,—
Nearer to thee.

3 There let the way appear,
Steps unto heaven;
All that thou send'st to me,
In mercy given;
Angels to beckon me
Nearer, my God! to thee,—
Nearer to thee.

4 Or if, on joyful wing,
Cleaving the sky,
Sun, moon, and stars forgot,
Upward I fly,
Still all my song shall be,
Nearer, my, God! to thee,—
Nearer to thee.

MRS. SARAH FLOWER ADAMS, 1841.

312 [FIRST VERSE IN MUSIC BELOW.]
Parting with the World. (582)

2 Tempt not my soul away:
Jesus is mine;
Here would I ever stay;
Jesus is mine:
Perishing things of clay,
Born but for one brief day!
Pass from my heart away,
Jesus is mine.

3 Farewell, ye dreams of night!
Jesus is mine:
Mine is a dawning bright,
Jesus is mine:
All that my soul has tried,
Left but a dismal void;
Jesus has satisfied;
Jesus is mine.

4 Farewell, mortality!
Jesus is mine:
Welcome, eternity!
Jesus is mine:
Welcome, ye scenes of rest!
Welcome, ye mansions blest!
Welcome, a Savior's breast;
Jesus is mine.

MRS. HORATIUS BONAR, 1845.
THEODORE E. PERKINS, 1858.

HOPE. 6s & 4s.

Fade, fade, each earthly joy, Je-sus is mine; Break, ev-'ry mortal tie, Je-sus is mine.

Dark is the wil-der-ness, Distant the resting-place; Je-sus a-lone can bless, Je-sus is mine.

313 HENDON. 7s.
C. H. A. MALAN.

1. Ask ye what great thing I know That delights and stirs me so? What the high re-
2. What is faith's foundation strong? What awakes my lips to song? He who bore my
3. Who is life in life to me? Who the death of death will be? Who will place me
4. This is that great thing I know; This delights and stirs me so; Faith in him who

ward I win? Whose the name I glo-ry in? Je-sus Christ, the cru-ci-fied.
sin-ful load, Purchased for me peace with God, Je-sus Christ, the cru-ci-fied.
on his right With the countless hosts of light? Je-sus Christ, the cru-ci-fied.
died to save, Him who triumphed o'er the grave, Je-sus Christ, the cru-ci-fied.

REV. B. H. KENNEDY, 1863.

314(554) WOODWORTH. L. M.
WILLIAM B. BRADBURY, 1849.

1. Oh, that I could for-ev - er dwell De-light - ed at the Savior's feet,
2. The world shut out from all my soul, And heav'n bro't in with all its bliss,
3. This is the hid-den life I prize, A life of pen-i-ten-tial love,

Be-hold the form I love so well, And all his ten-der words re - peat.
Oh! is there aught, from pole to pole, One moment to compare with this?
When most my fol-lies I despise, And raise my highest tho'ts a - bove

4 When all I am I clearly see,
  And freely own with deepest shame;
  When the Redeemer's love to me
  Kindles within a deathless flame.

5 Thus would I live till nature fail
  And all my former sins forsake:
  Then rise to God within the veil,
  And of eternal joys partake.

ANDREW REED, 1841.

315 (529) **REVIVE US AGAIN.** 10s & 11s.

J. J. HUSBAND.

1. We praise thee, O God! for the Son of thy love, For Jesus who
2. We praise thee, O God! for thy Spirit of light, Who has shown us our
3. All glory and praise to the Lamb that was slain, Who has borne all our

CHORUS.

died, and is now gone above.
Savior, and scattered our night. Hal-le-lu-jah! thine the glo-ry, Hal-le-
sins, and has cleansed ev-'ry stain.

lu-jah! A-men. Hal-le-lu-jah! thine the glo-ry, Re-vive us a-gain.

4 All glory and praise to the God of all grace,
Who has bought us, and sought us, and guided our ways.

5 Revive us again; fill each heart with thy love;
May each soul be rekindled with fire from above.

WM. P. MACKAY, 1863.

316

Rejoicing in Christ.

REJOICE and be glad: the Redeemer has come!
Go look on his cradle, his cross and his tomb.

CHORUS.—Sound his praises, tell the story,
Of him who was slain,
Sound his praises, tell with gladness,
He liveth again.

2 Rejoice and be glad: for the blood has been shed;
Redemption is finished, the price has been paid.

3 Rejoice and be glad: for the Lamb that was slain,
O'er death is triumphant, and liveth again.

4 Rejoice and be glad: for our King is on high;
He pleadeth for us on his throne in the sky.

5 Rejoice and be glad: for he cometh again—
He cometh in glory, the Lamb that was slain.

H. BONAR, 1874.

317   WELCOME VOICE. S. M.   REV. L. HARTSOUGH.

1. I hear thy welcome voice That calls me, Lord, to thee For cleansing in thy
2. Tho' coming weak and vile, Thou dost my strength assure; Thou dost my vileness
3. 'T is Jesus calls me on   To perfect faith and love,   To perfect hope, and
4. 'T is Jesus who confirms   The blessed work within,   By adding grace to
5. And he the witness gives   To loyal hearts and free,   That every promise
6. All hail, atoning blood!   All hail, redeeming grace! All hail, the Gift of

CHORUS.

precious blood That flowed on Cal - va - ry.
ful - ly cleanse, Till spot - less all and pure.
peace, and trust, For earth and heaven above.
welcomed grace, Where reigned the power of sin.
is ful-filled,   If faith but brings the plea.
Christ, our Lord, Our Strength and Righteousness!
                              REV. L. HARTSOUGH.

I am com-ing, Lord!

Com-ing now to thee! Wash me, cleanse me, in the blood That flowed on Calvary.

318   *Christ the Guide and Counselor.* (688)

JESUS, my truth, my way,
  My sure, unerring light,
On thee my feeble steps I stay,
  Which thou wilt guide aright.

2 My wisdom and my guide,
  My counselor thou art;
Oh, never let me leave thy side,
  Or from thy paths depart.

3 Never will I remove
  Out of thy hands my cause;
But rest in thy redeeming love,
  And hang upon thy cross.

4 Oh, make me all like thee,
  Before I hence remove;
Settle, confirm, and 'stablish me,
  And build me up in love.
                    CHARLES WESLEY.

LOVING-KINDNESS. L. M.   WESTERN MELODY.

A-wake, my soul, to joy-ful lays, And sing thy great Redeemer's praise;

He just-ly claims a song from me; His lov-ing-kind-ness, oh, how free!

CHORUS.

Lov-ing kindness, lov-ing kindness, His lov-ing kind-ness, oh, how free!

319 *Loving Kindness.* (599)

AWAKE, my soul, to joyful lays,
And sing thy great Redeemer's praise;
He justly claims a song from me,
His loving kindness, oh, how free!

2 He saw me ruined in the fall,
Yet loved me notwithstanding all;
He saved me from my lost estate—
His loving kindness, oh, how great!

3 Though num'rous hosts of mighty foes—
Though earth and hell my way oppose;
He safely leads my soul along—
His loving kindness, oh, how strong!

4 When trouble, like a gloomy cloud,
Has gathered thick and thundered loud,
He near my soul has always stood—
His loving kindness, oh, how good!
S. MEDLEY, 1787.

320 *Love Which Passeth Knowledge.*

OF him who did salvation bring,
I could forever think and sing;
Arise, ye needy, he'll relieve;
Arise, ye guilty, he'll forgive.

2 Ask but his grace, and lo, 'tis given!
Ask, and he turns your hell to heaven;
Though sin and sorrow wound my soul,
Jesus, thy balm will make me whole.

3 'Tis thee I love, for thee alone,
I shed my tears, and make my moan!
Where'er I am, where'er I move,
I meet the object of my love.

4 Insatiate to this spring I fly;
I drink, and yet am ever dry;
Ah! who against thy charms is proof?
Ah, who that loves can love enough?
BERNARD OF CLAIRVAUX,
tr. by A. W. BOEHM, 1712.

—

321   THE SOLID ROCK. L. M.   WILLIAM B. BRADBURY.

1. My hope is built on noth-ing less Than Jesus' blood and righteousness; I
2. When darkness veils His lovely face, I   rest on his unchanging grace: In
3. His oath, his cov-enant, his blood, Support me in the whelming flood: When
4. When he shall come with trumpet sound, O,   may I then in him be found; Dressed

dare not trust the sweetest frame, But wholly lean on Jesus' name.
ev - ery high and stormy gale, My anchor holds within the vail. On Christ, the Solid
all around my soul gives way, He then is all my hope and stay.
in   his righteousness alone, Faultless to stand before the throne.

REV. EDWARD MOTE, 1825.

CHORUS.

Rock, I stand; All other ground is sinking sand, All other ground is sinking sand.

MY BELOVED. 11s & 8s.   FREEMAN LEWIS, 1813.

Oh, thou, in whose presence my soul takes delight, On whom in af-flic-tion I call,

My comfort by day, and my song in the night, My hope, my sal-va-tion, my all.

322 HOW CAN I BUT LOVE HIM. 6s & 5s.

E. S. Lorenz.

1. So ten - der, so pre-cious, My Sav - ior to me; So true, and so
2. So pa - tient, so kind - ly Tow'rd all of my ways; I blun - der so
3. Of all friends the fair - est And tru - est is he; His love is the
4. His beau-ty, tho' bleed-ing And circled with thorns, Is then most ex-

gra - cious, I've found him to be;
blind - ly, He love still re - pays; How can I but love him? But
rar - est, That ev - er can be.
ceed - ing: For grief him a - dorns.

J. E. Rankin, D. D.

love him, but love him? There's no friend above him, Poor sinner, for thee.

---

323 *My Beloved.*

O thou, in whose presence my soul takes delight,
　On whom in affliction I call;
My comfort by day, and my song in the night,
　My hope, my salvation, my all.

2 Where dost thou at noon-tide resort with thy sheep,
　To feed in the pastures of love?
And why in the valley of death should I weep,
　Or alone in the wilderness rove?

3 O, why should I wander an alien from thee,
　Or cry in the desert for bread?
Thy foes will rejoice when my sorrows they see,
　And smile at the tears I have shed.

4 He looks, and ten thousands of angels rejoice,
　And myriads wait for his word;
He speaks, and eternity, fill'd with his voice,
　Re-echoes the praise of the Lord.

Jos. Swain, 1792.

DE FLEURY. 8s. D.   LEWIS EDSON.

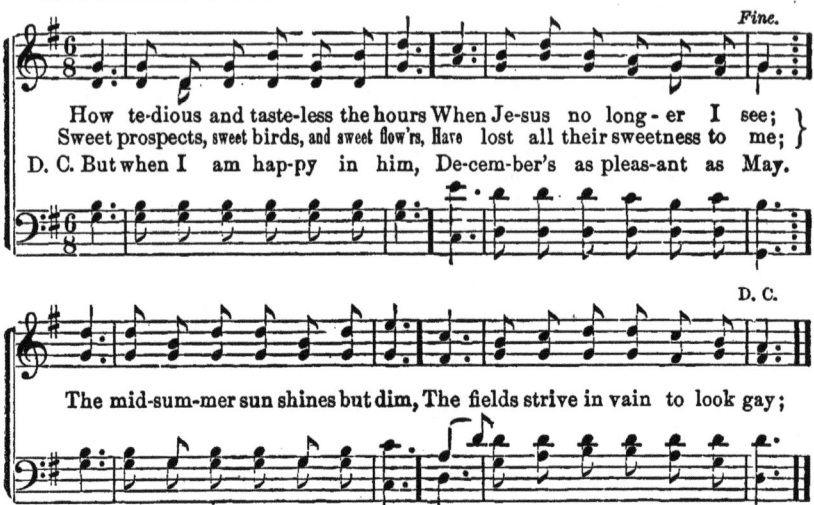

How te-dious and taste-less the hours When Je-sus no long-er I see;
Sweet prospects, sweet birds, and sweet flow'rs, Have lost all their sweetness to me;
D. C. But when I am hap-py in him, De-cem-ber's as pleas-ant as May.

The mid-sum-mer sun shines but dim, The fields strive in vain to look gay;

324 *The Presence of Christ Desired.*

How tedious and tasteless the hours
  When Jesus no longer I see!
Sweet prospects, sweet birds, and sweet flowers
  Have lost all their sweetness to me:
The midsummer sun shines but dim;
  The fields strive in vain to look gay;
But when I am happy in him,
  December's as pleasant as May.

2 His name yields the richest perfume,
  And sweeter than music his voice;
His presence disperses my gloom,
  And makes all within me rejoice:
I should, were he always so nigh,
  Have nothing to wish or to fear;
No mortal so happy as I;
  My summer would last all the year.

3 Content with beholding his face,
  My all to his pleasure resigned,
No changes of season or place
  Would make any change in my mind:
While blest with a sense of his love,
  A palace a toy would appear;
And prisons would palaces prove,
  If Jesus would dwell with me there.

4 Dear Lord, if indeed I am thine,
  If thou art my sun and my song,
Say, why do I languish and pine?
  And why are my winters so long?

O, drive these dark clouds from my sky;
  Thy soul-cheering presence restore;
Or take me unto thee on high,
  Where winter and clouds are no more.
                              JOHN NEWTON.

325   *Phil.* 1 : 23.   (571)

My Savior, whom absent I love,
  Whom, not having seen, I adore,
Whose name is exalted above
  All glory, dominion, and power,—
Dissolve thou these bands that detain
  My soul from her portion in thee;
Ah! strike off this adamant chain,
  And make me eternally free!

2 When that happy era begins,
  When arrayed in thy glories I shine,
Nor grieve any more, by my sins,
  The bosom on which I recline,
Oh! then shall the veil be removed,
  And round me thy brightness be poured!
I shall meet him, whom absent I loved,
  I shall see, whom unseen I adored.

3 And then, nevermore shall the fears,
  The trials, temptations, and woes,
Which darken this valley of tears,
  Intrude on my blissful repose:
To Jesus, the crown of my hope,
  My soul is in haste to be gone;
Oh! bear me, ye cherubim, up,
  And waft me away to his throne!
                              W. COWPER.

326 I NEED THEE EVERY HOUR. P. M.

ROBERT LOWRY.

1. I need thee ev'ry hour, Most gracious Lord; No ten - der voice like
2. I need thee ev'ry hour; Stay thou near by; Temp - ta - tions lose their
3. I need thee ev'ry hour, In joy or pain; Come quick-ly and a-
4. I need thee ev'ry hour; Teach me thy will; And thy rich prom - is-
5. I need thee ev'ry hour, Most ho - ly One; Oh, make me thine in-

REFRAIN.

thine Can peace af - ford.
pow'r When thou art nigh.
bide, Or life is vain.   I need thee, oh, I need thee, Ev - 'ry hour I
es In me ful - fill.
deed, Thou bless - ed Son.

ANNIE S. HAWKS.

need thee; Oh, bless me now, my Sav - ior, I come to thee.

327 *Altogether Lovely.* (572)

My gracious Redeemer I love,
  His praises aloud I'll proclaim:
And join with the armies above,
  To shout his adorable name.
To gaze on his glories divine
  Shall be my eternal employ;
To see them incessantly shine,
  My boundless, ineffable joy.

2 He freely redeemed with his blood
  My soul from the confines of hell,
To live on the smiles of my God,
  And in his sweet presence to dwell:—
To shine with the angels in light,
  With saints and with seraphs to sing,
To view, with eternal delight,
  My Jesus, my Savior, my King!

B. FRANCIS.

328   THE LILY OF THE VALLEY.   P. M.   ENGLISH MELODY.

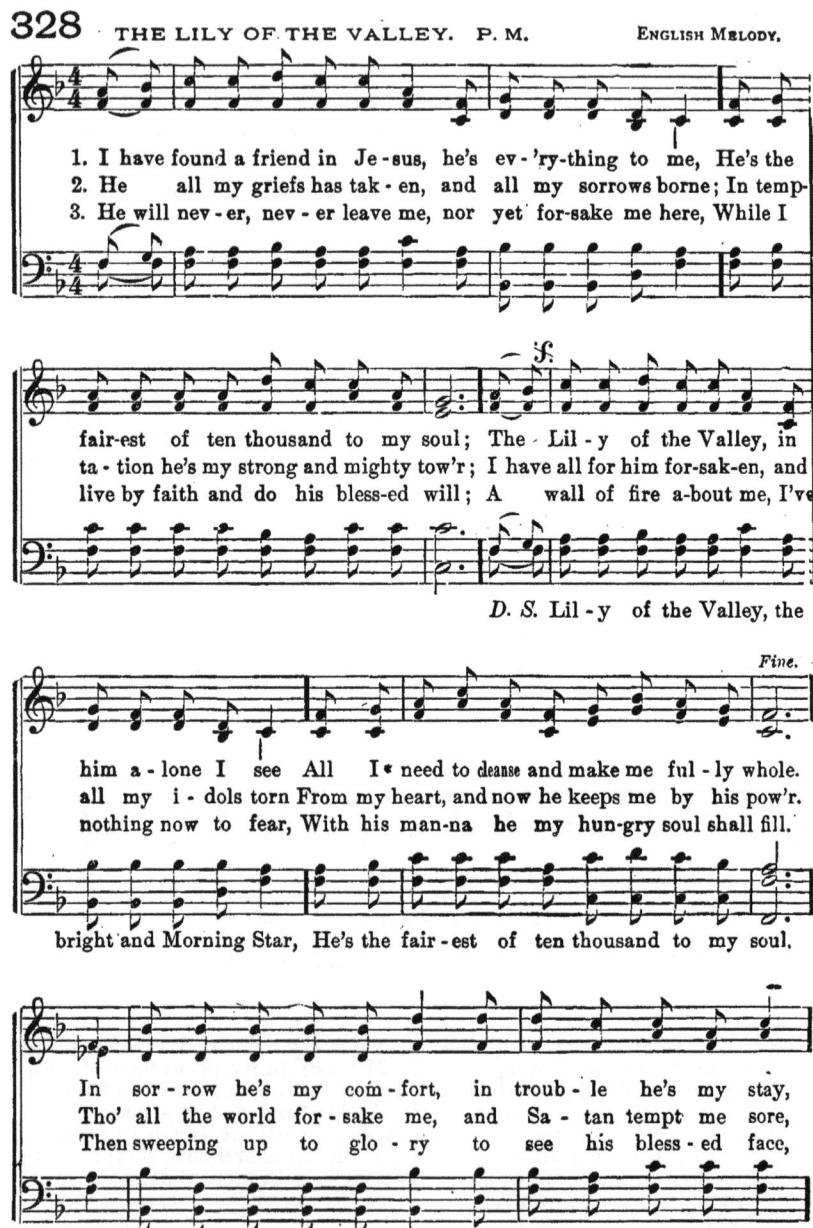

1. I have found a friend in Je-sus, he's ev-'ry-thing to me, He's the
2. He all my griefs has tak-en, and all my sorrows borne; In temp-
3. He will nev-er, nev-er leave me, nor yet for-sake me here, While I

fair-est of ten thousand to my soul; The Lil-y of the Valley, in
ta-tion he's my strong and mighty tow'r; I have all for him for-sak-en, and
live by faith and do his bless-ed will; A wall of fire a-bout me, I've

D. S. Lil-y of the Valley, the

Fine.

him a-lone I see All I need to cleanse and make me ful-ly whole.
all my i-dols torn From my heart, and now he keeps me by his pow'r.
nothing now to fear, With his man-na he my hun-gry soul shall fill.

bright and Morning Star, He's the fair-est of ten thousand to my soul.

In sor-row he's my com-fort, in troub-le he's my stay,
Tho' all the world for-sake me, and Sa-tan tempt me sore,
Then sweeping up to glo-ry to see his bless-ed face,

THE LILY OF THE VALLEY. Concluded.

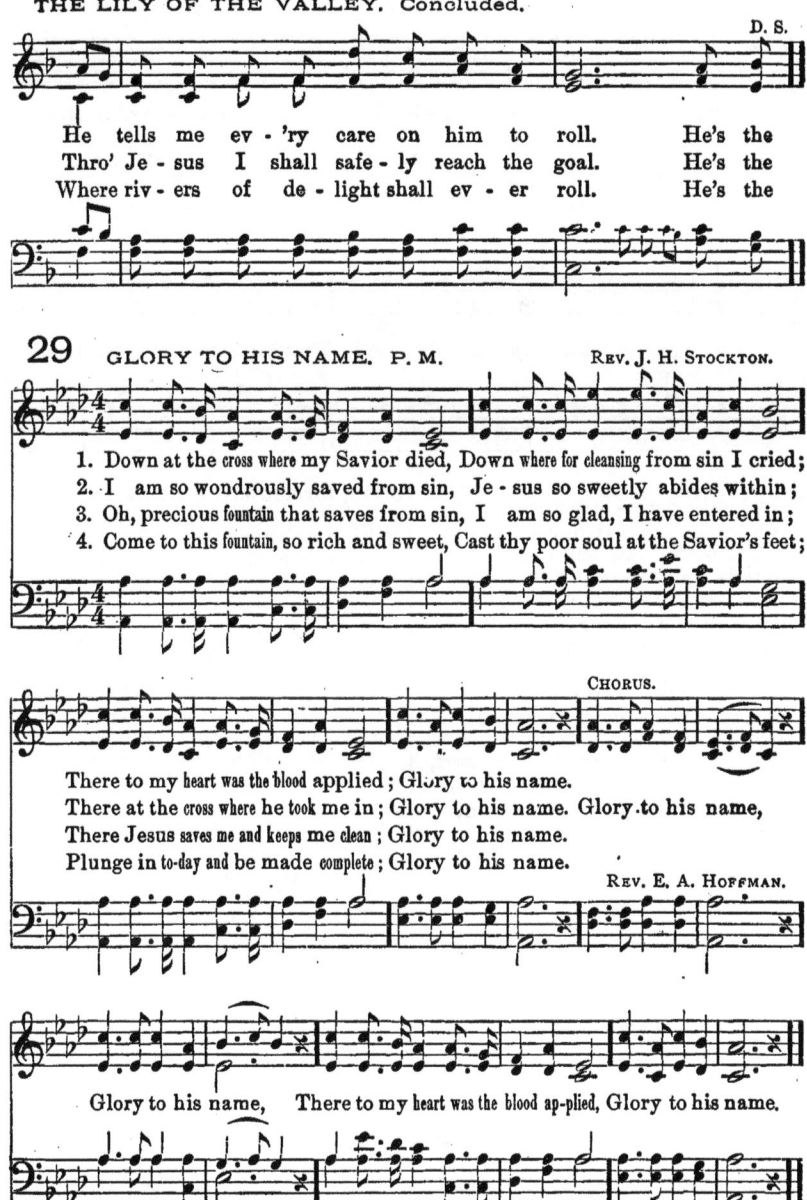

He tells me ev - 'ry care on him to roll.   He's the
Thro' Je - sus I shall safe - ly reach the goal.   He's the
Where riv - ers of de - light shall ev - er roll.   He's the

29 GLORY TO HIS NAME. P. M.   Rev. J. H. Stockton.

1. Down at the cross where my Savior died, Down where for cleansing from sin I cried;
2. I am so wondrously saved from sin, Je - sus so sweetly abides within;
3. Oh, precious fountain that saves from sin, I am so glad, I have entered in;
4. Come to this fountain, so rich and sweet, Cast thy poor soul at the Savior's feet;

CHORUS.

There to my heart was the blood applied ; Glory to his name.
There at the cross where he took me in ; Glory to his name. Glory to his name,
There Jesus saves me and keeps me clean ; Glory to his name.
Plunge in to-day and be made complete ; Glory to his name.

Rev. E. A. Hoffman.

Glory to his name,   There to my heart was the blood ap-plied, Glory to his name.

BALERMA. C. M.   Adapted by R. SIMPSON.

Oh, for a clo - ser walk with God! A calm and heaven-ly frame!

A light to shine up-on the road That leads me to the Lamb!

330 [FIRST VERSE IN MUSIC.]   (625)
Lamenting the Absence of the Spirit.

2 Where is the blessedness I knew
  When first I saw the Lord?
Where is the soul-refreshing view
  Of Jesus and his word?

3 What peaceful hours I then enjoyed!
  How sweet their memory still!
But now I find an aching void
  The world can never fill.

4 Return, oh, holy Dove, return,
  Sweet messenger of rest;
I hate the sins that made thee mourn,
  And drove thee from my breast.

5 The dearest idol I have known,
  Whate'er that idol be,
Help me to tear it from thy throne,
  And worship only thee.

6 So shall my walk be close with God,
  Calm and serene my frame;
So purer light shall mark the road
  That leads me to the Lamb.
                 W. COWPER, 1772.

331   *A Perfect Heart.*   (645)

OH, for a heart to praise my God,
  A heart from sin set free—
A heart that always feels thy blood,
  So freely spilt for me;—

2 A heart resigned, submissive, meek,
  My great Redeemer's throne,
Where only Christ is heard to speak,
  Where Jesus reigns alone.

3 Oh, for a lowly, contrite heart,
  Believing, true, and clean,
Which neither life nor death can part
  From him that dwells within;—

4 A heart in every thought renewed,
  And full of love divine;
Perfect, and right, and pure, and good,
  A copy, Lord, of thine.

5 Thy nature, gracious Lord, impart;
  Come quickly from above;
Write thy new name upon my heart—
  Thy new, best name of Love.
           CHARLES WESLEY, 1742.

332   *Triumphant Grace.*   (847)

AMAZING grace! how sweet the sound,
  That saved a wretch like me!
I once was lost, but now am found,
  Was blind, but now I see.

2 'Twas grace that taught my heart to fear,
  And grace my fears relieved:
How precious did that grace appear:
  The hour I first believed!

3 Through many dangers, toils, and snares,
  I have already come:
'Tis grace has brought me safe thus far,
  And grace will lead me home.

4 The Lord has promised good to me,
  His word my hope secures;
He will my shield and portion be,
  As long as life endures.

EVAN. C. M.   Arr., WILLIAM HENRY HAVERGAL, 1846.

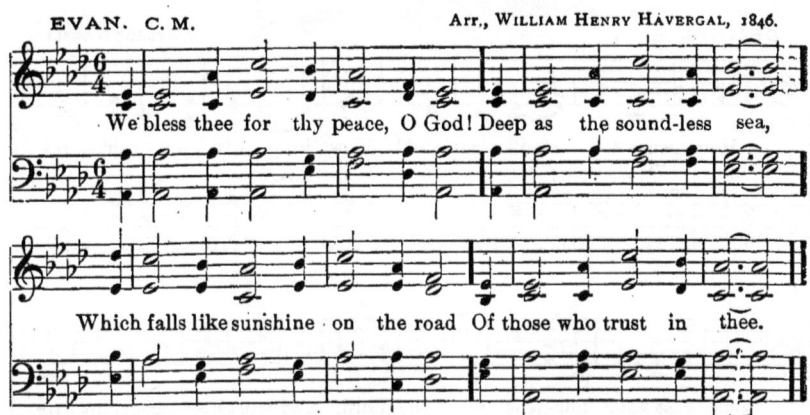

We bless thee for thy peace, O God! Deep as the sound-less sea,

Which falls like sunshine on the road Of those who trust in thee.

33 [FIRST VERSE IN MUSIC ABOVE.]
  The Peace of God. (725)

That peace which suffers and is strong,
Trusts where it can not see,
eems not the trial way too long,
But leaves the end with thee;—
That peace which flows serene and deep,
A river in the soul,
Whose banks a living verdure keep;
God's sunshine o'er the whole.

4 Such, Father! give our hearts such peace,
Whate'er the outward be,
Till all life's discipline shall cease,
And we go home to thee.
  ANON. 1862.

334 [FIRST TWO VERSES IN MUSIC BELOW.]
  The Voice of Jesus. (666)

3 I heard the voice of Jesus say
  "Behold! I freely give

The living water; thirsty one!
Stoop down, and drink, and live."

4 I came to Jesus, and I drank
Of that life-giving stream;
My thirst was quenched, my soul revived,
And now I live in him.

5 I heard the voice of Jesus say,
"I am this dark world's Light;
Look unto me; thy morn shall rise,
And all thy day be bright."

6 I looked to Jesus, and I found,
In him my Star, my Sun;
And, in that light of life, I'll walk
Till traveling days are done.
  HORATIUS BONAR, 1857.

VARINA. C. M. D.
Not too fast.   From CHRISTIAN HEINRICH RINK, 1770-1840.
                                   Arr., GEORGE F. ROOT, 1846.

I heard the voice of Jesus say, "Come unto me and rest;
Lay down, thou wear-y one, lay down Thy head upon my breast." 2 I came to Je-sus as I was,

Weary, and worn, and sad; I found in him a resting-place, And he has made me glad.

DENNIS. S. M.   HANS GEORGE NAGELI.

How gen - tle God's command! How kind his pre - cepts are!

Come, cast your bur-dens on the Lord, And trust his constant care.

335   *The Lord's Guardianship.*   (855)

How gentle God's commands!
  How kind his precepts are!
Come, cast your burdens on the Lord,
  And trust his constant care.

2 His bounty will provide;
  His saints securely dwell;
That hand which bears creation up,
  Shall guard his children well.

3 Why should this anxious load
  Press down your weary mind?
Oh, seek your heavenly Father's throne,
  And peace and comfort find.

4 His goodness stands approved,
  Unchanged from day to day;
I'll drop my burden at his feet,
  And bear a song away.
                PHILIP DODDRIDGE, 1740.

336   *Grace.—Eph. 2: 8.*   (744)

GRACE! 'tis a charming sound
  Harmonious to the ear!
Heaven with the echo shall resound,
  And all the earth shall hear.

2 Grace first contrived a way
  To save rebellious man;
And all the steps that grace display,
  Which drew the wondrous plan.

3 Grace led my roving feet
  To tread the heavenly road;

And new supplies each hour I meet
  While pressing on to God.

4 Grace all the work shall crown,
  Through everlasting days;
It lays in heaven the topmost stone,
  And well deserves the praise.
                PHILIP DODDRIDGE, 1755.

337   *Adoption.—1 John 3: 1-3.*   (742)

BEHOLD what wondrous grace
  The Father has bestowed
On sinners of a mortal race,
  To call them sons of God!

2 Nor doth it yet appear
  How great we must be made;
But when we see our Savior there,
  We shall be like our Head.

3 A hope so much divine
  May trials well endure,
May purge our souls from sense and sin,
  As Christ the Lord is pure.

4 If in my Father's love
  I share a filial part,
Send down thy Spirit, like a dove,
  To rest upon my heart.

5 We would no longer lie
  Like slaves beneath the throne;
Our faith shall Abba, Father! cry,
  And thou the kindred own.
                ISAAC WATTS. 1709.

NETTLETON. 8s & 7s. 6 or 8 lines. ASAHEL NETTLETON, 1825.

Come, thou Fount of ev - 'ry bless-ing, Tune my heart to sing thy grace;
Streams of mer - cy, nev - er ceas-ing, Call for songs of loud-est praise.
D. C. Praise the mount—I'm fixed up-on it, Mount of thy re-deem-ing love.

Teach me some me - lo - dious son - net, Sung by flaming tongues a-bove;

338 [FIRST VERSE INSERTED IN MUSIC.]
Memorial of Praise. (617)

2 Here I'll raise mine Ebenezer,
  Hither by thy help I'm come;
And I hope by thy good pleasure,
  Safely to arrive at home.
Jesus sought me when a stranger,
  Wand'ring from the fold of God,
He, to rescue me from danger,
  Interposed his precious blood.

3 Oh! to grace how great a debtor,
  Daily I'm constrained to be!
Let thy goodness, like a fetter,
  Bind my wand'ring heart to thee.
Prone to wander, Lord, I feel it;
  Prone to leave the God I love—
Here's my heart, oh, take and seal it;
  Seal it for thy courts above.
ROBERT ROBINSON, 1758.

339 (188) BRADEN. S. M.
WILLIAM B. BRADBURY, 1844.

1. The pit - y of the Lord, To those that fear his name,
2. He knows we are but dust, Scat- tered with ev - 'ry breath;
3. Our days are as the grass, Or like the morn ing flow'r;
4. But thy com-pas - sions, Lord, To end - less years en - dure;

Is such as ten - der par - ents feel; He knows our fee - ble frame.
His an - ger, like a ris - ing wind, Can send us swift to death.
If one sharp blast sweep o'er the field, It with - ers in an hour.
And chil-dren's children ev - er find, Thy words of prom-ise sure.
ISAAC WATTS, 1719.

12

REFUGE. 7s. D.   J. P. Holbrook, 1862.

Je-sus, Lov-er of my soul, Let me to thy bo-som fly, While the

near-er waters roll, While the tempest still is high! Hide me, O my Savior, hide

Till the storm of life is past; Safe into the haven guide, O receive my soul at last.

340   *The Only Refuge.*   (532)

JESUS, Lover of my soul,
  Let me to thy bosom fly,
While the nearer waters roll,
  While the tempest still is high!
Hide me, O my Savior, hide,
  Till the storm of life is past;
Safe into the haven guide,
  O receive my soul at last!

2 Other refuge have I none;
  Hangs my helpless soul on thee:
Leave, O leave me not alone,
  Still support and comfort me:
All my trust on thee is stayed,
  All my help from thee I bring;
Cover my defenseless head
  With the shadow of thy wing!

3 Thou, O Christ, art all I want;
  More than all in thee I find;
Raise the fallen, cheer the faint,
  Heal the sick, and lead the blind.
Just and holy is thy name,
  I am all unrighteousness:
False and full of sin I am,
  Thou art full of truth and grace.

4 Plenteous grace with thee is found,
  Grace to cover all my sin:
Let the healing streams abound:
  Make and keep me pure within.
Thou of life the fountain art,
  Freely let me take of thee:
Spring thou up within my heart,
  Rise to all eternity.

CHARLES WESLEY, 1740.

SIMEON BUTLER MARSH, 1834.

MARTYN. 7s. D.

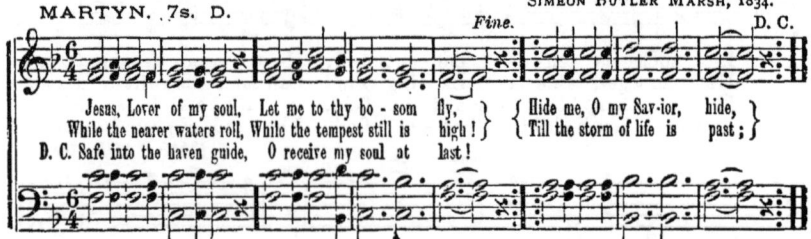

Jesus, Lover of my soul, Let me to thy bo-som fly, } { Hide me, O my Sav-ior, hide, }
While the nearer waters roll, While the tempest still is high! } { Till the storm of life is past; }
D. C. Safe into the haven guide, O receive my soul at last!

341 PILOT. 7s, 6 l. J. E. GOULD,

1. Je-sus, Savior, pilot me, Over life's tempestuous sea ; Unknown waves before me
2. As a mother stills her child, Thou canst hush the ocean wild ; Boist'rous waves obey thy
3. When at last I near the shore, And the fearful breakers roar 'Twixt me and the peaceful

roll, Hiding rock and treach'rous shoal ; Chart and compass come from thee : Jesus, Savior, pilot me.
will, When thou sayst to them " Be still ! " Wondrous Sov'reign of the sea, Jesus, Savior, pilot me.
rest, Then, while leaning on thy breast, May I hear thee say to me, " Fear not, I will pilot thee ! '

REV. EDWARD HOPPER.

342(577) FULTON. 7s. W. B. BRADBURY.

1. Sav - ior ! teach me, day by day, Love's sweet les - son to o - bey ;
2. With a child-like heart of love, At thy bid - ding may I move ;
3. Teach me all thy steps to trace, Strong to fol - low in thy grace ;
4. Love in lov - ing finds em - ploy— In o - be-dience all her joy ;

Sweet - er les - son can not be, Lov - ing him who first loved me.
Prompt to serve and fol - low thee, Lov - ing him who first loved me.
Learn-ing how to love from thee, Lov - ing him who first loved me.
Ev - er new that joy will be, Lov - ing him who first loved me.

MISS JANE E. LEESON, 1842.

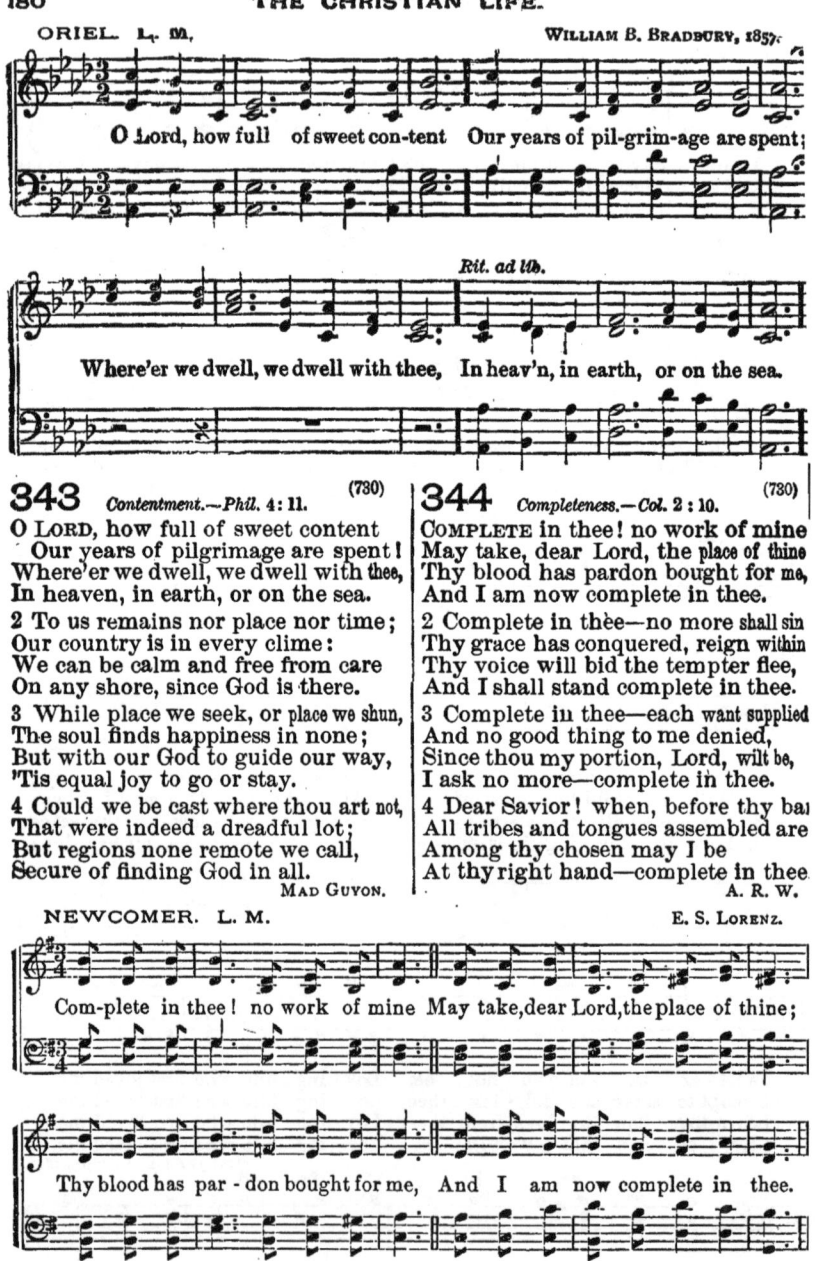

ORIEL. L. M.

WILLIAM B. BRADBURY, 1857.

O Lord, how full of sweet con-tent Our years of pil-grim-age are spent;

Rit. ad lib.

Where'er we dwell, we dwell with thee, In heav'n, in earth, or on the sea.

343 *Contentment.—Phil. 4: 11.* (730)

O LORD, how full of sweet content
 Our years of pilgrimage are spent!
Where'er we dwell, we dwell with thee,
In heaven, in earth, or on the sea.

2 To us remains nor place nor time;
Our country is in every clime:
We can be calm and free from care
On any shore, since God is there.

3 While place we seek, or place we shun,
The soul finds happiness in none;
But with our God to guide our way,
'Tis equal joy to go or stay.

4 Could we be cast where thou art not,
That were indeed a dreadful lot;
But regions none remote we call,
Secure of finding God in all.
                                MAD GUYON.

344 *Completeness.—Col. 2 : 10.* (730)

COMPLETE in thee! no work of mine
May take, dear Lord, the place of thine
Thy blood has pardon bought for me,
And I am now complete in thee.

2 Complete in thee—no more shall sin
Thy grace has conquered, reign within
Thy voice will bid the tempter flee,
And I shall stand complete in thee.

3 Complete in thee—each want supplied
And no good thing to me denied,
Since thou my portion, Lord, wilt be,
I ask no more—complete in thee.

4 Dear Savior! when, before thy bar
All tribes and tongues assembled are
Among thy chosen may I be
At thy right hand—complete in thee
                                A. R. W.

NEWCOMER. L. M.

E. S. LORENZ.

Com-plete in thee! no work of mine May take, dear Lord, the place of thine;

Thy blood has par-don bought for me, And I am now complete in thee.

WARING. 7s & 6s. D.　　　　　　　　FELIX MENDELSSOHN BARTHOLDY.

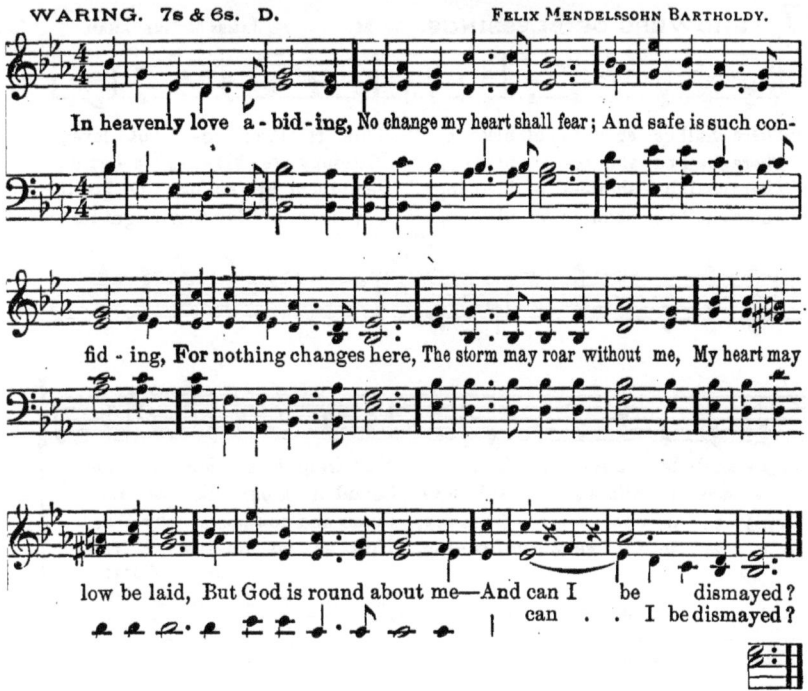

In heavenly love a-bid-ing, No change my heart shall fear; And safe is such con-

fid - ing, For nothing changes here, The storm may roar without me, My heart may

low be laid, But God is round about me—And can I be dismayed?
can . . I be dismayed?

45 *Safe in Jesus.* (696)

ı heavenly love abiding,
No change my heart shall fear,
nd safe is such confiding,
For nothing changes here;
he storm may roar without me,
My heart may low be laid,
ut God is round about me,—
And can I be dismayed?

Wherever he may guide me,
No want shall turn me back;
Iy Shepherd is beside me,
And nothing can I lack;
is wisdom ever waketh,
His sight is never dim,
e knows the way he taketh,
And I will walk with him.

Green pastures are before me,
Which yet I have not seen;
ɔright skies will soon be o'er me,
Where darkest clouds have been;

My hope I can not measure,
My path to life is free;
My Savior has my treasure,
And he will walk with me.
ANNA LETITIA WARING, 1850.

346 *Light after Darkness.*

SOMETIMES a light surprises
The Christian while he sings:
It is the Lord who rises
With healing on his wings;
When comforts are declining,
He grants the soul again
A season of clear shining,
To cheer it after rain.

2 In holy contemplation,
We sweetly then pursue
The theme of God's salvation,
And find it ever new:
Set free from present sorrow,
We cheerfully can say,
Let the unknown to-morrow
Bring with it what it may.
WM. COWPER.

347   SHOWERS OF BLESSINGS. P. M.   James McGranahan.

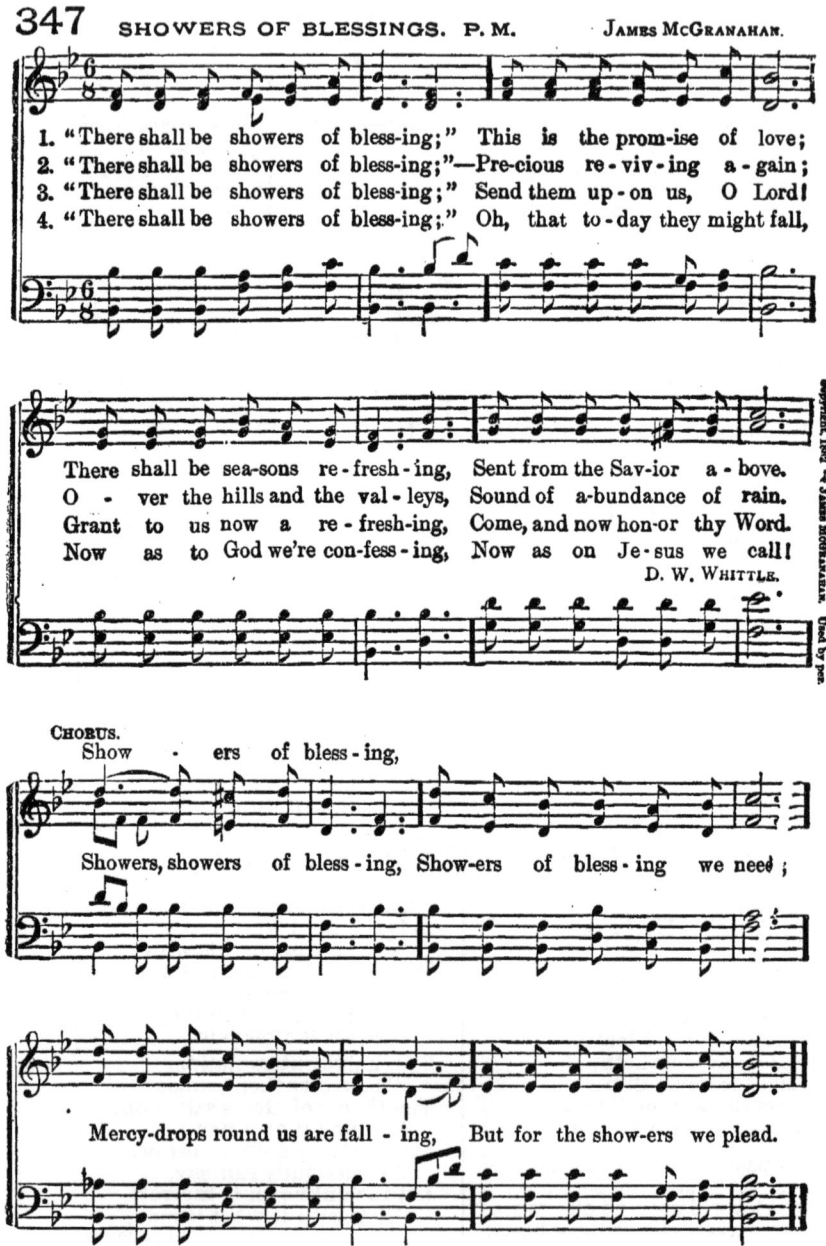

1. "There shall be showers of bless-ing;" This is the prom-ise of love;
2. "There shall be showers of bless-ing;"—Pre-cious re-viv-ing a-gain;
3. "There shall be showers of bless-ing;" Send them up-on us, O Lord!
4. "There shall be showers of bless-ing;" Oh, that to-day they might fall,

There shall be sea-sons re-fresh-ing, Sent from the Sav-ior a-bove.
O-ver the hills and the val-leys, Sound of a-bundance of rain.
Grant to us now a re-fresh-ing, Come, and now hon-or thy Word.
Now as to God we're con-fess-ing, Now as on Je-sus we call!

D. W. Whittle.

Chorus.

Show-ers of bless-ing,

Showers, showers of bless-ing, Show-ers of bless-ing we need;

Mercy-drops round us are fall-ing, But for the show-ers we plead.

48(706) OH, SING OF HIS MIGHTY LOVE. 11s.

WILLIAM B. BRADBURY.

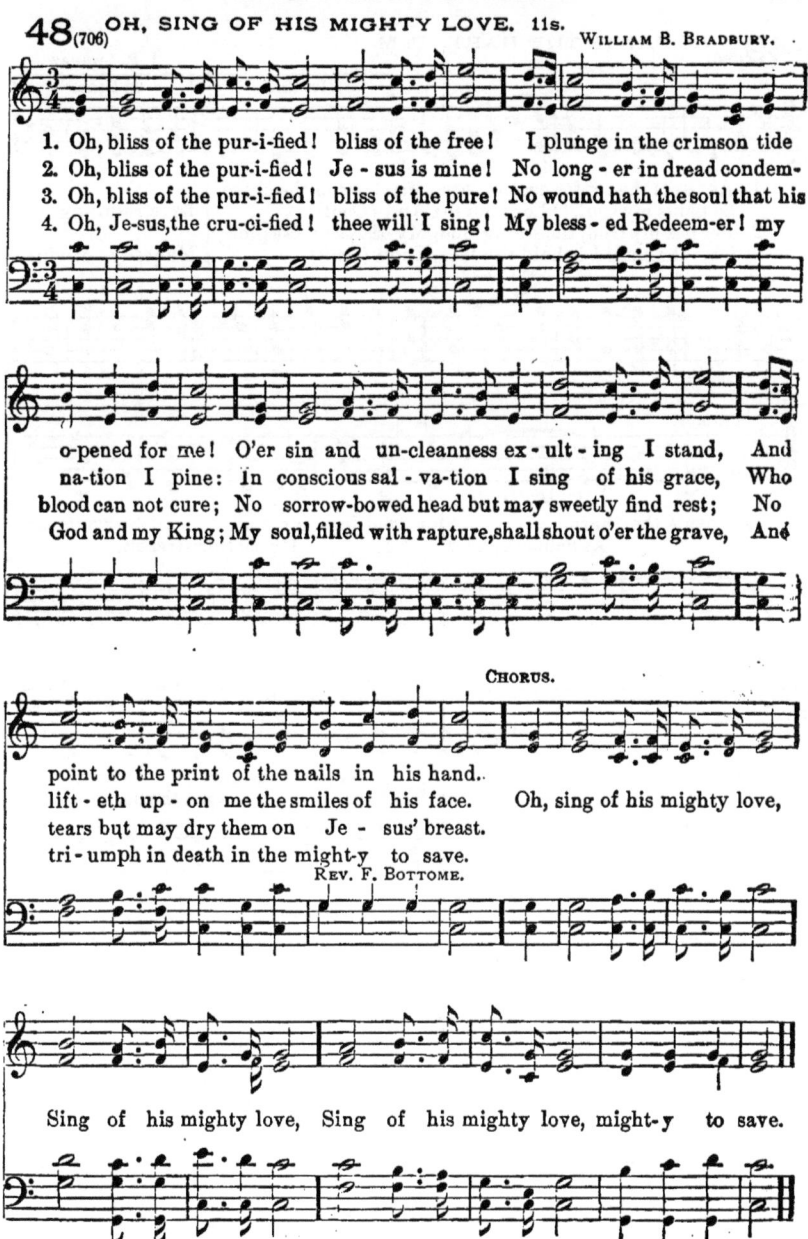

1. Oh, bliss of the pur-i-fied! bliss of the free! I plunge in the crimson tide
2. Oh, bliss of the pur-i-fied! Je - sus is mine! No long - er in dread condem-
3. Oh, bliss of the pur-i-fied! bliss of the pure! No wound hath the soul that his
4. Oh, Je-sus,the cru-ci-fied! thee will I sing! My bless - ed Redeem-er! my

o-pened for me! O'er sin and un-cleanness ex - ult - ing I stand, And
na-tion I pine: In conscious sal - va-tion I sing of his grace, Who
blood can not cure; No sorrow-bowed head but may sweetly find rest; No
God and my King; My soul,filled with rapture,shall shout o'er the grave, And

CHORUS.

point to the print of the nails in his hand.
lift - eth up - on me the smiles of his face. Oh, sing of his mighty love,
tears but may dry them on Je - sus' breast.
tri - umph in death in the might-y to save.

REV. F. BOTTOME.

Sing of his mighty love, Sing of his mighty love, might-y to save.

349 (660) AS PANTS THE HART. C. M.

J. R. SWENEY.

1. As pants the hart for cooling streams, When heated in the chase,
So pants my soul, O Lord, for thee, And (*Omit*) . . . } thy refreshing grace.
2. For thee, my God, the living God, My thirsty soul doth pine;
Oh, when shall I behold thy face, Thou (*Omit*) . . . } Ma-jes-ty di-vine?

CHORUS.

As pants the hart . . . . for cool-ing streams, . . So pants my
As pants the hart   for cooling streams,

soul, . . . O Lord, for thee; . . As pants the hart . . for cooling
So pants my soul,   O Lord, for thee;   As pants the hart

streams, . . . So pants my soul, . . . O Lord, for thee.
for cool-ing streams,   So pants my soul,

3 I sigh to think of happier days,
  When thou, O Lord, wast nigh,
When ev'ry heart was tuned to praise,
  And none more blest than I.

4 Why restless, why cast down, my soul?
  Trust God, and thou shalt sing
His praise again, and find him still
  Thy health's eternal spring.

HENRY F. LYTE, 1834.

350 HIDE THOU ME. P. M.

REV. ROBERT LOWRY.

1. In thy cleft, O Rock of A - ges, Hide thou me;
2. From the snare of sin - ful pleas - ure Hide thou me;
3. In the lone - ly night of sor - row, Hide thou me;

When the fit - ful tem - pest ra - ges, Hide thou me; Where no
Thou, my soul's e - ter - nal treas - ure, Hide thou me; When the
Till in glo - ry dawns the mor - row, Hide thou me; In the

mor - tal arm can sev - er From my heart thy love for - ev - er,
world its pow'r is wield-ing, And my heart is al - most yield-ing,
sight of Jor-dan's bil - low, Let thy bo - som be my pil - low,

Hide me, O thou Rock of A - ges, Safe in thee.

FANNY J. CROSBY.

---

351 *Godly Sincerity.—Eph. 5 : 8.* (724)

WALK in the light! so shalt thou know
  That fellowship of love,
His Spirit only can bestow,
  Who reigns in light above.

2 Walk in the light! and thou shalt find
  Thy heart made truly his,
Who dwells in cloudless light enshrined,
  In whom no darkness is.

3 Walk in the light! and ev'n the tomb
  No fearful shade shall wear;
Glory shall chase away its gloom,
  For Christ hath conquered there.

4 Walk in the light! and thou shalt see
  Thy path, though thorny, bright,
For God by grace shall dwell in thee,
  And God himself is light.

BERNARD BARTON.

352 THE CHILD OF A KING. Jno. A. Sumner. Arr.

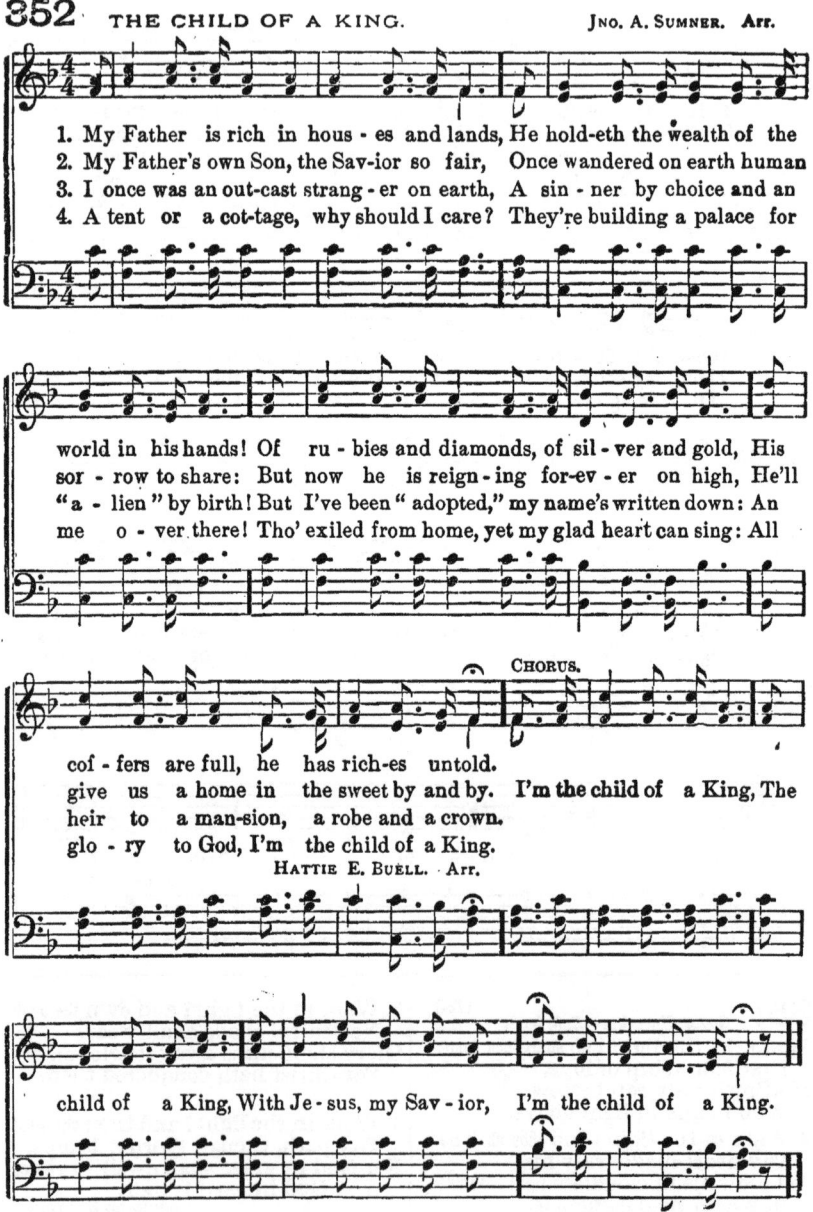

1. My Father is rich in hous - es and lands, He hold-eth the wealth of the
2. My Father's own Son, the Sav-ior so fair, Once wandered on earth human
3. I once was an out-cast strang - er on earth, A sin - ner by choice and an
4. A tent or a cot-tage, why should I care? They're building a palace for

world in his hands! Of ru - bies and diamonds, of sil - ver and gold, His
sor - row to share: But now he is reign-ing for-ev - er on high, He'll
"a - lien" by birth! But I've been " adopted," my name's written down: An
me o - ver there! Tho' exiled from home, yet my glad heart can sing: All

CHORUS.

cof - fers are full, he has rich-es untold.
give us a home in the sweet by and by. I'm the child of a King, The
heir to a man-sion, a robe and a crown.
glo - ry to God, I'm the child of a King.

Hattie E. Buell. Arr.

child of a King, With Je - sus, my Sav - ior, I'm the child of a King.

353 THOU THINKEST, LORD, OF ME. 8s & 6s. E. S. LORENZ.

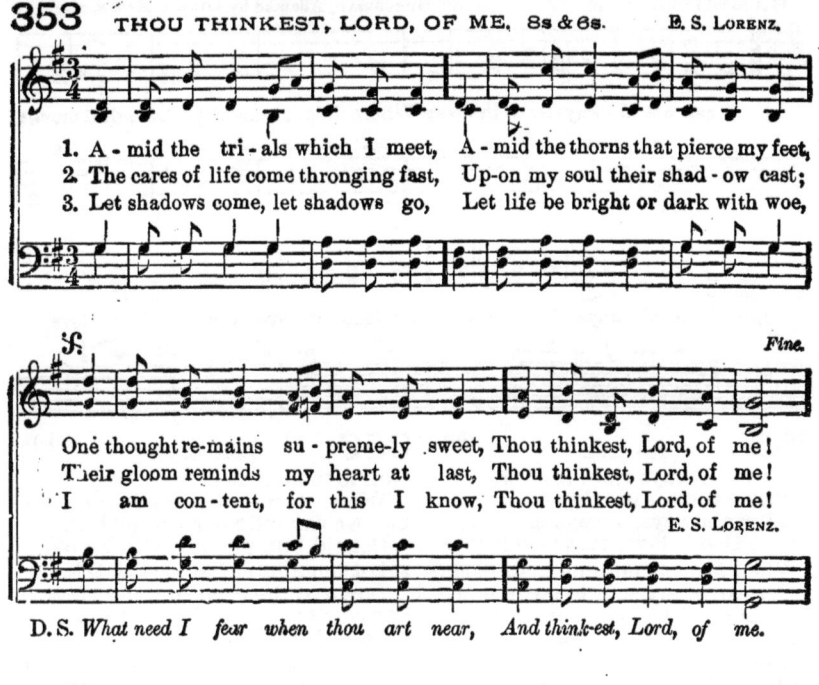

1. A - mid the tri - als which I meet, A - mid the thorns that pierce my feet,
2. The cares of life come thronging fast, Up-on my soul their shad - ow cast;
3. Let shadows come, let shadows go, Let life be bright or dark with woe,

S.   *Fine.*

One thought re-mains su - preme-ly sweet, Thou thinkest, Lord, of me!
Their gloom reminds my heart at last, Thou thinkest, Lord, of me!
I am con - tent, for this I know, Thou thinkest, Lord, of me!

E. S. LORENZ.

D. S. *What need I fear when thou art near, And think-est, Lord, of me.*

CHORUS.   . D. S.

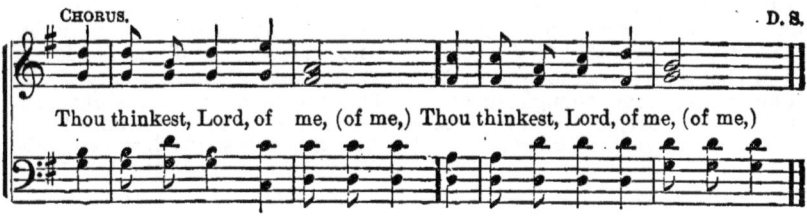

Thou thinkest, Lord, of me, (of me,) Thou thinkest, Lord, of me, (of me,)

354 *Plead For Me.* (633)

O THOU, the contrite sinner's Friend,
Who loving, lov'st them to the end,
On this alone my hopes depend
    That thou wilt plead for me.

CHORUS.—‖: O Savior, plead for me (for me),:‖
  On this alone my hopes depend
That thou wilt plead for me.

2 When weary in the Christian race,
Far off appears my resting place,
And, fainting, I mistrust thy grace,
    Then, Savior, plead for me.

3 When I have erred and gone astray,
Afar from thine and wisdom's way,
And see no glimmering, guiding ray,
    Still, Savior, plead for me.

4 When Satan, by my sins made bold,
Strives from thy cross to loose my hold,
Then with thy pitying arms enfold,
    And plead, oh, plead for me!

5 And when my dying hour draws near,
Darkened with anguish, guilt and fear,
Then to my fainting sight appear,
    Pleading in heaven for me.

CHARLOTTE ELLIOTT.

HAMBURG. L. M. GREGORIAN, Adapted by LOWELL MASON, 182..

I can not al - ways trace the way Where thou, Al-might-y One, dost move;

But I can al - ways, al - ways say That God is love, that God is love.

---

355   *Heb.* 12: 6.   (852)

I CAN not always trace the way
   Where thou, Almighty One, dost move;
But I can always, always say,
   That God is love, that God is love.

2 When fear her chilling mantle flings
   O'er earth, my soul to heaven above,
As to her native home, upsprings,
   For God is love, for God is love.

8 When mystery clouds my darkened path,
   I'll check my dread, my doubts reprove;
In this my soul sweet comfort hath,
   That God is love, that God is love.

4 Yes, God is love;—a thought like this,
   Can every gloomy thought remove,
And turn all tears, all woes, to bliss,
   For God is love, for God is love.
                  ANON.

356   *Psalm 46.*   (849)

GOD is the refuge of his saints,
   When storms of sharp distress invade.
Ere we can offer our complaints,
   Behold him present with his aid

2 Let mountains from their seats be hurled,
   Down to the deep, and buried there,
Convulsions shake the solid world ;—
   Our faith shall never yield to fear.

3 There is a stream, whose gentle flow
   Supplies the city of our God;
Life, love, and joy still gliding through
   And watering our divine abode :—

4 That sacred stream, thy holy word,—
   That all our raging fear controls:
Sweet peace thy promises afford,
   And give new strength to fainting souls
              ISAAC WATTS, 1710

WARD. L. M. SCOTCH, ARR. by LOWELL MASON, 1830.

God is the Ref-uge of his saints When storms of sharp dis-tress in - vade;

Ere we can of - fer our complaints, Be-hold him pres - ent with his aid.

357 SESSIONS. L. M.

L. O. EMERSON, 1847.

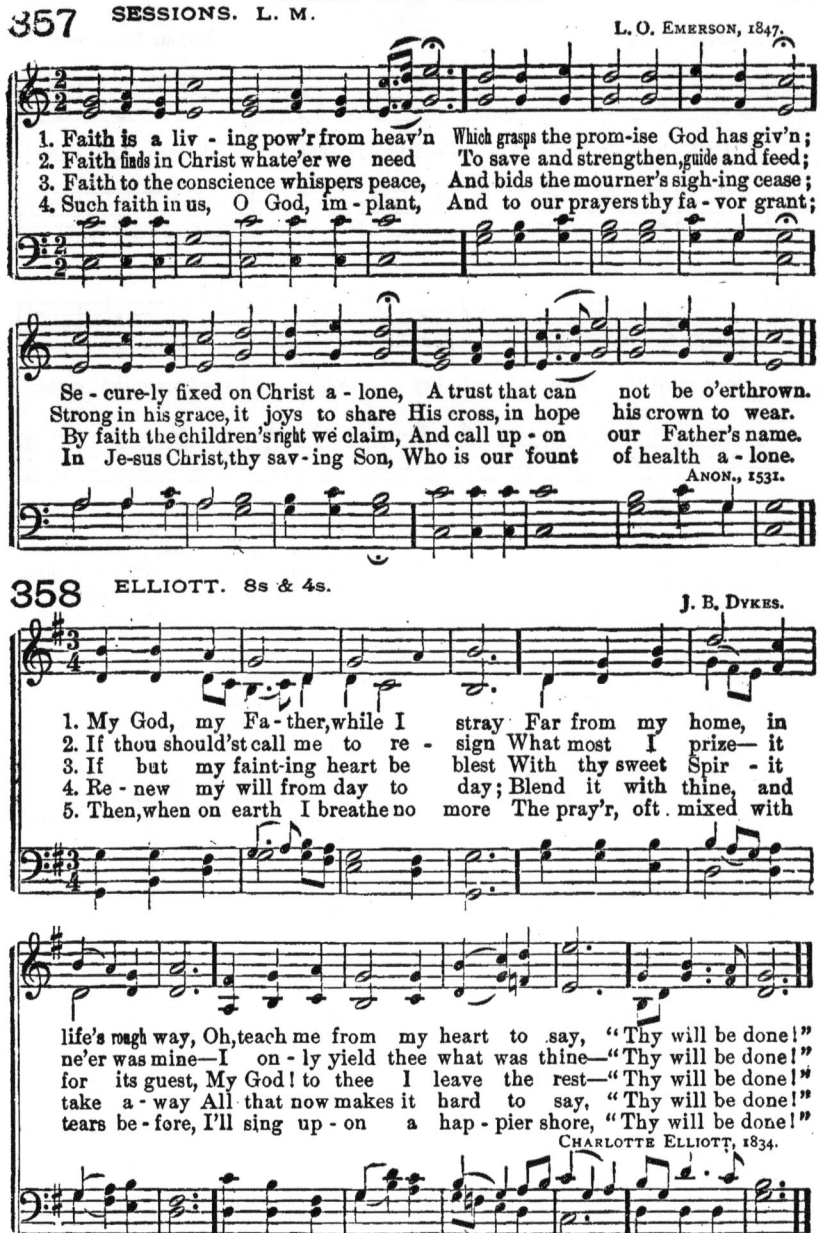

1. Faith is a liv - ing pow'r from heav'n   Which grasps the prom-ise God has giv'n;
2. Faith finds in Christ whate'er we need   To save and strengthen, guide and feed;
3. Faith to the conscience whispers peace,   And bids the mourner's sigh-ing cease;
4. Such faith in us, O God, im - plant,   And to our prayers thy fa - vor grant;

Se - cure-ly fixed on Christ a - lone, A trust that can   not be o'erthrown.
Strong in his grace, it joys to share His cross, in hope   his crown to wear.
By faith the children's right we claim, And call up - on   our Father's name.
In   Je-sus Christ, thy sav - ing Son, Who is our fount of health a - lone.

ANON., 1531.

358   ELLIOTT. 8s & 4s.

J. B. DYKES.

1. My God, my Fa - ther, while I   stray Far from my   home, in
2. If thou should'st call me to re - sign What most   I   prize— it
3. If   but my faint-ing heart be   blest With thy sweet Spir - it
4. Re - new my will from day to   day; Blend it with thine, and
5. Then, when on earth I breathe no   more The pray'r, oft . mixed with

life's rough way, Oh, teach me from my heart to .say, "Thy will be done!"
ne'er was mine—I on - ly yield thee what was thine—"Thy will be done!"
for its guest, My God! to thee I leave the rest—"Thy will be done!"
take a - way All that now makes it hard to say, "Thy will be done!"
tears be - fore, I'll sing up - on   a hap - pier shore, "Thy will be done!"

CHARLOTTE ELLIOTT, 1834.

LISBON. S. M.   DANIEL READ, 1785.

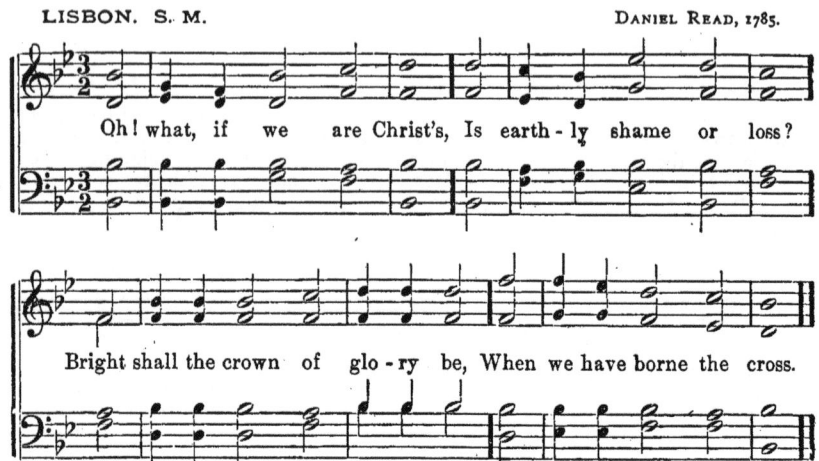

Oh! what, if we are Christ's, Is earth-ly shame or loss?

Bright shall the crown of glo-ry be, When we have borne the cross.

359 *The Cross and Crown.*   (858)

OH! what, if we are Christ's,
  Is earthly shame or loss?
Bright shall the crown of glory be,
  When we have borne the cross.

2 Keen was the trial once,
    Bitter the cup of woe,
  When martyred saints, baptized in blood,
    Christ's sufferings shared below.

3 Bright is their glory now,
    Boundless their joy above,
  Where, on the bosom of their God,
    They rest in perfect love.

4 Lord! may that grace be ours,
    Like them, in faith, to bear
  All that of sorrow, grief, or pain
    May be our portion here.
                        HENRY W. BAKER, 1852.

360 *God our Shepherd. Ps. 23.*   (859)

THE Lord my Shepherd is;
  I shall be well supplied:
Since he is mine, and I am his,
  What can I want beside?

2 He leads me to the place
    Where heavenly pasture grows,
  Where living waters gently pass,
    And full salvation flows.

3 If e'er I go astray,
    He doth my soul reclaim,
  And guides me, in his own right way,
    For his most holy name.

4 While he affords his aid,
    I can not yield to fear;
  Tho' I should walk thro' death's dark shade,
    My Shepherd 's with me there.
                        ISAAC WATTS, 1719.

361   *Psalm 37 : 3–7.*   (745)

HERE I can firmly rest;
  I dare to boast of this,
That God, the highest and the best,
  My Friend and Father is.

2 Naught have I of my own,
    Naught in the life I lead;
  What Christ hath given, that alone
    I dare in faith to plead.

3 I rest upon the ground
    Of Jesus and his blood;
  It is through him that I have found
    My soul's eternal good.

4 At cost of all I have,
    At cost of life and limb,
  I cling to God who yet shall save;
    I will not turn from him.

5 His Spirit in me dwells,
    O'er all my mind he reigns;
  My care and sadness he dispels,
    And soothes away my pains.

6 He prospers day by day
    His work within my heart,
  Till I have strength and faith to say,
    Thou, God, my Father art!
                        PAUL GERHARDT, 1650.
                    Tr. by MISS C. WINKWORTH, 1855.

362 (807) SEGUR. 8s, 7s & 4s.

J. P. HOLBROOK.

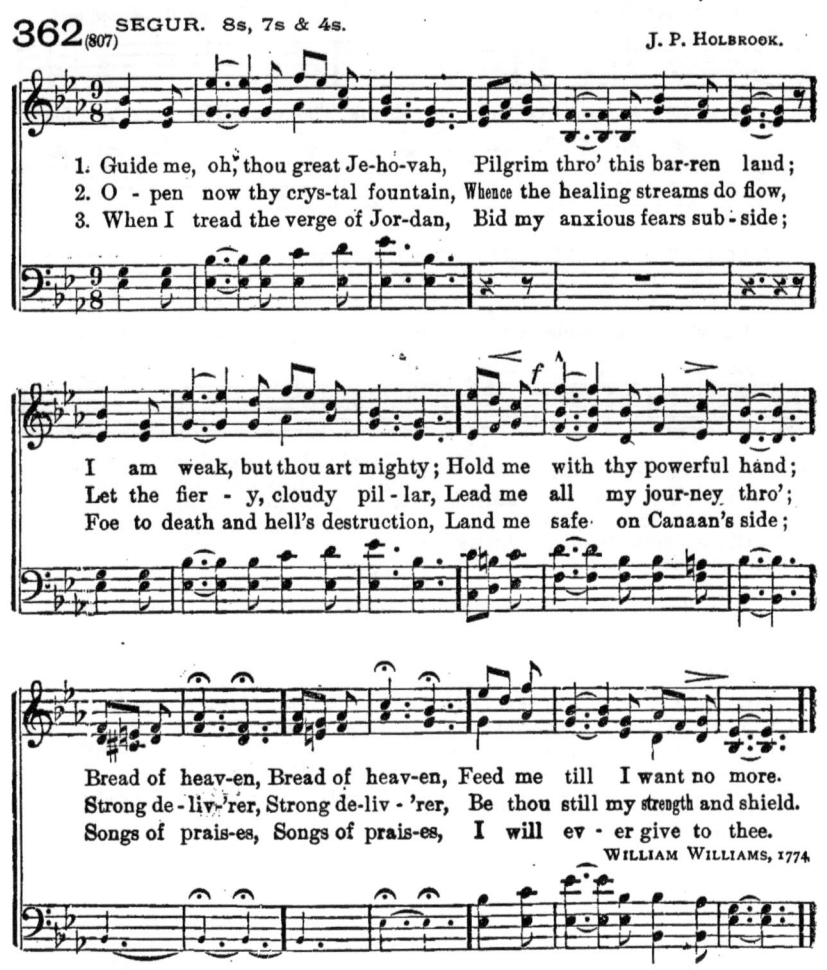

1. Guide me, oh, thou great Je-ho-vah, Pilgrim thro' this bar-ren land;
2. O - pen now thy crys-tal fountain, Whence the healing streams do flow,
3. When I tread the verge of Jor-dan, Bid my anxious fears sub - side;

I am weak, but thou art mighty; Hold me with thy powerful hand;
Let the fier - y, cloudy pil - lar, Lead me all my jour-ney thro';
Foe to death and hell's destruction, Land me safe on Canaan's side;

Bread of heav-en, Bread of heav-en, Feed me till I want no more.
Strong de - liv-'rer, Strong de-liv - 'rer, Be thou still my strength and shield.
Songs of prais-es, Songs of prais-es, I will ev - er give to thee.

WILLIAM WILLIAMS, 1774.

---

363 *Hope Thou in God.* (860)

GIVE to the winds thy fears;
　Hope, and be undismayed;
God hears thy sighs and counts thy tears,
　God shall lift up thy head.

2 Through waves, and clouds, and storms,
　He gently clears thy way;
Wait thou his time; so shall this night
　Soon end in joyous day.

3 What, though thou rulest not?
　Yet heaven, and earth, and hell
Proclaim,—God sitteth on the throne,
　And ruleth all things well.

4 Leave to his sovereign sway
　To choose, and to command;
So shalt thou wondering own, his way
　How wise, how strong his hand!

Ger., PAUL GERHARDT, 1666.
Tr. JOHN WESLEY, 1739.

PETERBOROUGH. C. M.   RALPH HARRISON, 1786.

Oh! for a faith that will not shrink, Tho' pressed by ev - 'ry foe;

That will not trem-ble on the brink Of an - y earth-ly woe!—

364   *Unwavering Faith.*   (713)

OH! for a faith that will not shrink,
 Though pressed by every foe;
That will not tremble on the brink
 Of any earthly woe!—

2 That will not murmur nor complain,
 Beneath the chastening rod,
But, in the hour of grief or pain,
 Will lean upon its God;—

3 A faith, that shines more bright and clear
 When tempests rage without;
That, when in danger, knows no fear,
 In darkness, feels no doubt;—

4 A faith, that keeps the narrow way
 'Till life's last hour is fled,
And, with a pure and heavenly ray,
 Lights up a dying bed!

5 Lord! give us such a faith as this;
 And then, whate'er may come,
We'll taste, ev'n here, the hallowed bliss
 Of an eternal home.
          WILLIAM H. BATHURST, 1831.

365   *Resignation.*   (841)

FATHER! whate'er of earthly bliss
 Thy sovereign hand denies,
Accepted at thy throne of grace,
 Let this petition rise:—

2 "Give me a calm, a thankful heart,
 From every murmur free;
The blessings of thy grace impart,
 And let me live to thee.

3 "Let the sweet hope that thou art mine
 My path of life attend;
Thy presence through my journey shine,
 And bless its happy end."
          ANNE STEELE, 1760.

NAOMI. C. M.   LOWELL MASON, 1836.

Fa-ther! whate'er of earth-ly bliss Thy sov'reign hand de-nies,

Ac-cept-ed at thy throne of grace, Let this pe - ti - tion rise:—

366 (861) HORTON. 7s.

XAVIER SCHNYDER VON WARTENSEE, 1786.

1. Cast thy bur-den on the Lord, On - ly lean up-on his word;
2. He sus-tains thee by his hand, He en - a - bles thee to stand;
3. Heaven and earth may pass a-way, God's free grace shall not de - cay;
4. Je - sus! Guardian of thy flock, Be thy-self our con-stant Rock;

Thou wilt soon have cause to bless His e-ter - nal faith-ful-ness.
Those whom Jesus once hath loved, From his grace are nev - er moved.
He hath prom-ised to ful-fill All the pleas-ure of his will.
Make us, by thy powerful hand, Strong as Zi - on's mount-ain stand.

ROWLAND HILL, 1783.

367 THE LORD WILL PROVIDE. P. M.

E. S. LORENZ.

1. In some way or oth - er The Lord will provide; It may not be my way,
2. At some time or oth - er The Lord will provide; It may not be my time,
3. Despond then no long - er, The Lord will provide; And this be the to-ken—
4. March on, then, right boldly, The sea shall di - vide; The pathway made glorious

It may not be thy way, And yet in his own way, The Lord will provide.
It may not be thy time, And yet in his own time, The Lord will provide.
No word he hath spoken, Was ev - er yet brok-en, The Lord will provide.
With shoutings victorious, We'll join in the cho - rus, The Lord will provide.

MRS. M. A. W. COOK.

13

CONSOLATION. 11s.   W. H. Lanthurn, 1874.

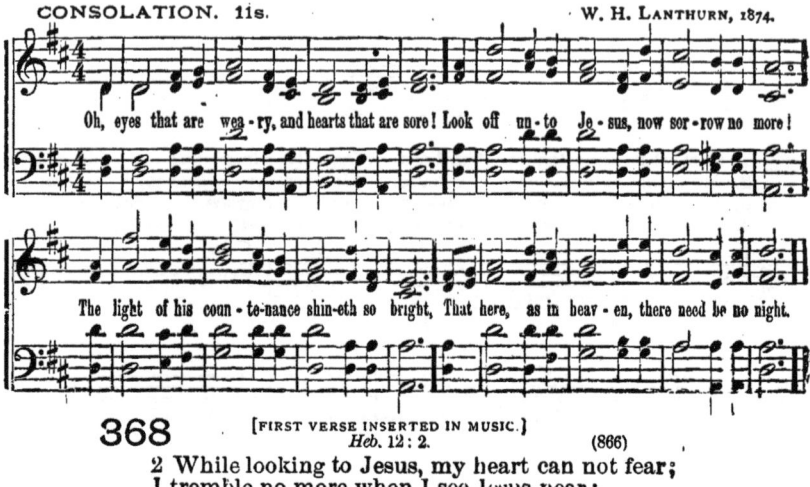

Oh, eyes that are wea-ry, and hearts that are sore! Look off un-to Je-sus, now sor-row no more!

The light of his coun-te-nance shin-eth so bright, That here, as in heav-en, there need be no night.

368   [FIRST VERSE INSERTED IN MUSIC.]
Heb. 12: 2.   (866)

2 While looking to Jesus, my heart can not fear;
I tremble no more when I see Jesus near;
I know that his presence my safeguard will be,
For, "Why are you troubled?" he saith unto me.

3 Still looking to Jesus, oh, may I be found,
When Jordan's dark waters encompass me round!
They bear me away in his presence to be:
I see him still nearer whom always I see.

4 Then, then shall I know the full beauty and grace
Of Jesus, my Lord, when I stand face to face;
Shall know how his love went before me each day,
And wonder that ever my eyes turned away.

PORTUGUESE HYMN. 11s.   Marc Antoine Portogallo.

How firm a foun-da-tion, ye saints of the Lord, Is laid for your faith in his

excellent word! What more can he say than to you he has said, You who unto

Je-sus for ref-uge have fled, You who unto Je-sus for ref-uge have fled.

FOUNDATION. 11s. AMERICAN SPIRITUAL.

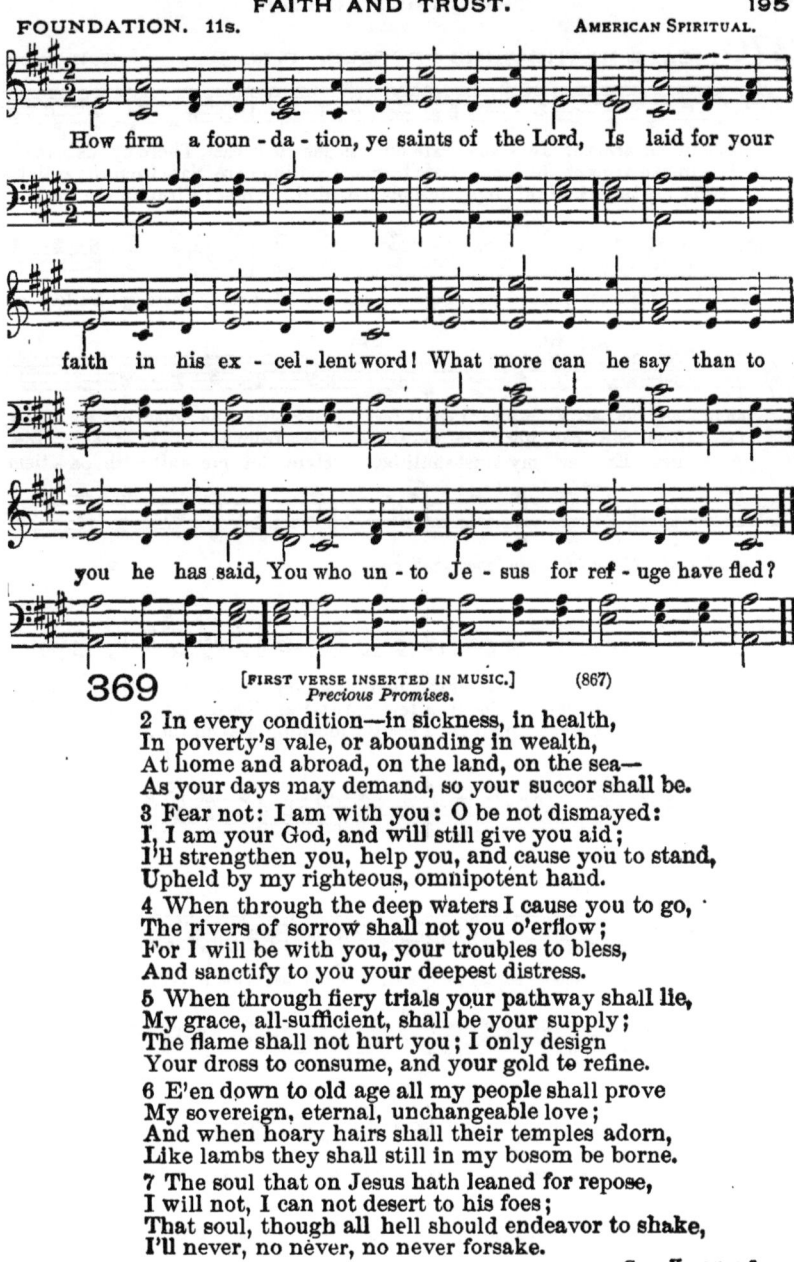

How firm a foun - da - tion, ye saints of the Lord, Is laid for your

faith in his ex - cel - lent word! What more can he say than to

you he has said, You who un - to Je - sus for ref - uge have fled?

369 [FIRST VERSE INSERTED IN MUSIC.] (867)
Precious Promises.

2 In every condition—in sickness, in health,
In poverty's vale, or abounding in wealth,
At home and abroad, on the land, on the sea—
As your days may demand, so your succor shall be.

3 Fear not: I am with you: O be not dismayed:
I, I am your God, and will still give you aid;
I'll strengthen you, help you, and cause you to stand,
Upheld by my righteous, omnipotent hand.

4 When through the deep waters I cause you to go,
The rivers of sorrow shall not you o'erflow;
For I will be with you, your troubles to bless,
And sanctify to you your deepest distress.

5 When through fiery trials your pathway shall lie,
My grace, all-sufficient, shall be your supply;
The flame shall not hurt you; I only design
Your dross to consume, and your gold to refine.

6 E'en down to old age all my people shall prove
My sovereign, eternal, unchangeable love;
And when hoary hairs shall their temples adorn,
Like lambs they shall still in my bosom be borne.

7 The soul that on Jesus hath leaned for repose,
I will not, I can not desert to his foes;
That soul, though all hell should endeavor to shake,
I'll never, no never, no never forsake.

GEO. KEITH, 1787.

370   SAFE IN THE ARMS OF JESUS.   P. M.   W. H. DOANE.

1. Safe in the arms of Je - sus, Safe on his gen-tle breast, There by his love o'er-
2. Safe in the arms of Je - sus, Safe from corrod-ing care, Safe from the world's temp-
3. Je-sus, my heart's dear ref - uge, Je - sus has died for me; Firm on the Rock of

CHO.—*Safe in the arms of Je - sus, Safe on his gen-tle breast, There by his love o'er-*

Rit.   *Fine.*

shad - ed, Sweet-ly my soul shall rest. Hark! 'tis the voice of an - gels,
ta - tions, Sin can not harm me there. Free from the blight of sor - row,
A - ges Ev - er my trust shall be. Here let me wait with pa - tience,

shad - ed, Sweet-ly my soul shall rest.

D. C. Chorus.

Borne in a song to me,   O-ver the fields of glo-ry, O-ver the jasper sea.
Free from my doubts and fears;   On-ly a few more tri-als, On-ly a few more tears!
Wait till the night is o'er;   Wait till I see the morning Break on the golden shore.

FANNY J. CROSBY.

JEWETT. 6s. D.   C. M. VON WEBER, 1820.

My Je - sus, as thou wilt—O may thy will be mine! In- to thy hand of love I would my all re - sign.

Thro' sor-row, or thro' joy, Conduct me as thine own, And help me still to say, My Lord, thy will be done.

371   HE LEADETH ME. L. M.   WM. B. BRADBURY.

1. He leadeth me! oh! blessed tho't, Oh! words with heav'nly comfort fraught; What-
2. Sometimes 'mid scenes of deepest gloom, Sometimes where Eden's bowers bloom, By
3. Lord, I would clasp thy hand in mine, Nor ev - er mur-mur or repine—Con-
4. And when my task on earth is done, When by thy grace, the vict'ry's won, E'en

e'er I do, where'er I be, Still 'tis God's hand that leadeth me.
waters still, o'er troubled sea—Still 'tis his hand that leadeth me. He leadeth me! he
tent, whatever lot I see, Since 'tis my God that leadeth me.
death's cold wave I will not flee, Since God thro' Jordan leadeth me.

REV. JOS. H. GILMORE, 1861.

leadeth me! By his own hand he leadeth me; His faithful follower I would be, For by his hand he leadeth me.

---

372   *Mark 14: 36.*   (864)

My Jesus, as thou wilt—
  O may thy will be mine!
Into thy hand of love
  I would my all resign;
Through sorrow, or through joy,
  Conduct me as thine own,
And help me still to say,
  My Lord, thy will be done!

2 My Jesus, as thou wilt—
  If needy here and poor,
Give me thy people's bread,
  Their portion rich and sure;

The manna of thy word,
  Let my soul feed upon,
And, if all else should fail,
  My Lord, thy will be done!

3 My Jesus, as thou wilt:
  If among thorns I go,
Still sometimes here and there
  Let a few roses blow.
But thou, on earth, along
  The thorny path hast gone:
Then lead me after thee;
  My Lord, thy will be done!

BENJAMIN SCHMOLKE.
Tr. by JANE BORTHWICK, 1853.

373 TRUSTING IN THE PROMISE. P. M.

E. S. Lorenz.

1. I have found repose for my wea-ry soul, Trusting in the promise of the Savior;
2. I will sing my song as the days go by, Trusting in the promise of the Savior;
3. Oh, the peace and joy of the life I live, Trusting in the promise of the Savior;

And a har-bor safe when the billows roll, Trusting in the promise of the Savior.
And rejoice in hope, while I live or die, Trusting in the promise of the Savior.
Oh, the strength and grace on-ly God can give, Trusting in the promise of the Savior.

I will fear no foe in the deadly strife, Trusting in the promise of the Savior;
I can smile at grief and a-bide in pain, Trusting in the promise of the Savior;
Who-so-ev-er will may be saved to-day, Trusting in the promise of the Savior;

I will bear my lot in the toil of life, Trusting in the promise of the Savior.
And the loss of all shall be highest gain, Trusting in the promise of the Savior.
And be-gin to walk in the ho-ly way, Trusting in the promise of the Savior.

Rev. H. B. Hartzler.

TRUSTING IN THE PROMISE. Concluded.

REFRAIN.

Resting on his mighty arm for-ev-er, Nev-er from his lov-ing heart to sev - er,

I will rest by grace in his strong em-brace, Trusting in the promise of the Sav-ior.

374 (868) **COME, YE DISCONSOLATE.** 11s & 10s.

SAMUEL WEBBE, 1800.

Choir.

1. Come, ye dis-con-so-late, wher-e'er ye lan-guish; Come to the
2. Joy. of the des - o- late, light of the stray-ing, Hope when all
3. Here see the bread of life; see wa-ters flow-ing Forth from the

Congregation.

mer - cy - seat, fer - vent - ly kneel; Here bring your wound-ed hearts,
oth - ers die, fade - less and pure— Here speaks the Com - fort - er,
throne of God, bound- less in love; Come to the feast pre - pared,

here tell your an-guish; Earth has no sor - row that heaven can not heal.
in God's name say-ing, Earth has no sor - row that heaven can not cure.
come, ev - er know-ing Earth has no sor - row but heaven can re-move.

Vs. 1, 2, by THOMAS MOORE, 1816; V. 3, by THOS. HASTINGS.

375 FOLLOW ON! P. M.   R**OBERT** L**OWRY**.

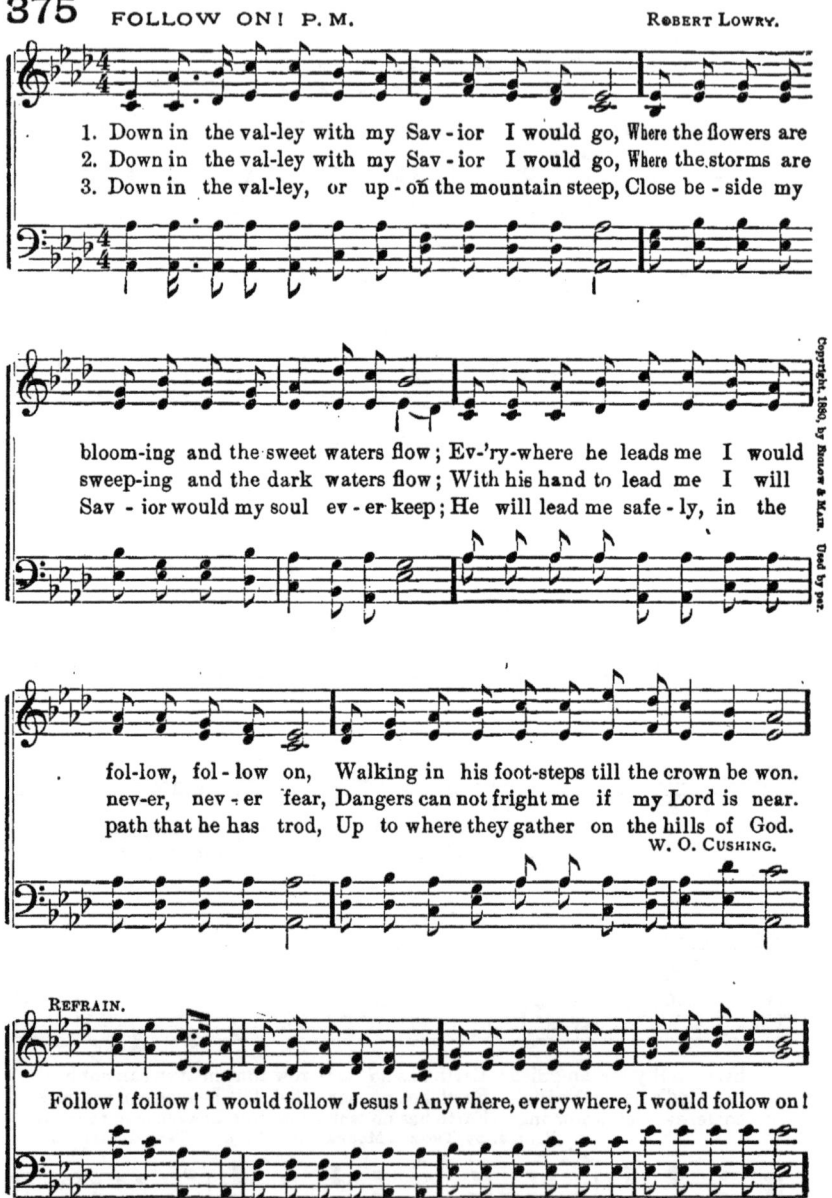

1. Down in the val-ley with my Sav-ior I would go, Where the flowers are
2. Down in the val-ley with my Sav-ior I would go, Where the storms are
3. Down in the val-ley, or up-on the mountain steep, Close be-side my

bloom-ing and the sweet waters flow; Ev-'ry-where he leads me I would
sweep-ing and the dark waters flow; With his hand to lead me I will
Sav-ior would my soul ev-er keep; He will lead me safe-ly, in the

fol-low, fol-low on, Walking in his foot-steps till the crown be won.
nev-er, nev-er fear, Dangers can not fright me if my Lord is near.
path that he has trod, Up to where they gather on the hills of God.

W. O. C**USHING**.

REFRAIN.

Follow! follow! I would follow Jesus! Anywhere, everywhere, I would follow on!

FOLLOW ON! Concluded.

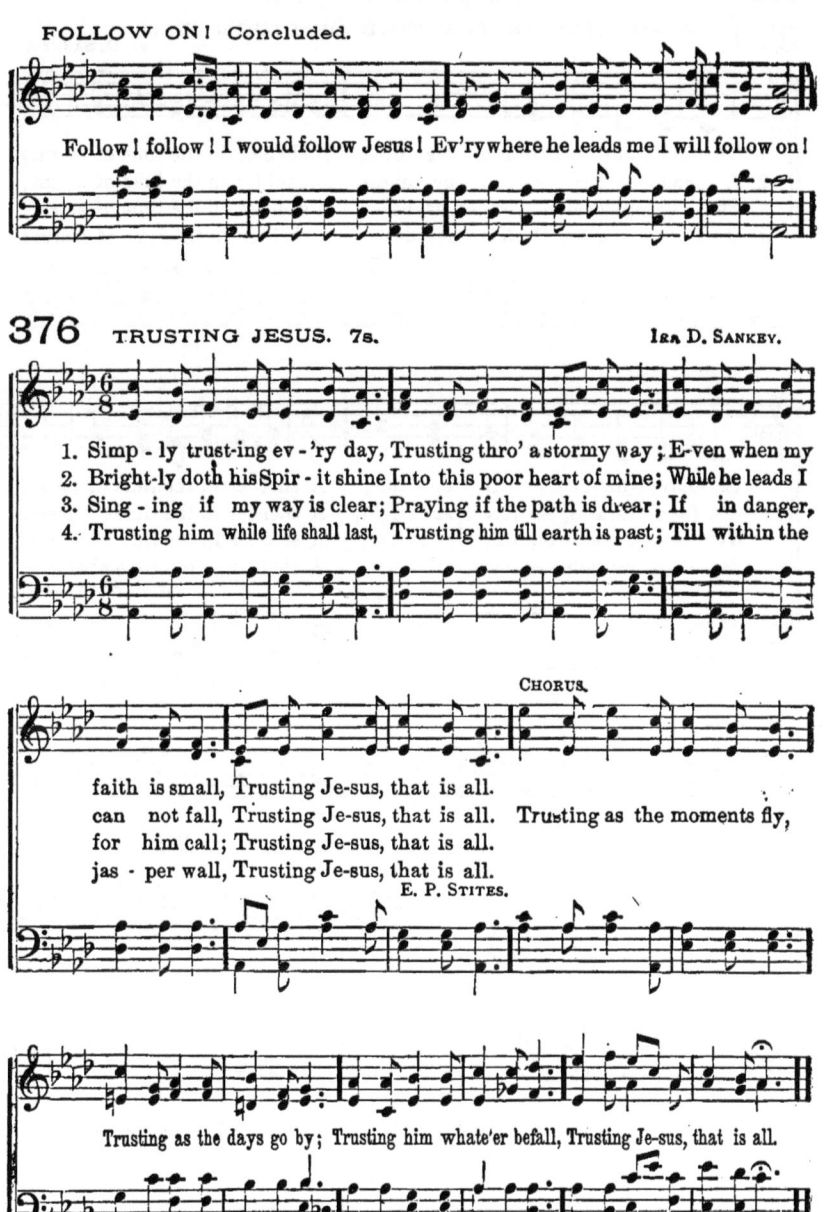

Follow! follow! I would follow Jesus! Ev'rywhere he leads me I will follow on!

376 TRUSTING JESUS. 7s.   Ira D. Sankey.

1. Simp - ly trust-ing ev - 'ry day, Trusting thro' a stormy way; E-ven when my
2. Bright-ly doth his Spir - it shine Into this poor heart of mine; While he leads I
3. Sing - ing if my way is clear; Praying if the path is drear; If in danger,
4. Trusting him while life shall last, Trusting him till earth is past; Till within the

CHORUS.

faith is small, Trusting Je-sus, that is all.
can not fall, Trusting Je-sus, that is all.   Trusting as the moments fly,
for him call; Trusting Je-sus, that is all.
jas - per wall, Trusting Je-sus, that is all.
             E. P. Stites.

Trusting as the days go by; Trusting him whate'er befall, Trusting Je-sus, that is all.

377   A SHELTER IN THE TIME OF STORM. L. M.
IRA D. SANKEY.

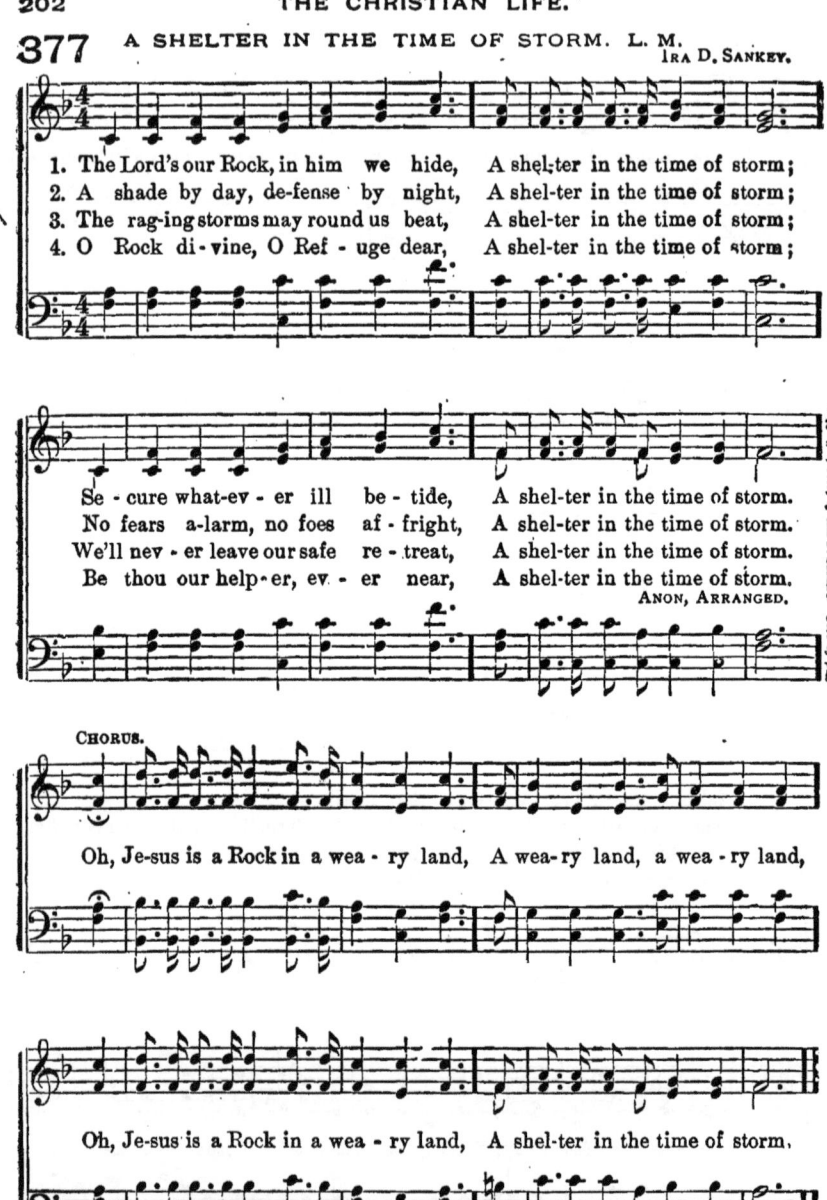

1. The Lord's our Rock, in him we hide,   A shel-ter in the time of storm;
2. A shade by day, de-fense by night,   A shel-ter in the time of storm;
3. The rag-ing storms may round us beat,   A shel-ter in the time of storm;
4. O Rock di-vine, O Ref-uge dear,   A shel-ter in the time of storm;

Se - cure what-ev - er ill be - tide,   A shel-ter in the time of storm.
No fears a-larm, no foes af - fright,   A shel-ter in the time of storm.
We'll nev - er leave our safe re - treat,   A shel-ter in the time of storm.
Be thou our help-er, ev - er near,   A shel-ter in the time of storm.

ANON, ARRANGED.

CHORUS.

Oh, Je-sus is a Rock in a wea - ry land, A wea-ry land, a wea-ry land,

Oh, Je-sus is a Rock in a wea - ry land, A shel-ter in the time of storm.

378 UNDER HIS WINGS. 8s.

Asa Hull, 1872.

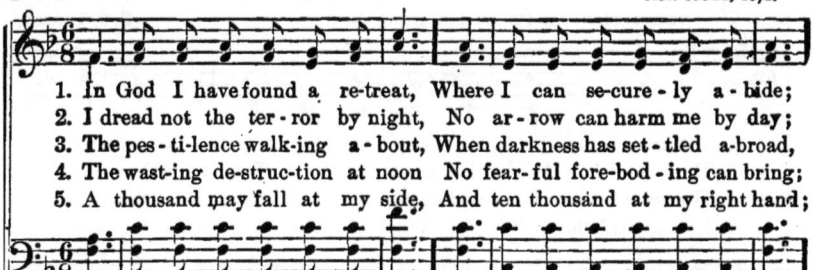

1. In God I have found a re-treat, Where I can se-cure-ly a-bide;
2. I dread not the ter-ror by night, No ar-row can harm me by day;
3. The pes-ti-lence walk-ing a-bout, When darkness has set-tled a-broad,
4. The wast-ing de-struc-tion at noon No fear-ful fore-bod-ing can bring;
5. A thousand may fall at my side, And ten thousand at my right hand;

No ref-uge nor rest so complete; And here I in-tend to re-side.
His shad-ow has cov-ered me quite, My fears he has driv-en a-way.
Can nev-er com-pel me to doubt The presence and pow-er of God.
With Je-sus my soul doth commune, His per-fect sal-va-tion I sing.
A-bove me his wings are spread wide, Beneath them in safe-ty I stand.

James Nicholson.

CHORUS.

h, what com-fort it brings, As my sol sweet-ly sings,

m all dan-ger While un-der his wings.

379 HE KNOWS IT ALL. 8s & 4s. E. S. LORENZ.

1. He knows the bit - ter, wea - ry way, The end - less striv - ing
2. He knows how hard the fight has been, The clouds that come our
3. He knows, when, faint and worn, we sink, How deep the pain, how
4. He knows! oh, tho't so full of bliss! For though on earth our

day by day, The souls that weep, the souls that pray—He knows it all.
lives between, The wounds the world has nev - er seen—He knows it all.
near the brink Of dark de-spair, we pause and shrink—He knows it all.
joys we miss, We still can bear it, feel - ing this—He knows it all.

UNKNOWN.

REFRAIN.

He knows it all, . . The bit - ter, wea - ry way;
He knows it all,

O souls that weep, O souls that pray, He knows it all.

Lord, Cast thy burden on the Lord, And he will sustain thee, and strengthen thee, and

comfort thee; He will sustain thee and com-fort thee. He will sustain thee, and

com - fort thee. He will sus - tain thee, he will com-fort thee:

Repeat pp.

Cast thy bur - den on the Lord! Cast thy bur - den on the Lord.

381   LUX BENIGNA. 10s & 4s.   J. B. DYKES.

1. Lead, kind-ly Light, a - mid th' en-cir-cling gloom, Lead thou me on; The night is
2. I was not ev-er thus, nor prayed that thou Shouldst lead me on; I loved to
3. So long thy pow'r has blessed me, sure it still Will lead me on; O'er moor and

dark, and I am far from home, Lead thou me on; Keep thou my feet; I
choose and see my path, but now Lead thou me on; I loved the gar-ish
fen, o'er crag and torrent, till The night is gone; And with the morn those

do not ask to see The dis-tant scene; one step e - nough for me.
day, and spite of fears, Pride ruled my will. Re-mem-ber not past years.
an-gel fa - ces smile Which I have loved long since, and lost a - while.

CARDINAL J. H. NEWMAN.

LANDIS. S. M.   E. S. LORENZ.

How ten - der is thy hand, Oh, thou be - lov - ed Lord!

Af - flic - tions come at thy command, And leave us at thy word.

382 JOY COMETH IN THE MORNING. P. M.

E. S. Lorenz.

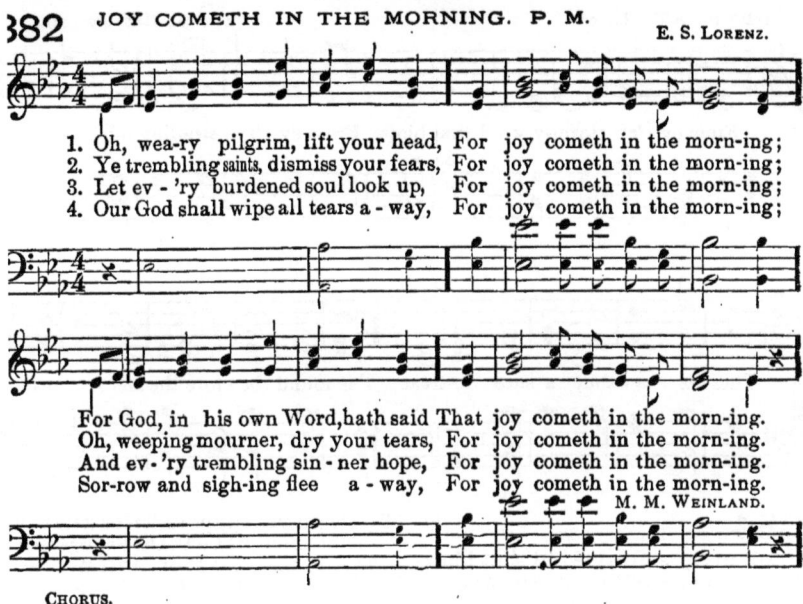

1. Oh, wea-ry pilgrim, lift your head, For joy cometh in the morn-ing;
2. Ye trembling saints, dismiss your fears, For joy cometh in the morn-ing;
3. Let ev - 'ry burdened soul look up, For joy cometh in the morn-ing;
4. Our God shall wipe all tears a - way, For joy cometh in the morn-ing;

For God, in his own Word, hath said That joy cometh in the morn-ing.
Oh, weeping mourner, dry your tears, For joy cometh in the morn-ing.
And ev - 'ry trembling sin - ner hope, For joy cometh in the morn-ing.
Sor-row and sigh-ing flee a - way, For joy cometh in the morn-ing.

M. M. Weinland.

Chorus.

m-eth in the morn - ing;

joy com-eth in the morn-ing.

383 *God's Tenderness in our Grief.* (883)

ow tender is thy hand,
Oh, thou beloved Lord !
fflictions come at thy command,
And leave us at thy word.

How gentle was the rod
That chastened us for sin !
ow soon we found a smiling God,
Where deep distress had been !

3 A Father's hand we felt,
A Father's heart we knew ;
With tears of penitence we knelt,
And found his word was true.

4 We told him all our grief,
We thought of Jesus' love ;
A sense of pardon brought relief,
And bade our pains remove.

Thomas Hastings.

RETREAT. L. M.   THOMAS HASTINGS, 1822.

From ev - 'ry storm-y wind that blows, From ev - 'ry swelling tide of woes,

There is   a calm,   a sure re-treat ; 'T is found be - fore the mer - cy seat.

384   *The Mercy-Seat.*   (787)

FROM every stormy wind that blows,
From every swelling tide of woes,
There is a calm, a sure retreat ;—
'Tis found before the mercy-seat.

2 There is a place, where Jesus sheds
The oil of gladness on our heads,—
A place, than all besides, more sweet ;
It is the blood-bought mercy-seat.

3 There is a spot where spirits blend,
Where friend holds fellowship with friend ;
Though sundered far, by faith they meet
Around one common mercy-seat.

4 There, there, on eagle's wings we soar,
And time, and sense seem all no more ;
And heaven comes down our souls to greet,
And glory crowns the mercy-seat !

5 Oh ! may my hand forget her skill,
My tongue be silent, cold, and still,
This bounding heart forget to beat,
If I forget the mercy-seat !
                            HUGH STOWELL, 1827.

385   *Design of Prayer.*   (796)

PRAYER is appointed to convey
   The blessings God designs to give :
Long as they live should Christians pray ;
   They learn to pray when first they live.

2 If pain afflict, or wrongs oppress ;
   If cares distract, or fears dismay ;
If guilt deject ; if sin distress ;
   In every case, still watch and pray.

3 'Tis prayer supports the soul that's weak :
   Tho' thought be broken, language lame,
Pray, if thou canst or canst not speak ;
   But pray with faith in Jesus' name.

4 Depend on him ; thou canst not fail ;
   Make all thy wants and wishes known ;
Fear not ; his merits must prevail ;
   Ask but in faith, it shall be done.
                            JOSEPH HART. D. 1768.

386   *Psalm 104 : 34.*   (794)

MY God, is any hour so sweet,
   From blush of morn to evening star,
As that which calls me to thy feet,
   The calm and holy hour of prayer ?

2 Blest is the tranquil break of morn,
   And blest the hush of solemn eve,
When on the wings of prayer up-borne,
   This fair, but transient, world I leave.

3 Then is my strength by thee renewed ;
   Then are my sins by thee forgiven ;
Then dost thou cheer my solitude,
   With clear and beauteous hopes of heaven.

4 No words can tell what sweet relief,
   There for my every want I find ;
What strength for warfare, balm for grief,
   What deep and cheerful peace of mind.

5 Lord, till I reach the blissful shore,
   No privilege so dear shall be,
As thus my inmost soul to pour
   In faithful filial prayer to thee !
                            CHARLOTTE ELLIOTT, 1854.

387 (799) SWEET HOUR OF PRAYER. L. M. D.

WILLIAM B. BRADBURY, 1859.

1. Sweet hour of prayer! sweet hour of prayer! That calls me from a world of care,
2. Sweet hour of prayer! sweet hour of prayer! Thy wings shall my pe-ti-tion bear
3. Sweet hour of prayer! sweet hour of prayer! May I thy con-so-la-tion share,

And bids me at my Father's throne Make all my wants and wishes known:
To him whose truth and faithfulness En-gage the wait-ing soul to bless.
Till, from Mount Pisgah's lofty height, I view my home and take my flight:

In sea-sons of dis-tress and grief, My soul has oft-en found re-lief;
And since He bids me seek his face, Believe his word, and trust his grace,
This robe of flesh I'll drop, and rise To seize the ev-er-last-ing prize;

And oft es-caped the tempter's snare, By thy re-turn, sweet hour of prayer!
I'll cast on him my ev-'ry care And wait for thee, sweet hour of prayer!
And shout, while passing thro' the air, Farewell, farewell, sweet hour of prayer!

REV. W. W. WALFORD, 1846.

14

BROWN, C. M.

WILLIAM B. BRADBURY, 1840.

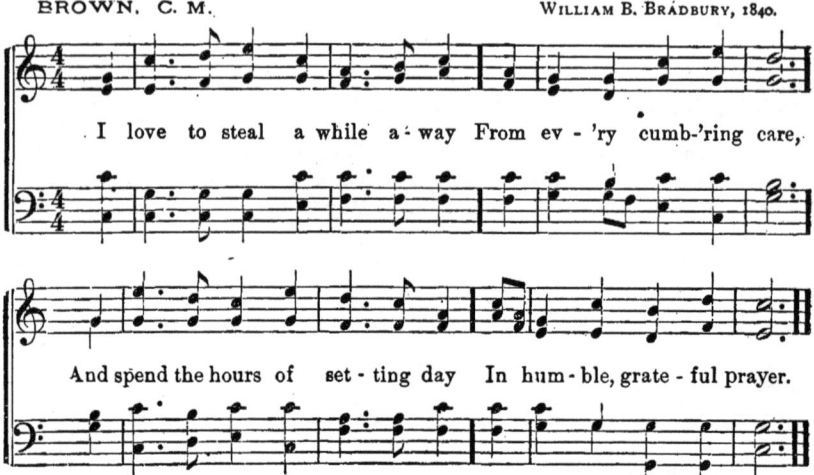

I love to steal a while a - way From ev - 'ry cumb-'ring care,

And spend the hours of set - ting day In hum - ble, grate - ful prayer.

388 *Secret Prayer.* (775)

1 LOVE to steal awhile away
  From ev'ry cumb'ring care,
And spend the hours of setting day
  In humble, grateful prayer.

2 I love in solitude to shed
  The penitential tear,
And all his promises to plead,
  Where none but God can hear.

3 I love to think on mercies past,
  And future good implore,
And all my cares and sorrows cast
  On him whom I adore.

4 I love by faith to take a view
  Of brighter scenes in heaven;
The prospect doth my strength renew,
  While here by tempests driven.

5 Thus, when life's toilsome day is o'er,
  May its departing ray
Be calm as this impressive hour,
  And lead to endless day!
          MRS. PHŒBE H. BROWN, 1825.

389 *Graces Sought in Prayer.* (786)

LORD! teach us how to pray aright,
  With reverence and with fear;
Though dust and ashes in thy sight,
  We may, we must draw near.

2 God of all grace, we come to thee,
  With broken, contrite hearts.

Give, what thine eye delights to see,
  Truth in the inward parts:

3 Patience, to watch, and wait, and weep,
  Though mercy long delay;
Courage, our fainting souls to keep,
  And trust thee though thou slay.

4 Give these, and then—thy will be done—
  Thus strengthened with all might,
We by thy Spirit and thy Son,
  Shall pray, and pray aright.
          JAMES MONTGOMERY, 1819.

390 *Mark 13: 33.* (784)

THE Savior bids thee watch and pray
  Through life's momentous hour;
And grants the Spirit's quickening ray
  To those who seek his power.

2 The Savior bids thee watch and pray,
  Maintain a warrior's strife;
Oh, Christian! hear his voice to-day:
  Obedience is thy life.

3 The Savior bids thee watch and pray,
  For soon the hour will come
That calls thee from the earth away
  To thy eternal home.

4 The Savior bids thee watch and pray,
  Oh, hearken to his voice,
And follow where he leads the way,
  To heaven's eternal joys.
          T. HASTINGS.

DEVIZES. C. M.   ISRAEL TUCKER, 1800.

Prayer is the soul's sin- cere de- sire, Uttered or un - ex-pressed; The motion

of a hid-den fire, That trembles in the breast, That trembles in the breast.

391   *Prayer.*   (781)

PRAYER is the soul's sincere desire,
  Uttered or unexpressed;
The motion of a hidden fire,
  That trembles in the breast.

2 Prayer is the burden of a sigh,
  The falling of a tear,
The upward glancing of an eye,
  When none but God is near.

3 Prayer is the simplest form of speech,
  That infant lips can try;
Prayer, the sublimest strains that reach
  The Majesty on high.

4 Prayer is the Christian's vital breath,
  The Christian's native air:
His watchword at the gates of death;
  He enters heaven with prayer.

5 Oh,Thou, by whom we come to God,—
  The Life, the Truth, the Way!
The path of prayer thyself hast trod;
  Lord! teach us how to pray.
        JAMES MONTGOMERY, 1819.

392   *A Throne of Grace.*   (778)

A THRONE of grace! then let us go
  And offer up our prayer;
A gracious God will mercy show
  To all that worship there.

2 A throne of grace! oh, at that throne
  Our knees have often bent,
And God has showered his blessings down
  As often as we went.

3 A throne of grace! rejoice, ye saints!
  That throne is open still;
To God unbosom your complaints,
  And then inquire his will.
        CORBIN.

MARLOW. C. M.   JOHN CHETHAM, 1718.

A throne of grace; then let us go And of-fer up our prayer;

A gracious God will mer - cy show To all that wor-ship there.

393 (777) NOTTING HILL. C. M.

C. H. PURDAY.

1. Talk with us, Lord, thy-self re-veal, While here o'er earth we rove;
2. With thee con-vers-ing, we for-get All time, and toil, and care:
3. Here, then, my God, vouchsafe to stay, And bid my heart re-joice:
4. Thou call-est me to seek thy face—'T is all I wish to seek;

Speak to our hearts, and let us feel The kind-ling of thy love.
La - bor is rest, and pain is sweet, If thou, my God! art here.
My bounding heart shall own thy sway, And e-cho to thy voice.
T' at-tend the whisperings of thy grace, And hear thee on-ly speak.

CHARLES WESLEY, 1740.

394 (804) ALETTA. 7s.

WILLIAM B. BRADBURY, 1856.

1. Come, my soul! thy suit pre-pare; Je-sus loves to an-swer prayer;
2. Thou art com-ing to a King, Large pe-ti-tions with thee bring;
3. Lord! I come to thee for rest, Take pos-ses-sion of my breast:
4. While I am a pil-grim here, Let thy love my spir-it cheer;

He him-self has bid thee pray, Therefore will not say thee nay.
For his grace and power are such, None can ev-er ask too much.
There thy blood-bought right maintain, And with-out a ri-val reign.
As my Guide, my Guard, my Friend, Lead me to my jour-ney's end.

JOHN NEWTON, 1779.

395

WHAT A FRIEND WE HAVE IN JESUS. 8s & 7s. D.

C. C. CONVERSE, 1871.

1. What a friend we have in Jesus, All our sins and griefs to bear; What a privilege to
2. Have we trials and temptations? Is there trouble anywhere? We should never be dis-
3. Are we weak and heavy laden, Cumbered with a load of care?—Precious Savior, still our

car - ry   Ev-'rything to God in prayer! O what peace we often forfeit, O what
couraged,   Take it to the Lord in prayer. Can we find a friend so faithful, Who will
ref - uge,— Take it to the Lord in prayer. Do thy friends despise, forsake thee? Take it

needless pain we bear, All because we do not carry Ev-'rything to God in prayer!
all our sorrows share? Jesus knows our ev'ry weakness, Take it to the Lord in prayer!
to the Lord in prayer; In his arms he'll take and shield thee, Thou wilt find a solace there.

UNKNOWN.

396   THE LORD'S PRAYER.

GREGORIAN.

1 Our Father who art in heaven, | Hallowed | be thy | name,‖
   Thy kingdom come: thy will be done in | earth, as it | is in | heaven,

2 Give us this | day our—|daily | bread:‖
   And forgive us our debts, as | we for-| give our | debtors.

3 Lead us not into temptation, but de- | liver | us from | evil; ‖
   For thine is the kingdom, and the power, and the glory, for | ever. | A- —|men.

THATCHER. S. M.　　　　　　　　　　GEO. FRED'K HANDEL, 1732.

Come at the morn - ing hour, Come, let us kneel and pray;

Pray'r is the Chris-tian pil-grim's staff To walk with God all day.

397 [FIRST VERSE INSERTED IN MUSIC.]
1 *Tim.* 2: 8.　　　　　(1168)

2 At noon beneath the Rock
　Of ages, rest and pray;
Sweet is that shelter from the sun
　In weary heat of day.

3 At evening, in thy home,
　Around its altar, pray;
And finding there the house of God,
　With heaven then close the day.

4 When midnight veils our eyes,
　Oh, it is sweet to say,
I sleep, but my heart waketh, Lord!
　With thee to watch and pray.
　　　　　　　　　　　　　ANON.

398　　*The Throne of Grace.*　　(801)
BEHOLD the throne of grace!
　The promise calls me near;

There Jesus shows a smiling face,
　And waits to answer prayer.

2 That rich atoning blood,
　Which sprinkled round I see,
Provides, for those who come to God,
　An all-prevailing plea.

3 My soul! ask what thou wilt;
　Thou canst not be too bold;
Since his own blood for thee he spilt,
　What else can he withhold?

4 Thine image, Lord! bestow,
　Thy presence and thy love;
I ask to serve thee here below,
　And reign with thee above.

5 Teach me to live by faith;
　Conform my will to thine;
Let me victorious be in death,
　And then in glory shine.
　　　　　　　　　　JOHN NEWTON, 1779.

CAPELLO. S. M.　　　　　　　　　　LOWELL MASON.

Be - hold the throne of grace! The prom - ise calls me near;

There Je - sus shows a smil - ing face, And waits to an - swer pray'r.

399 TELL IT TO JESUS ALONE. P. M.

E. S. LORENZ.

1. Are you wea-ry, are you heav-y-heart-ed? Tell it to Je-sus,
2. Do the tears flow down your cheeks unbid-den? Tell it to Je-sus,
3. Do you fear the gath'ring clouds of sor-row? Tell it to Je-sus,
4. Are you trou-bled at the tho't of dy-ing? Tell it to Je-sus,

Tell it to Je-sus. Are you griev-ing o-ver joys de-part-ed?
Tell it to Je-sus. Have you sins that to man's eye are hid-den?
Tell it to Je-sus. Are you anx-ious what shall be to-mor-row?
Tell it to Je-sus. For Christ's com-ing king-dom are you sigh-ing?

CHORUS.

Tell it to Je-sus a-lone. Tell it to Je-sus, Tell it to Je-sus,

J. E. RANKIN, D. D.

He is a Friend that's well-known: You have no oth-er

such a friend or broth-er? Tell it to Je-sus a-lone.

MAITLAND. C. M.   George N. Allen, 1849.

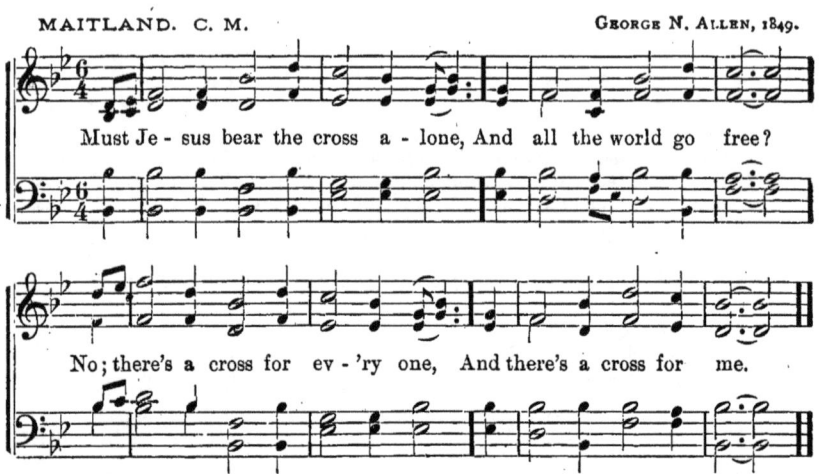

Must Je - sus bear the cross a - lone, And all the world go free?

No; there's a cross for ev - 'ry one, And there's a cross for me.

400 *The Cross and the Crown.* (835)

Must Jesus bear the cross alone,
  And all the world go free?
No, there's a cross for every one,
  And there's a cross for me.

2 How happy are the saints above,
  Who once went mourning here!
But now they taste unmingled love,
  And joy without a tear.

3 This consecrated cross I'll bear,
  Till death shall set me free,
And then go home my crown to wear,
  For there's a crown for me.

4 Upon the crystal pavement, down
  At Jesus' pierced feet,
Joyful, I'll cast my golden crown,
  And his dear name repeat.

5 And palms shall wave, and harps shall ring
  Beneath heaven's arches high;
The Lord, that lives, the ransomed sing,
  That lives no more to die.

6 Oh! precious cross! oh! glorious crown!
  Oh! resurrection day!
Ye angels! from the skies come down,
  And bear my soul away.
            V. 1, Thomas Shepherd, 1692.
            Vs. 2-3, G. N. Allen, 1849, a.

401 *The Christian Race.* (783)

Awake, my soul—stretch every nerve,
  And press with vigor on;
A heavenly race demands thy zeal,
  A bright, immortal crown.

2 'Tis God's all-animating voice
  That calls thee from on high:
'Tis his own hand presents the prize
  To thine aspiring eye.

3 A cloud of witnesses around,
  Hold thee in full survey:
Forget the steps already trod,
  And onward urge thy way.

4 Blest Savior, introduced by thee
  Have we our race begun;
And, crowned with vict'ry, at thy feet
  We'll lay our laurels down.
            P. Doddridge, 1740.

402 *Christian Charity.* (809)

Blest is the man, whose softening heart
  Feels all another's pain;
To whom the supplicating eye
  Was never raised in vain;—

2 Whose breast expands with generous warmth,
  A stranger's woes to feel,
And bleeds in pity o'er the wound
  He wants the power to heal.

3 He spreads his kind supporting arms
  To every child of grief;
His secret bounty largely flows,
  And brings unasked relief.

4 To gentle offices of love,
  His feet are never slow;
He views, through mercy's melting eye,
  A brother in a foe.
            Mrs. Anna L Barbauld, 1772.

BOYLSTON. S. M.   LOWELL MASON, 1832.

A charge to keep I have, A God to glo-ri-fy;

A nev-er-dy-ing soul to save, And fit it for the sky.

403 *The Christian's Life-Work.* (798)

A CHARGE to keep I have,
  A God to glorify;
A never-dying soul to save,
  And fit it for the sky:—

2 To serve the present age,
  My calling to fulfill,—
Oh! may it all my powers engage—
  To do my Master's will.

3 Arm me with jealous care,
  As in thy sight to live;
And, oh! thy servant, Lord! prepare
  A strict account to give.

4 Help me to watch and pray,
  And on thyself rely;
Assured, if I my trust betray,
  I shall forever die.
          CHARLES WESLEY, 1762.

404 *Sowing and Reaping.* (1014)

Sow in the morn thy seed,
  At eve hold not thy hand;
To doubt and fear give thou no heed;
  Broad-cast it o'er the land.

And duly shall appear,
  In verdure, beauty, strength,
The tender blade, the stalk, the ear,
  And the full corn at length.

3 Thou canst not toil in vain;
  Cold, heat, and moist, and dry,

Shall foster and mature the grain,
  For garners in the sky.

4 Thence, when the glorious end,
  The day of God, shall come,
The angel-reapers shall descend,
  And heaven cry "Harvest-home!"
        JAMES MONTGOMERY, 1825.

405 *Doing Good.* (821)

WE give thee but thine own,
  Whate'er the gift may be:
All that we have is thine alone,
  A trust, O Lord! from thee.

2 O, hearts are bruised and dead,
  And homes are bare and cold,
And lambs, for whom the Shepherd bled,
  Are straying from the fold.

3 To comfort and to bless,
  To find a balm for woe,
To tend the lone and fatherless
  Is angels' work below.

4 The captive to release,
  To God the lost to bring,
To teach the way of life and peace,
  It is a Christ-like thing.

5 And we believe thy word,
  Though dim our faith may be:
Whate'er for thine we do, O Lord,
  We do it unto thee.
        WILLIAM WALSHAM HOW, 1854.

TRIUMPH. L. M.   L. O. EMERSON.

Go, la-bor on; spend, and be spent,—Thy joy to do the Fa-ther's will;

It is the way the Master went; Should not the servant tread it still?

406 [FIRST VERSE INSERTED IN MUSIC.]
The Useful Life.   (818)

2 Go, labor on; 'tis not for naught;
   Thine earthly loss is heavenly gain;
Men heed thee, love thee, praise thee not,
   The Master praises;—what are men?

3 Go, labor on; enough, while here,
   If he shall praise thee, if he deign
Thy willing heart to mark and cheer:
   No toil for him shall be in vain.

4 Toil on, and in thy toil rejoice;
   For toil comes rest, for exile home;
Soon shalt thou hear the Bridegroom's voice,
   The midnight peal,—"Behold! I come!"
                         HORATIUS BONAR, 1857.

407 Consistency.—Titus 2: 10-13.   (737)

So let our lips and lives express
The holy gospel we profess;
So let our works and virtues shine,
To prove the doctrine all divine.

2 Thus shall we best proclaim abroad
The honors of our Savior God;
When his salvation reigns within,
And grace subdues the power of sin.

5 Religion bears our spirits up,
While we expect that blessed hope,—
The bright appearance of the Lord:
And faith stands leaning on his word.
                         ISAAC WATTS, 1709.

JUST AS I AM. L. M.   From "MUSICAL PIONEER,"

Go, la-bor on; spend, and be spent; Thy joy to do the Father's will;

It is the way the Mas-ter went; Should not the servant tread it still?

408   ESSEX. 8s & 7s.   THOMAS CLARK.

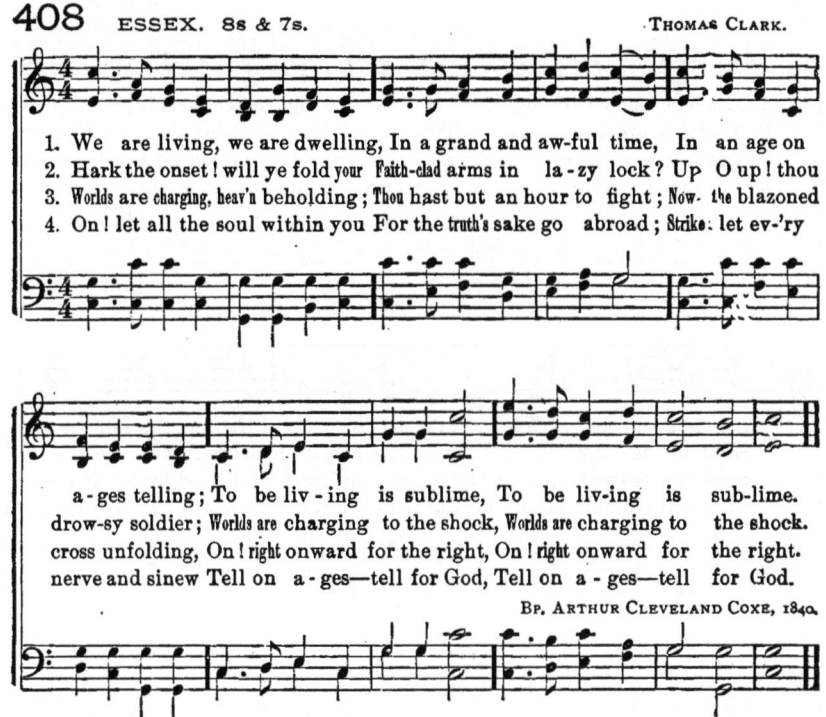

1. We are living, we are dwelling, In a grand and aw-ful time, In an age on
2. Hark the onset! will ye fold your Faith-clad arms in la-zy lock? Up O up! thou
3. Worlds are charging, heav'n beholding; Thou hast but an hour to fight; Now· the blazoned
4. On! let all the soul within you For the truth's sake go abroad; Strike: let ev-'ry

a-ges telling; To be liv-ing is sublime, To be liv-ing is sub-lime.
drow-sy soldier; Worlds are charging to the shock, Worlds are charging to the shock.
cross unfolding, On! right onward for the right, On! right onward for the right.
nerve and sinew Tell on a-ges—tell for God, Tell on a-ges—tell for God.

BP. ARTHUR CLEVELAND COXE, 1840.

---

409   Zeal.—John 9 : 4.   (1009)

Go, labor on, while it is day;
  The world's dark night is hastening on :
Speed, speed thy work,—cast sloth away!
  It is not thus that souls are won.

2 Men die in darkness at your side,
  Without a hope to cheer the tomb :
Take up the torch and wave it wide—
  The torch that lights time's thickest gloom.

3 Toil on, faint not;—keep watch and pray!
  Be wise the erring soul to win;
Go forth into the world's highway;
  Compel the wanderer to come in.

4 Go, labor on; your hands are weak;
  Your knees are faint, your soul cast down,
Yet falter not; the prize you seek
  Is near,—a kingdom and a crown !
              H. BONAR, 1857.

410   Psalm 41.   (819)

BLEST is the man whose heart doth move,
  And melt with pity, to the poor;
Whose soul, by sympathizing love,
  Feels what his fellow-saints endure.

2 His heart contrives, for their relief,
  More good than his own hands can do;
He, in the time of general grief,
  Shall find the Lord has pity too.

3 His soul shall live secure on earth,
  With secret blessings on his head,
When drought, and pestilence, and dearth
  Around him multiply their dead.

4 Or, if he languish on his couch,
  God will pronounce his sins forgiven,
Will save him with a healing touch,
  Or take his willing soul to heaven.
              ISAAC WATTS, 1719.

411   RESCUE THE PERISHING. P. M.

W. H. DOANE.

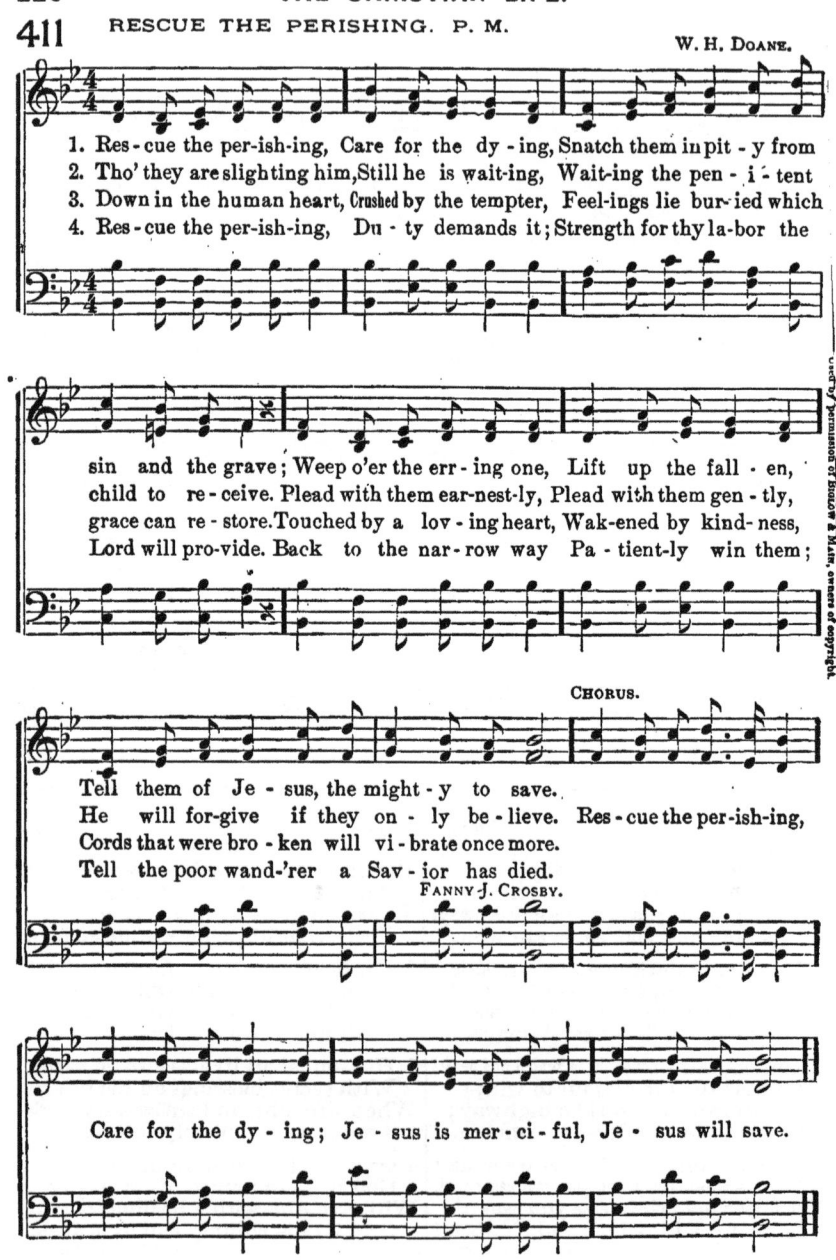

1. Res - cue the per-ish-ing, Care for the dy - ing, Snatch them in pit - y from
2. Tho' they are slighting him, Still he is wait-ing, Wait-ing the pen - i - tent
3. Down in the human heart, Crushed by the tempter, Feel-ings lie bur-ied which
4. Res - cue the per-ish-ing, Du - ty demands it; Strength for thy la-bor the

sin and the grave; Weep o'er the err - ing one, Lift up the fall - en,
child to re - ceive. Plead with them ear-nest-ly, Plead with them gen - tly,
grace can re - store. Touched by a lov - ing heart, Wak-ened by kind- ness,
Lord will pro-vide. Back to the nar - row way Pa - tient-ly win them;

CHORUS.

Tell them of Je - sus, the might - y to save.
He will for-give if they on - ly be - lieve. Res - cue the per-ish-ing,
Cords that were bro - ken will vi - brate once more.
Tell the poor wand-'rer a Sav - ior has died.

FANNY J. CROSBY.

Care for the dy - ing; Je - sus is mer - ci - ful, Je - sus will save.

412 WHILE THE DAYS ARE GOING BY. P. M.

IRA D. SANKEY.

1. There are lone - ly hearts to cher-ish, While the days are going by;
There are wea - ry souls who per-ish, While the days are going by;
2. There's no time for i - dle scorn-ing, While the days are going by:
Let your face be like the morn-ing, While the days are going by;
3. All the lov - ing links that bind us, While the days are going by;
One by one we leave be - hind us, While the days are going by;

If a smile we can re-new, As our jour-ney we pur - sue, Oh, the good we
Oh, the world is full of sighs, Full of sad and weeping eyes; Help your fall - en
But the seeds of good we sow Both in shade and shine will grow, And will keep our

REFRAIN.

all may do, While the days are going by. Go-ing by, go-ing by,
brother rise, While the days are going by.
hearts aglow, While the days are going by. going by, going by,

GEORGE COOPER.

Going by, going by, Oh, the good we all may do, While the days are go-ing by.
Going by, going by,

413 I WANT TO BE A WORKER. P. M.   I. BALTZELL.

1. I want to be a work-er for the Lord, I want to love and
2. I want to be a work-er ev - 'ry day, I want to lead the
3. I want to be a work-er strong and brave, I want to trust in
4. I want to be a work-er; help me, Lord, To lead the lost and

trust his ho-ly word; I want to sing and pray, and be busy ev'ry day In the
err - ing in the way That leads to heav'n above, where all is peace and love, In the
Je-sus' pow'r to save; All who will truly come, shall find a happy home In the
err - ing to thy word That points to joys on high, where pleasures never die, In the

CHORUS.

vine-yard of the Lord. I will work, I will pray,
king-dom of the Lord.
king-dom of the Lord.
king-dom of the Lord. I will work and pray, I will work and pray,

ISAIAH BALTZELL.

In the vine-yard, in the vineyard of the Lord, (of the Lord;) I will

work, I will pray, I will la-bor ev-'ry day In the vineyard of the Lord.

414   SEEDS OF PROMISE. C. M.   FRED. A. FILLMORE.

1. Oh, scat-ter seeds of lov-ing deeds, A-long the fer-tile field,
2. Tho' sown in tears the wea-ry years, The seed will sure-ly live;
3. The harv-est-home of God will come; And af-ter toil and care,

For grain will grow from what you sow, And fruit-ful har-vest yield.
Tho' great the cost it is not lost, For God will fruit-age give.
With joy un-told your sheaves of gold Will all be gar-nered there.

JESSIE H. BROWN.

CHORUS.

Then day by day . . . . a-long your way, . . . The seeds of

Then day by day   along your way,

prom - - ise cast, ... That ripened grain . . from hill and

The seeds of promise cast, the seeds of prom-ise cast,   That ripened grain

plain, . . . Be gathered home . . . at last.

from hill and plain,   Be gathered home at last, be gathered home at last.

Be gathered home at   last . . . .

415　WE'RE MARCHING TO ZION. S. M.　Rev. Robert Lowry.

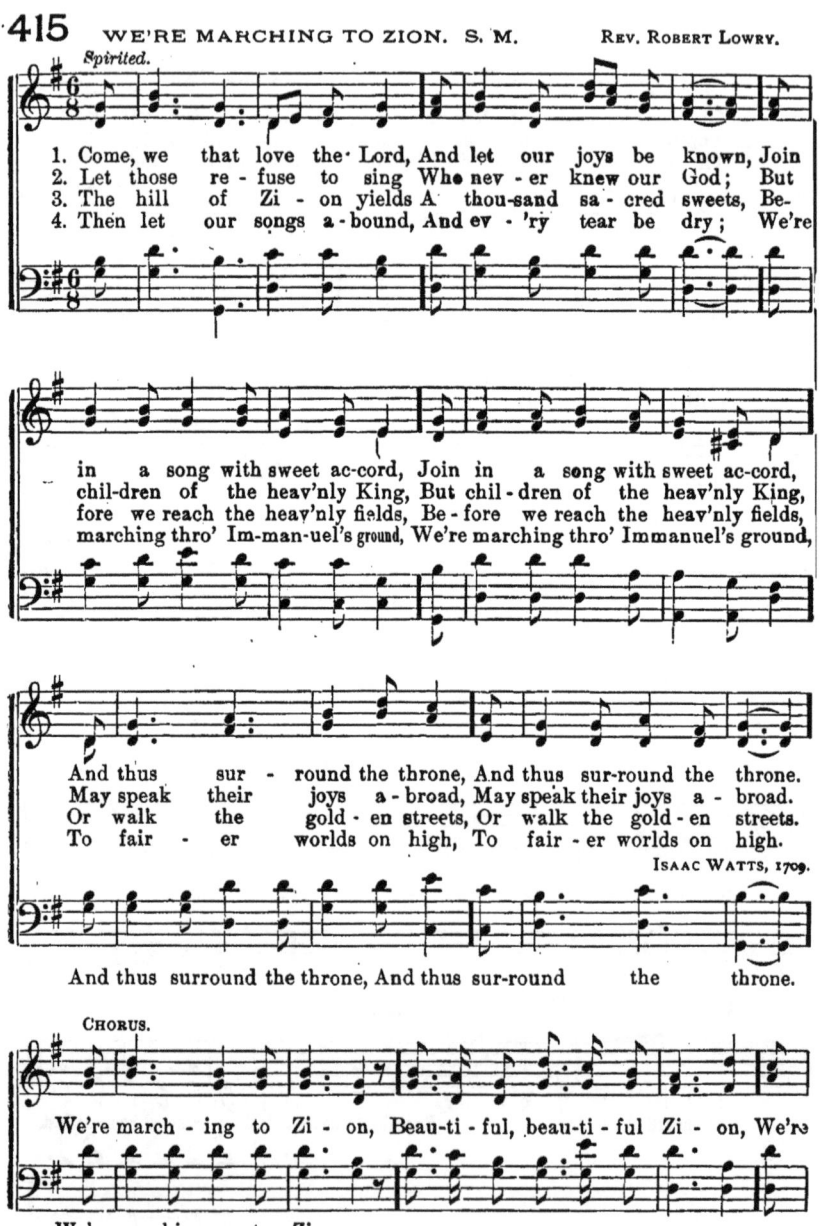

Spirited.

1. Come, we that love the Lord, And let our joys be known, Join
2. Let those re - fuse to sing Who nev - er knew our God; But
3. The hill of Zi - on yields A thou-sand sa - cred sweets, Be-
4. Then let our songs a - bound, And ev - 'ry tear be dry; We're

in a song with sweet ac-cord, Join in a song with sweet ac-cord,
chil-dren of the heav'nly King, But chil-dren of the heav'nly King,
fore we reach the heav'nly fields, Be - fore we reach the heav'nly fields,
marching thro' Im-man-uel's ground, We're marching thro' Immanuel's ground,

And thus sur - round the throne, And thus sur-round the throne.
May speak their joys a - broad, May speak their joys a - broad.
Or walk the gold - en streets, Or walk the gold-en streets.
To fair - er worlds on high, To fair - er worlds on high.

Isaac Watts, 1709.

And thus surround the throne, And thus sur-round the throne.

CHORUS.

We're march - ing to Zi - on, Beau-ti - ful, beau-ti - ful Zi - on, We're

We're marching on to Zi - on,

WE'RE MARCHING TO ZION. Concluded.

marching upward to Zi - on, The beau-ti-ful cit-y of God.

Zi - on, Zi-on,

16 WORK, FOR THE NIGHT IS COMING. P. M. LOWELL MASON.

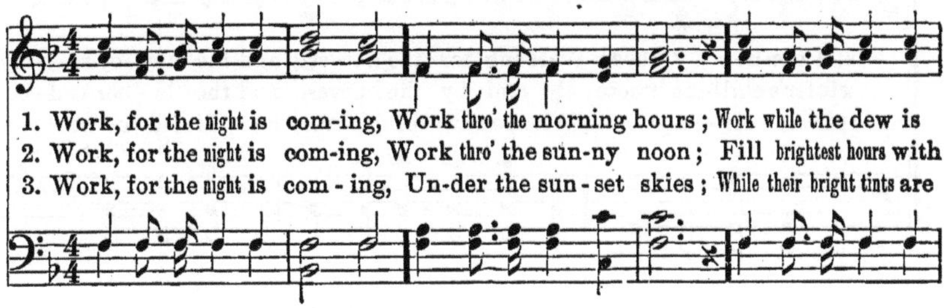

1. Work, for the night is com-ing, Work thro' the morning hours; Work while the dew is
2. Work, for the night is com-ing, Work thro' the sun-ny noon; Fill brightest hours with
3. Work, for the night is com - ing, Un-der the sun - set skies; While their bright tints are

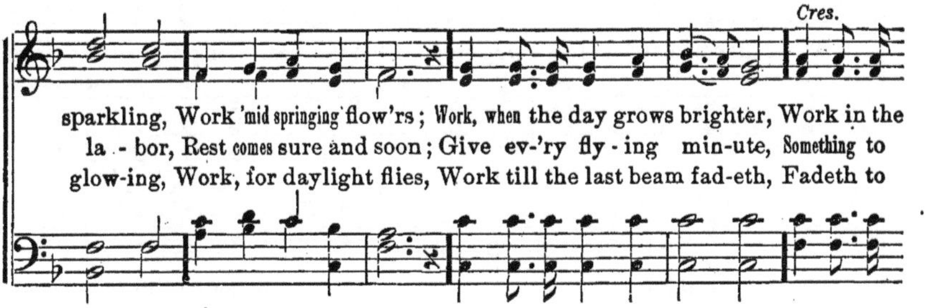

Cres.

sparkling, Work 'mid springing flow'rs; Work, when the day grows brighter, Work in the
la - bor, Rest comes sure and soon; Give ev-'ry fly - ing min-ute, Something to
glow-ing, Work, for daylight flies, Work till the last beam fad-eth, Fadeth to

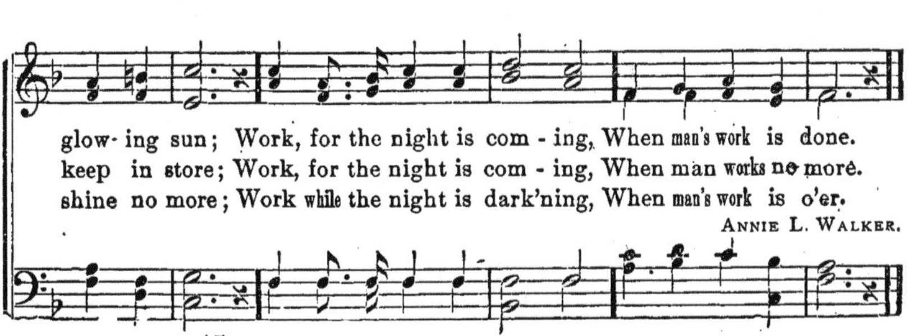

glow- ing sun; Work, for the night is com - ing, When man's work is done.
keep in store; Work, for the night is com - ing, When man works no more.
shine no more; Work while the night is dark'ning, When man's work is o'er.

ANNIE L. WALKER.

15

417   BRINGING IN THE SHEAVES. P. M.

GEORGE A. MINOR.

1. Sowing in the morning, sowing seeds of kindness, Sow-ing in the noon-tide
2. Sowing in the sunshine, sowing in the shadows, Fear-ing neither clouds nor
3. Going forth with weeping, sowing for the Master, Tho' the loss sustained our

and the dew-y eve; Wait-ing for the harvest, and the time of reap-ing,
winter's chill-ing breeze; By and by the harvest, and the la-bor end-ed,
spir-it oft-en grieves; When our weeping's over, he will bid us wel-come;

KNOWLES SHAW.

CHORUS.

We shall come, re-joic-ing, bring-ing in the sheaves. Bringing in the sheaves,

bring-ing in the sheaves, We shall come, re-joic-ing, bring-ing in the sheaves;

Bring-ing in the sheaves, bring-ing in the sheaves; We shall come, re-joic-ing, bring-ing in the sheaves.

418 CROWN AFTER CROSS. P. M.

E. S. LORENZ.

1. Light af-ter darkness, Gain af-ter loss, Strength af-ter wea-ri-ness,
2. Sheaves af-ter sow-ing, Sun af-ter rain, Sight af-ter mys-te-ry,
3. Near af-ter dis-tant, Gleam af-ter gloom, Love af-ter lone-li-ness,

Crown af-ter cross, Sweet af-ter bit-ter, Song af-ter sigh,
Peace af-ter pain, Joy af-ter sor-row, Calm af-ter blast,
Life af-ter tomb; Af-ter long ag-o-ny, Rapt-ure of bliss;

CHORUS.

Home af-ter wandering, Praise af-ter cry.
Rest af-ter wea-ri-ness, Sweet rest at last. Now comes the weeping,
Right was the path-way Lead-ing to this.

FRANCES R. HAVERGAL.

419 I LOVE TO TELL THE STORY. 7s & 6s. D. W. G. FISCHER.

1. I love to tell the sto-ry Of unseen things a-bove, Of Je-sus and his
2. I love to tell the sto-ry! More wonderful it seems, Than all the golden
3. I love to tell the sto-ry! 'Tis pleas-ant to re-peat What seems, each time I
4. I love to tell the sto-ry! For those who know it best Seem hungering and

glo - ry, Of Je - sus and his love! I love to tell the sto - ry! Be-
fan - cies Of all our golden dreams. I love to tell the sto - ry! It
tell it, More won-der-ful-ly sweet. I love to tell the sto - ry! For
thirsting To hear it like the rest. And when, in scenes of glo - ry, I

cause I know it's true; It sat-is-fies my longings, As nothing else would do.
did so much for me! And that is just the rea-son, I tell it now to thee.
some have nev-er heard The message of sal - va-tion From God's own Holy Word.
sing the New, New Song, 'Twill be—the Old, Old Story That I have loved so long.

MISS KATE HANKEY, 1867.

CHORUS.

I love to tell the sto - ry! 'Twill be my theme in glo - ry,

To tell the Old, Old Sto - ry Of Je - sus and his love.

By permission of author.

420 ONLY A WORD. P. M.

E. S. LORENZ.

1. On - ly a word for Je - sus, Spo-ken in fear with sense of need;
2. On - ly a word for Je - sus, Gen-tle and low with falt'ring breath;
3. On - ly a word for Je - sus, On - ly a wav-'ring soul to hear;
4. On - ly a word for Je - sus, Fee-ble the love and praise ap - pear;

Yet, with the Mas.-ter's bless-ing, Thousands that word may feed.
Yet, with the Spir - it's thrill-ing, Win - ning a soul from death.
Yet, thro' in - creas-ing a - ges, Wid - en its help and cheer.
An - gels their songs are ceas-ing, Glad the new note to hear.

E. S. LORENZ.

CHORUS.

Give me a word for thee, Mas - ter! Give me a word for thee!

To speak thy praise, Some soul to raise, Oh, give me a word for thee.

421   IS YOUR LAMP STILL BURNING? P. M.   I. BALTZELL.

1. Are you Christ's light bearer? Of his joy a shar-er? Is this dark world
2. Is your heart warm glow-ing, With his love o'er-flow-ing, And his good-ness
3. Keep your al-tars burn-ing, Wait your Lord's return-ing, While your heart's deep

fair-er For your cheer-ing ray; Is your bea-con light-ed, Guid-ing
showing More and more each day? Are you press-ing on-ward, With Christ's
yearning Draws him ev-er near; With his ra-diance splen-did Shall your

D. S. Are you ev-er wait-ing For your

Fine. CHORUS.

souls be-night-ed To the land of per-fect day?
faith-ful vanguard, In the safe and nar-row way?   Oh, broth-er, is your
light be blend-ed When his glo-ry shall ap-pear?
            PRISCILLA J. OWENS.

Lord's re-turn-ing? Are you watch-ing day by day?

                                    D. S.

lamp trimmed and burning? Is the world made brighter by its cheer-ing ray?

422   WILL JESUS FIND US WATCHING? P. M.   W. H. DOANE.

1. When Je - sus comes to re-ward his serv-ants, Wheth-er it be
2. If at the dawn of the ear - ly morn-ing, He shall call us
3. Have we been true to the trust he left us? Do we seek to
4. Bless - ed are those whom the Lord finds watching, In his glo - ry

noon or night, Faith-ful to him will he find us watch-ing,
one by one, When to the Lord we re - store our tal - ents,
do our best? If in our hearts there is naught con-demns us,
they shall share; If he shall come at the dawn or mid-night,

Rit.   REFRAIN.

With our lamps all trimm'd and bright?
Will he an - swer thee—Well done? Oh, can we say we are
We shall have a glo-rious rest.
Will he find us watch-ing there?

FANNY J. CROSBY.

read-y, broth-er? Read-y for the soul's bright home? Say, will he

find you and me still watching, Waiting, waiting when the Lord shall come?

LABAN. S. M.   LOWELL MASON, 1839.

My soul, be on thy guard, Ten thou-sand foes a-rise;

The hosts of sin are press-ing hard To draw thee from the skies.

423   *Watchfulness and Prayer.*   (763)

MY soul, be on thy guard,
  Ten thousand foes arise:
The hosts of sin are pressing hard
  To draw thee from the skies.

2 Oh, watch, and fight, and pray;
  The battle ne'er give o'er;
Renew it boldly every day,
  And help divine implore.

3 Ne'er think the vict'ry won,
  Nor lay thine armor down;
Thy arduous work will not be done
  Till thou obtain thy crown.

4 Fight on, my soul, till death
  Shall bring thee to thy God;
He'll take thee, at thy parting breath,
  To his divine abode.

           GEORGE HEATH, 1806.

424   *The Panoply of God.*   (761)

SOLDIERS of Christ! arise,
  And put your armor on,—
Strong, in the strength which God supplies,
  Through his eternal Son :—

2 Strong, in the Lord of hosts,
  And in his mighty power;
Who in the strength of Jesus trusts,
  Is more than conqueror.

3 Stand, then, in his great might,
  With all his strength endued;
And take, to arm you for the fight,
  The panoply of God :—

4 That, having all things done,
  And all your conflicts past,
You may o'ercome through Christ alone,
  And stand entire at last.

5 From strength to strength go on;
  Wrestle, and fight, and pray;
Tread all the powers of darkness down,
  And win the well-fought day.

6 Still let the Spirit cry,
  In all his soldiers, "Come,"
Till Christ, the Lord, descends from high,
  And takes the conquerors home.

           CHARLES WESLEY, 1749.

425   *Victory is on the Lord's Side.*   (765)

ARISE, ye saints, arise!
  The Lord our leader is :
The foe before his banner flies,
  And victory is his.

2 We soon shall see the day
  When all our toils shall cease;
When we shall cast our arms away,
  And dwell in endless peace.

3 This hope supports us here;
  It makes our burdens light;
'Twill serve our drooping hearts to cheer,
  Till faith shall end in sight :—

4 Till, of the prize possess'd,
  We hear of war no more;
And ever with our Leader rest,
  On yonder peaceful shore.

           THOMAS KELLY, 1809.

426(751) MAITLAND. C. M.

GEORGE N. ALLEN, 1849.

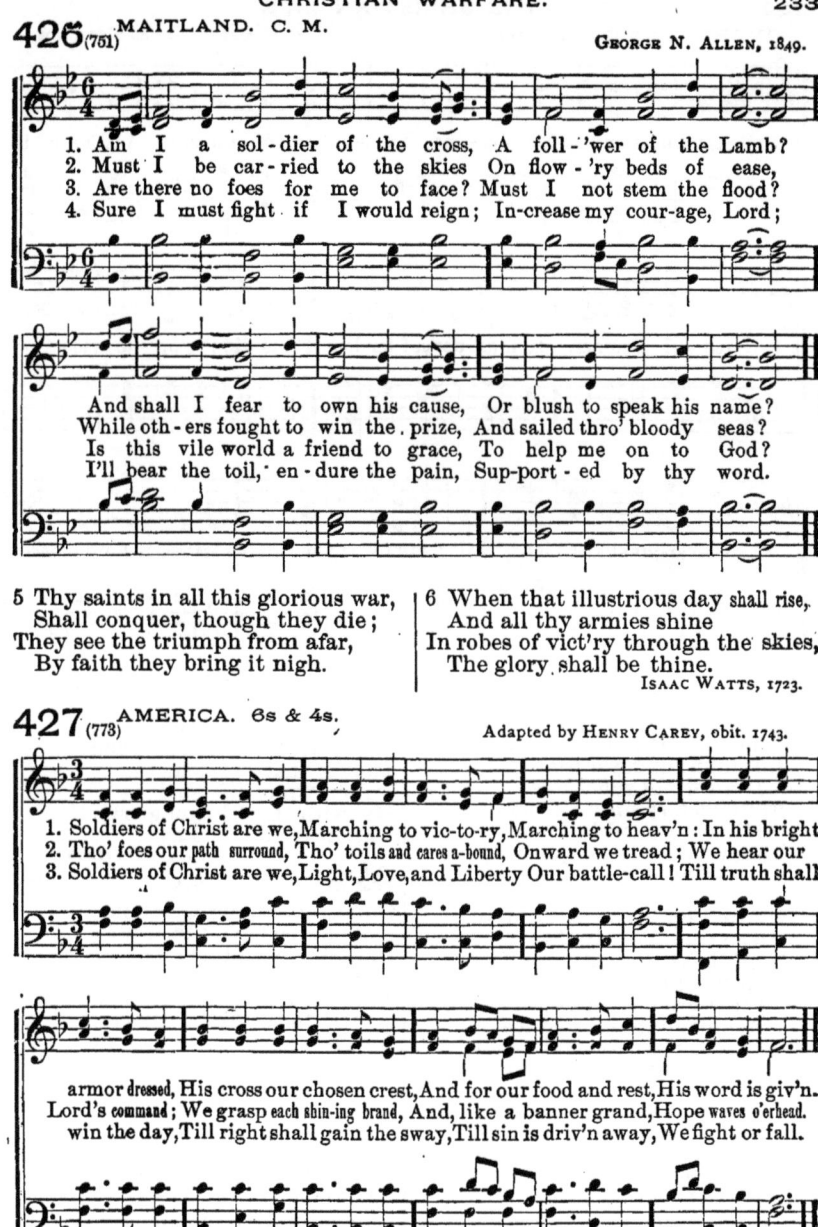

1. Am I a sol-dier of the cross, A foll-'wer of the Lamb?
2. Must I be car-ried to the skies On flow-'ry beds of ease,
3. Are there no foes for me to face? Must I not stem the flood?
4. Sure I must fight if I would reign; In-crease my cour-age, Lord;

And shall I fear to own his cause, Or blush to speak his name?
While oth-ers fought to win the prize, And sailed thro' bloody seas?
Is this vile world a friend to grace, To help me on to God?
I'll bear the toil, en-dure the pain, Sup-port-ed by thy word.

5 Thy saints in all this glorious war,
  Shall conquer, though they die;
They see the triumph from afar,
  By faith they bring it nigh.

6 When that illustrious day shall rise,
  And all thy armies shine
In robes of vict'ry through the skies,
  The glory shall be thine.

ISAAC WATTS, 1723.

427(773) AMERICA. 6s & 4s.

Adapted by HENRY CAREY, obit. 1743.

1. Soldiers of Christ are we, Marching to vic-to-ry, Marching to heav'n: In his bright
2. Tho' foes our path surround, Tho' toils and cares a-bound, Onward we tread; We hear our
3. Soldiers of Christ are we, Light, Love, and Liberty Our battle-call! Till truth shall

armor dressed, His cross our chosen crest, And for our food and rest, His word is giv'n.
Lord's command; We grasp each shin-ing brand, And, like a banner grand, Hope waves o'erhead.
win the day, Till right shall gain the sway, Till sin is driv'n away, We fight or fall.

WEBB. 7s & 6s. 8 lines.   GEORGE JAMES WEBB, 1830.

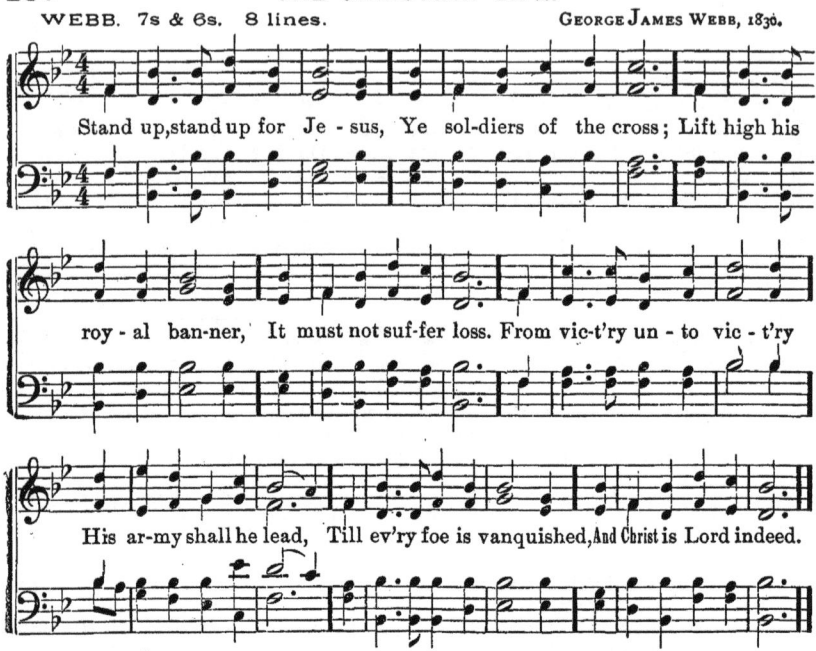

Stand up, stand up for Je - sus, Ye sol-diers of the cross; Lift high his
roy - al ban-ner, It must not suf-fer loss. From vic-t'ry un - to vic - t'ry
His ar-my shall he lead, Till ev'ry foe is vanquished, And Christ is Lord indeed.

428   *Good Soldiers.*   (771)

STAND up, stand up for Jesus,
  Ye soldiers of the cross!
Lift high his royal banner,
  It must not suffer loss:
From victory unto victory
  His army shall he lead,
Till every foe is vanquished,
  And Christ is Lord indeed.

2 Stand up, stand up for Jesus,
  The trumpet call obey;
Forth to the mighty conflict,
  In this his glorious day:
Ye that are men! now serve him,
  Against unnumbered foes;
Your courage rise with danger,
  And strength to strength oppose.

3 Stand up, stand up for Jesus;
  Stand in his strength alone;
The arm of flesh will fail you;
  Ye dare not trust your own:
Put on the gospel armor,
  And, watching unto prayer,
Where duty calls, or danger,
  Be never wanting there.

4 Stand up, stand up for Jesus;
  The strife will not be long;
This day, the noise of battle,—
  The next, the victor's song:
To him that overcometh,
  A crown of life shall be;
He, with the King of glory,
  Shall reign eternally!
           GEORGE DUFFIELD, 1858.

429   *Psalm 27.*   (772)

GOD is my strong salvation;
  What foe have I to fear?
In darkness and temptation,
  My Light, my Help is near:
Though hosts encamp around me,
  Firm to the fight I stand;
What terror can confound me,
  With God at my right hand?

2 Place on the Lord reliance;
  My soul! with courage wait;
His truth be thine affiance,
  When faint and desolate;
His might thy heart shall strengthen,
  His love thy joy increase;
Mercy thy days shall lengthen;
  The Lord will give thee peace.
         JAMES MONTGOMERY, 1822.

430   YIELD NOT TO TEMPTATION.   P. M.

H. R. PALMER.

1. Yield not to temp-ta-tion, For yield-ing is sin; Each vic-t'ry will
2. Shun e-vil com-pan-ions, Bad language dis-dain, God's name hold in
3. To him that o'er-com-eth, God giv-eth a crown; Thro' faith we shall

help you Some oth-er to win. Fight man-ful-ly on-ward,
rev-'rence, Nor take it in vain; Be thoughtful and ear-nest,
con-quer, Though oft-en cast down; He who is our Sav-ior

Dark passions sub-due; Look ev-er to Je-sus, He'll car-ry you through.
Kind-hearted and true; Look ev-er to Je-sus, He'll car-ry you through.
Our strength will renew; Look ev-er to Je-sus, He'll car-ry you through.

H. R. PALMER.

CHORUS.

Ask the Sav-ior to help you, Com-fort,strengthen, and keep you;

He is will-ing to aid you, He will car-ry you through.

ST. MARTIN'S. C. M. WILLIAM TANSUR, 1735.

With state - ly tow'rs and bul-warks strong, Un - ri - valed and a - lone,

Loved theme of ma - ny a sa - cred song, God's ho - ly cit - y shone.

431 [FIRST VERSE INSERTED IN MUSIC.]
Founded on a Rock. (892)

2 Thus fair was Zion's chosen seat,
The glory of all lands;
Yet fairer and in strength complete,
The Christian temple stands.

3 The faithful of each clime and age
This glorious church compose;
Built on a Rock, with idle rage
The threat'ning tempest blows.

4 Fear not; though hostile bands alarm,
Thy God is thy defense;
And weak and powerless every arm
Against Omnipotence.
ISAAC WATTS.

432 *The Church Immovable.* (891)

OH! where are kings and empires now,
Of old that went and came?
But, Lord! thy church is praying yet,
A thousand years the same.

2 We mark her goodly battlements,
And her foundations strong;
We hear within the solemn voice
Of her unending song.

3 For, not like kingdoms of the world,
Thy holy church, O God!
Though earthquake shocks are threatening her,
And tempests are abroad;

4 Unshaken as eternal hills,
Immovable she stands,
A mountain that shall fill the earth,
A house not made by hands.
ARTHUR CLEVELAND COXE, 1839, a.

433 *Returning to Zion.* (894)

DAUGHTER of Zion, from the dust
Exalt thy fallen head;
Again in thy Redeemer trust—
He calls thee from the dead.

2 Awake, awake, put on thy strength,
Thy beautiful array;
The day of freedom dawns at length—
The Lord's appointed day.

3 Rebuild thy walls, thy bounds enlarge,
And send thy heralds forth;
Say to the south, Give up thy charge!
And, Keep not back, O north!

4 They come, they come; thine exiled bands,
Where'er they rest or roam,
Have heard thy voice in distant lands,
And hasten to their home.
JAMES MONTGOMERY, 1825.

434 *Little Flock.*

CHURCH of the ever-living God,
The Father's gracious choice,
Amid the voices of this earth
How feeble is thy voice!

2 Not many rich or noble called,
Not many great or wise;
They whom God makes his kings and priests
Are poor in human eyes.

3 But the chief Shepherd comes at length;
Their feeble days are o'er,
No more a handful in the earth,
A little flock no more.
H. BONAR, ab.

LABAN. S. M.   L. MASON, 1830.

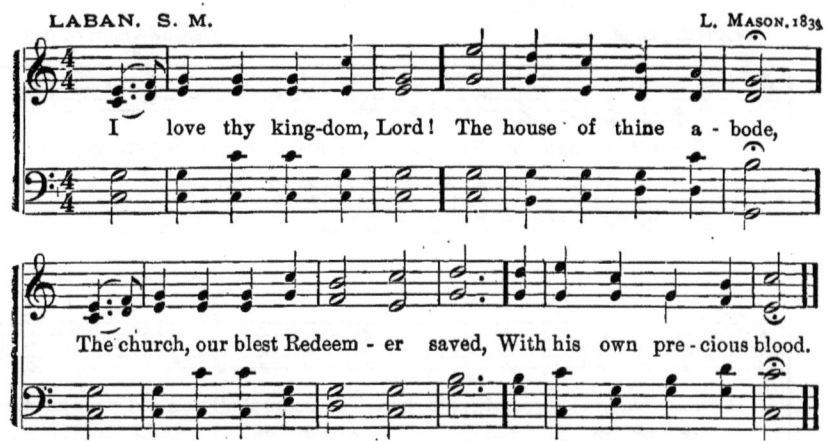

I love thy king-dom, Lord! The house of thine a - bode,

The church, our blest Redeem - er saved, With his own pre - cious blood.

435 [FIRST VERSE INSERTED IN MUSIC.]
Psalm 137. (914)

2 I love thy church, O God!
  Her walls before thee stand,
Dear as the apple of thine eye,
  And graven on thy hand.

3 For her my tears shall fall,
  For her my prayers ascend;
To her my cares and toils be given,
  Till toils and cares shall end.

4 Beyond my highest joy
  I prize her heavenly ways,
Her sweet communion, solemn vows,
  Her hymns of love and praise.

5 Sure as thy truth shall last,
  To Zion shall be given
The brightest glories earth can yield,
  And brighter bliss of heaven.
          TIMOTHY DWIGHT, 1800.

436 A Revival Sought. (912)

REVIVE thy work, O Lord!
  Thy mighty arm make bare;
Speak, with the voice that wakes the dead,
  And make thy people hear.

2 Revive thy work, O Lord!
  Disturb this sleep of death;
Quicken the smoldering embers now,
  By thine almighty breath,

3 Revive thy work, O Lord!
  Exalt thy precious name;
And, by the Holy Ghost, our love
  For thee and thine inflame.

4 Revive thy work, O Lord!
  And give refreshing showers;
The glory shall be all thine own,
  The blessing, Lord! be ours.
          ALBERT MIDLANE, 1861.

STATE STREET. S. M.   J. C. WOODMAN, 1844.

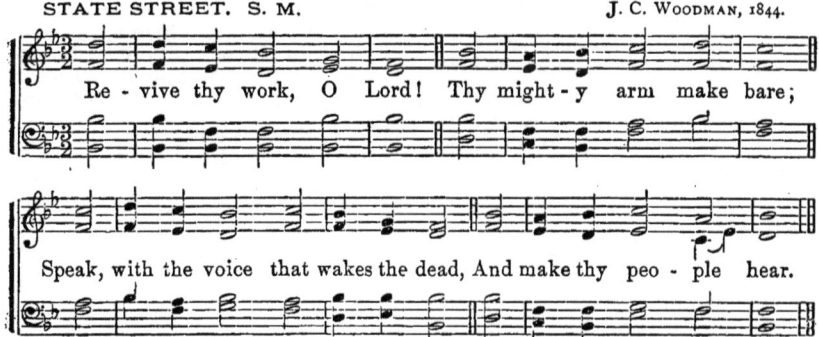

Re - vive thy work, O Lord! Thy might - y arm make bare;

Speak, with the voice that wakes the dead, And make thy peo - ple hear.

WARE. L. M.   GEORGE KINGSLEY, 1838.

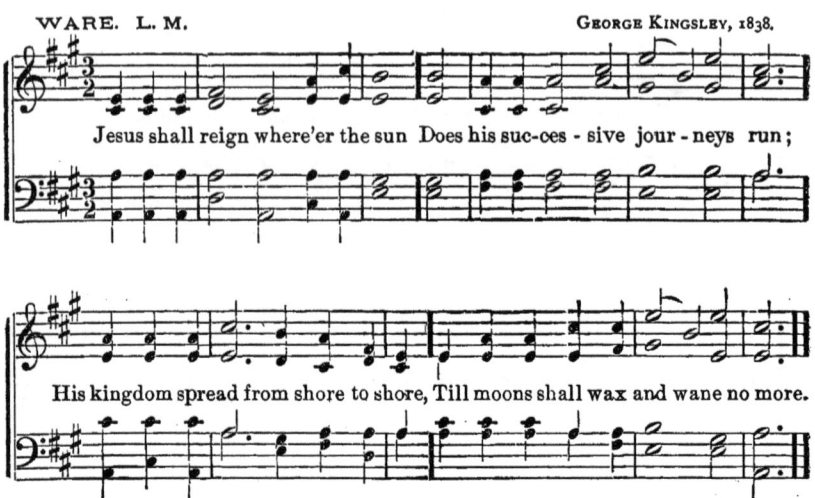

Jesus shall reign where'er the sun Does his suc-ces-sive jour-neys run;

His kingdom spread from shore to shore, Till moons shall wax and wane no more.

437 [FIRST VERSE INSERTED IN MUSIC.]
Christ's Everlasting Kingdom.   (895)

2 From north to south the princes meet,
To pay their homage at his feet;
While western empires own their Lord,
And savage tribes attend his word.

3 To him shall endless prayer be made,
And endless praises crown his head;
His name, like sweet perfume, shall rise
With every morning sacrifice.

4 People and realms of every tongue
Dwell on his love with sweetest song,
And infant voices shall proclaim
Their early blessings on his name.

5 Blessings abound where'er he reigns;
The prisoner leaps to lose his chains;
The weary find eternal rest,
And all the sons of want are blest.

6 Let every creature rise and bring
Peculiar honors to our King;
Angels descend with songs again,
And earth repeat the loud Amen!
ISAAC WATTS, 1719.

438 *The Glory of the Church.*   (904)
TRIUMPHANT Zion! lift thy head
From dust, and darkness, and the dead;
Though humbled long, awake at length,
And gird thee with thy Savior's strength.

2 Put all thy beauteous garments on,
And let thy various charms be known;
The world thy glories shall confess,
Decked in the robes of righteousness.

3 No more shall foes unclean invade,
And fill thy hallowed walls with dread;
No more shall hell's insulting host
Their vict'ry and thy sorrows boast.

4 God, from on high, thy groans will hear;
His hand thy ruins shall repair;
Nor will thy watchful Monarch cease
To guard thee in eternal peace.
PHILIP DODDRIDGE, 1740.

439   *Rev. 11: 15.*   (1028)
SOON may the last glad song arise
Through all the millions of the skies—
That song of triumph which records
That all the earth is now the Lord's!

2 Let thrones and powers and kingdoms be
Obedient, mighty God, to thee!
And, over land and stream and main,
Wave thou the scepter of thy reign!

3 Oh, let that glorious anthem swell,
Let host to host the triumph tell,
That not one rebel heart remains,
But over all the Savior reigns!
MRS. VOKE, 1816.

ZION. 8s, 7s & 4s.   THOMAS HASTINGS, 1830.

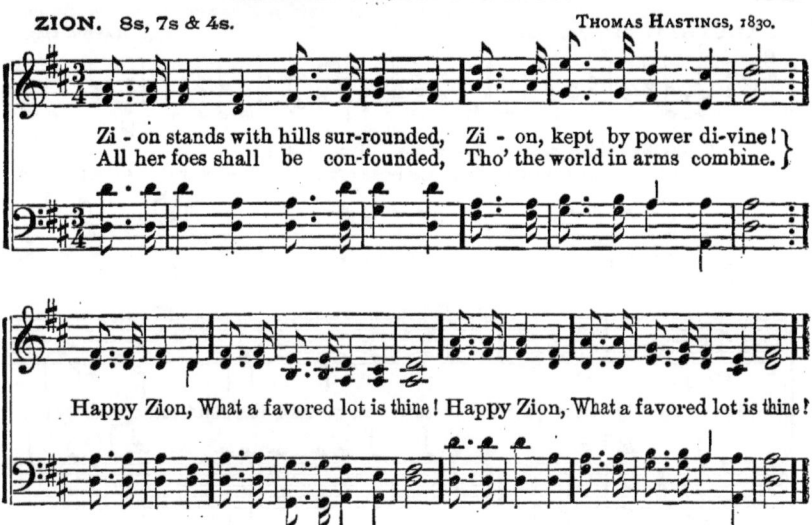

Zi - on stands with hills sur-rounded, Zi - on, kept by power di-vine!
All her foes shall be con-founded, Tho' the world in arms combine.

Happy Zion, What a favored lot is thine! Happy Zion, What a favored lot is thine!

440 [FIRST VERSE INSERTED IN MUSIC.]
Her Enemies Confounded. (925)

2 Ev'ry human tie may perish,
  Friend to friend unfaithful prove,
Mothers cease their own to cherish,
  Heaven and earth at last remove;
    But no changes
  Can attend Jehovah's love.

3 In the furnace God may prove thee,
  Thence to bring thee forth more bright
But can never cease to love thee—
  Thou art precious in his sight:
    God is with thee—
  God, thine everlasting light.
                    THOMAS KELLY, 1804.
                              (926)
441   *The Gospel Herald.*

ON the mountain's top appearing,
  Lo! the sacred herald stands,
Welcome news to Zion bearing—
  Zion long in hostile lands:
    Mourning captive!
  God himself shall loose thy bands.

2 Has thy night been long and mournful?
  Have thy friends unfaithful proved?
Have thy foes been proud and scornful?
  By thy sighs and tears unmoved?
    Cease thy mourning;
  Zion still is well beloved.

3 God, thy God, will now restore thee;
  He himself appears thy Friend;

All thy foes shall flee before thee;
  Here their boasts and triumph end:
    Great deliverance
  Zion's King will surely send.
                    THOMAS KELLY, 1804.

442   *Prayer for a Revival.*   (923)

SAVIOR, visit thy plantation;
  Grant us, Lord, a gracious rain;
All will come to desolation,
  Unless thou return again.
    Lord, revive us!
  All our help must come from thee.

2 Keep no longer at a distance;
  Shine upon us from on high,
Lest, for want of thine assistance,
  Every plant should droop and die.
    Lord, revive us!
  All our help must come from thee.

3 Let our mutual love be fervent!
  Make us prevalent in prayers;
Let each one, esteemed thy servant,
  Shun the world's bewitching snares.
    Lord, revive us!
  All our help must come from thee.

4 Break the tempter's fatal power,
  Turn the stony heart to flesh,
And begin, from this good hour,
  To revive thy work afresh.
    Lord, revive us!
  All our help must come from thee.
                    JOHN NEWTON, 1779.

AUSTRIA. 8s, 7s. D.　　　　　　　　　　　F. J. HAYDN, 1797.

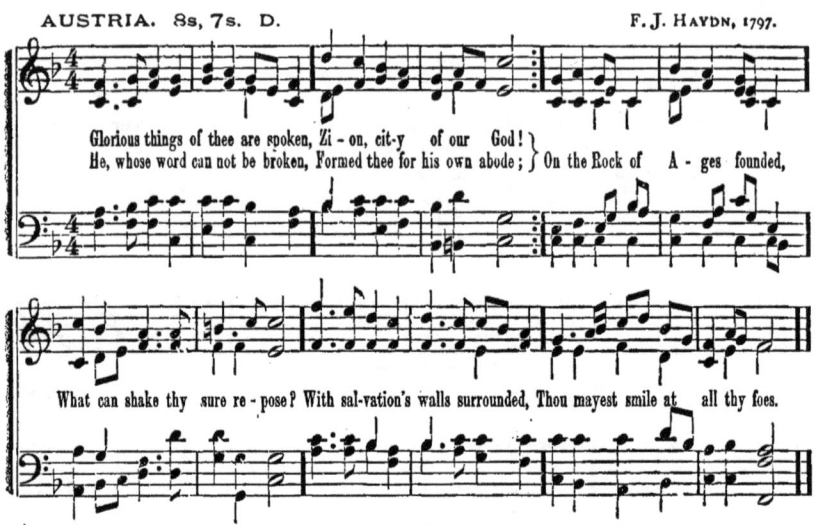

Glorious things of thee are spoken, Zi - on, cit-y　of our　God ! }
He, whose word can not be broken, Formed thee for his own abode ; } On the Rock of　A - ges founded,

What can shake thy sure re-pose ? With sal-vation's walls surrounded, Thou mayest smile at　all thy foes.

443　*The Glory of the Church.*　(921)

GLORIOUS things of thee are spoken,
　Zion, city of our God !
He, whose word can not be broken,
　Formed thee for his own abode :
On the Rock of ages founded,
　What can shake thy sure repose ?
With salvation's walls surrounded,
　Thou mayest smile at all thy foes.

2 See ! the streams of living waters,
　Springing from eternal love,
Well supply thy sons and daughters,
　And all fear of want remove :
Who can faint, while such a river,
　Ever flows their thirst t' assuage ?—
Grace, which, like the Lord, the Giver,
　Never fails from age to age.

3 Round each habitation hovering,
　See the cloud and fire appear,
For a glory and a covering,
　Showing that the Lord is near !
Thus deriving from their banner,
　Light by night, and shade by day,
Safe they feed upon the manna
　Which he gives them when they pray.
　　　　　　　　　　JOHN NEWTON, 1779.

444　　　*Isa.* 54 : 10.

ZION, dreary and in anguish,
　'Mid the desert hast thou strayed !
Oh, thou weary, cease to languish;
　Jesus shall lift up thy head.

Still lamenting and bemoaning,
　'Mid thy follies and thy woes !
Soon repenting and returning,
　All thy solitude shall close.

2 Though benighted and forsaken,
　Though afflicted and distressed ;
His almighty arm shall waken ;
　Zion's King shall give thee rest :
Cease thy sadness, unbelieving ;
　Soon his glory shalt thou see !
Joy and gladness, and thanksgiving
　And the voice of melody !
　　　　　　　　　　THOS. HASTINGS.

445　*The Heralds of the Gospel.*　(1048)

ONWARD, onward, men of heaven !
　Bear the gospel's banner high ;
Rest not, till its light is given,
　Star of every pagan sky :
Send it where the pilgrim stranger
　Faints beneath the torrid ray ;
Bid the red-browed forest-ranger
　Hail it, ere he fades away.

2 Rude in speech, or grim in feature
　Dark in spirit, though they be,
Show that light to every creature—
　Prince or vassal, bond or free :
Lo ! they haste to every nation :
　Host on host the ranks supply :
Onward ! Christ is your salvation,
　And your death is victory.
　　　　　　　　　　MRS. LYDIA H. SIGOURNEY.

BACA. L. M.
Moderato.
W. B. BRADBURY.

The heathen perish ; day by day, Thousands on thousands pass away ! O Christians,

to their rescue fly, Preach Jesus to them ere they die ! Preach Jesus to them ere they die !

446 [FIRST VERSE INSERTED IN MUSIC.]
Save the Perishing. (1021)

2 Wealth, labor, talents freely give,
 Yea, life itself, that they may live ;
What hath your Savior done for you ?
 And what for him will ye not do ?

3 Oh, Spirit of the Lord ! go forth,
 Call in the south, wake up the north ;
From every clime, from sun to sun,
 Gather God's children into one !
 J. MONTGOMERY.

447 *Home Missions.* (1022)

LOOK from thy sphere of endless day,
 O God of mercy and of might !
In pity look on those who stray,
 Benighted, in this land of light.

2 In peopled vale, in lonely glen,
 In crowded mart, by stream or sea,
How many of the sons of men
 Hear not the message sent from thee !

3 Send forth thy heralds, Lord ! to call
 The thoughtless young, the hardened old,
A scattered, homeless flock, till all
 Be gathered to thy peaceful fold.

4 Send them thy mighty word to speak,
 Till faith shall dawn, and doubt depart,
To awe the bold, to stay the weak,
 And bind and heal the broken heart.

5 Then all these wastes, a dreary scene,
 That make us sadden as we gaze,
Shall grow with living waters green,
 And lift to heaven the voice of praise.
 16 WILLIAM C. BRYANT 1840.

448 *Missionary Charged and Encouraged.* (1024)

GO, messenger of peace and love,
 To people plunged in shades of night,
Like angels sent from fields above,
 Be thine to shed celestial light.

2 Go to the hungry—food impart ;
 To paths of peace the wand'rer guide,
And lead the thirsty, panting heart,
 Where streams of living water glide.

3 Oh, faint not in the day of toil,
 When harvest waits the reaper's hand ;
Go, gather in the glorious spoil,
 And joyous in his presence stand.

4 Thy love a rich reward shall find
 From him who sits enthroned on high ;
For they who turn the erring mind
 Shall shine like stars above the sky.
 A. BALFOUR.

449 *Ascend thy Throne.*

ASCEND thy throne, almighty King,
 And spread thy glories all abroad ;
Let thine own arm salvation bring,
 And be thou known the gracious God.

2 Let millions bow before thy seat,
 Let humble mourners seek thy face,
Bring daring rebels to thy feet,
 Subdued by thy victorious grace.

3 Oh, let the kingdoms of the world
 Become the kingdoms of the Lord !
Let saints and angels praise thy name,
 Be thou through heaven and earth adored.
 BENJAMIN BEDDOME.

MISSIONARY CHANT. L. M.   HEINRICH CHARLES ZEUNER, 1832.

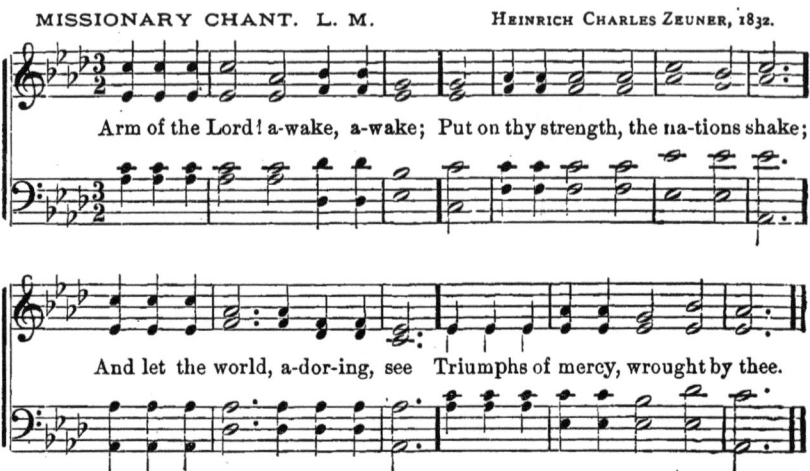

Arm of the Lord! a-wake, a-wake; Put on thy strength, the na-tions shake;

And let the world, a-dor-ing, see   Triumphs of mercy, wrought by thee.

450 *The Universal Reign of Christ.* (1033)
ARM of the Lord! awake, awake;
Put on thy strength, the nations shake;
And let the world, adoring, see
Triumphs of mercy, wrought by thee.

2 Say to the heathen, from thy throne,
"I am Jehovah—God alone!"
Thy voice their idols shall confound,
And cast their altars to the ground.

3 No more let human blood be spilt,
Vain sacrifice for human guilt;
But to each conscience be applied
The blood, that flowed from Jesus' side.

4 Almighty God! thy grace proclaim,
In every clime, of every name,
Till adverse powers before thee fall,
And crown the Savior—Lord of all.
          WILLIAM SHRUBSOLE, 1776.

451 *Mission to the Heathen.* (1030)
BEHOLD, the heathen waits to know
The joy the gospel will bestow;
The exiled captive to receive
The freedom Jesus has to give.

2 Come, let us, with a grateful heart,
In this blest labor share a part;
Our prayers and offerings gladly bring
To aid the triumphs of our King.

3 Our hearts exult in songs of praise,
That we have seen these latter days,
When our Redeemer shall be known
Where Satan long has held his throne.

4 Where'er his hand hath spread the skies,
Sweet incense to his name shall rise,
And slave and freeman, Greek and Jew,
By sovereign grace be formed anew.
          MRS. VOKE.

452 *The Gospel Banner.* (1027)
FLING out the banner! let it float
Skyward and seaward, high and wide,
The sun that lights its shining folds,
The cross on which the Savior died.

2 Fling out the banner! angels bend
In anxious silence o'er the sign,
And vainly seek to comprehend
The wonder of the Love Divine.

3 Fling out the banner! heathen lands
Shall see from far the glorious sight;
And nations, crowding to be born,
Baptize their spirits in its light.

4 Fling out the banner! sin-sick souls,
That sink and perish in the strife,
Shall touch in faith its radiant hem,
And spring immortal, into life.

5 Fling out the banner! let it float
Skyward and seaward, high and wide;
Our glory, only in the Cross,
Our only hope, the Crucified.

6 Fling out the banner! wide and high,
Seaward and skyward let it shine;
Nor skill, nor might, nor merit, ours;
We conquer only in that sign.
          GEO. W. DOANE, 1848.

453 (1042) ZION. 8s, 7s & 4s.

1. Yes, we trust the day is breaking; Joyful times are near at hand; }
   God, the mighty God, is speaking By his word in ev'ry land; } When he chooses,
2. While the foe becomes more dar-ing, While he enters like a flood, }
   God, the Sav-ior, is pre-par-ing Means to spread his truth abroad; } Ev'ry language

Darkness flies at his com-mand, When he chooses, Darkness flies at his command.
Soon shall tell the love of God, Ev'-ry language Soon shall tell the love of God.

3 Oh, 'tis pleasant, 'tis reviving
  To our hearts, to hear, each day,
Joyful news, from far arriving,
  How the gospel wins its way,
    Those enlight'ning
  Who in death and darkness lay.

4 God of Jacob, high and glorious,
  Let thy people see thy hand;
Let the gospel be victorious,
  Through the world in every land;
    Then shall idols
  Perish, Lord, at thy command.
    THOMAS KELLY, 1809.

454 ANVERN. L. M.

German, adapted by LOWELL MASON, 1840.

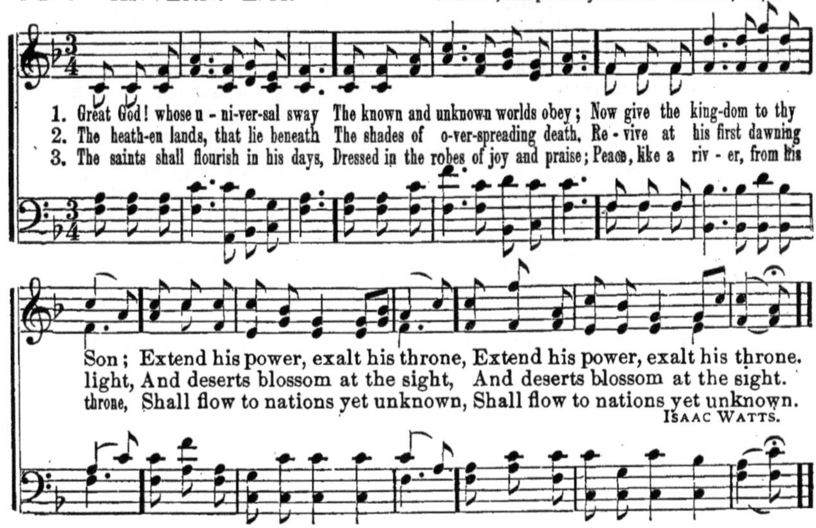

1. Great God! whose u-ni-ver-sal sway The known and unknown worlds obey; Now give the king-dom to thy
2. The heath-en lands, that lie beneath The shades of o-ver-spreading death, Re-vive at his first dawning
3. The saints shall flourish in his days, Dressed in the robes of joy and praise; Peace, like a riv-er, from his

Son; Extend his power, exalt his throne, Extend his power, exalt his throne.
light, And deserts blossom at the sight, And deserts blossom at the sight.
throne, Shall flow to nations yet unknown, Shall flow to nations yet unknown.
    ISAAC WATTS.

MISSIONARY HYMN. 7s & 6s. Double. LOWELL MASON, 1824.

From Greenland's icy mountains, From India's coral strand; Where Afric's sunny fountains Roll down their golden sand; From many an ancient riv-er, From many a palmy plain, They call us to de-liv-er Their land from er-ror's chain.

455 *Condition of the Heathen.* (1061)

FROM Greenland's icy mountains,
  From India's coral strand—
Where Afric's sunny fountains
  Roll down their golden sand—
From many an ancient river,
  From many a palmy plain—
They call us to deliver
  Their land from error's chain.

2 Shall we, whose souls are lighted
  By wisdom from on high,
Shall we to man benighted
  The light of life deny?
Salvation! oh, salvation!
  The joyful sound proclaim,
Till earth's remotest nation
  Has learned Messiah's name.

3 Waft, waft, ye winds, his story,
  And you, ye waters, roll,
Till like a sea of glory
  It spreads from pole to pole,
Till o'er our ransomed nature
  The Lamb, for sinners slain,
Redeemer, King, Creator,
  In bliss returns to reign.
         REGINALD HEBER, 1819.

456 *Home Missions.* (1062)

OUR country's voice is pleading,
  Ye men of God, arise!
His providence is leading,
  The land before you lies;
Day gleams are o'er it brightening,
  And promise clothes the soil;
Wide fields for harvest whitening,
  Invite the reaper's toil.

2 Go where the waves are breaking
  On California's shore,
Christ's precious gospel taking,
  More rich than golden ore;
On Allegheny's mountains,
  Through all the western vale,
Beside Missouri's fountains,
  Rehearse the wondrous tale.

3 The love of Christ unfolding,
  Speed on from east to west,
Till all, his cross beholding,
  In him are fully blest.
Great Author of salvation,
  Haste, haste the glorious day,
When we, a ransomed nation,
  Thy scepter shall obey.
         MRS. G. W. ANDERSON.

WEBB. 7s & 6s. 8 lines. GEORGE JAMES WEBB, 1830.

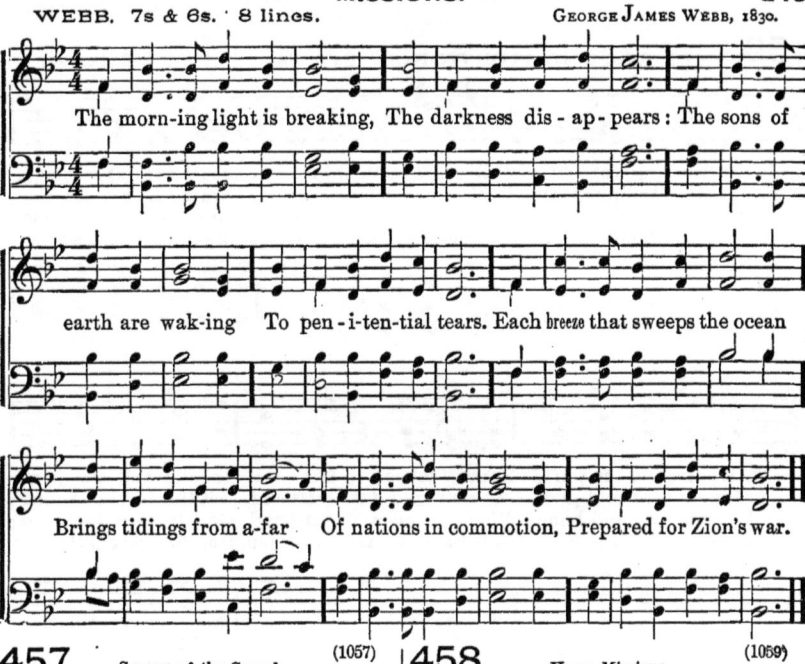

The morn-ing light is breaking, The darkness dis - ap - pears : The sons of

earth are wak-ing To pen - i-ten-tial tears. Each breeze that sweeps the ocean

Brings tidings from a-far Of nations in commotion, Prepared for Zion's war.

457 *Success of the Gospel.* (1057)

2 Rich dews of grace come o'er us,
 In many a gentle shower,
And brighter scenes before us
 Are opening every hour ;
Each cry, to heaven going,
 Abundant answers brings,
And heavenly gales are blowing,
 With peace upon their wings.

3 See heathen nations bending
 Before the God we love,
And thousand hearts ascending
 In gratitude above ;
While sinners, now confessing,
 The gospel call obey,
And seek the Savior's blessing,—
 A nation in a day.

4 Blest river of salvation !
 Pursue thine onward way ;
Flow thou to every nation,
 Nor in thy richness stay :—
Stay not, till all the lowly
 Triumphant reach their home ;
Stay not, till all the holy
 Proclaim " The Lord is come."
 SAMUEL F. SMITH, 1845.

458 *Home Missions.* (1059)

Go preach the blest salvation
 · To every sinful race,
And bid each guilty nation
 Accept the Savior's grace ;
But bear, oh, quickly bear it
 Where thronging millions roam,
And bid them freely share it,
 Who dwell with us at home.

2 Where blooms the broad savanna,
 Where mighty waters roll,
There let the gospel banner
 Beam hope on every soul ;
Go where the west is teeming,
 And yet behold they come !
The fields all ripe are gleaming
 For those who reap at home !

3 Our children there are dwelling,
 Neglected and astray,
Whose hearts are often swelling
 To learn of Zion's way.
Bear, bear to them the treasure
 And bid the exiles come ;
There is no sweeter pleasure,
 Than preaching Christ at home.
 SIDNEY DYER.

459 ALL AROUND THE WORLD. 6s & 5s.

E. S. LORÉNZ.

1. See the flag of Je - sus O'er the earth unfurled! Sabbath schools are singing,
2. Lit - tle Indian diamonds, Precious island pearls; Learning Bi - ble les- sons,
3. Sunday schools are singing, France and Spain and Rome; Hear their joyous mu-sic,
4. Sunday schools in Chi - li, Reaching down the coast; Mex - i - co is lead-ing,

All around the world : Sunday schools in Chi - na, In - dia and Ja - pan;
Hap-py boys and girls. Af-ric's gold dust scattered, 'Neath the feet of wrong;
Songs of heav'n and home. Where the martyrs suf-fered, Ho - ly seed is spread;
Gal-lant lit - tle host. Glad Bra - zil - ian chil-dren, Praise to God shall sing;

D. S. *See the flag of Je - sus, O'er the earth unfurled!*

Fine. CHORUS.

Training souls for glo - ry, By the gos - pel plan.
Ris - es up in brightness, From the darkness long. Lift the cross of Je - sus,
Gather up these ru - bies, Dyed in life-blood red.
Far - off Pat - a - gon - ia Answers Christ is King.

PRISCILLA J. OWENS.

Sunday schools are sing-ing, All a-round the world.

D. S.

Bear the Bi - ble on ; Soon the world will ech - o, With the vic-t'ry won.

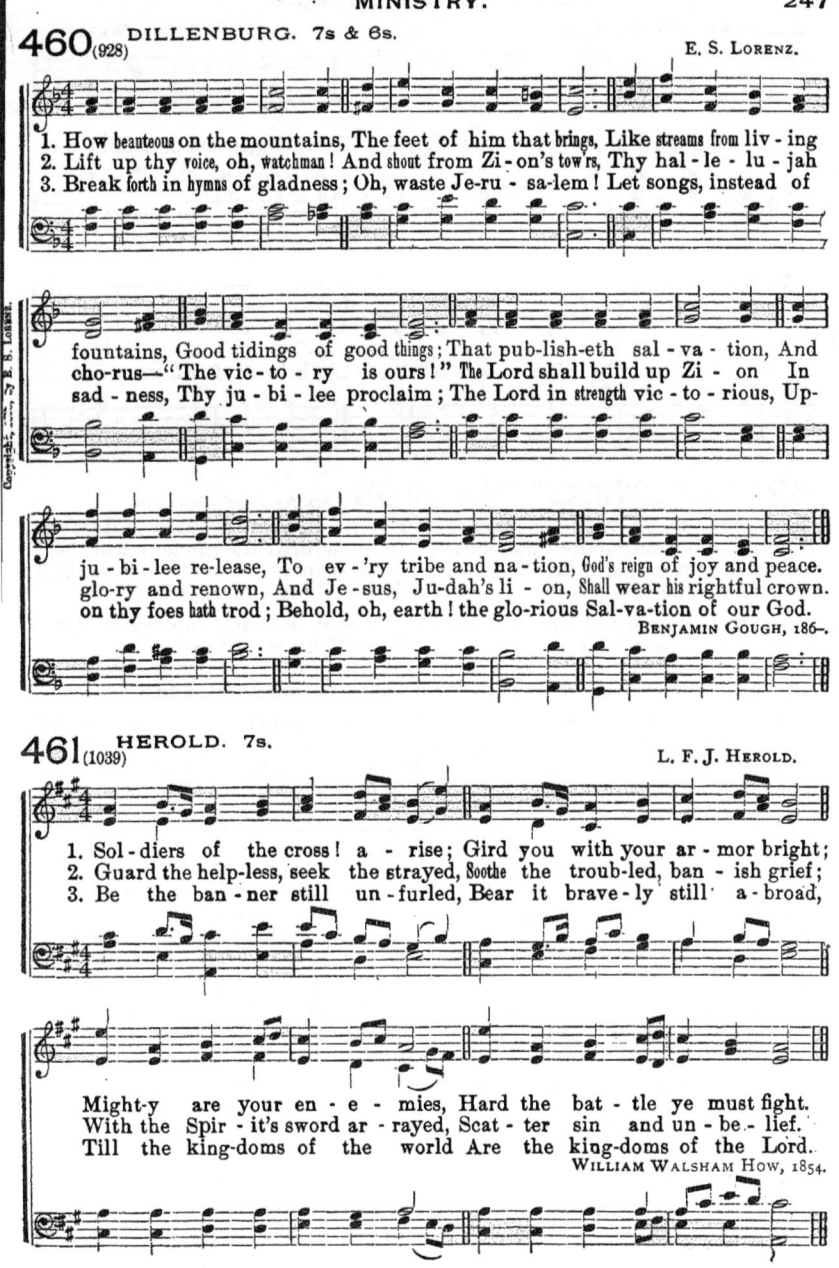

460(928) DILLENBURG. 7s & 6s.

E. S. LORENZ.

1. How beauteous on the mountains, The feet of him that brings, Like streams from liv - ing
2. Lift up thy voice, oh, watchman! And shout from Zi - on's tow'rs, Thy hal - le - lu - jah
3. Break forth in hymns of gladness; Oh, waste Je - ru - sa - lem! Let songs, instead of

fountains, Good tidings of good things; That pub-lish-eth sal - va - tion, And
cho-rus—"The vic-to - ry is ours!" The Lord shall build up Zi - on In
sad - ness, Thy ju - bi - lee proclaim; The Lord in strength vic - to - rious, Up-

ju - bi - lee re-lease, To ev - 'ry tribe and na - tion, God's reign of joy and peace.
glo-ry and renown, And Je - sus, Ju-dah's li - on, Shall wear his rightful crown.
on thy foes hath trod; Behold, oh, earth! the glo-rious Sal-va-tion of our God.

BENJAMIN GOUGH, 186-.

461(1039) HEROLD. 7s.

L. F. J. HEROLD.

1. Sol - diers of the cross! a - rise; Gird you with your ar - mor bright;
2. Guard the help-less, seek the strayed, Soothe the troub-led, ban - ish grief;
3. Be the ban - ner still un - furled, Bear it brave - ly still a - broad,

Might-y are your en - e - mies, Hard the bat - tle ye must fight.
With the Spir - it's sword ar - rayed, Scat - ter sin and un - be - lief.
Till the king-doms of the world Are the king-doms of the Lord.

WILLIAM WALSHAM HOW, 1854.

ALLHALLOWS. C. M.   SAMUEL WEBBE.

With thine own pit-y, Sav-ior, see The thronged and darkening way!

We go to win the lost to thee, Oh, help us, Lord, we pray!

462 [FIRST VERSE INSERTED IN MUSIC.]
In the Strength of Jesus. (983)

2 Thou bid'st us go, with thee to stand
  Against hell's marshalled powers;
And heart to heart, and hand to hand,
  To make thine honor ours.

3 Teach thou our lips of thee to speak,
  Of thy sweet love to tell;
Till they who wander far shall seek
  And find and serve thee well.

4 O'er all the world thy Spirit send,
  And make thy goodness known,
Till earth and heaven together blend
  Their praises at thy throne.
               RAY PALMER.

463 *Zeal for Souls.—John 4: 35.*

OH! still in accents sweet and strong
  Sounds forth the ancient word,—
"More reapers for white harvest fields,
  More laborers for the Lord!"

2 We hear the call; in dreams no more
  In selfish ease we lie,
But girded for our Father's work,
  Go forth beneath his sky.

3 Where prophets' word, and martyrs' blood,
  And prayers of saints were sown,
We, to their labors entering in,
  Would reap where they have strown.
             S. LONGFELLOW.

464 *A Meeting of Ministers.* (1006)

POUR out thy Spirit from on high;
  Lord! thine assembled servants bless;
Graces and gifts to each supply,
  And clothe thy priests with righteousness.

2 Wisdom and zeal, and faith impart,
  Firmness with meekness from above,
To bear thy people on our heart,
  And love the souls whom thou dost love:

3 To watch and pray, and never faint;
  By day and night, strict guard to keep;
To warn the sinner, cheer the saint,
  Nourish thy lambs, and feed thy sheep.

4 Then, when our work is finished here,
  In humble hope, our charge resign;
When the chief Shepherd shall appear,
  O God! may they and we be thine.
        JAMES MONTGOMERY, 1825.

465 *An Ordination Service.* (1011)

THE solemn service now is done;
  The vow is pledged, the toil begun;
Seal thou, O God! the oath above,
  And ratify the pledge of love.

2 The shepherd of thy people bless;
  Gird him with thine own holiness;
In duty may his pleasure be,
  His glory in his zeal for thee.

3 Here let the ardent prayer arise,
  Faith fix its grasp beyond the skies,
The tear of penitence be shed,
  And myriads to the Savior led.

4 Come, Spirit! here consent to dwell;
  The mists of earth and sin dispel:
Blest Savior! thine own rights maintain;
  Supreme in every bosom reign.
        SAMUEL F. SMITH, 1843.

HAPPY DAY. L. M.

Oh, happy day, that fixed my choice On thee, my Savior and my God !
Well may this glowing heart rejoice, And tell its raptures all a-broad. } Hap-py

day, happy day, When Je - sus washed my sins away ; { He taught me how to watch and pray,
And live rejoicing ev'ry day ! }

466 [FIRST VERSE INSERTED IN MUSIC.]
Rejoicing in Entire Consecration. (937)

2 Oh, happy bond, that seals my vows
   To him who merits all my love !
Let cheerful anthems fill the house,
   While to his altar now I move.

3 'Tis done—the great transaction's done ;
   I am my Lord's, and he is mine ;
He drew me, and I followed on,
   Rejoiced to own the call divine.

4 Now rest—my long divided heart—
   Fixed on this blissful center, rest—
Here have I found a nobler part,
   Here heavenly pleasures fill my breast.

5 High Heaven, that heard the solemn vow,
   That vow renewed shall daily hear,
Till, in life's latest hour, I bow,
   And bless in death a bond so dear.
                         PHILIP DODDRIDGE, 1740.

467   *Converts Welcomed.*   (940)

COME in, thou blessed of the Lord !
   Enter in Jesus' precious name ;
We welcome thee, with one accord,
   And trust the Savior does the same.

2 Those joys, which earth can not afford,
   We'll seek in fellowship to prove,
Joined in one spirit to our Lord,
   Together bound by mutual love.

3 And, while we pass this vale of tears,
   We'll make our joys and sorrows known ;
We'll share each other's hopes and fears,
   And count a brother's case our own.

4 Once more, our welcome we repeat ;
   Receive assurance of our love ;
Oh ! may we all together meet,
   Around the throne of God above.
                         THOMAS KELLY, 1812.

WELTON. L. M.   C. H. A. MALAN.

The sol-emn serv-ice now is done ; The vow is pledged, the toil be-gun ;

Seal thou, O God ! the oath a - bove, And rat - i - fy the pledge of love.

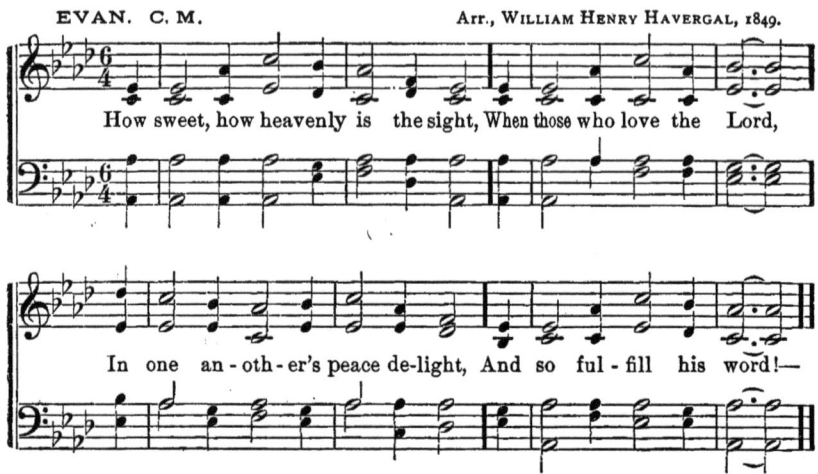

EVAN. C. M.   Arr., William Henry Havergal, 1849.

How sweet, how heavenly is the sight, When those who love the Lord,

In one an-oth-er's peace de-light, And so ful-fill his word!—

468   *Brotherly Love.*   (983)

How sweet, how heavenly is the sight,
  When those who love the Lord,
In one another's peace delight,
  And so fulfill his word!—

2 When each can feel his brother's sigh,
  And with him bear a part;
When sorrow flows from eye to eye,
  And joy from heart to heart:

3 When, free from envy, scorn, and pride,
  Our wishes all above,
Each can his brother's failings hide,
  And show a brother's love:

4 When love, in one delightful stream,
  Through every bosom flows;
When union sweet, and dear esteem,
  In every action glows.

5 Love is the golden chain, that binds
  The happy souls above;
And he's an heir of heaven, that finds
  His bosom glow with love.
                    Joseph Swain, 1792.

469   *Gen.* 24: 31.   (931)

Come in, beloved of the Lord,
  Stranger nor foe art thou;
We welcome thee with warm accord,
  Our friend, our brother, now.

2 The hand of fellowship, the heart
  Of love, we offer thee:

Leaving the world, thou dost but part
  From lies and vanity.

3 Come with us,—we will do thee good,
  As God to us hath done;
Stand but in him, as those have stood
  Whose faith the victory won.

4 And when, by turns, we pass away,
  And star by star grows dim,
May each, translated into day,
  Be lost and found in him.
                    James Montgomery.

470   *Covenant Vows.*   (933)

Witness, ye men and angels! now,
  Before the Lord we speak;
To him we make our solemn vow,
  A vow we dare not break;—

2 That, long as life itself shall last,
  Ourselves to Christ we yield;
Nor from his cause will we depart,
  Or ever quit the field.

3 We trust not in our native strength,
  But on his grace rely;
That, with returning wants, the Lord
  Will all our need supply.

4 Oh! guide our doubtful feet aright,
  And keep us in thy ways;
And, while we turn our vows to prayers,
  Turn thou our prayers to praise.
                    Benjamin Beddome, 1790.

DENNIS. S. M.

HANS GEORGE NAGELI, 1773-1836.

Blest be the tie that binds Our hearts in Chris-tian love!

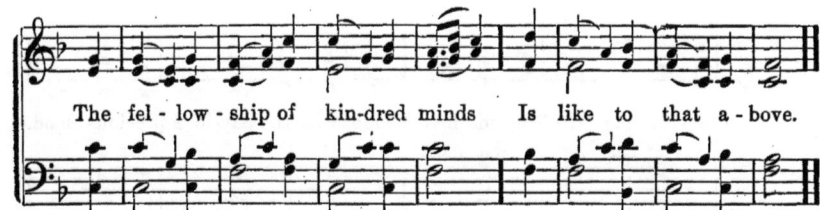

The fel-low-ship of kin-dred minds Is like to that a-bove.

471 [FIRST VERSE INSERTED IN MUSIC.]
Love to the Brethren. (992)

2 Before our Father's throne,
  We pour our ardent prayers;
Our fears, our hopes, our aims are one,
  Our comforts and our cares.

3 We share our mutual woes;
  Our mutual burdens bear:
And often for each other flows
  The sympathizing tear.

4 When we asunder part,
  It gives us inward pain:
But we shall still be joined in heart,
  And hope to meet again.

5 This glorious hope revives
  Our courage by the way;
While each in expectation lives,
  And longs to see the day.

6 From sorrow, toil, and pain,
  And sin we shall be free;
And perfect love and friendship reign
  Through all eternity.
  JOHN FAWCETT, 1772.

472 *Laborers in the Vineyard.* (995)

AND let our bodies part—
  To diff'rent climes repair;
Inseparably joined in heart
  The friends of Jesus are.

2 Oh, let us still proceed
  In Jesus' work below;
And following our triumphant Head,
  To further conquests go.

3 The vineyard of the Lord
  Before his laborers lies;
And lo! we see the vast reward
  Which waits us in the skies.

4 Oh, let our heart and mind
  Continually ascend,
That haven of repose to find,
  Where all our labors end.
  CHARLES WESLEY.

473 *Meeting After Absence.* (996)

AND are we yet alive,
  And see each other's face?
Glory and praise to Jesus give,
  For his redeeming grace.

2 Preserved by power divine
  To full salvation here,
Again in Jesus' praise we join,
  And in his sight appear.

3 What troubles have we seen!
  What conflicts have we passed!
Fightings without, and fears within,
  Since we assembled last!

4 But out of all the Lord
  Hath brought us by his love;
And still he doth his help afford,
  And hides our life above.

5 Let us take up the cross,
  Till we the crown obtain;
And gladly reckon all things loss,
  So we may Jesus gain.
  CHARLES WESLEY.

ROCKINGHAM. L. M.   Lowell Mason, 1830.

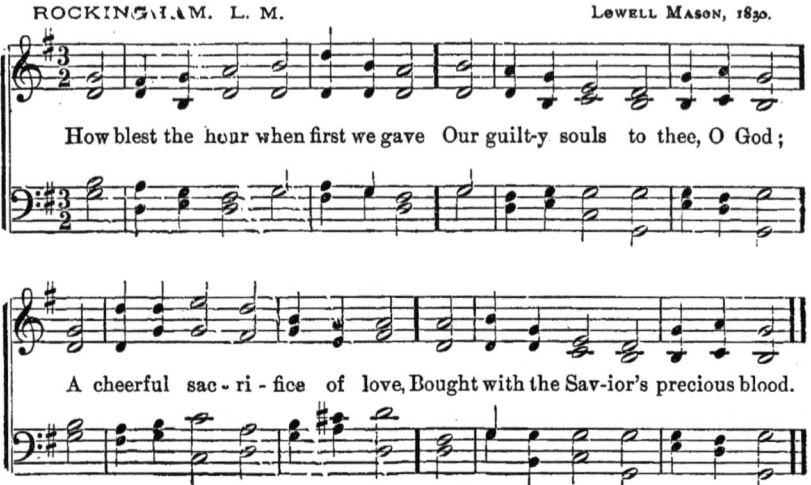

How blest the hour when first we gave Our guilt-y souls to thee, O God;

A cheerful sac - ri - fice of love, Bought with the Sav-ior's precious blood.

474   *The Likeness of His Death.*   (974)

How blest the hour when first we gave
  Our guilty souls to thee, O God;
A cheerful sacrifice of love,
  Bought with the Savior's precious blood.

2 How blest the vow we here record!
  How blest the grace we now receive!
Buried in baptism with our Lord,
  New lives of holiness to live.

3 How blest the solemn rite that seals
  Our death to sin, our guilt forgiven;—
How blest the emblem that reveals
  God reconciled, and peace with heaven.

4 Thus through the emblematic grave
  The glorious, suffering Savior trod;
Thou art our pattern, through the wave
  We follow thee, blest Son of God.
                      S. F. Smith.

475   *The Feast of Love.*   (961)

My God! and is thy table spread?
  And does thy cup with love o'erflow?
Thither be all thy children led,
  And let them all its sweetness know.

2 Hail! sacred feast, which Jesus makes!
  Rich banquet of his flesh and blood;
Thrice happy he, who here partakes
  That sacred stream, that heavenly food!

3 Oh! let thy table honored be,
  And furnished well with joyful guests;

And may each soul salvation see,
That here its sacred pledges tastes.

4 Let crowds approach, with hearts prepared:
  With hearts inflamed let all attend;
Nor, when we leave our Father's board,
  The pleasure or the profit end.
                Philip Doddridge, 1740.

476   *Jesu, Dulcedo Cordium!*   (963)

Jesus, thou Joy of loving hearts!
  Thou Fount of life! thou Light of men!
From the best bliss that earth imparts,
  We turn unfilled to thee again.

2 Thy truth unchanged hath ever stood;
  Thou savest those that on thee call;
To them that seek thee, thou art good,
  To them that find thee,—All in all!

3 We taste thee, Oh, thou living Bread!
  And long to feast upon thee still;
We drink of thee, the Fountain Head,
  And thirst our souls from thee to fill.

4 Our restless spirits yearn for thee,
  Where'er our changeful lot is cast;
Glad, when thy gracious smile we see,
  Blest, when our faith can hold thee fast.

5 O Jesus! ever with us stay;
  Make all our moments calm and bright;
Chase the dark night of sin away;
  Shed o'er the world thy holy light.
      Lat., Bernard, of Clairvaux, 1140.
           Tr., Ray Palmer, 1822.

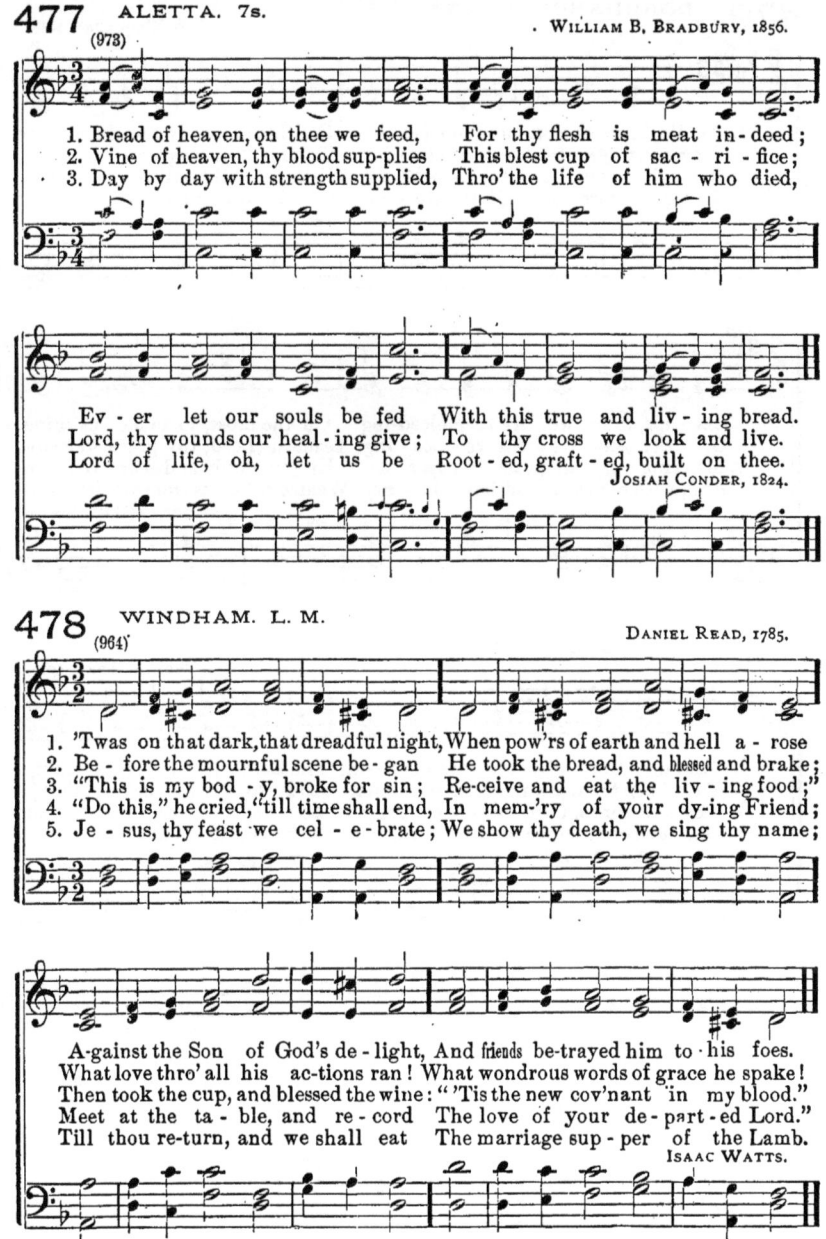

477 ALETTA. 7s.
(978)

WILLIAM B. BRADBURY, 1856.

1. Bread of heaven, on thee we feed, For thy flesh is meat in-deed;
2. Vine of heaven, thy blood sup-plies This blest cup of sac - ri - fice;
3. Day by day with strength supplied, Thro' the life of him who died,

Ev - er let our souls be fed With this true and liv - ing bread.
Lord, thy wounds our heal - ing give; To thy cross we look and live.
Lord of life, oh, let us be Root - ed, graft - ed, built on thee.

JOSIAH CONDER, 1824.

478 WINDHAM. L. M.
(964)

DANIEL READ, 1785.

1. 'Twas on that dark, that dreadful night, When pow'rs of earth and hell a - rose
2. Be - fore the mournful scene be - gan He took the bread, and blessed and brake;
3. "This is my bod - y, broke for sin; Re-ceive and eat the liv - ing food;"
4. "Do this," he cried, "till time shall end, In mem-'ry of your dy-ing Friend;
5. Je - sus, thy feast we cel - e - brate; We show thy death, we sing thy name;

A-gainst the Son of God's de - light, And friends be-trayed him to his foes.
What love thro' all his ac-tions ran! What wondrous words of grace he spake!
Then took the cup, and blessed the wine: "'Tis the new cov'nant in my blood."
Meet at the ta - ble, and re-cord The love of your de-part-ed Lord."
Till thou re-turn, and we shall eat The marriage sup-per of the Lamb.

ISAAC WATTS.

479(977) DORRNANCE. 8s & 7s.

I. B. WOODBURY, 1845.

1. While, in sweet com-mun-ion, feed-ing   On this earth - ly bread and wine,
2. Now, our eyes for - ev - er clos- ing   To this fleet - ing world be - low,
3. Though unseen, be   ev - er near us,   With the still small voice of   love,
4. Bring be - fore us   all the sto - ry   Of thy life, and death of   woe;

Sav - ior, may we   see thee bleed-ing   On the cross, to make   us thine.
On   thy gen - tle breast re - pos - ing,   Teach us, Lord, thy grace to know.
Whisp'ring words of peace to cheer us,   Ev - 'ry doubt and fear   re-move.
And, with hopes of end-less glo - ry,   Wean our hearts from all   be - low.

EDWARD DENNY, 1839.

480(958) ARLINGTON C. M.

THOS. A. ARNE, 1762.

1. That dreadful night be - fore his death,   The Lamb, for sin - ners slain,
2. To   keep the feast, Lord, we have met,   And to   re - mem-ber thee,
3. Thy suff-'rings, Lord, each sa-cred sign   To   our   re - mem-brance brings,
4. Oh, tune our tongues, and set in frame   Each heart that pants for   thee,

Did, al-most with his dy - ing breath,   This sol - emn feast or - dain.
Help each poor trembler to   re - peat—   For me   he died, for me.
We   eat the bread and drink the wine,   But think on no - bler things.
To sing, Ho - san - na to the Lamb,   The Lamb that died for   me.

JOSEPH HART, d. 1768.

481 TILL HE COME. 7s. 6 lines.

P. P. BLISS.

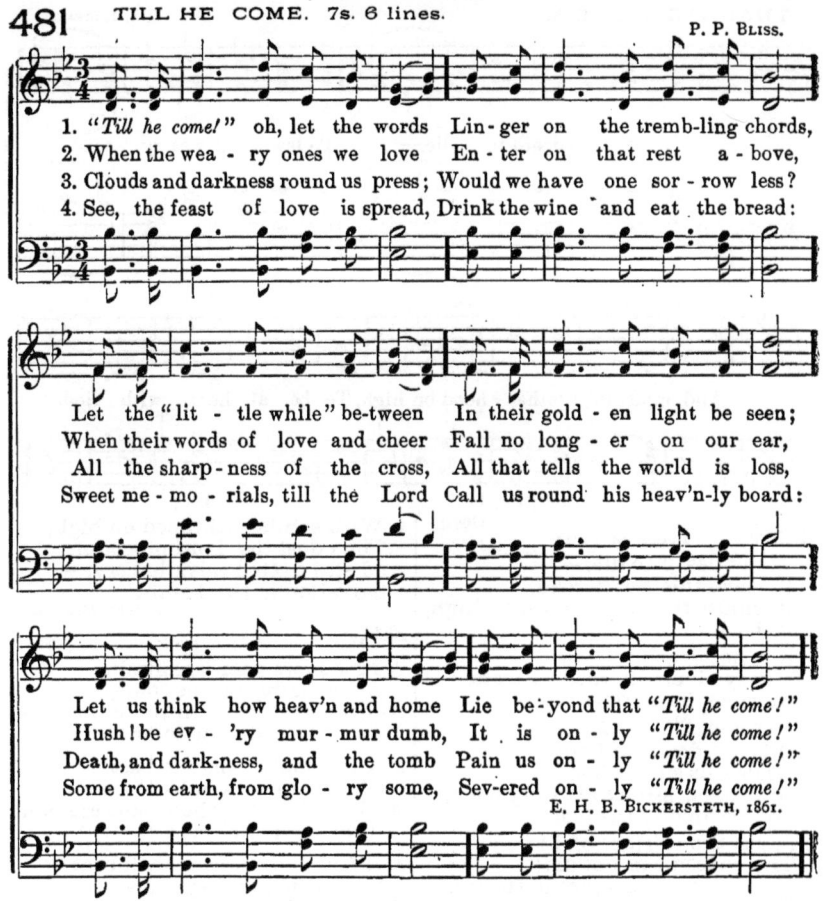

1. *"Till he come!"* oh, let the words Lin-ger on the tremb-ling chords,
2. When the wea - ry ones we love En - ter on that rest a - bove,
3. Clouds and darkness round us press; Would we have one sor - row less?
4. See, the feast of love is spread, Drink the wine and eat the bread:

Let the "lit - tle while" be-tween In their gold - en light be seen;
When their words of love and cheer Fall no long - er on our ear,
All the sharp-ness of the cross, All that tells the world is loss,
Sweet me - mo - rials, till the Lord Call us round his heav'n-ly board:

Let us think how heav'n and home Lie be-yond that *"Till he come!"*
Hush! be ev - 'ry mur - mur dumb, It is on - ly *"Till he come!"*
Death, and dark-ness, and the tomb Pain us on - ly *"Till he come!"*
Some from earth, from glo - ry some, Sev-ered on - ly *"Till he come!"*

E. H. B. BICKERSTETH, 1861.

---

482 *Baptized into His Death.* (945)

WE long to move and breathe in thee,
  Inspired with thine own breath,
To live thy life, O Lord, and be
  Baptized into thy death.

2 Thy death to sin we die below,
  But we shall rise in love;
We here are planted in thy woe,
  But we shall bloom above.

3 Above we shall thy glory share,
  As we thy cross have borne;
E'en we shall crowns of honor wear,
  When we the thorns have worn.

483 *Baptism of Children.* (946).

OUR children, Lord, in faith and prayer
  We now devote to thee;
Let them thy covenant mercies share,
  And thy salvation see.

2 In early days their hearts secure
  From worldly snares, we pray;
And let them to the end endure
  In every righteous way.

3 Grant us before them, Lord, to live
  In holy faith and fear;
And then to heaven our souls receive
  And bring our children there.

THANATOPSIS. S. M.

E. S. LORENZ.

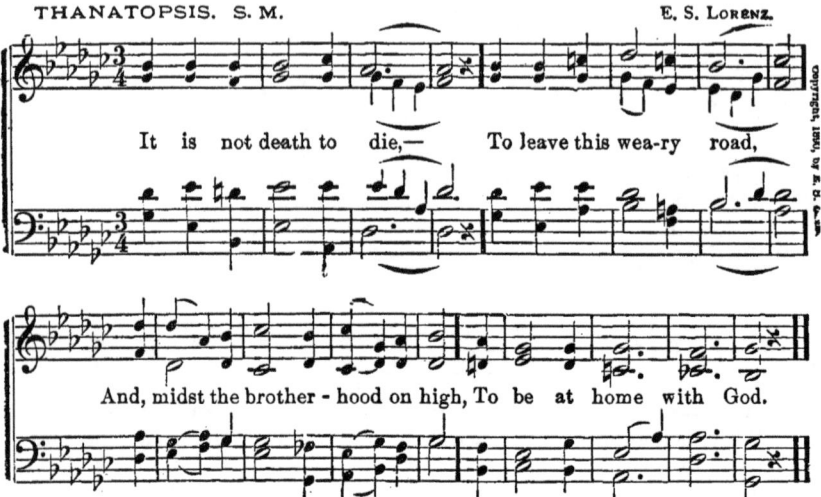

It is not death to die,— To leave this wea-ry road,

And, midst the brother - hood on high, To be at home with God.

484 *Dying, not Death.* (1088)

IT is not death to die,—
To leave this weary road,
And, midst the brotherhood on high,
To be at home with God.

2 It is not death to close
The eye long dimmed by tears,
And wake, in glorious repose
To spend eternal years.

3 It is not death to fling
Aside this sinful dust,
And rise, on strong exulting wing,
To live among the just.

4 Jesus, thou Prince of life!
Thy chosen can not die;
Like thee, they conquer in the strife,
To reign with thee on high.
GEORGE W. BETHUNE, 1847.

485 *The Crowning Hour.* (1086)

SERVANT of God, well done!
Thy glorious warfare's past;
The battle's fought, the race is won,
And thou art crown'd at last;—

2 Of all thy heart's desire
Triumphantly possess'd;
Lodged by the ministerial choir
In thy Redeemer's breast.

3 In condescending love,
Thy ceaseless prayer he heard,
And bade thee suddenly remove
To thy complete reward.

4 With saints enthroned on high,
Thou dost thy Lord proclaim,
And still to God salvation cry,—
Salvation to the Lamb!
CHARLES WESLEY.

486 *A Little While.* (1089)

A FEW more years shall roll,
A few more seasons come,
And we shall be with those that rest
Asleep within the tomb:

2 A few more suns shall set
O'er these dark hills of time,
And we shall be where suns are not,
A far serener clime:

3 A few more storms shall beat
On this wild rocky shore,
And we shall be where tempests cease,
And surges swell no more:

4 A few more struggles here,
A few more partings o'er,
A few more toils, a few more tears,
And we shall weep no more:

5 'Tis but a little while
And he shall come again,
Who died that we might live, who lives
That we with him may reign:

6 Then, O my Lord, prepare
My soul for that great day;
Oh, wash me in thy precious blood,
And take my sins away.
HORATIUS BONAR, 1856.

187 ST. SYLVESTER. 8s & 7s. J. B. DYKES, 1861.

1. Days and moments quickly fly - ing Blend the liv - ing with the dead;
2. Soon our souls to God who gave them Will have sped their rap-id flight;
3. Je - sus, in - fi - nite Re-deem-er, Mak - er of this might-y frame;
4. Whence we came, and whither wending; Soon we must through darkness go,

Soon shall we who sing be ly - ing, Each within our nar-row bed.
A - ble now by grace to save them, Oh, that while we can we might.
Teach, oh, teach us to re - mem-ber What we are, and whence we came:—
To in - her - it bliss un - end - ing, Or e - ter - ni - ty of woe.

REV. EDWARD CASWELL, 1849.

After fourth verse.

As the tree falls so must it lie; As the man lives so will he die; As the man dies,

such must he be, All through the days of e - ter - - - ni - ty. A - men.

488 *Matt.* 6: 10. (1097)

ᴊᴇꜱᴜꜱ, while our hearts are bleeding
O'er the spoils that death has won,
We would at this solemn meeting,
Calmly say,—thy will be done.
Though cast down, we're not forsaken;
Though afflicted, not alone;
Thou didst give, and thou hast taken;
Blessed Lord,—thy will be done.

3 Tho' to-day we're filled with mourning
Mercy still is on the throne;
With thy smiles of love returning,
We can sing—thy will be done.

4 By thy hands the boon was given,
Thou hast taken but thine own:
Lord of earth, and God of heaven,
Evermore,—thy will be done!

THOMAS HASTINGS.

17

REST. L. M.   WILLIAM B. BRADBURY, 1844.

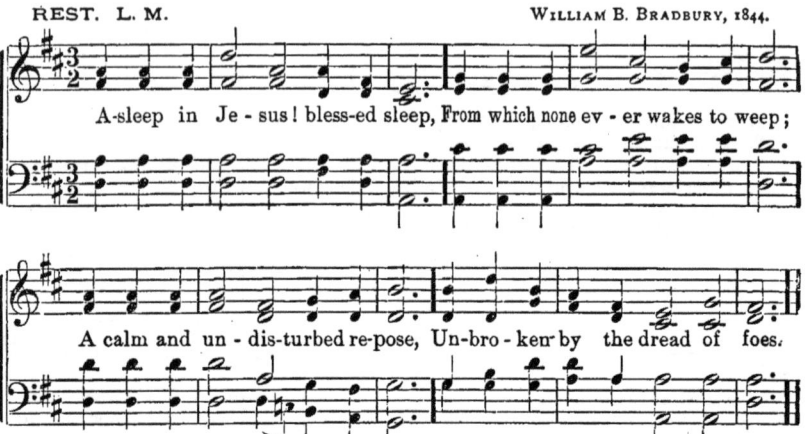

A-sleep in Je - sus! bless-ed sleep, From which none ev - er wakes to weep;

A calm and un - dis-turbed re-pose, Un-bro - ken by the dread of foes.

489 [FIRST VERSE INSERTED IN MUSIC.]
Sleeping in Jesus.   (1077)

2 Asleep in Jesus! peaceful rest,
Whose waking is supremely blest;
No fear, no woes, shall dim the hour,
Which manifests the Savior's power.

3 Asleep in Jesus! oh, for me
May such a blissful refuge be;
Securely shall my ashes lie,
And wait the summons from on high.

4 Asleep in Jesus! far from thee
Thy kindred and their graves may be;
But thine is still a blessed sleep,
From which none ever wakes to weep.
          MRS. MARGARET MACKAY, 1832.

490 *The End of that Man is Peace.* (1078)

How blest the righteous when he dies!
  When sinks a weary soul to rest!
How mildly beam the closing eyes!
  How gently heaves the expiring breast!

2 So fades a summer cloud away;
  So sinks the gale when storms are o'er;
So gently shuts the eye of day;
  So dies a wave along the shore.

3 A holy quiet reigns around,
  A calm which life nor death destroys;
And naught disturbs that peace profound
  Which his unfettered soul enjoys.

4 Life's labor done, as sinks the clay,
  Light from its load the spirit flies,
While heaven and earth combine to say,
  How blest the righteous when he dies!
          MRS. A. L. BARBAULD, 1773.

491 *Death and Burial of a Christian.* (1080)

UNVEIL thy bosom, faithful tomb;
  Take this new treasure to thy trust
And give these sacred relics room,
  To slumber in the silent dust.

2 Nor pain, nor grief, nor anxious fear,
  Invades thy bounds; no mortal woes
Can reach the peaceful sleeper here,
  While angels watch the soft repose.

3 So Jesus slept; God's dying Son
  Passed thro' the grave, and blest the bed;
Rest here, blest saint, till from his throne
  The morning break, and pierce the shade.

4 Break from his throne, illustrious morn;
  Attend, O earth, his sovereign word;
Restore thy trust; a glorious form
  Shall then arise to meet the Lord.
          ISAAC WATTS, 1734.

492 *The Fading Flower.* (1084)

So fades the lovely, blooming flower—
Frail smiling solace of an hour!
So soon our transient comforts fly,
And pleasure only blooms to die.

2 Is there no kind, no lenient art,
To heal the anguish of the heart?
Spirit of grace! be ever nigh,
Thy comforts are not made to die.

3 Bid gentle patience smile on pain,
Till dying hope shall live again;
Hope wipes the tear from sorrow's eye,
And faith points upward to the sky.
          ANNE STEELE, 1760.

CHINA. C. M.   THOMAS SWAN, 1799.

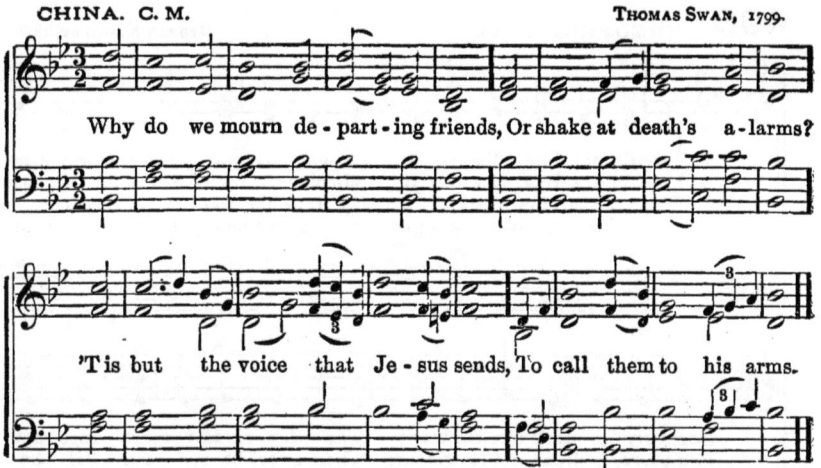

Why do we mourn de-part-ing friends, Or shake at death's a-larms?

'T is but the voice that Je-sus sends, To call them to his arms.

493 *We are Confident.* (1067)

WHY do we mourn departing friends,
  Or shake at death's alarms?
'T is but the voice that Jesus sends,
  To call them to his arms.

2 Are we not tending upward, too,
  As fast as time can move?
Nor would we wish the hours more slow,
  To keep us from our love.

8 Why should we tremble to convey
  Their bodies to the tomb?
There the dear flesh of Jesus lay,
  And scattered all the gloom.

4 The graves of all the saints be blessed,
  And softened every bed;
Where should the dying members rest,
  But with the dying Head?

5 Thence he arose, ascending high,
  And showed our feet the way;
Up to the Lord we, too, shall fly
  At the great rising-day.

6 Then let the last loud trumpet sound,
  And bid our kindred rise;
Awake! ye nations under ground;
  Ye saints! ascend the skies.
                        ISAAC WATTS, 1707.

494 *Cheerful Submission to Death.* (1065)

AND let this feeble body fail,
  And let it faint or die;
My soul shall quit the mournful vale,
  And soar to worlds on high—

2 Shall join the disembodied saints,
  And find its long-sought rest;
That only bliss for which it pants,
  In the Redeemer's breast.

3 In hope of that immortal crown,
  I now the cross sustain;
And gladly wander up and down,
  And smile at toil and pain.

4 I suffer on my three-score years,
  Till my Deliverer come,
And wipes away his servant's tears,
  And takes his exile home.
                        CHARLES WESLEY, 1759.

495 *Mourning with Hope.* (1066)

WHY should our tears in sorrow flow
  When God recalls his own,
And bids them leave a world of woe,
  For an immortal crown?

2 Is not e'en death a gain to those
  Whose life to God was given?
Gladly to earth their eyes they close
  To open them in heaven.

3 Their toils are past, their work is done,
  And they are fully blest!
They fought the fight, the victory won,
  And entered into rest.

4 Then let our sorrows cease to flow,—
  God has recalled his own;
But let our hearts, in every woe,
  Still say, "Thy will be done!"
                        WM. H. BATHURST, 1829.

496   FREDERICK. 11s.   GEORGE KINGSLEY, 1838.

1. I would not live al-way; I ask not to stay Where storm af-ter
2. I would not live al-way; no, wel-come the tomb! Since Je-sus has
3. Who, who would live al-way, a - way from his God, A - way from yon
4. Where the saints of all a - ges in harmony meet, Their Sav-ior and

storm ris - es dark o'er the way; The few cloud-y morn - ings that
lain there, I dread not its gloom; There sweet be my rest, till he
heav-en, that bliss - ful a - bode, Where the rivers of pleas - ure flow
breth-ren trans-ported to greet; While the anthems of rapt-ure un-

dawn on us here Are enough for life's woes, full enough for its cheer.
bid me a - rise, To hail him in tri-umph de - scend-ing the skies.
o'er the bright plains, And the noontide of glory e - ter - nal - ly reigns;
ceas - ing - ly roll, And the smile of the Lord is the feast of the soul?

W. A. MUHLENBERG.

497   THY WILL BE DONE. Chant.   LOWELL MASON.

Close. Thy will be done!

Mark 14: 36.

"Thy will be | done!" ‖ In devious way
The hurrying stream of | life may | run; ‖
Yet still our grateful hearts shall say, |
   "Thy will be | done."

2 " Thy will be | done!" ‖ If e'er us shine
A laddening and a | prosperous | sun. ‖

This prayer will make it more divine—|
   "Thy will be | done!"

3 "Thy will be | done!" ‖ Tho' shrouded o'er
Our | path with | gloom, | one comfort, one
Is ours :—to breathe, while we adore,|
   "Thy will be | done."

SIR J. BOWRING. 1825

498 (1146) SHINING-SHORE. 8s & 7s. Trochaic.
GEORGE F. ROOT, 1859.

1. My days are glid-ing swift-ly by, And I, a pil-grim stranger,
2. We'll gird our loins, my breth-ren dear! Our heav'nly home dis-cern-ing;
3. Should com-ing days be cold and dark, We need not cease our sing-ing;
4. Let sorrow's rud-est tem-pest blow, Each cord on earth to sev-er;

Would not de-tain them as they fly, Those hours of toil and dan-ger:
Our ab-sent Lord has left us word,—"Let ev-'ry lamp be burn-ing:"
That per-fect rest none can mo-lest, Where gold-en harps are ring-ing:
Our King says,—"Come!"—and there's our home, For-ev-er, oh! for-ev-er!

DAVID NELSON, 1835.

CHORUS.

For, oh! we stand on Jor-dan's strand, Our friends are pass-ing o-ver;

And, just be-fore, the shin-ing shore We may al-most dis-cov-er.

499   *Wayfarers.*   (1147)

WAYFARERS in the wilderness,
  By morn, and noon, and even,
Day after day, we journey on,
  With weary feet toward heaven:
CHO.—O land above! O land of love!
  The glory shineth o'er thee;
O Christ, our King! in mercy bring
  Us thither, we implore thee!

2 By day the cloud before us goes,
    By night the cloud of fire,
  To guide us o'er the trackless waste,
    To Canaan ever nigher:

3 The sea was riven from our feet,
    And so shall be the river;
  And, by the King's highway brought home,
    We'll praise his name forever:
ALEXANDER R. THOMPSON, 1869.

500 (1189) NEARER HOME. 6s.

JOHN M. EVANS, 1860.

1. One sweet - ly sol - emn tho't Comes to me o'er and o'er;
2. Near - er my Fa - ther's house Where the blest man - sions be;
3. Near - er the bound where we Must lay our bur - dens down
4. The waves of that deep sea Roll dark be - fore my sight,
5. Oh! if my mor - tal feet Have al - most gained the brink,
6. Fa - ther! per - fect my trust, That I may rest, in death,

I'm near - er home to - day Than e'er I've been be - fore:
Near - er the great white throne, Near - er the crys - tal sea;
Near - er to leave the cross, Near - er to gain the crown.
But break, the oth - er side, Up - on a shore of light.
If I am near - er home To - day than e'en I think,
On Christ, my Lord, a - lone, And thus re - sign my breath.

PHŒBE CARY, 1852, a.

CODA.

I'm near-er my home, near-er my home, Nearer my home to - day; Yes,

near-er my home in heav'n to - day, Than ev - er I've been be - fore.

501 CONSOLATION. P. M. E. S. Lorenz.

Slowly and with feeling.

1. There is no flock, how-ever watched and tended, But one dead lamb is there!
2. Let us be patient, these severe afflictions Not from the ground a-rise,
3. She is not dead, the child of our af-fection, But gone un - to that school
4. And tho' at times, impetuous with e-mo-tion, And anguish long suppressed,

There is no fire-side, how-so-e'er de-fend- ed, But has one va-cant chair!
But oft - en-times ce - les-tial ben-e - dic-tions Assume this dark disguise.
Where she no long - er needs our poor pro-tection, And Christ himself doth rule.
The swelling heart heaves moaning like the o-cean That can not be at rest:

The air is full of farewells to the dy-ing, And mournings for the dead;
We see but dim - ly thro' the mists and va-pors, A-mid these earthly damps,
In that great cloister's stillness and-se-clu-sion, By guardian an-gels led,
We will be patient—and assuage the feel-ing We can not whol-ly stay,

The heart of Ra-chel for her children cry-ing Will not be comfort - ed!
What seem to us but sad, fu - ne-real ta-pers, May be heav'n's distant lamps.
Safe from tempta-tion, safe from sin's pollu-tion, She lives whom we call dead.
By si-lence sanc-ti - fy-ing, not con-ceal-ing The grief that must have way.

Henry W. Longfellow, 1849.

502   PEACE, BE STILL. P. M.

E. S. LORENZ.

1. Peace, be still! In this night of sor-row bow; Oh, my heart, con-
2. Hold thee still! Tho' the Fa-ther scourge thee sore, Cling thou to him
3. Lord, my God! Give me grace, that I may be Thy true child, and
4. Shep-herd mine! From thy fullness give me still Faith to do and

tend not thou; What be-falls is God's own will; Peace, be still!
all the more; Let him mer-cy's work ful-fill; Hold thee still!
si-lent-ly Own thy scep-ter and thy rod; Lord, my God!
bear thy will Till the morning light shall shine; Shep-herd mine!

SCHILLER.

Copyright, 1876, by W. J. Shory, Agt.

503   REST, WEARY PILGRIM. 10s.

J. H. TENNEY.

Softly and slowly.

1. Rest, weary pilgrim, thy journey is o'er, Rest, sweetly rest, on the beautiful shore;
2. Never again shall thy storm-beat-en breast Sigh, deeply sigh, for the sweet "land of rest;"
3. Rest, weary pilgrim, thy journey is o'er, Rest, sweetly rest, on the beautiful shore;

Rit. e dim.

Safely at last thou hast reached the bright goal, Fa - - - ther-land, home of the soul.
Land of our Father, the home of the soul.

Gone to the Savior's bright mansion above, Rest (ev-er rest) in the light of his love.
Dangers and troubles shall harm thee no more, Rest (sweetly rest) on the beau-ti-ful shore.

MARIA STRAUB.

504 AS FADE THE STARS. P. M.

E. S. LORENZ.

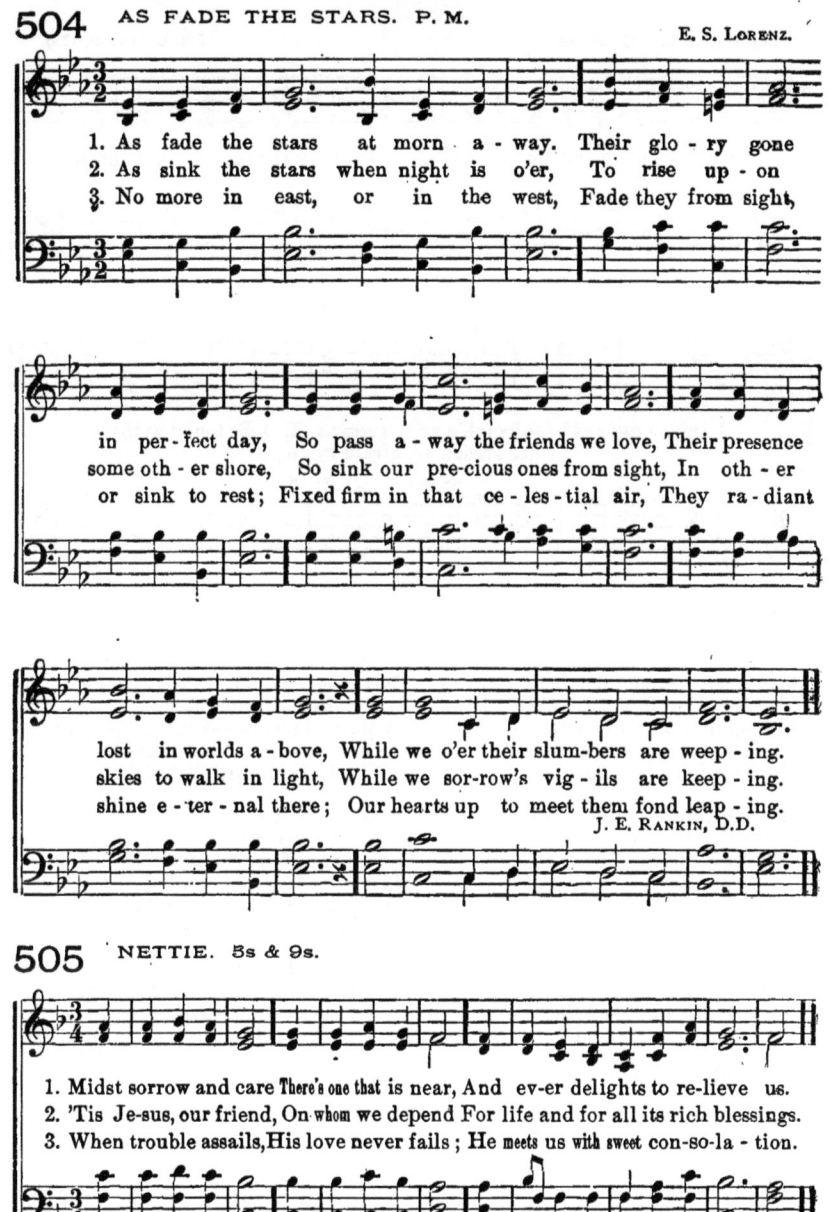

1. As fade the stars at morn a - way. Their glo - ry gone
2. As sink the stars when night is o'er, To rise up - on
3. No more in east, or in the west, Fade they from sight,

in per - fect day, So pass a - way the friends we love, Their presence
some oth - er shore, So sink our pre-cious ones from sight, In oth - er
or sink to rest; Fixed firm in that ce - les - tial air, They ra - diant

lost in worlds a - bove, While we o'er their slum-bers are weep - ing.
skies to walk in light, While we sor-row's vig - ils are keep - ing.
shine e - ter - nal there; Our hearts up to meet them fond leap - ing.

J. E. RANKIN, D.D.

505 NETTIE. 5s & 9s.

1. Midst sorrow and care There's one that is near, And ev - er delights to re-lieve us.
2. 'Tis Je-sus, our friend, On whom we depend For life and for all its rich blessings.
3. When trouble assails, His love never fails ; He meets us with sweet con-so-la - tion.

MERIBAH. C. P. M.   DR. L. MASON, 1839.

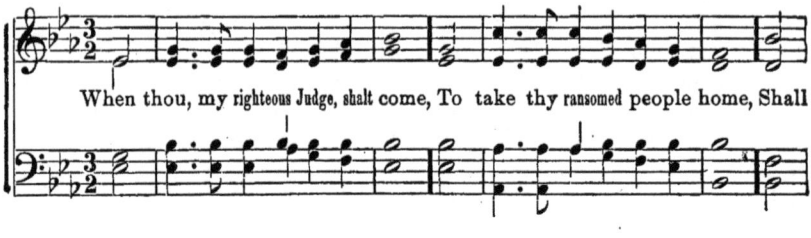

When thou, my righteous Judge, shalt come, To take thy ransomed people home, Shall

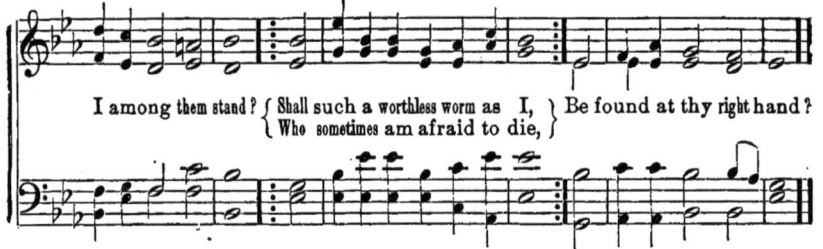

I among them stand? { Shall such a worthless worm as I, } Be found at thy right hand?
                    { Who sometimes am afraid to die, }

506 *Pleading for Acceptance.*   (1114)

WHEN thou, my righteous Judge, shalt come,
To take thy ransomed people home,
  Shall I among them stand?
Shall such a worthless worm as I,
Who sometimes am afraid to die,
  Be found at thy right hand?

2 I love to meet thy people now,
Before thy feet with them to bow,
  Though vilest of them all;
But—can I bear the piercing thought?—
What if my name should be left out,
  When thou for them shalt call?

3 O Lord, prevent it by thy grace;
Be thou my only hiding-place,
  In this th' accepted day;
Thy pardoning voice, oh, let me hear,
To still my unbelieving fear,
  Nor let me fall, I pray.

4 And when the final trump shall sound,
Among thy saints let me be found,
  To bow before thy face;
Then in triumphant strains I'll sing,
While heaven's resounding mansions ring
  With praise of sovereign grace.
            MRS. SELINA SHIRLEY, 1772.

507 *Present and Future Realities.*   (1115)

LO! on a narrow neck of land,
Between two boundless seas I stand,—
  Yet how insensible!
A point of time—a moment's space—
Removes me to yon heavenly place,
  Or shuts me up in hell!

2 O God! my inmost soul convert,
And deeply on my thoughtless heart
  Eternal things impress;
Give me to feel their solemn weight,
And save me, ere it be too late!
  Wake me to righteousness.

3 Be this my one great business here,
With holy trembling, holy fear,
  To make my calling sure;
Thine utmost counsel to fulfill,
To suffer all thy righteous will,
  And to the end endure!

4 Then Savior! then my soul receive,
Transported from the earth, to live
  And reign with thee above;
Where faith is sweetly lost in sight,
And hope, in full supreme delight,
  And everlasting love.
            CHARLES WESLEY, 1749.

MARLOW. C. M.

JOHN CHETHAM, 1832.

That aw-ful day will sure-ly come, Th'ap-point-ed hour makes haste,

When I must stand be-fore my Judge, And pass the sol-emn test.

508 Certainty of Judgment. (1103)

THAT awful day will surely come,
Th' appointed hour makes haste,
When I must stand before the Judge
And pass the solemn test.

2 Thou lovely Chief of all my joys,
Thou Sovereign of my heart,
How could I bear to hear thy voice
Pronounce the sound, " Depart!"

3 Oh, wretched state of deep despair,
To see my God remove,
And fix my dreadful station where
I must not taste his love!

4 Oh, tell me that my worthless name
Is graven on thy hands;
Show me some promise in thy book
Where my salvation stands.
ISAAC WATTS, 1707.

509 The Judgment Day. (1106)

AND must I be to judgment brought
And answer in that day,
For every vain and idle thought,
And every word I say?

2 Yes, every secret of my heart
Shall shortly be made known,
And I receive my just desert
For all that I have done.

3 How careful then I ought to live!
With what religious fear,
Who such a strict account must give
For my behavior here.

4 Thou awful Judge of quick and dead,
The watchful power bestow;
So shall I to my ways take heed,
To all I speak or do.
CHARLES WESLEY.

JUDGMENT. C. M.

E. S. LORENZ.

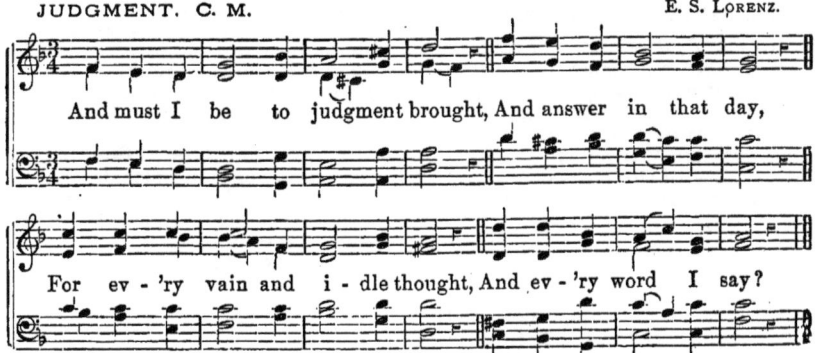

And must I be to judgment brought, And answer in that day,

For ev-'ry vain and i-dle thought, And ev-'ry word I say?

EWING. 7s & 6s. D.   A. EWING, 1853.

Je-ru-sa-lem, the golden, With milk and honey blest! Beneath thy contem-

pla - tion Sink heart and voice oppressed: I know not, oh, I know not

What social joys are there, What radiancy of glo-ry, What light beyond compare.

510   *The New Jerusalem.*

JERUSALEM, the golden,
  With milk and honey blest!
Beneath thy contemplation
  Sink heart and voice oppressed:
I know not, oh, I know not,
  What social joys are there,
What radiancy of glory,
  What light beyond compare.

2 They stand, those halls of Zion,
  All jubilant with song,
And bright with many an angel,
  And all the martyr throng;
The Prince is ever in them,
  The daylight is serene;
The pastures of the blessed
  Are decked in glorious sheen.

3 There is the throne of David;
  And there, from care released,
The song of them that triumph,
  The shout of them that feast;
And they who, with their Leader,
  Have conquered in the fight,

For ever and for ever
Are clad in robes of white.
          BERNARD OF CLUNY, 1145.
            J. M. NEALE, *tr.*, 1751.

511   *Paradise of Joy.*

FOR thee, O dear, dear Country,
  Mine eyes their vigils keep;
For very love, beholding
  Thy happy name, they weep.
The mention of thy glory
  Is unction to the breast,
And medicine in sickness,
  And love, and life, and rest.

2 Oh, sweet and blessed Country,
  The home of God's elect!
Oh, sweet and blessed Country,
  That eager hearts expect!
Jesus, in mercy bring us
  To that dear land of rest;
Who art, with God the Father,
  And Spirit, ever blest.
          BERNARD OF CLUNY, 1145.
            NEALE, *tr.*, 1751.

512

IMMANUEL'S LAND. 7s & 6s. D.

E. S. LORENZ, 1882.

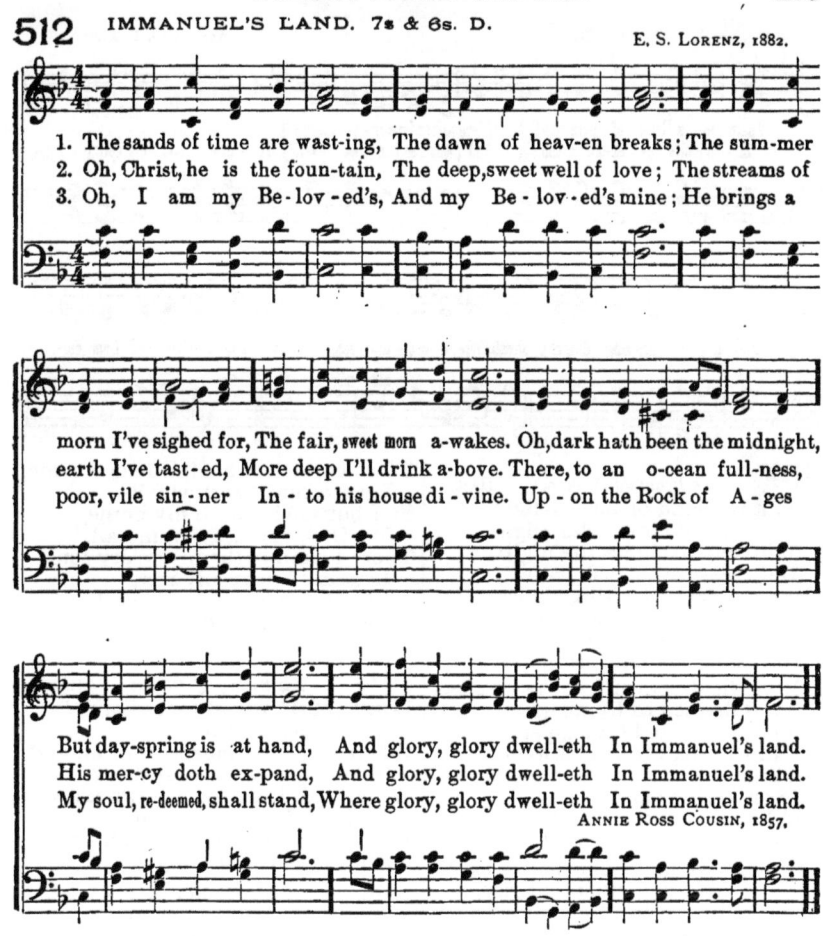

1. The sands of time are wast-ing, The dawn of heav-en breaks; The sum-mer morn I've sighed for, The fair, sweet morn a-wakes. Oh, dark hath been the midnight, But day-spring is at hand, And glory, glory dwell-eth In Immanuel's land.

2. Oh, Christ, he is the foun-tain, The deep, sweet well of love; The streams of earth I've tast-ed, More deep I'll drink a-bove. There, to an o-cean full-ness, His mer-cy doth ex-pand, And glory, glory dwell-eth In Immanuel's land.

3. Oh, I am my Be-lov-ed's, And my Be-lov-ed's mine; He brings a poor, vile sin-ner In-to his house di-vine. Up-on the Rock of A-ges My soul, re-deemed, shall stand, Where glory, glory dwell-eth In Immanuel's land.

ANNIE ROSS COUSIN, 1857.

513   Heb. 11:14.

JERUSALEM, the glorious!
  The glory of th' elect,—
O dear and future vision
  That eager hearts expect!
Ev'n now by faith I see thee,
  Ev'n here thy walls discern;
To thee my thoughts are kindled,
  And strive, and pant, and yearn!

2 The Cross is all thy splendor,
  The Crucified, thy praise;
His laud and benediction
  Thy ransomed people raise;—

Jerusalem! exulting
  On that securest shore,
I hope thee, wish thee, sing thee,
  And love thee evermore!

3 O sweet and blessed Country!
  Shall I e'er see thy face?
O sweet and blessed Country!
  Shall I e'er win thy grace?—
Exult, O dust and ashes!
  The Lord shall be thy part;
His only, his forever,
  Thou shalt be, and thou art!

BERNARD OF CLUNY, 1145.
NEALE, tr. 1739.

VARINA. C. M. D.　　　　　　　　　　Arr. by G. F. ROOT.

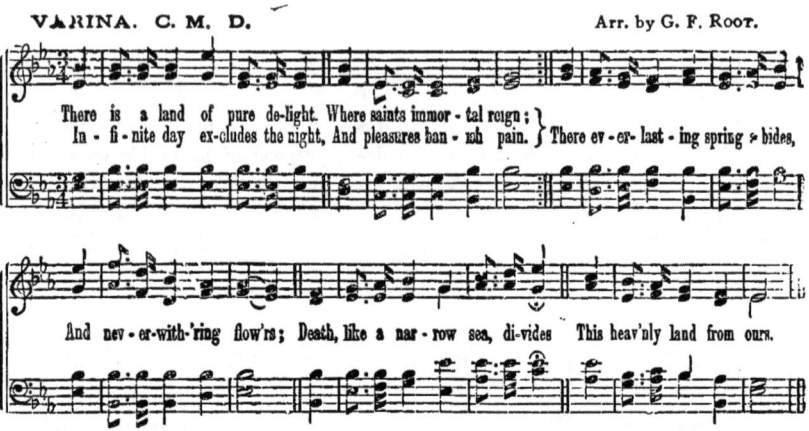

There is a land of pure delight. Where saints immor-tal reign;
In-fi-nite day ex-cludes the night, And pleasures ban-ish pain. } There ev-er-last-ing spring a-bides,

And nev-er-with-'ring flow'rs; Death, like a nar-row sea, di-vides This heav'nly land from ours.

514 *The Heavenly Canaan.* (1116)

THERE is a land of pure delight,
　Where saints immortal reign;
Infinite day excludes the night,
　And pleasures banish pain.
There everlasting spring abides,
　And never-withering flowers;
Death, like a narrow sea, divides
　This heavenly land from ours.

2 Sweet fields beyond the swelling flood
　Stand dressed in living green;
So to the Jews old Canaan stood,
　While Jordan rolled between.
But timorous mortals start and shrink
　To cross this narrow sea,
And linger, shivering on the brink,
　And fear to launch away.

3 O could we make our doubts remove,
　Those gloomy doubts that rise,
And see the Canaan that we love,
　With unbeclouded eyes—
Could we but climb where Moses stood,
　And view the landscape o'er,
Not Jordan's stream, nor death's cold flood,
　Should fright us from the shore.
　　　　　ISAAC WATTS, 1709.

515 *Heavenly Rest in Anticipation.* (1118)

WHEN I can read my title clear
　To mansions in the skies,
I'll bid farewell to every fear,
　And wipe my weeping eyes.
Should earth against my soul engage,
　And fiery darts be hurled,
Then I can smile at Satan's rage,
　And face a frowning world.

2 Let cares like a wild deluge come,
　Let storms of sorrow fall—
So I but safely reach my home,
　My God, my heaven, my all.
There I shall bathe my weary soul
　In seas of heavenly rest,
And not a wave of trouble r ll
　Across my peaceful breast.
　　　　　ISAAC WATTS, 1707.

516 *The Society of Heaven* (1126)

JERUSALEM! my glorious home!
　Name ever dear to me!
When shall my labors have an end,
　In joy, and peace, and thee?
When shall these eyes thy heaven-built walls
　And pearly gates behold?
Thy bulwarks with salvation strong,
　And streets of shining gold?

2 Oh, when, thou city of my God,
　Shall I thy courts ascend,
Where congregations ne'er break up,
　And Sabbaths have no end?
There happier bowers than Eden's bloom,
　Nor sin nor sorrow know:
Blest seats! through rude and stormy scenes
　I onward press to you.

3 Why should I shrink at pain and woe
　Or feel at death dismay?
I've Canaan's goodly land in view,
　And realms of endless day.
Jerusalem! my glorious home!
　My soul still pants for thee;
Then shall my labors have an end,
　When I thy joys shall see.
　　　　　FRANCIS BAKER (?), 1801.

517 (1141) OVER THERE. P. M.

TULLIUS C. O'KANE.

By permission.

1. Oh, think of the home over there, By the side of the riv-er of light,
2. Oh, think of the friends over there, Who before us the journey have trod,
3. My Sav-ior is now o-ver there, There my kindred and friends are at rest;
4. I'll soon be at home o-ver there, For the end of my journey I see;

o-ver there,

Where the saints, all immortal and fair, Are robed in their gar-ments of white, o-ver there.
Of the songs that they breathe on the air, In their home in the palace of God, o-ver there.
Then away from my sorrow and care, Let me fly to the land of the blest, o-ver there.
Many dear to my heart, o-ver there, Are watching and waiting for me, o-ver there.

REV. D. W. C. HUNTINGTON.

REFRAIN.

Over there, over there, Oh, think of the home over there, o-ver there;
Oh, think of the friends over there, o-ver there;
My Sav-ior is now over there, o-ver there;
Over there, over there, I'll soon be at home over there, o-ver there;

Over there, over there, over there, Oh, think of the home over there.
Oh, think of the friends over there.
My Sav-ior is now over there.
Over there, over there, I'll soon be at home over there.

518(1150) SWEET BY AND BY. P. M.

J. P. WEBSTER.

1. There's a land that is fair-er than day, And by faith we can see it a - far;
2. We shall sing on that beautiful shore The me - lo - di-ous songs of the blest,
3. To our boun-ti - ful Fa-ther a-bove We will of - fer the trib-ute of praise,
4. We shall rest on that beautiful shore, In the joys of the saved we shall share;
5. We shall meet, we shall sing, we shall reign, In the land where the saved never die;

For the Fa-ther waits o - ver the way, To prepare us a dwelling-place there.
And our spir - its shall sorrow no more, Not a sigh for the blessing of rest.
For the glo - ri-ous gift of his love, And the blessings that hallow our days.
All our pil-grim-age toil will be o'er, And the conqueror's crown we shall wear.
We shall rest, free from sorrow and pain, Safe at home in the sweet by and by.

S. F. BENNETT.

CHORUS.

In the sweet   by and by,   We shall meet on that beautiful shore;
by and by, in the sweet by and by,   by and by;

Repeat Chorus pp.

In the sweet   by and by,   We shall meet on that beau-ti-ful shore.
by and by, in the sweet by and by,

519 (1148) REST FOR THE WEARY. 8s & 7s. J. W. DADMUN, 1858.

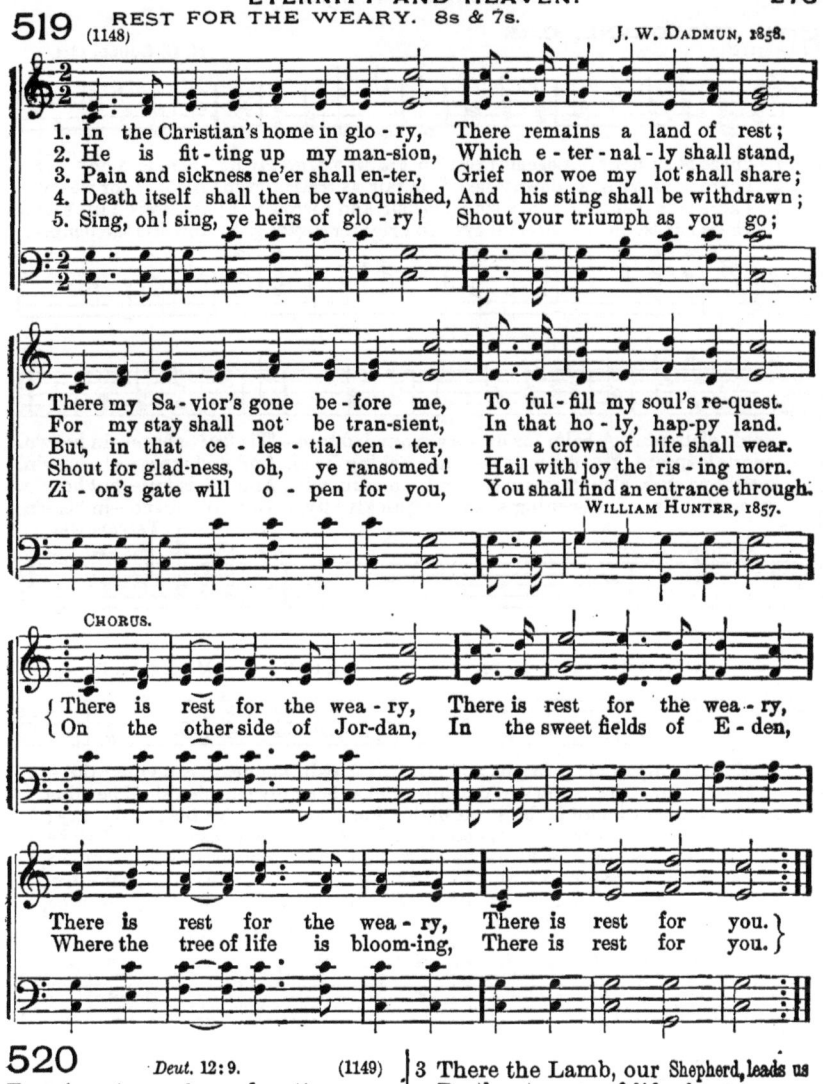

1. In the Christian's home in glo - ry, There remains a land of rest;
2. He is fit - ting up my man-sion, Which e - ter - nal - ly shall stand,
3. Pain and sickness ne'er shall en-ter, Grief nor woe my lot shall share;
4. Death itself shall then be vanquished, And his sting shall be withdrawn;
5. Sing, oh! sing, ye heirs of glo - ry! Shout your triumph as you go;

There my Sa - vior's gone be - fore me, To ful - fill my soul's re-quest.
For my stay shall not be tran-sient, In that ho - ly, hap-py land.
But, in that ce - les - tial cen - ter, I a crown of life shall wear.
Shout for glad-ness, oh, ye ransomed! Hail with joy the ris - ing morn.
Zi - on's gate will o - pen for you, You shall find an entrance through.

WILLIAM HUNTER, 1857.

CHORUS.

There is rest for the wea - ry, There is rest for the wea - ry,
On the other side of Jor-dan, In the sweet fields of E - den,

There is rest for the wea - ry, There is rest for you.
Where the tree of life is bloom-ing, There is rest for you.

520 Deut. 12: 9. (1149)

THIS is not my place of resting,—
  Mine 's a city yet to come;
Onward to it I am hasting—
  On to my eternal home.

2 In it all is light and glory;
  O'er it shines a nightless day :
Every trace of sin's sad story,
  All the curse hath passed away ;

3 There the Lamb, our Shepherd, leads us
  By the streams of life along—
On the freshest pastures feeds us,
  Turns our sighing into song.

4 Soon we pass this desert dreary,
  Soon we bid farewell to pain ;
Never more are sad or weary,
  Never, never sin again !

H. BONAR.

18

521 (1121) WOODLAND. C. M.

N. D. GOULD, 1832.

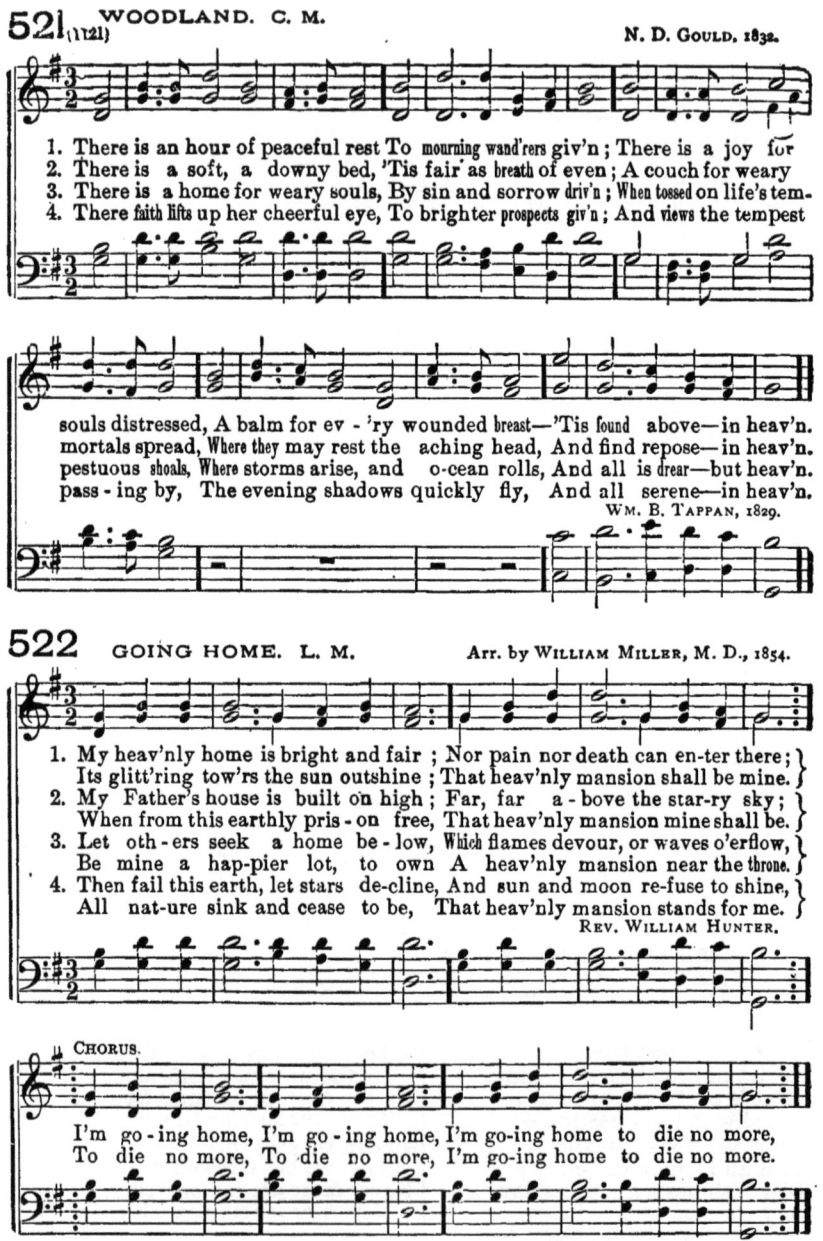

1. There is an hour of peaceful rest To mourning wand'rers giv'n; There is a joy for
2. There is a soft, a downy bed, 'Tis fair as breath of even; A couch for weary
3. There is a home for weary souls, By sin and sorrow driv'n; When tossed on life's tem-
4. There faith lifts up her cheerful eye, To brighter prospects giv'n; And views the tempest

souls distressed, A balm for ev - 'ry wounded breast—'Tis found above—in heav'n.
mortals spread, Where they may rest the aching head, And find repose—in heav'n.
pestuous shoals, Where storms arise, and o-cean rolls, And all is drear—but heav'n.
pass - ing by, The evening shadows quickly fly, And all serene—in heav'n.

WM. B. TAPPAN, 1829.

522 GOING HOME. L. M.

Arr. by WILLIAM MILLER, M. D., 1854.

1. My heav'nly home is bright and fair; Nor pain nor death can en-ter there; ⎫
   Its glitt'ring tow'rs the sun outshine; That heav'nly mansion shall be mine. ⎭
2. My Father's house is built on high; Far, far a - bove the star-ry sky; ⎫
   When from this earthly pris - on free, That heav'nly mansion mine shall be. ⎭
3. Let oth - ers seek a home be - low, Which flames devour, or waves o'erflow, ⎫
   Be mine a hap-pier lot, to own A heav'nly mansion near the throne. ⎭
4. Then fail this earth, let stars de-cline, And sun and moon re-fuse to shine, ⎫
   All nat-ure sink and cease to be, That heav'nly mansion stands for me. ⎭

REV. WILLIAM HUNTER.

CHORUS.

I'm go - ing home, I'm go - ing home, I'm go-ing home to die no more,
To die no more, To die no more, I'm go-ing home to die no more.

523₍₁₁₄₂₎ SWEET HOME. 11s.

Sir Henry Rowley Bishop.

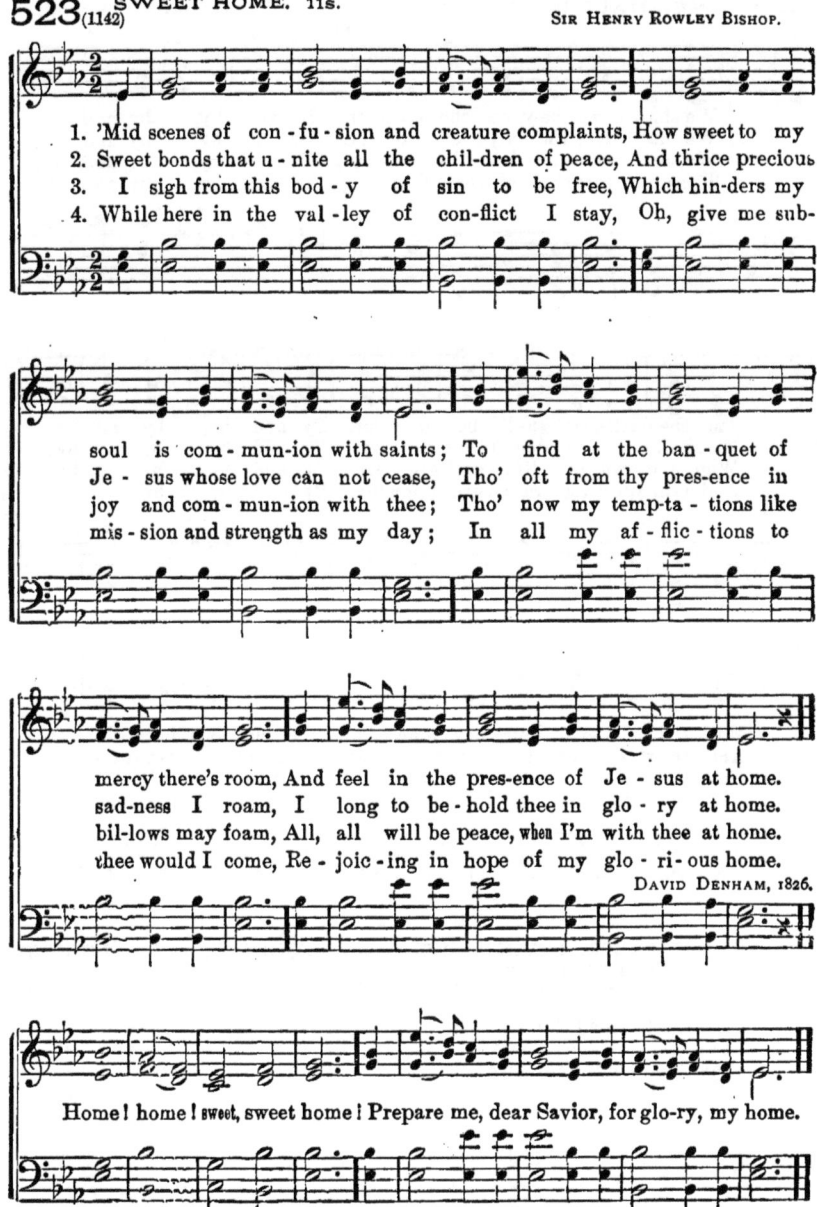

1. 'Mid scenes of con-fu-sion and creature complaints, How sweet to my
2. Sweet bonds that u-nite all the chil-dren of peace, And thrice precious
3. I sigh from this bod-y of sin to be free, Which hin-ders my
4. While here in the val-ley of con-flict I stay, Oh, give me sub-

soul is com-mun-ion with saints; To find at the ban-quet of
Je-sus whose love can not cease, Tho' oft from thy pres-ence in
joy and com-mun-ion with thee; Tho' now my temp-ta-tions like
mis-sion and strength as my day; In all my af-flic-tions to

mercy there's room, And feel in the pres-ence of Je-sus at home.
sad-ness I roam, I long to be-hold thee in glo-ry at home.
bil-lows may foam, All, all will be peace, when I'm with thee at home.
thee would I come, Re-joic-ing in hope of my glo-ri-ous home.

David Denham, 1826.

Home! home! sweet, sweet home! Prepare me, dear Savior, for glo-ry, my home.

524 WE SHALL MEET. P. M. HUBERT P. MAIN, 1867.

1. We shall meet be-yond the riv - er, By and by, by and by;
2. We shall strike the harps of glo - ry, By and by, by and by;
3. We shall see . and be like Je - sus, By and by, by and by;
4. There our tears shall all cease flow - ing, By and by, by and by;

And the dark-ness shall be o - ver, By and by, by and by;
We shall sing re - demption's sto - ry, By and by, by and by;
Who a crown of life will give us, By and by, by and by;
And with sweet-est rapt - ure knowing, By and by, by and by;

With the toil - some jour - ney done, And the glo-rious bat - tle won,
And the strains for ev - er - more Shall re-sound in sweet-ness o'er,
And the an - gels who ful - fill All the mandates of his will
All the blest ones who have gone To the land of life and song,—

We shall shine forth as the sun, By and by, by and by.
Yon - der ev - er - last - ing shore, By and by, by and by.
Shall at - tend, and love us still, By and by, by and by.
We with shoutings shall re - join, By and by, by and by.

REV. JOHN ATKINSON.

525 DELIVERANCE WILL COME. .7s & 6s.

REV. JNO. B. MATTHIAS, 1836.

1. I saw a way-worn trav-'ler, In tat-tered gar-ments clad,
His back was la-den heav-y, His strength was al-most gone,

2. The sum-mer sun was shin-ing, The sweat was on his brow,
But he kept press-ing on-ward, For he was wend-ing home;

3. The song-sters in the ar-bor That stood be-side the way
His watchword be-ing "On-ward," He stopped his ears and run,

And strug-gling up the moun-tain, It seemed that he was sad; }
Yet he shout-ed as he jour-neyed, De-liv-er-ance will come. }

His gar-ments worn and dust-y, His step seemed ver-y slow; }
Still shout-ing as he jour-neyed, De-liv-er-ance will come. }

At-tract-ed his at-ten-tion, In-vit-ing his de-lay: }
Still shout-ing as he jour-neyed, De-liv-er-ance will come. }

REFRAIN.

Then palms of vic-to-ry, crowns of glo-ry, Palms of vic-to-ry I shall wear.

4 I saw him in the evening,
  The sun was bending low,
He'd overtopped the mountain
  And reached the vale below;
He saw the golden city,—
  His everlasting home,—
And shouted loud, Hosanna,
  Deliverance will come!

5 While gazing on that city,
  Just o'er the narrow flood,
A band of holy angels
  Came from the throne of God;

They bore him on their pinions
  Safe o'er the dashing foam,
And joined him in his triumph,—
  Deliverance has come!

6 I heard the song of triumph
  They sang upon that shore,
Saying, Jesus has redeemed us
  To suffer nevermore:
Then, casting his eyes backward
  On the race which he had run,
He shouted loud, Hosanna,
  Deliverance has come!

J. B. MATTHIAS.

526   HOME OF THE SOUL. P. M.

PHILIP PHILLIPS.

1. I will sing you a song of that beau-ti-ful land, The far a-way home
2. Oh, that home of the soul, in my vis-ions and dreams Its bright jasper walls
3. That unchangeable home is for you and for me, Where Je - sus of Naz-
4. Oh, how sweet it will be in that beau-ti-ful land, So free from all sor-

of the soul; Where no storms ev-er beat on the glit-ter-ing strand, While the years
I can see; Till I fan - cy but thin-ly the veil in-ter-venes   Be - tween
a-reth stands; The King of all kingdoms for-ev - er is he, And he hold-
row and pain; With songs on our lips and with harps in our hands, To meet

of e - ter - ni - ty   roll, While the years of e - ter - ni - ty roll; Where no storms
the fair cit - y and me,   Be-tween the fair cit - y and me; Till I fan-
eth our crowns in his hands, And he holdeth our crowns in his hands; The King
one an-oth - er a-gain,   To meet one an - oth - er a-gain; With songs

ev - er beat on the glit-ter-ing strand, While the years of e - ter - ni - ty roll.
cy but thin-ly the veil in-ter-venes   Be-tween the fair cit - y and me.
of all kingdoms for-ev - er is   he, And he hold-eth our crowns in his hands.
on our lips and with harps in our hands, To meet one an - oth - er a - gain.

MRS. ELLEN H. GATES.

527(1134) FOREVER WITH THE LORD. S. M. D.

I. B. WOODBURY.

1. "For-ev - er with the Lord!" A-men, so let it be; Life from the
2. My Father's house on high, Home of my soul, how near, At times, to
3. Yet doubts still in - ter - vene, And all my com-fort flies; Like No - ah's

dead is in that word, 'Tis im-mor-tal - i - ty. Here in the bod - y pent,
faith's as-pir-ing eye Thy gold-en gates ap-pear. Ah! then my spir-it faints
dove, I flit between Rough seas and stormy skies. A - non the clouds de-part,

Ab-sent from him, I roam, Yet night - ly pitch my mov-ing tent A day's march
To reach the land I love; The bright in - her - it-ance of saints—Je - ru - sa-
The wind and waters cease, While sweet-ly o'er my gladdened heart Expands the

near-er home; Near-er home, near-er home, A day's march near - er home.
lem a-bove; Home a-bove, home a-bove, Je - ru - sa - lem a - bove.
bow of peace: Bow of peace, bow of peace, Ex-pands the bow of peace.

JAMES MONTGOMERY, 1835.

528(1117) ON JORDAN'S STORMY BANKS. C. M.

T. C. O'KANE.

1. On Jor-dan's storm-y banks I stand, And cast a wish-ful eye
2. O'er all those wide - ex-tend - ed plains Shines one e - ter - nal day;
3. When shall I reach that hap - py place, And be for - ev - er blest?
4. Filled with de-light, my raptured soul Would here no long - er stay;

To Canaan's fair and hap - py land, Where my pos - ses - sions lie.
There God the Son for - ev - er reigns, And scat-ters night a - way.
When shall I see my Fa-ther's face, And in his bo - som rest?
Tho' Jor-dan's waves a-round me roll, Fear-less I'd launch a - way.

SAMUEL STENNETT, 1787.

CHORUS.

We will rest in the fair and hap-py land, (by and by), Just a-cross on the ev - er-green shore, . . . Sing the song of Mo-ses
ev - er-green shore,

and the Lamb, by and by, And dwell with Je - sus ev - er-more.

529 SHALL WE GATHER. 8s & 7s.   ROBERT LOWRY, 1864.

1. Shall we gath-er at the riv - er Where bright an - gel feet have trod;
2. On the mar-gin of the riv - er Wash-ing up its sil - ver spray,
3. Ere we reach the shin-ing riv - er Lay we ev -'ry bur-den down;
4. At the smil-ing of the riv - er Mir - ror of the Sav-ior's face,
5. Soon we'll reach the sil - ver riv - er, Soon our pil-grim-age will cease;

With its crys-tal tide for - ev - er Flowing by the throne of God.
We will walk and worship ev - er, All the hap - py, gold-en day.
Grace our spir-its will de - liv - er, And pro-vide a robe and crown.
Saints whom death will nev - er sev - er Lift their songs of sav - ing grace.
Soon our hap-py hearts will quiv - er With the mel - o - dy of peace.

ROBERT LOWRY.

CHORUS.

Yes, we'll gath-er at the riv - er, The beauti-ful, the beauti-ful riv - er,—

Gath-er with the saints at the riv - er That flows by the throne of God.

530 THE FUTURE. 8s & 7s. D.

A. A. ARMEN.

1. Oh, I oft-en sit and ponder, When the sun is sink-ing low, Where shall
2. Shall I be at work for Je-sus, Whilst he leads me by the hand, And to
3. But perhaps my work for Jesus Soon in fu-ture may be done, All my

yon-der fu-ture find me? Does but God in heaven know? Shall I be a-
those around be saying, Come and join this hap-py band? Come, for all things
earth-ly tri-als end-ed, And my crown in heav-en won; Then for-ev-er

mong the liv-ing? Shall I be a-mong the free? Where-so-e'er my path be
now are read-y, Come, his faithful foll'wer be; Oh, where'er my path be
with the ran-somed Thro' e-ter-ni-ty I'd be Chanting hymns to him who

CHORUS.

leading, Savior, keep my heart with thee.
leading, Savior, keep my heart with thee. Oh, the fu- -ture lies before me,
bo't me With his blood, shed on a tree. Oh, the future lies before me, and I know not where I'll be,

MISS JENNIE STOUT.

And I know .... not where I'll be; But where'er .... my
Oh, the fu-ture lies be-fore me, and I know not where I'll be; But wher-e'er my path be lead-ing,

THE FUTURE. Concluded.

path be lead - - ing, Savior, keep . . . . . my heart with thee.

Savior, keep my heart with thee, But wher-e'er my path be lead-ing, Sav - ior, keep my heart with thee.

531   GOING HOME AT LAST. 7s & 6s.

E. S. LORENZ.

1. The eve - ning shades are fall-ing, The sun is sink - ing fast: The
2. The road's been long and drea-ry, The toils came thick and fast; In
3. We now are near - ing heav - en, And soon shall be at rest; Our
4. Oh, praise the Lord for - ev - er, Our sor - rows are all past; We'll

CHORUS.

Ho - ly One is call-ing, We're go-ing home at last.
bod - y weak and wea-ry, We're go-ing home at last.   Going home at last,
crowns will soon be giv - en, We're go-ing home at last.
part no more, no, nev - er; We are at home at last.

REV. W. GOSSETT.

Going home at last; The march will soon be over, We're going home at last.

532 THE SWEET STORY. P. M.　　　J. C. Englebrecht.

1. I think when I read that sweet sto-ry of old, When Je-sus was here a-mong
2. I wish that his hands had been placed on my head, His arms had been thrown around
3. Yet still to his footstool in pray'r I may go, And ask for a share in his

men, How he called lit-tle chil-dren as lambs to his fold, I should
me, And that I might have seen his kind look when he said, "Let the
love; And if I now earn-est-ly seek him be-low, I shall

Fine. REFRAIN.　　　D. S.

like to have been with them then. I should like to have been with them then,
lit-tle ones come un-to me." "Let the lit-tle ones come un-to me,"
see him and hear him a-bove. I shall see him and hear him a-bove,

MRS. JEMIMA LUKE, 1841.

533(1180) SILOAM. C. M.　　　I. B. WOODBURY, 1850.

With gentleness.

1. By cool Si-lo-am's sha-dy rill How fair the lil-y grows!
2. Lo! such the child whose ear-ly feet The paths of peace have trod,
3. By cool Si-lo-am's sha-dy rill The lil-y must de-cay;
4. And soon, too soon, the win-try hour Of man's ma-tur-er age

How sweet the breath, be-neath the hill, Of Shar-on's dew-y rose!
Whose se-cret heart, with influence sweet, Is up-ward drawn to God.
The rose that blooms be-neath the hill, Must short-ly fade a-way.
Will shake the soul with sor-row's pow'r, And storm-y pas-sion's rage.

REGINALD HEBER, 1812.

SWANWICK. C. M.   J. LUCAS, 1805.

God of the u - ni-verse! to thee This sa-cred house we rear, And now, with songs and bended knee, In-voke thy presence here, Invoke thy presence here.

534 *A New House of Worship.*   (1176)

GOD of the universe! to thee
  This sacred house we rear,
And now, with songs and bended knee,
  Invoke thy presence here.

2 Long may this echoing dome resound
  The praises of thy name,
These hallowed walls to all around
  The Triune God proclaim.

3 Here let thy love, thy presence dwell;
  Thy glory here make known ;
Thy people's home, oh! come and fill,
  And seal it as thine own.

4 And, when the last long Sabbath morn
  Upon the just shall rise,
May all who own thee here be borne
  To mansions in the skies.
                          MISS MARY O——, 1841.

535   *Church Opening.*

ARISE, O King of grace, arise,
  And enter to thy rest;
Lo! thy church waits, with longing eyes,
  Thus to be owned and blest.

2 Enter with all thy glorious train,
  Thy Spirit and thy word ;
All that the ark did once contain
  Could no such grace afford.

3 Here, mighty God, accept our vows,
  Here let thy praise be spread ;
Bless the provisions of thy house,
  And fill thy poor with bread.

4 Here let the Son of David reign,
  Let God's Anointed shine ;
Justice and truth his court maintain,
  With love and power divine.

5 Here let him hold a lasting throne,
  And as his kingdom grows,
Fresh honors shall adorn his crown,
  And shame confound his foes.
                              ISAAC WATTS.

536   *Temperance Meeting.*   (1186)

'T IS thine alone, almighty Name,
  To raise the dead to life,
The lost inebriate to reclaim
  From passion's fearful strife.

2 What ruin hath intemperance wrought,
  How widely roll its waves !
How many myriads hath it brought
  To fill dishonored graves !

3 And see, O Lord! what numbers still
  Are maddened by the bowl,
Led captive at the tyrant's will,
  In bondage heart and soul !

4 Stretch forth thy hand, O God, our King!
  And break the galling chain;
Deliverance to the captive bring,
  And end th' usurper's reign.

5 The cause of Temperance is thine own.
  Our plans and efforts bless;
We trust, O Lord! in thee alone
  To crown them with success.
                          EDWIN F. HATFIELD, 1872.

537 LET US ARISE. P. M.

E., S. LORENZ.

1. Do you slumber in your tent, Christian soldier, While the foe is spread-ing
2. Can you sleep while homes are rent, Christian soldier? Are not heavens turned to
3. Can you lin-ger in your tent, Christian soldier? Sa - tan's smiling o'er your
4. Let us rise in ho- ly wrath, Christian soldiers, Crush the e - vil 'neath the

woe thro' the land? Do you note his ris-ing pow'r, Growing bolder ev - 'ry
hells by his pow'r? Mark you not the mother's sigh? Hear you not the children's
i - dle de - lay; Thousands perish while you wait, While you counsel and de-
heel of our might! Counting cost, no longer wait; Forward, manhood of the

D. S. *Tho' our numbers may be few, God will lead us grand-ly*

Fine. CHORUS.

hour? Will he not our land devour while you stand?
cry? See you not their loved ones die ev - 'ry hour? Let us a-rise! all u-nite!
bate; Heed you not their aw-ful fate as they stray?
state! For in God your strength is great for the right.

E. S. LORENZ.

thro'. And our arms with strength endue by his might.

D. S.

Let us a-rise in our might! Let us a-rise! speak for God and the right.

WEBB. 7s & 6s. D. GEORGE JAMES WEBB, 1830.

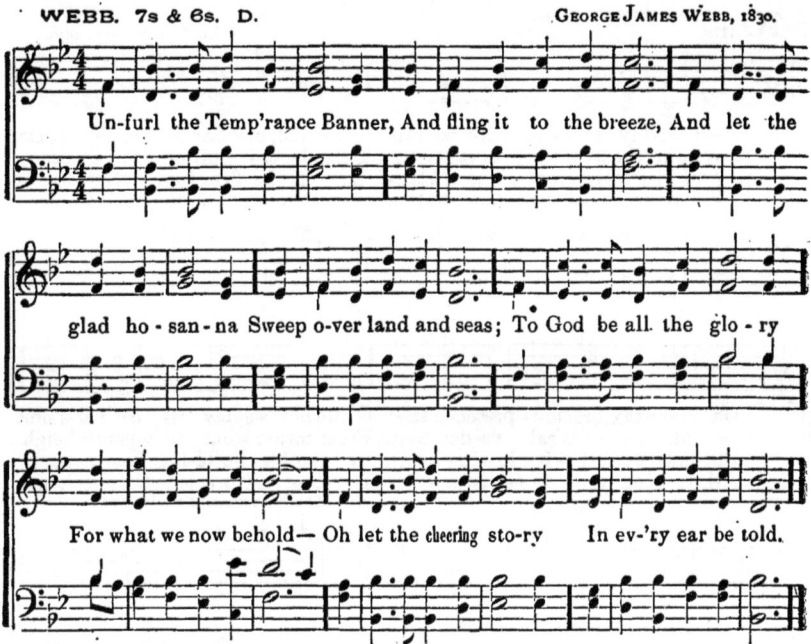

Un-furl the Temp'rance Banner, And fling it to the breeze, And let the

glad ho-san-na Sweep o-ver land and seas; To God be all the glo-ry

For what we now behold— Oh let the cheering sto-ry In ev-'ry ear be told.

538 *The Temperance Banner* (1192)

UNFURL the Temp'rance Banner,
 And fling it to the breeze,
And let the glad hosanna
 Sweep over land and seas;
To God be all the glory
 For what we now behold—
Oh, let the cheering story
 In every ear be told.

2 The drunkard shall not perish
 In Alcohol's dire chain,
But wife and children cherish
 Within his home again;
And sobered men, repenting,
 Will bow at Jesus' feet,
Their thankful hearts relenting
 Before the mercy-seat.

3 A new-waked zeal is burning
 In this and every land,
And thousands now are turning
 To join our temp'rance band;
The light of truth is shining
 In many a darkened soul;
Ere long its rays combining
 Will blaze from pole to pole.

539 *The Crystal Fountain.* (1193)

FROM brightest crystal fountain
 That flows in beauty free,
By shady hill and mountain
 Fill high the cup for me!
Sing of the sparkling waters,
 Sing of the cooling spring—
Let freedom's sons and daughters
 Their joyous tribute bring.

2 From many a happy dwelling
 Late misery's dark abode,
The joyous peal is swelling—
 The hymn of praise to God,
Glad songs are now ascending
 From many a thankful heart,
Hope, Joy, and Peace are blending
 And each their aid impart.

3 We'll join the tuneful chorus
 And raise our song on high!
The cheering view before us
 Delights the raptured eye;
The glorious cause is gaining
 New strength from day to day,
The drunkard host is waning
 Before cold water's sway.

540 (1178) **HEBRON. L. M.**

LOWELL MASON, 1830.

1. An earthly tem-ple here we raise, Lord God, our Sav-ior! to thy praise;
2. Within the house thy servants rear, Deign by thy Spir-it to ap-pear;
3. And when this temple, "made with hands," Up-on its firm foun-dation stands,
4. Where every polished stone shall be A hu-man soul won back to thee;

Oh! make thy gracious presence known, While now we lay its cor-ner-stone.
On all its walls sal-va-tion write, From corner-stone to topmost height.
Oh! may we all with lov-ing heart, In no-bler build-ing bear a part:
All rest-ing up-on Christ a-lone,—The chief and precious Corner-Stone.

MRS. CATHERINE H. JOHNSON, 1866.

541 (1217) **CHESTERFIELD. C. M.**

THOMAS HAWEIS, 1792.

1. Lord! while for all man-kind we pray, Of ev-'ry clime and coast,
2. Oh! guard our shore from ev-'ry foe, With peace our bor-ders bless,
3. U-nite us in the sa-cred love Of knowledge, truth, and thee;
4. Lord of the na-tions! thus to thee Our coun-try we commend;

Oh! hear us for our na-tive land,—The land we love the most.
With prosperous times our cit-ies crown, Our fields with plenteous-ness.
And let our hills and val-leys shout The songs of lib-er-ty.
Be thou her Ref-uge and her Trust, Her ev-er-last-ing friend.

JOHN REYNELL WREFORD, 1837.

AMERICA. 6s & 4s.   Adapted by HENRY CAREY, *obit.* 1743.

My coun-try! 'tis of thee, Sweet land of lib - er - ty, Of thee I sing: Land where my
fa-thers died! Land of the pilgrim's pride! From ev - 'ry mount-ain side Let free-dom ring!

42 [FIRST VERSE INSERTED IN MUSIC.]
America. (1226)

2 My native country, thee,—
Land of the noble, free,—
  Thy name—I love;
I love thy rocks and rills,
Thy woods and templed hills:
My heart with rapture thrills
  Like that above.

3 Let music swell the breeze,
And ring, from all the trees,
  Sweet freedom's song:
Let mortal tongues awake;
Let all that breathe partake;
Let rocks their silence break,—
  The sound prolong.

4 Our fathers' God! to thee,
Author of liberty,
  To thee we sing:
Long may our land be bright,
With freedom's holy light;
Protect us, by thy might,
  Great God, our King!
                SAMUEL F. SMITH, 1832.

43 *Our Native Land.* (1227)

GOD bless our native land!
Firm may she ever stand,
  Through storm and night;
When the wild tempests rave,
Ruler of winds and wave!
Do thou our country save,
  By thy great might.

2 For her our prayer shall rise
To God above the skies;
  On him we wait;
Thou, who art ever nigh,
Guardian with watchful eye!
To thee aloud we cry,—
  God save the state!
                JOHN S. DWIGHT, 1844

544 *The Poor.*

LORD, from thy blessed throne,
Sorrow look down upon!
  God save the poor!
Teach them true liberty,
Make them from tyrants free,
Let their homes happy be!
  God save the poor!

2 The arms of wicked men
Do thou with might restrain—
  God save the poor!
Raise thou their lowliness,
Succor thou their distress,
Thou whom the meanest bless!
  God save the poor!

3 Give them stanch honesty,
Let their pride manly be—
  God save the poor!
Help them to hold the right,
Give them both truth and might,
Lord of all life and light!
  God save the poor!
                NICOLL.

19

545　　OUR GLAD JUBILEE. P. M.　　　　　　WM. F. SHERWIN.

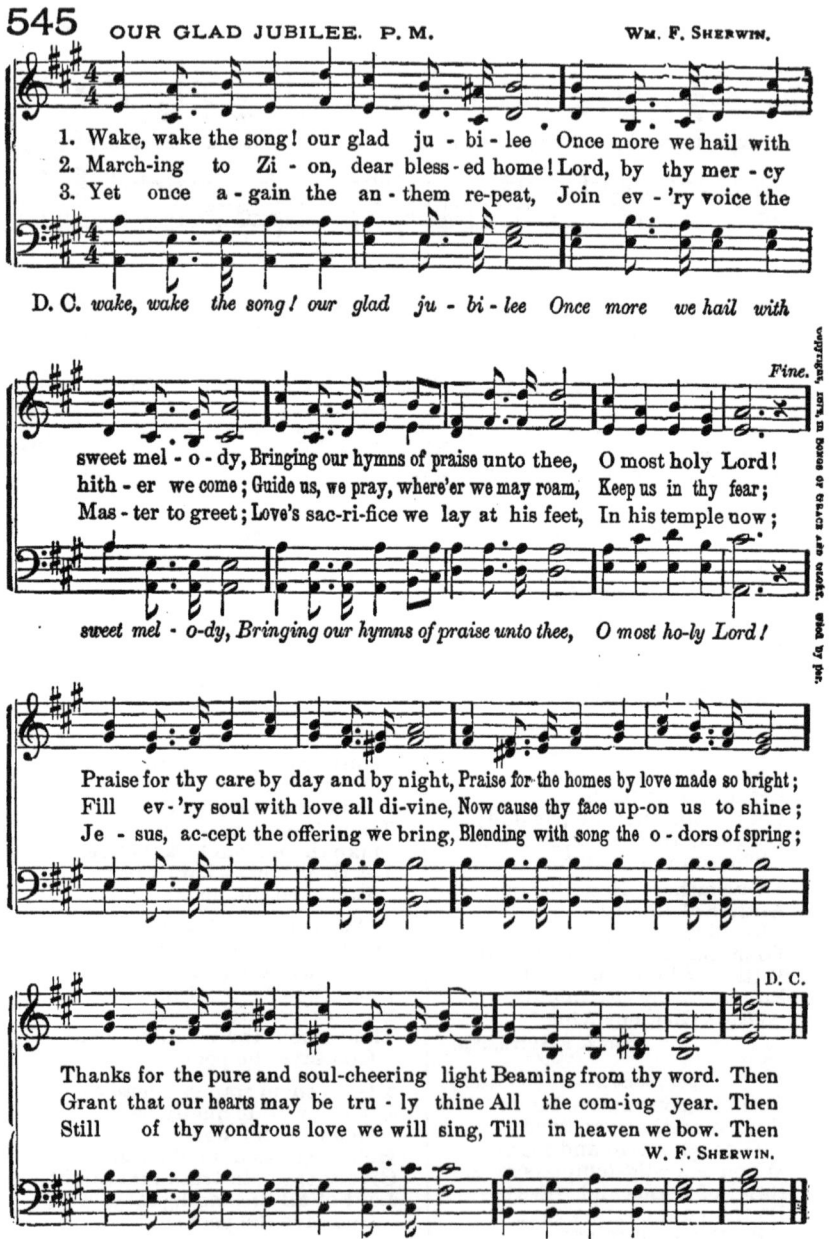

1. Wake, wake the song! our glad ju - bi - lee Once more we hail with
2. March-ing to Zi - on, dear bless - ed home! Lord, by thy mer - cy
3. Yet once a - gain the an - them re-peat, Join ev - 'ry voice the

D. C. *wake, wake the song! our glad ju - bi - lee Once more we hail with*

sweet mel - o - dy, Bringing our hymns of praise unto thee, O most holy Lord!
hith - er we come; Guide us, we pray, where'er we may roam, Keep us in thy fear;
Mas - ter to greet; Love's sac-ri-fice we lay at his feet, In his temple now;

sweet mel - o-dy, Bringing our hymns of praise unto thee, O most ho-ly Lord!

Praise for thy care by day and by night, Praise for the homes by love made so bright;
Fill ev - 'ry soul with love all di-vine, Now cause thy face up-on us to shine;
Je - sus, ac-cept the offering we bring, Blending with song the o - dors of spring;

D. C.

Thanks for the pure and soul-cheering light Beaming from thy word. Then
Grant that our hearts may be tru - ly thine All the com-ing year. Then
Still of thy wondrous love we will sing, Till in heaven we bow. Then

W. F. SHERWIN.

546(1223) LAUDO. 7s.

E. S. LORENZ.

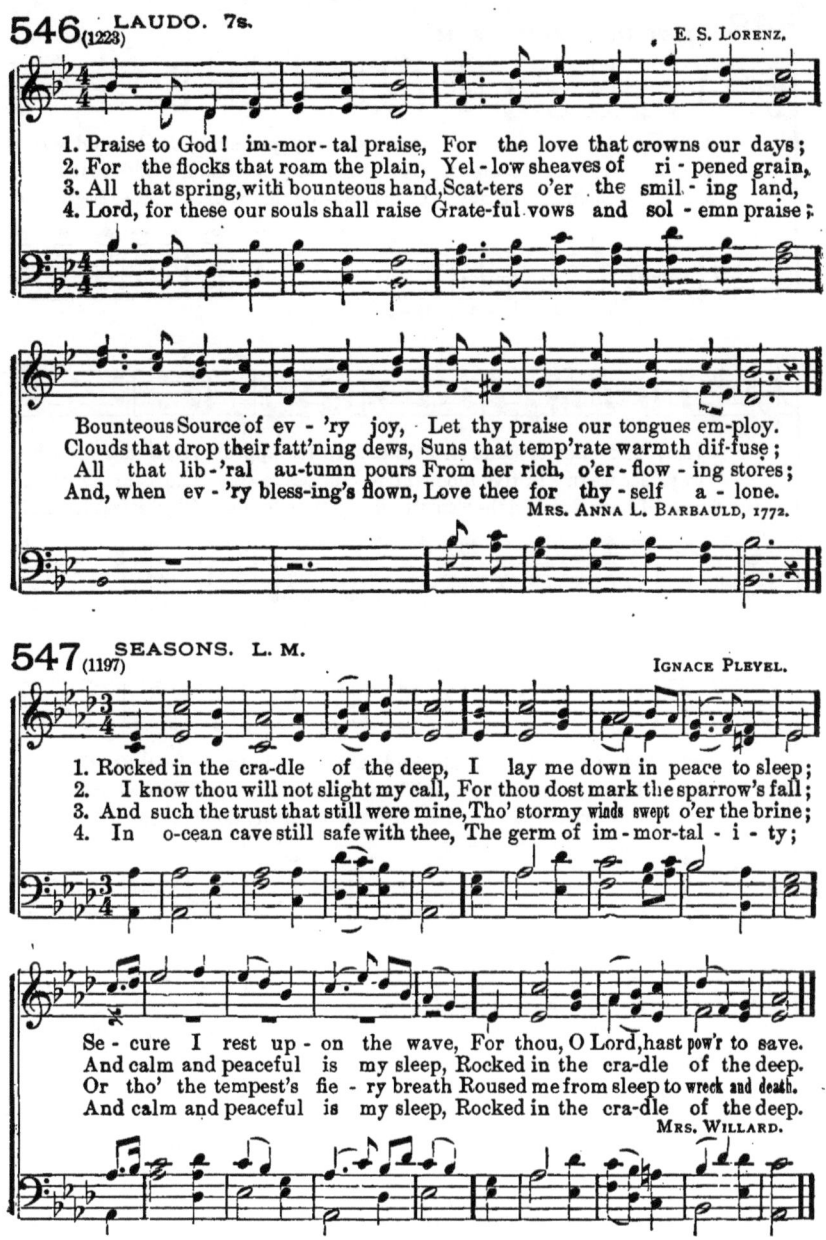

1. Praise to God! im-mor-tal praise, For the love that crowns our days;
2. For the flocks that roam the plain, Yel-low sheaves of ri-pened grain,
3. All that spring,with bounteous hand,Scat-ters o'er the smil-ing land,
4. Lord, for these our souls shall raise Grate-ful vows and sol-emn praise;

Bounteous Source of ev-'ry joy, Let thy praise our tongues em-ploy.
Clouds that drop their fatt'ning dews, Suns that temp'rate warmth dif-fuse;
All that lib-'ral au-tumn pours From her rich, o'er-flow-ing stores;
And, when ev-'ry bless-ing's flown, Love thee for thy-self a-lone.

MRS. ANNA L. BARBAULD, 1772.

547(1197) SEASONS. L. M.

IGNACE PLEYEL.

1. Rocked in the cra-dle of the deep, I lay me down in peace to sleep;
2. I know thou will not slight my call, For thou dost mark the sparrow's fall;
3. And such the trust that still were mine,Tho' stormy winds swept o'er the brine;
4. In o-cean cave still safe with thee, The germ of im-mor-tal-i-ty;

Se-cure I rest up-on the wave, For thou, O Lord,hast pow'r to save.
And calm and peaceful is my sleep, Rocked in the cra-dle of the deep.
Or tho' the tempest's fie-ry breath Roused me from sleep to wreck and death.
And calm and peaceful is my sleep, Rocked in the cra-dle of the deep.

MRS. WILLARD.

548　LET US ANEW. P. M.

UNKNOWN.

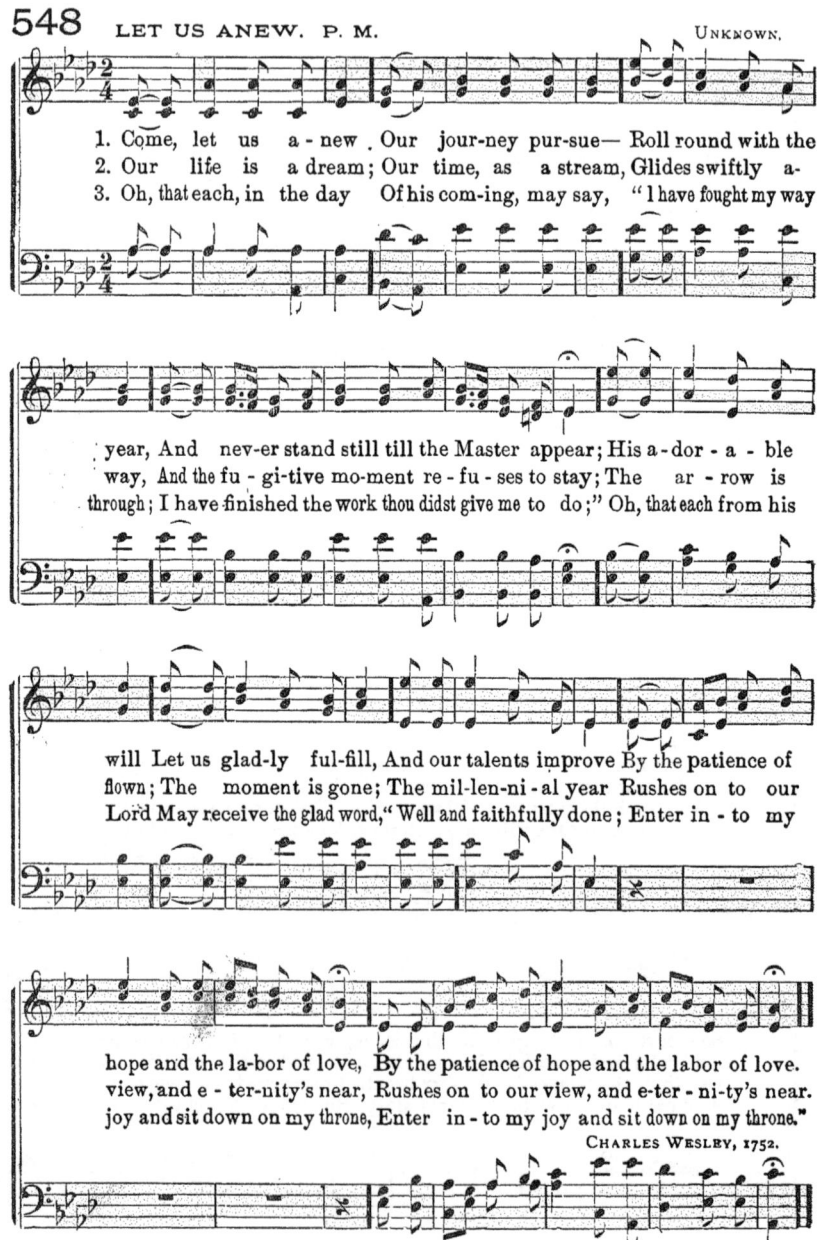

1. Come, let us a-new . Our jour-ney pur-sue— Roll round with the
2. Our life is a dream; Our time, as a stream, Glides swiftly a-
3. Oh, that each, in the day Of his com-ing, may say, "I have fought my way

year, And nev-er stand still till the Master appear; His a-dor-a-ble
way, And the fu-gi-tive mo-ment re-fu-ses to stay; The ar-row is
through; I have finished the work thou didst give me to do;" Oh, that each from his

will Let us glad-ly ful-fill, And our talents improve By the patience of
flown; The moment is gone; The mil-len-ni-al year Rushes on to our
Lord May receive the glad word, "Well and faithfully done; Enter in-to my

hope and the la-bor of love, By the patience of hope and the labor of love.
view, and e-ter-ni-ty's near, Rushes on to our view, and e-ter-ni-ty's near.
joy and sit down on my throne, Enter in-to my joy and sit down on my throne."

CHARLES WESLEY, 1752.

INDEX OF TUNES.

METRICAL INDEX.

INDEX OF SUBJECTS.

INDEX OF FIRST LINES.

1

CHANTS AND RESPONSIVE READINGS.

1   THE APOSTLES' CREED.

I BELIEVE in God the Father Almighty, maker of heaven and earth; and in Jesus Christ his only Son our Lord; who was conceived by the Holy Ghost, born of the Virgin Mary, suffered under Pontius Pilate; was crucified, dead, and buried; the third day he rose from the dead; he ascended into heaven, and sitteth on the right hand of God the Father Almighty; from thence he shall come to judge the quick and the dead.

I believe in the Holy Ghost; the Holy Catholic Church; the communion of saints, the forgiveness of sins; the resurrection of the body; and the life everlasting. *Amen.*

2   THE LORD'S PRAYER.

OUR Father who art in heaven, Hallowed be thy name. Thy kingdom come. Thy will be done in earth as it is in heaven. Give us this day our daily bread; and forgive us our trespasses, as we forgive them that trespass against us. And lead us not into temptation; but deliver us from evil; for thine is the kingdom, and the power, and the glory, forever. *Amen.*

3 THE TEN COMMANDMENTS.

I. Thou shalt have no other gods before me.
Response.

II. Thou shalt not make unto thee any graven image, or any likeness of any thing that is in heaven above, or that is in the earth beneath, or that is in the water under the earth: thou shalt not bow down thyself to them nor serve them; for I, the Lord, thy God, am a jealous God, visiting the iniquity of the fathers upon the children unto the third and fourth generation of them that hate me; and showing mercy unto thousands of them that love me and keep my commandments.
Response.

III. Thou shalt not take the name of the Lord, thy God, in vain; for the Lord will not hold him guiltless that taketh his name in vain.
Response.

IV. Remember the Sabbath day to keep it holy. Six days shalt thou labor and do all thy work: but the seventh day is the Sabbath of the Lord, thy God; in it thou shalt not do any work, thou, nor thy son, nor thy daughter, thy man-servant, nor thy maid-servant, nor thy cattle, nor thy stranger that is within thy gates. For in six days the Lord made heaven and earth, the sea, and all that in them is, and rested on the seventh day; wherefore the Lord blessed the seventh day, and hallowed it.
Response.

V. Honor thy father and thy mother: that thy days may be long upon the land which the Lord, thy God, giveth thee.
Response.

VI. Thou shalt not kill.
Response.

VII. Thou shalt not commit adultery.
Response.

VIII. Thou shalt not steal.
Response.

IX. Thou shalt not bear false witness against thy neighbor.
Response.

X. Thou shalt not covet thy neighbor's house, thou shalt not covet thy neighbor's wife, nor his man-servant, nor maid servant, nor his ox, nor his ass, nor any thing that is thy neighbor's.
Last Response.

RESPONSE.   TALLIS.

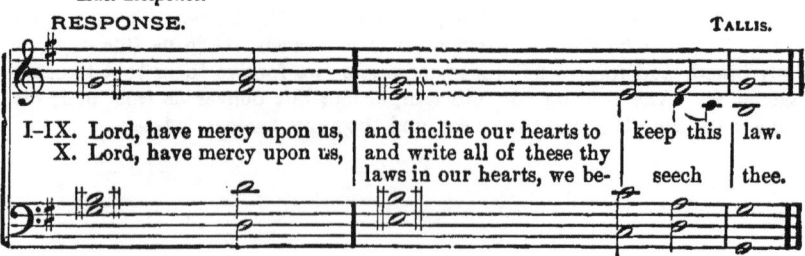

I-IX. Lord, have mercy upon us, | and incline our hearts to | keep this | law.
X. Lord, have mercy upon us, | and write all of these thy | |
| laws in our hearts, we be- | seech | thee.

CHANTS.

4 GLORIA IN EXCELSIS.

1. Glory be to | God on | high, ‖ and on earth | peace, good- | will toward | men.
2. We praise thee, we bless thee, we | worship | thee, ‖ we glorify thee, we give thanks to | thee for | thy great | glory.

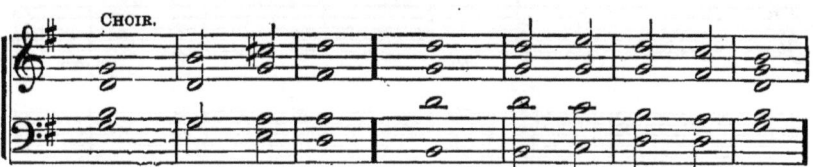

3. O Lord God, | heavenly | King, ‖ God the | Father | al- | mighty.
4. O Lord, the only begotten Son, | Jesus | Christ; ‖ O Lord God, Lamb of | God, Son | of the | Father.

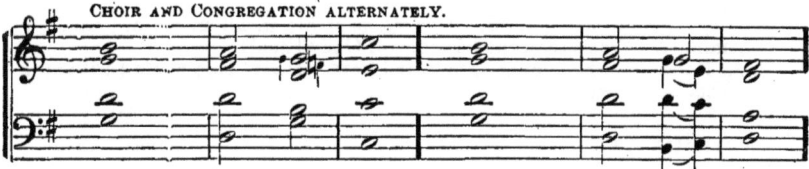

5. That takest away the | sins ·· of the | world, ‖ have mercy | upon | us.
6. Thou that takest away the | sins ·· of the | world, ‖ have mercy | upon | us.
7. Thou that takest away the | sins ·· of the | world, ‖ re- | ceive our | prayer.
8. Thou that sittest at the right hand of | God the | Father, ‖ have mercy | upon | us.

9. For thou | only ·· art | holy: ‖ thou | only | art the | Lord;
10. Thou only, O Christ! with the | Holy | Ghost, ‖ art most high in the | glory of | God the | Father. ‖ A- | men.

(3)

5   BENEDIC ANIMA MEA.

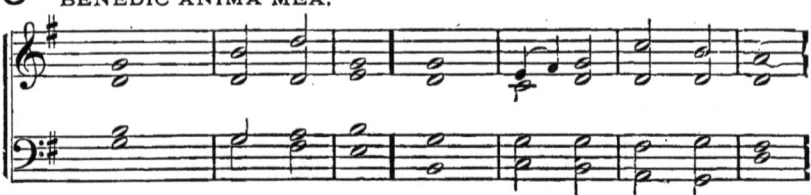

1. Praise the Lord, | O my | soul, ‖ and all that is within me | praise his | holy | name.
3. Who forgiveth | all thy | sin, ‖ and healeth | all " thine in- | firmi- | ties.
5. O praise the Lord, ye angels of his, ye that ex- | cel .in | strength, ‖ ye that fulfill his commandment and hearken un- | to the | voice " of his | word
8. Glory be to the Father, and | to the | Son, ‖ and | to the | Holy | Ghost;

2. Praise the Lord, | O my | soul, ‖ and forget not | all his | bene- | fits;
4. Who saveth thy life | from de- | struction, ‖ and crowneth thee with | mercy " and | loving- | kindness.
6. O praise the Lord, all | ye his | hosts, ‖ ye servants of | his that | do his | pleasure.
7. O speak good of the Lord, all ye works of his, in all places of | his do- | minion. ‖ Praise thou the | Lord, — | O my | soul!
9. As it was in the beginning, is now, and | ever " shall | be, ‖ world | without | end. A- | men.

6   DOMINUS REGIT ME.   LOWELL MASON.

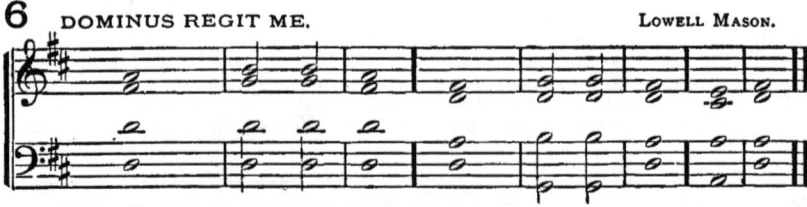

1. The Lord is my Shepherd: I | shall not | want;
2. He maketh me to lie down in green pastures; he leadeth me beside the still | wa- — | ters.
3. He restoreth my soul; he leadeth me in the paths of righteousness for his | names' — | sake;
4. Yea, though I walk through the valley of the shadow of death, I will fear no evil: for thou art with me; thy rod and thy staff they | comfort | me.
5. Thou preparest a table before me in the presence of mine enemies, thou anointest my head with oil ; my | cup " runneth | over.
6. Surely goodness and mercy shall follow me all the days of my life: and I will dwell in the house of the Lord for | ev- — | er. ‖ A- | men.

7 JUBILATE DEO.

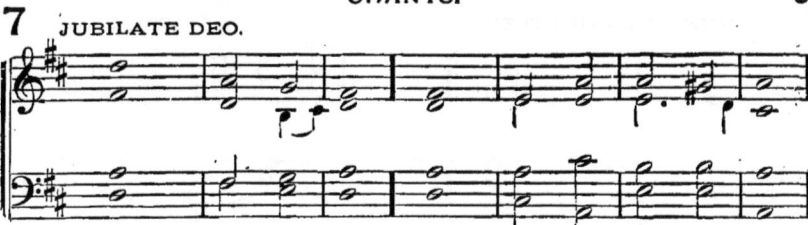

1. Make a joyful noise unto the Lord, | all ye | lands ; ‖ serve the Lord with glad-
   ness ; come before his | pres - ence | with — | singing.
3. Enter into his gates with thanksgiving, and into his | courts with | praise ; ‖
   be thankful unto him, | and — | bless his | name.
5. Glory be to the Father, and | to the | Son, ‖ and | to the | Ho - ly | Ghost;

2. Know ye that the Lord | he is | God ; ‖ it is he that hath made us, and not we
   ourselves ; we are his people, | and the | sheep " of his | pasture.
4. For the Lord is good ; his mercy is | ev - er- | lasting, ‖ and his truth endureth
   to | all — | gen - e - | rations.
6. As it was in the beginning, is now, and | ever " shall | be, ‖ world | without |
   end. A- | men.

8 VENITE AD ME.

1. Come unto me, all ye that labor and are | heav - y- | laden, ‖ and | I will |
   give you | rest.
2. Take my yoke upon you, and learn of me ; for I am meek and | lowly " in |
   heart, ‖ and ye shall find | rest— | unto " your | souls.
3. For my | yoke is | easy, ‖ and- | my— | burden " is | light.
4. Glory be to the Father, and | to the | Son, ‖ and | to the | Ho - ly | Ghost.
5. As it was in the beginning, is now, and | ever " shall | be, ‖ world | without
   end. A- | men.

9 BONUM EST CONFITERI.   T. S. DUPUIS.

1. It is a good thing to give thanks un- | to the | Lord; ‖ and to sing praises
   unto thy | name, — | O Most | High!
3. Upon an instrument of ten strings, and up- | on the | psaltery; ‖ upon the
   harp, | with a | solemn | sound.

2. To show forth thy loving-kindness | in the | morning, ‖ and thy | faithful-
   ness | every | night.
4. For thou, Lord, hast made me glad | through thy | work: ‖ I will triumph
   in the | works — | of thy | hands.

10 LEVAVI OCULOS.   HENRY ALDRICH.

1. I will lift up mine eyes | un-to the | hills, ‖ from whence | com-eth | my— |
   help.
2. My help cometh | from " the | Lord ‖ which | made — | heaven " and | earth.
3. He will not suffer thy | foot " to be | moved; ‖ he that | keepeth " thee | will"
   not | slumber.
4. Behold, he that | keepeth | Israel ‖ shall neither | slumber | nor — | sleep.
5. The Lord | is " thy | keeper; ‖ the Lord is thy shade up- | on " thy | right— |
   hand.
6. The sun shall not | smite thee " by | day, ‖ nor the | moon — | by — | night.
7. The Lord shall preserve thee from | all — | evil; ‖ he | shall " pre- | serve " thy |
   soul.
8. The Lord shall preserve thy going out and thy | coming | in ‖ from this time
   forth, and | even " for | ever- | more.

11 BAPTISMAL CHANT.

Before the Administration.

1. The mercy of the Lord is from everlasting to everlasting upon | them that | fear him, ‖ and his righteousness | unto | children's | children.

2. To such as keep his | cov - e- | nant; ‖ and to those that remember his com- | mandments ·· to | do — | them.

3. Suffer little children to come unto me, and for- | bid them | not: ‖ For of | such ·· is the | kingdom ·· of | heaven.

4. For the promise is unto you, and | to your | children; ‖ and to all that are afar off, even as many as the | Lord our | God shall | call.

BAPTISMAL CHANT.

After the Administration.

1. Then will I sprinkle clean | water ·· up- | on you, ‖ and | ye shall | be — | clean:

2. A new heart also | will I | give you, ‖ and a new spirit | will I | put with- | in you,

3. And I will take away the stony heart | out of ·· your | flesh, ‖ and I will | give ·· you a ! heart of | flesh.

4. I will pour my Spirit up- | on thy | seed, ‖ and my | blessing ·· up- | on thine | offspring:

5. And they shall spring up as a- | mong the | grass, ‖ As | willows ·· by the | water- | courses.

6. Glory be to the Father, and ! to the | Son, ‖ and | to the | Holy | Ghost;

7. As it was in the beginning, is now, and | ever ·· shall | be, ‖ world | without | end. A- | men.

PRAISE.

12   JOB XXXVI. 26-32; XXXVII. 21-24.

BEHOLD, God is great, and we know him not, neither can the number of his years be searched out.

For he maketh small the drops of water: they pour down rain according to the vapour thereof:

Which the clouds do drop and distil upon man abundantly.

Also can any understand the spreadings of the clouds, or the noise of his tabernacle?

Behold, he spreadeth his light upon it, and covereth the bottom of the sea.

For by them judgeth he the people; he giveth meat in abundance.

With clouds he covereth the light; and commanded it not to shine by the cloud that cometh betwixt.

And now men see not the bright light which is in the clouds: but the wind passeth, and cleanseth them.

Fair weather cometh out of the north: with God is terrible majesty.

Touching the Almighty, we cannot find him out:

He is excellent in power, and in judgment, and in plenty of justice: he will not afflict.

Men do therefore fear him: he respecteth not any that are wise of heart.

13   PSALM II.

WHY do the heathen rage, and the people imagine a vain thing?

The kings of the earth set themselves, and the rulers take counsel together, against the Lord, and against his Anointed, saying,

Let us break their bands asunder, and cast away their cords from us.

He that sitteth in the heavens shall laugh: the Lord shall have them in derision.

Then shall he speak unto them in his wrath, and vex them in his sore displeasure.

Yet have I set my King upon my holy hill of Zion.

I will declare the decree: the Lord hath said unto me, Thou art my Son; this day have I begotten thee.

Ask of me, and I shall give thee the heathen for thine inheritance, and the uttermost parts of the earth for thy possession.

Thou shalt break them with a rod of iron; thou shalt dash them in pieces like a potter's vessel.

Be wise now therefore, O ye kings: be instructed, ye judges of the earth.

Serve the Lord with fear, and rejoice with trembling.

Kiss the Son, lest he be angry, and ye perish from the way, when his wrath is kindled but a little. Blessed are all they that put their trust in him.

14   PSALM XVIII. 1-17; 30-35

I will love thee, O Lord, my strength.

The Lord is my rock, and my fortress, and my deliverer; my God, my strength, in whom I will trust; my buckler, and the horn of my salvation, and my high tower.

I will call upon the Lord, who is worthy to be praised: so shall I be saved from mine enemies.

The sorrows of death compassed me, and the floods of ungodly men made me afraid.

The sorrows of hell compassed me about: the snares of death prevented me.

In my distress I called upon the Lord, and cried unto my God: he heard my voice out of his temple, and my cry came before him, even into his ears.

Then the earth shook and trembled; the foundations also of the hills moved and were shaken, because he was wroth.

There went up a smoke out of his nostrils, and fire out of his mouth devoured: coals were kindled by it.

He bowed the heavens also, and came down: and darkness was under his feet.

And he rode upon a cherub, and did fly: yea, he did fly upon the wings of the wind.

He made darkness his secret place;

His pavilion round about him were dark waters and thick clouds of the skies.

At the brightness that was before him his thick clouds passed, hail stones and coals of fire.

The Lord also thundered in the heavens, and the Highest gave his voice; hail stones and coals of fire.

Yea, he sent out his arrows, and scattered them; and he shot out lightnings, and discomfited them.

Then the channels of waters were seen, and the foundations of the world were discovered at thy rebuke, O Lord, at the blast of the breath of thy nostrils.

He sent from above, he took me, he drew me out of many waters.

He delivered me from my strong enemy, and from them which hated me: for they were too strong for me. As for God, his way is perfect: the word of the Lord is tried:

He is a buckler to all those that trust in him.

For who is God save the Lord?

Or who is a rock save our God?

It is God that girdeth me with strength, and maketh my way perfect.

He maketh my feet like hinds' feet, and setteth me upon my high places.

He teacheth my hands to war, so that a bow of steel is broken by mine arms.

Thou hast also given me the shield of thy salvation:

And thy right hand hath holden me up, and thy gentleness hath made me great.

15   PSALM XIX

THE heavens aeclare the glory of God·
And the firmament sheweth his handywork.
Day unto day uttereth speech
And night unto night sheweth knowledge.
There is no speech nor language, where their voice is not heard
Their line is gone out through all the earth, and their words to the end of the world.
In them hath he set a tabernacle for the sun, which is as a bridegroom coming out of his chamber, and rejoiceth as a strong man to run a race
His going forth is from the end of the heaven, and his circuit unto the ends of it: and there is nothing hid from the heat thereof
The law of the Lord is perfect, converting the soul
The testimony of the Lord is sure, making wise the simple.
The statutes of the Lord are right, rejoicing the heart:
The commandment of the Lord is pure, enlightening the eyes.
The fear of the Lord is clean, enduring forever:
The judgments of the Lord are true and righteous altogether.
More to be desired are they than gold, yea, than much fine gold:
Sweeter also than honey and the honeycomb.
Moreover by them is thy servant warned: and in keeping of them there is great reward.
Who can understand his errors? cleanse thou me from secret faults.
Keep back thy servant also from presumptuous sins; let them not have dominion over me: then shall I be upright, and I shall be innocent from the great transgression.
Let the words of my mouth, and the meditation of my heart, be acceptable in thy sight, O Lord, my strength, and my redeemer.

16   PSALM XXIV.

THE earth is the Lord's, and the fulness thereof; the world, and they that dwell therein.
For he ha 'h founded it upon the seas, and established it upon the floods.
Who shall ascend into the hill the Lord? and who shall stand in his holy place?
He that hath clean hands, and a pure heart; who hath not lifted up his soul unio vanity, nor sworn deceitfully.
He shall receive the blessing from the Lord, and righteousness from the God of his salvation.
This is the generation of them that seek him, that seek thy face, O Jacob
Lift up your heads, O ye gates; and be ye lift up, ye everlasting doors;
And the King of glory shall come in.
Who is this King of glory?
The Lord, strong and mighty, the Lord mighty in battle.

Lift up your heads, O ye gates; even lift them up, ye everlasting doors,
And the King of glory shall come in.
Who is this King of glory?
The Lord of hosts, he is the King of glory.

17 PSALM XXIX.

GIVE unto the Lord, O ye mighty, give unto the Lord glory and strength.
Give unto the Lord the glory due unto his name; worship the Lord in the
beauty of holiness.
The voice of the Lord is upon the waters: the God of glory thundereth:
the Lord is upon many waters.
The voice of the Lord is powerful; the voice of the Lord is full of majesty.
The voice of the Lord breaketh the cedars;
Yea, the Lord breaketh the cedars of Lebanon.
The voice of the Lord divideth the flames of fire.
The voice of the Lord shaketh the wilderness; the Lord shaketh the wilder-
ness of Kadesh.
The voice of the Lord maketh the hinds to calve, and discovereth the
forests:
And in his temple doth every one speak of his glory.
The Lord sitteth upon the flood;
Yea, the Lord sitteth King for ever.
The Lord will give strength unto his people;
The Lord will bless his people with peace.

18 PSALM LXV.

PRAISE waiteth for thee, O God, in Zion: and unto thee shall the vow be
performed.
O thou that hearest prayer, unto thee shall all flesh come.
Iniquities prevail against me: as for our transgressions, thou shalt purge
them away.
Blessed is the man whom thou choosest, and causest to approach unto thee,
that he may dwell in thy courts: we shall be satisfied with the goodness of
thy house, even of thy holy temple.
By terrible things in righteousness wilt thou answer us, O God of our
salvation;
Who art the confidence of all the ends of the earth, and of them that are
afar off upon the sea:
Which by his strength setteth fast the mountains; being girded with
power:
Which stilleth the noise of the seas, the noise of their waves, and the
tumult of the people.
They also that dwell in the uttermost parts are afraid at thy tokens:
Thou makest the outgoings of the morning and evening to rejoice.

Thou visited the earth, and waterest it: thou greatly enrichest it with the river of God, which is full of water:

Thou preparest them corn, when thou hast so provided for it.

Thou waterest the ridges thereof abundantly: thou settlest the furrows thereof:

Thou makest it soft with showers: thou blessest the springing thereof.

Thou crownest the year with thy goodness; and thy paths drop fatness.

They drop upon the pastures of the wilderness: and the little hills rejoice on every side.

The pastures are clothed with flocks;

The valleys also are covered over with corn; they shout for joy, they also sing.

19   PSALM LXXII.

GIVE the king thy judgments, O God, and thy righteousness unto the king's son.

He shall judge thy people with righteousness, and thy poor with judgment.

The mountains shall bring peace to the people, and the little hills, by righteousness.

He shall judge the poor of the people, he shall save the children of the needy, and shall break in pieces the oppressor.

They shall fear thee as long as the sun and moon endure, throughout all generations.

He shall come down like rain upon the mown grass: as showers that water the earth.

In his days shall the righteous flourish; and abundance of peace so long as the moon endureth.

He shall have dominion also from sea to sea, and from the river unto the ends of the earth.

They that dwell in the wilderness shall bow before him;

And his enemies shall lick the dust.

The kings of Tarshish and of the isles shall bring presents:

The kings of Sheba and Seba shall offer gifts.

Yea, all kings shall fall down before him:

All nations shall serve him.

For he shall deliver the needy when he crieth; the poor also, and him that hath no helper.

He shall spare the poor and needy, and shall save the souls of the needy.

He shall redeem their soul from deceit and violence: and precious shall their blood be in his sight.

And he shall live, and to him shall be given of the gold of Sheba: prayer also shall be made for him continually; and daily shall he be praised.

There shall be a handful of corn in the earth upon the top of the mountains; the fruit thereof shall shake like Lebanon: and they of the city shall flourish like grass of the earth.

His name shall endure for ever: his name shall be continued as long as the sun: and men shall be blessed in him: all nations shall call him. blessed.

Blessed be the Lord God, the God of Israel, who only doeth wondrous things.

And blessed be his glorious name for ever: and let the whole earth be filled with his glory. Amen, and Amen.

20 PSALM LXXXIV.

How amiable are thy tabernacles, O Lord of hosts!

My soul longeth, yea, even fainteth for the courts of the Lord: my heart and my flesh crieth out for the living God.

Yea, the sparrow hath found a house, and the swallow a nest for herself, where she may lay her young, even thine altars, O Lord of hosts, my King, and my God.

Blessed are they that dwell in thy house: they will be still praising thee.

Blessed is the man whose strength is in thee; in whose heart are the ways of them.

Who passing through the valley of Baca make it a well; the rain also filleth the pools

They go from strength to strength, every one of them in Zion appeareth before God.

O Lord God of hosts, hear my prayer: give ear, O God of Jacob.

Behold, O God our shield, and look upon the face of thine anointed.

For a day in thy courts is better than a thousand. I had rather be a doorkeeper in the house of my God, than to dwell in the tents of wickedness.

For the Lord God is a sun and shield: the Lord will give grace and glory: no good thing will he withhold from them that walk uprightly.

O Lord of hosts, blessed is the man that trusteth in thee

21 PSALM XCV.

Oh, come, let us sing unto the Lord; let us make a joyful noise to the Rock of our salvation.

Let us come before his presence with thanksgiving, and make a joyful noise unto him with psalms.

For the Lord is a great God, and a great King above all gods.

In his hand are the deep places of the earth; the strength of the hills is his also.

The sea is his, and he made it: and his hands formed the dry land.

Oh, come let us worship and bow down: let us kneel before the Lord, our Maker.

For he is our God;

And we are the people of his pasture, and the sheep of his hand.

22   PSALM XCIX.

THE Lord reigneth; let the people tremble:
He sitteth between the cherubims; let the earth be moved.
The Lord is great in Zion; and he is high above all the people.
Let them praise thy great and terrible name; for it is holy.
The king's strength also loveth judgment; thou dost establish equity,
Thou executest judgment and righteousness in Jacob.
Exalt ye the Lord our God, and worship at his footstool; for he is holy.
*Moses and Aaron among his priests, and Samuel among them that call
upon his name;*
They called upon the Lord, and he answered them.
He spake unto them in the cloudy pillar:
They kept his testimonies, and the ordinance that he gave them.
Thou answeredst them, O Lord our God:
Thou wast a God that forgavest them, though thou tookest vengeance of
their inventions.
*Exalt the Lord our God, and worship at his holy hill; for the Lord our
God is holy.*

23   PSALM CXLVI.

PRAISE ye the Lord.
Praise the Lord, O my soul.
While I live will I praise the Lord:
I will sing praises unto my God while I have any being.
Put not your trust in princes, nor in the son of man, in whom there is no help.
*His breath goeth forth, he returneth to his earth; in that very day his
thoughts perish.*
Happy is he that hath the God of Jacob for his help, whose hope is in the
Lord his God:
*Which made heaven, and earth, the sea, and all that therein is: which
keepeth truth for ever:*
Which executeth judgment for the oppressed: which giveth food to the
hungry. The Lord looseth the prisoners:
*The Lord openeth the eyes of the blind: the Lord raiseth them that are
bowed down: the Lord loveth the righteous:*
The Lord preserveth the strangers; he relieveth the fatherless and widow:
but the way of the wicked he turneth upside down.
*The Lord shall reign for ever, even thy God, O Zion, unto all generations
Praise ye the Lord.*

24   PSALM CXLVII.

PRAISE ye the Lord:
*For it is good to sing praises unto our God; for it is pleasant; and
praise is comely.*

The Lord doth build up Jerusalem: he gathereth together the outcasts of Israel.

He healeth the broken in heart, and bindeth up their wounds.

He telleth the number of the stars; he calleth them all by their names.

Great is our Lord, and of great power: his understanding is infinite.

The Lord lifteth up the meek: he casteth the wicked down to the ground.

Sing unto the Lord with thanksgiving; sing praise upon the harp unto our God:

Who covereth the heaven with clouds, who prepareth rain for the earth, who maketh grass to grow upon the mountains.

He giveth to the beast his food, and to the young ravens which cry.

He delighteth not in the strength of the horse: he taketh not pleasure in the legs of a man.

The Lord taketh pleasure in them that fear him, in those that hope in his mercy.

Praise the Lord, O Jerusalem; praise thy God, O Zion.

For he hath strengthened the bars of thy gates;

He hath blessed thy children within thee.

He maketh peace in thy borders, and filleth thee with the finest of the wheat.

He sendeth forth his commandment upon earth: his word runneth very swiftly.

He giveth snow like wool: he scattereth the hoar frost like ashes.

He casteth forth his ice like morsels: who can stand before his cold?

He sendeth out his word, and melteth them: he causeth his wind to blow, and the waters flow.

He sheweth his word unto Jacob, his statutes and his judgments unto Israel.

He hath not dealt so with any nation; and as for his judgments, they have not known them. Praise ye the Lord.

25 PSALM CXLVIII.

PRAISE ye the Lord. Praise ye the Lord from the heavens: praise him in the heights.

Praise ye him, all his angels: praise ye him, all his hosts.

Praise ye him, sun and moon: praise him, all ye stars of light.

Praise him, ye heavens of heavens, and ye waters that be above the heavens.

Let them praise the name of the Lord: for he commanded, and they were created.

He hath also stablished them for ever and ever: he hath made a decree which shall not pass.

Praise the Lord from the earth, ye dragons, and all deeps:

Fire, and hail; snow, and vapour; stormy wind fulfilling his word:

Mountains, and all hills; fruitful trees, and all cedars:

Beasts, and all cattle; creeping things, and flying fowl

Kings of the earth, and all people; princes, and all judges of the earth:

Both young men, and maidens; old men, and children:

Let them praise the name of the Lord: for his name alone is excellent; his glory is above the earth and heaven.

He also exalteth the horn of his people, the praise of all his saints; even of the children of Israel, a people near unto him. Praise ye the Lord.

26   PSALM CXLIX.

PRAISE ye the Lord. Sing unto the Lord a new song, and his praise in the congregation of saints.

Let Israel rejoice in him that made him: let the children of Zion be joyful in their King.

Let them praise his name in the dance: let them sing praises unto him with the timbrel and harp.

For the Lord taketh pleasure in his people: he will beautify the meek with salvation.

Let the saints be joyful in glory: let them sing aloud upon their beds.

Let the high praises of God be in their mouth, and a twoedged sword in their hand;

To execute vengeance upon the heathen, and punishments upon the people;

To bind their kings with chains, and their nobles with fetters of iron;

To execute upon them the judgment written: this honour have all his saints

Praise ye the Lord.

27   PSALM CL.

PRAISE ye the Lord. Praise God in his sanctuary

Praise him in the firmament of his power.

Praise him for his mighty acts:

Praise him according to his excellent greatness.

Praise him with the sound of the trumpet:

Praise him with the psaltery and harp.

Praise him with the timbrel and dance:

Praise him with stringed instruments and organs.

Praise him upon the loud cymbals:

Praise him upon the high sounding cymbals.

Let every thing that hath breath praise the Lord.

Praise ye the Lord.

28   ISAIAH XII.

AND in that day thou shalt say, O Lord, I will praise thee: though thou wast angry with me, thine anger is turned away, and thou comfortedst me.

Behold, God is my salvation; I will trust, and not be afraid: for the Lord Jehovah is my strength and my song; he also is become my salvation

Thererore with joy shall ye draw water out of the wells of salvation.

And in that day shall ye say, Praise the Lord, call upon his name, declare
his doings among the people, make mention that his name is exalted.

Sing unto the Lord; for he hath done excellent things:

This is known in all the earth.

Cry out and shout, thou inhabitant of Zion:

For great is the Holy One of Israel in the midst of thee.

29   REVELATION VII: 9–12; V: 9–14.

AFTER this I beheld, and, lo, a great multitude, which no man could
number, of all nations, and kindreds, and people, and tongues. stood before
the throne, and before the Lamb, clothed with white robes, and palms in
their hands;

And cried with a loud voice, saying, Salvation to our God which sitteth
upon the throne, and unto the Lamb.

And all the angels stood round about the throne, and about the elders and
the four beasts, and fell before the throne on their faces, and worshipped God,
saying,

Amen: Blessing, and glory, and wisdom, and thanksgiving, and honour,
and power, and might, be unto our God for ever and ever. Amen.

And they sung a new song, saying, Thou art worthy to take the book, and
to open the seals thereof: for thou wast slain, and hast redeemed us to God by
thy blood out of every kindred, and tongue, and people, and nation;

And hast made us unto our God kings and priests: and we shall reign on
the earth.

And I beheld, and I heard the voice of many angels round about the
throne, and the beasts, and the elders: and the number of them was ten thousand times ten thousand, and thousands of thousands;

Saying with a loud voice, Worthy is the Lamb that was slain to receive
power, and riches, and wisdom, and strength, and honour, and glory, and
blessing.

And every creature which is in heaven, and on the earth, and under the
earth, and such as are in the sea, and all that are in them, heard I saying,
Blessing, and honour, and glory, and power, be unto him that sitteth upon the
throne, and unto the Lamb for ever and ever.

And the four beasts said, Amen. And the four and twenty elders fell
down and worshipped him that liveth for ever and ever.

2

THANKSGIVING.

---

30   PSALM VIII

O LORD our Lord, how excellent is thy name in all the earth! who hast set thy glory above the heavens.

Out of the mouth of babes and sucklings hast thou ordained strength because of thine enemies, that thou mightest still the enemy and the avenger.

When I consider thy heavens, the work of thy fingers, the moon and the stars, which thou hast ordained;

What is man, that thou art mindful of him? and the son of man, that thou visitest him?

For thou hast made him a little lower than the angels, and hast crowned him with glory and honour.

Thou madest him to have dominion over the works of thy hands;
Thou hast put all things under his feet:

All sheep and oxen, yea, and the beasts of the field;

The fowl of the air, and the fish of the sea, and whatsoever passeth through the paths of the seas.

O Lord our Lord, how excellent is thy name in all the earth!

31   PSALM IX.

I WILL praise thee, O Lord, with my whole heart; I will shew forth all thy marvellous works.

I will be glad and rejoice in thee: I will sing praise to thy name, O thou Most High.

When mine enemies are turned back, they shall fall and perish at thy presence.

For thou hast maintained my right and my cause; thou satest in the throne judging right.

Thou hast rebuked the heathen, thou hast destroyed the wicked, thou hast put out their name for ever and ever.

O thou enemy, destructions are come to a perpetual end: and thou hast destroyed cities; their memorial is perished with them.

But the Lord shall endure for ever: he hath prepared his throne for judgment.

And he shall judge the world in righteousness, he shall minister judgment to the people in uprightness.

The Lord also will be a refuge for the oppressed, a refuge in times of trouble.

And they that know thy name will put their trust in thee: for thou, Lord, hast not forsaken them that seek thee.

Sing praises to the Lord, which dwelleth in Zion: declare among the people his doings.

When he maketh inquisition for blood, he remembereth them: he forgetteth not the cry of the humble.

Have mercy upon me, O Lord; consider my trouble which I suffer of them that hate me, thou that liftest me up from the gates of death:

That I may shew forth all thy praise in the gates of the daughter of Zion: I will rejoice in thy salvation.

The heathen are sunk down in the pit that they made: in the net which they hid is their own foot taken.

The Lord is known by the judgment which he executeth: the wicked is snared in the work of his own hands.

The wicked shall be turned into hell, and all the nations that forget God.

For the needy shall not always be forgotten: the expectation of the poor shall not perish forever.

Arise, O Lord; let not man prevail: let the heathen be judged in thy sight.

Put them in fear, O Lord: that the nations may know themselves to be but men.

32 PSALM XXXIV.

I WILL bless the Lord at all times: his praise shall continually be in my mouth.

My soul shall make her boast in the Lord: the humble shall hear thereof, and be glad.

O magnify the Lord with me, and let us exalt his name together.

I sought the Lord, and he heard me, and delivered me from all my fears.

They looked unto him, and were lightened: and their faces were not ashamed.

This poor man cried, and the Lord heard him, and saved him out of all his troubles.

The angel of the Lord encampeth round about them that fear him, and delivereth them.

O taste and see that the Lord is good: blessed is the man that trusteth in him.

O fear the Lord, ye his saints: for there is no want to them that fear him.

The young lions do lack, and suffer hunger: but they that seek the Lord shall not want any good thing.

Come, ye children, hearken unto me: I will teach you the fear of the Lord.

What man is he that desireth life, and loveth many days, that he may see good?

Keep thy tongue from evil, and thy lips from speaking guile.

Depart from evil, and do good; seek peace, and pursue it.

The eyes of the Lord are upon the righteous, and his ears are open unt their cry.

The face of the Lord is against them that do evil, to cut off the remem-brance of them from the earth.

The righteous cry, and the Lord heareth, and delivereth them out of all their troubles.

The Lord is nigh unto them that are of a broken heart; and saveth such as be of a contrite spirit.

Many are the afflictions of the righteous: but the Lord delivereth him out of them all.

He keepeth all his bones: not one of them is broken.

Evil shall slay the wicked: and they that hate the righteous shall be desolate.

The Lord redeemeth the soul of his servants: and none of them that trust in him shall be desolate.

33   PSALM XLVIII.

GREAT is the Lord, and greatly to be praised in the city of our God, in the mountain of his holiness.

Beautiful for situation, the joy of the whole earth, is mount Zion, on the sides of the north, the city of the great King.

God is known in her palaces for a refuge.

For, lo, the kings were assembled, they passed by together.

They saw it, and so they marvelled; they were troubled, and hasted away.

Fear took hold upon them there, and pain, as of a woman in travail.

Thou breakest the ships of Tarshish with an east wind.

As we have heard, so have we seen in the city of the Lord of hosts, in the city of our God: God will establish it for ever.

We have thought of thy lovingkindness, O God, in the midst of thy temple.

According to thy name, O God, so is thy praise unto the ends of the earth: thy right hand is full of righteousness.

Let mount Zion rejoice, let the daughters of Judah be glad, because of thy judgments.

Walk about Zion, and go round about her: tell the towers thereof.

Mark ye well her bulwarks, consider her palaces; that ye may tell it to the generation following.

For this God is our God for ever and ever: he will be our guide even unto death.

34   PSALM LXXVII.

I CRIED unto God with my voice, even unto God with my voice; and he gave ear unto me.

In the day of my trouble I sought the Lord: my sore ran in the night, and ceased not: my soul refused to be comforted.

I have considered the days of old, the years of ancient times.

I call to remembrance my song in the night: I commune with mine own heart: and my spirit made diligent search.

Will the Lord cast off for ever? and will he be favourable no more?

Is his mercy clean gone for ever? doth his promise fail for evermore?

Hath God forgotten to be gracious? hath he in anger shut up his tender mercies?

And I said, This is my infirmity: but I will remember the years of the right hand of the Most High.

I will remember the works of the Lord: surely I will remember thy wonders of old.

I will meditate also of all thy work, and talk of thy doings.

Thy way, O God, is in the sanctuary: who is so great a God as our God?

Thou art the God that doest wonders: thou hast declared thy strength among the people.

Thou hast with thine arm redeemed thy people, the sons of Jacob and Joseph.

The waters saw thee, O God, the waters saw thee; they were afraid: the depths also were troubled.

The clouds poured out water: the skies sent out a sound: thine arrows also went abroad.

The voice of thy thunder was in the heaven: the lightnings lightened the world: the earth trembled and shook.

Thy way is in the sea, and thy path in the great waters, and thy footsteps are not known.

Thou leddest thy people like a flock by the hand of Moses and Aaron.

35 PSALM LXXXVI.

Bow down thine ear, O Lord, hear me: for I am poor and needy.

Preserve my soul; for I am holy: O thou my God, save thy servant that trusteth in thee.

Be merciful unto me, O Lord: for I cry unto thee daily.

Rejoice the soul of thy servant: for unto thee, O Lord, do I lift up my soul.

For thou, Lord, art good, and ready to forgive; and plenteous in mercy unto all them that call upon thee.

Give ear, O Lord, unto my prayer; and attend to the voice of my supplications.

In the day of my trouble I will call upon thee: for thou wilt answer me.

Among the gods there is none like unto thee, O Lord; neither are there any works like unto thy works.

All nations whom thou hast made shall come and worship before thee, O Lord; and shall glorify thy name.

For thou art great, and doest wondrous things: thou art God alone.

Teach me thy way, O Lord; I will walk in thy truth: unite my heart to fear thy name.

I will praise thee, O Lord my God, with all my heart: and I will glorify thy name for evermore.

For great is thy mercy toward me: and thou hast delivered my soul from the lowest hell

O God, the proud are risen against me, and the assemblies of violent men have sought after my soul; and have not set thee before them.

But thou, O Lord, art a God full of compassion, and gracious, longsuffering, and plenteous in mercy and truth.

O turn unto me, and have mercy upon me;

Give thy strength unto thy servant, and save the son of thine handmaid.

Shew me a token for good; that they which hate me may see it, and be ashamed: because thou, Lord, hast holpen me, and comforted me.

36 PSALM C.

Make a joyful noise unto the Lord, all ye lands.

Serve the Lord with gladness: come before his presence with singing.

Know ye that the Lord he is God: it is he that hath made us, and not we ourselves;

We are his people, and the sheep of his pasture.

Enter into his gates with thanksgiving, and into his courts with praise;

Be thankful unto him, and bless his name.

For the Lord is good; his mercy is everlasting,

And his truth endureth to all generations.

37 PSALM CIII.

Bless the Lord, O my soul: and all that is within me, bless his holy name

Bless the Lord, O my soul, and forget not all his benefits

Who forgiveth all thine iniquities; who healeth all thy diseases;

Who redeemeth thy life from destruction; who crowneth thee with lovingkindness and tender mercies;

Who satisfieth thy mouth with good things; so that thy youth is renewed like the eagle's.

The Lord executeth righteousness and judgment for all that are oppressed

He made known his ways unto Moses, his acts unto the children of Israel

The Lord is merciful and gracious, slow to anger, and plenteous in mercy.

He will not always chide: neither will he keep his anger for ever.

He hath not dealt with us after our sins; nor rewarded us according to our iniquities.

For as the heaven is high above the earth, so great is his mercy toward them that fear him.

As far as the east is from the west, so far hath he removed our transgressions from us.

Like as a father pitieth his children, so the Lord pitieth them that fear him.

For he knoweth our frame; he remembereth that we are dust.

As for man, his days are as grass: as a flower of the field, so he flourisheth.

For the wind passeth over it, and it is gone; and the place thereof shall know it no more.

But the mercy of the Lord is from everlasting to everlasting upon them that fear him, and his righteousness unto children's children;

To such as keep his covenant, and to those that remember his commandments to do them.

The Lord hath prepared his throne in the heavens; and his kingdom ruleth over all.

Bless the Lord, ye his angels, that excel in strength, that do his commandments, hearkening unto the voice of his word.

Bless ye the Lord, all ye his hosts; ye ministers of his, that do his pleasure.

Bless the Lord, all his works in all places of his dominion: bless the Lord, O my soul.

38   PSALM CVII: 1-31.

O GIVE thanks unto the Lord, for he is good: for his mercy endureth for ever.

Let the redeemed of the Lord say so, whom he hath redeemed from the hand of the enemy;

And gathered them out of the lands, from the east, and from the west, from the north, and from the south.

They wandered in the wilderness in a solitary way; they found no city to dwell in.

Hungry and thirsty, their soul fainted in them.

Then they cried unto the Lord in their trouble, and he delivered them out of their distresses.

And he led them forth by the right way, that they might go to a city of

Then they cried unto the Lord in their trouble, and he saved them out of their distresses.

He brought them out of darkness and the shadow of. death, and brake their bands in sunder.

Oh, that men would praise the Lord for his goodness, and for his wonderful works to the children of men!

For he hath broken the gates of brass, and cut the bars of iron in sunder.

Fools, because of their transgression, and because of their iniquities, are afflicted.

Their soul abhorreth all manner of meat; and they draw near unto the gates of death.

Then they cry unto the Lord in their trouble, and he saveth them out of their distresses.

He sent his word, and healed them, and delivered them from their destruction.

Oh, that men would praise the Lord for his goodness, and for his wonderful works to the children of men!

And let them sacrifice the sacrifices of thanksgiving, and declare his works with rejoicing.

They that go down to the sea in ships, that do business in great waters;

These see the works of the Lord, and his wonders in the deep.

For he commandeth, and raiseth the stormy wind, which lifteth up the waves thereof.

They mount up to the heaven, they go down again to the depths: their soul is melted because of trouble.

They reel to and fro, and stagger like a drunken man, and are at their wit's end.

Then they cry unto the Lord in their trouble, and he bringeth them out of their distresses.

He maketh the storm a calm, so that the waves thereof are still.

Then are they glad because they be quiet; so he bringeth them unto their desired haven.

Oh, that men would praise the Lord for his goodness, and for his wonderful works to the children of men!

PENITENCE AND PRAYER.

***

39   PSALM VI.

O LORD, rebuke me not in thine anger, neither chasten me in thy hot displeasure.

Have mercy upon me, O Lord; for I am weak: O Lord, heal me; for my bones are vexed.

My soul is also sore vexed: but thou, O Lord, how long?

Return, O Lord, deliver my soul: oh save me for thy mercies' sake.

For in death there is no remembrance of thee: in the grave who shall give thee thanks?

I am weary with my groaning: all the night make I my bed to swim; I water my couch with my tears.

Mine eye is consumed because of grief; it waxeth old because of all mine enemies.

Depart from me, all ye workers of iniquity; for the Lord hath heard the voice of my weeping.

The Lord hath heard my supplication; the Lord will receive my prayer.

Let all mine enemies be ashamed and sore vexed: let them return and be ashamed suddenly.

40   PSALM XXII: 1–8; 15–19; 22–31.

MY God, my God, why hast thou forsaken me? why art thou so far from helping me, and from the words of my roaring?

O my God, I cry in the daytime, but thou hearest not; and in the night season, and am not silen

But thou art holy, O thou that inhabitest the praises of Israel.

Our fathers trusted in thee: they trusted, and thou didst deliver them.

They cried unto thee, and were delivered: they trusted in thee, and were not confounded.

But I am a worm, and no man; a reproach of men, and despised of the people.

All they that see me laugh me to scorn: they shoot out the lip, they shake the head, saying,

He trusted on the Lord that he would deliver him: let him deliver him, seeing he delighted in him.

My strength is dried up like a potsherd; and my tongue cleaveth to my jaws; and thou hast brought me into the dust of death.

For dogs have compassed me: the assembly of the wicked have enclosed me: they pierced my hands and my feet.

I may tell all my bones: they look and stare upon me.

They part my garments among them, and cast lots upon my vesture.

But be not thou far from me, O Lord: O my strength, haste thee to help me.

I will declare thy name unto my brethren: in the midst of the congregation will I praise thee.

Ye that fear the Lord, praise him; all ye the seed of Jacob, glorify him, and fear him, all ye the seed of Israel.

For he hath not despised nor abhorred the affliction of the afflicted, neither hath he hid his face from him; but when he cried unto him, he heard.

My praise shall be of thee in the great congregation: I will pay my vows before them that fear him.

The meek shall eat and be satisfied: they shall praise the Lord that seek him: your heart shall live for ever.

All the ends of the world shall remember and turn unto the Lord: and all the kindreds of the nations shall worship before thee.

For the kingdom is the Lord's: and he is the governor among the nations.

All they that be fat upon earth shall eat and worship: all they that go down to the dust shall bow before him:

And none can keep alive his own soul.

A seed shall serve him; it shall be accounted to the Lord for a generation.

They shall come, and shall declare his righteousness unto a people that shall be born, that he hath done this.

41   PSALM XXV.

UNTO thee, O Lord, do I lift up my soul.

O my God, I trust in thee: let me not be ashamed, let not mine enemies triumph over me.

Yea, let none that wait on thee be ashamed: let them be ashamed which transgress without cause.

Shew me thy ways, O Lord; teach me thy paths.

Lead me in thy truth, and teach me: for thou art the God of my salvation; on thee do I wait all the day.

Remember, O Lord, thy tender mercies and thy lovingkindnesses; for they have been ever of old.

Remember not the sins of my youth, nor my transgressions: according to thy mercy remember thou me for thy goodness' sake, O Lord.

Good and upright is the Lord: therefore will he teach sinners in the way.

The meek will he guide in judgment: and the meek will he teach his way.

All the paths of the Lord are mercy and truth unto such as keep his covenant and his testimonies.

For thy name's sake, O Lord, pardon mine iniquity; for it is great.

What man is he that feareth the Lord? him shall he teach in the way that he shall choose.

His soul shall dwell at ease; and his seed shall inherit the earth.

The secret of the Lord is with them that fear him; and he will shew them his covenant.

Mine eyes are ever toward the Lord; for he shall pluck my feet out of the net.

Turn thee unto me, and have mercy upon me; for I am desolate and afflicted.

The troubles of my heart are enlarged: O bring thou me out of my distresses.

Look upon mine affliction and my pain; and forgive all my sins.

Consider mine enemies; for they are many; and they hate me with cruel hatred.

O keep my soul, and deliver me: let me not be ashamed; for I put my trust in thee.

Let integrity and uprightness preserve me; for I wait on thee.

Redeem Israel, O God, out of all his troubles.

42   PSALM XXXIX.

I SAID, I will take heed to my ways, that I sin not with my tongue: I will keep my mouth with a bridle, while the wicked is before me.

I was dumb with silence, I held my peace, even from good; and my sorrow was stirred.

My heart was hot within me; while I was musing the fire burned: then spake I with my tongue,

Lord, make me to know mine end, and the measure of my days, what it is; that I may know how frail I am.

Behold, thou hast made my days as a handbreadth; and mine age is as nothing before thee:

Verily every man at his best state is altogether vanity

Surely every man walketh in a vain shew: surely they are disquieted in vain: *He heapeth up riches, and knoweth not who shall gather them.*

And now, Lord, what wait I for? my hope is in thee.

Deliver me from all my transgressions: make me not the reproach of the foolish.

I was dumb, I opened not my mouth; because thou didst it.

Remove thy stroke away from me: I am consumed by the blow of thine hand.

When thou with rebukes dost correct man for iniquity, thou makest his beauty to consume away like a moth: surely every man is vanity

Hear my prayer, O Lord, and give ear unto my cry; hold not thy peace at my tears:

For I am a stranger with thee, and a sojourner, as all my fathers were.

O spare me, that I may recover strength, before I go hence, and be no more.

43   PSALM XL.

I WAITED patiently for the Lord; and he inclined unto me, and heard my cry.
He brought me up also out of an horrible pit, out of the miry clay,
And set my feet upon a rock, and established my goings.
And he hath put a new song in my mouth, even praise unto our God:
Many shall see it, and fear, and shall trust in the Lord.
Blessed is that man that maketh the Lord his trust, and respecteth not the
proud, nor such as turn aside to lies.
Many, O Lord my God, are thy wonderful works which thou hast done, and
thy thoughts which are to usward:
They cannot be reckoned up in order unto thee:
If I would declare and speak of them, they are more than can be numbered.
Sacrifice and offering thou didst not desire; mine ears hast thou opened:
Burnt-offering and sin-offering hast thou not required.
Then said I, Lo, I come: in the volume of the book it is written of me,
I delight to do thy will, O my God: yea, thy law is within my heart.
I have preached righteousness in the great congregation:
Lo, I have not refrained my lips, O Lord, thou knowest.
I have not hid thy righteousness within my heart; I have declared thy
faithfulness and thy salvation:
I have not concealed thy lovingkindness and thy truth from the great
congregation.
Withhold not thou thy tender mercies from me, O Lord: let thy loving-
kindness and thy truth continually preserve me.
For innumerable evils have compassed me about: mine iniquities have
taken hold upon me, so that I am not able to look up;
They are more than the hairs of mine head: therefore my heart faileth me.
Be pleased, O Lord, to deliver me: O Lord, make haste to help me.
Let them be ashamed and confounded together that seek after my soul to
destroy it;
Let them be driven backward and put to shame that wish me evil.
Let them be desolate for a reward of their shame that say unto me,
Aha, aha.
Let all those that seek thee rejoice and be glad in thee: let such as love
thy salvation say continually, The Lord be magnified.
But I am poor and needy: yet the Lord thinketh upon me: thou art my
help and my deliverer; make no tarrying, O my God.

44   PSALM XLII.

As the hart panteth after the water brooks, so panteth my soul after thee,
O God.
My soul thirsteth for God, for the living God: when shall I come and
appear before God?

My tears have been my meat day and night, while they continually say unto me, Where is thy God?

When I remember these things, I pour out my soul in me: for I had gone with the multitude, I went with them to the house of God, with the voice of joy and praise, with a multitude that kept holy day.

Why art thou cast down, O my soul? and why art thou disquieted in me? hope thou in God: for I shall yet praise him for the help of his countenance.

O my God, my soul is cast down within me: therefore will I remember thee from the land of Jordan, and of the Hermonites, from the hill Mizar.

Deep calleth unto deep at the noise of thy waterspouts: all thy waves and thy billows are gone over me.

Yet the Lord will command his lovingkindness in the daytime, and in the night his song shall be with me, and my prayer unto the God of my life.

I will say unto God my rock, Why hast thou forgotten me? why go I mourning because of the oppression of the enemy?

As with a sword in my bones, mine enemies reproach me; while they say daily unto me, Where is thy God?

Why art thou cast down, O my soul? and why art thou disquieted within me? hope thou in God:

For I shall yet praise him, who is the health of my countenance, and my God.

45 PSALM LI.

HAVE mercy upon me, O God, according to thy lovingkindness: according unto the multitude of thy tender mercies blot out my transgressions.

Wash me thoroughly from mine iniquity, and cleanse me from my sin.

For I acknowledge my transgressions: and my sin is ever before me.

Against thee, thee only have I sinned, and done this evil in thy sight: that thou mightest be justified when thou speakest, and be clear when thou judgest.

Behold, I was shapen in iniquity; and in sin did my mother conceive me.

Behold, thou desirest truth in the inward parts: and in the hidden part thou shalt make me to know wisdom.

Purge me with hyssop, and I shall be clean. wash me, and I shall be whiter than snow.

Make me to hear joy and gladness; that the bones which thou hast broken may rejoice.

Hide thy face from my sins, and blot out all mine iniquities.

Create in me a clean heart, O God; and renew a right spirit within me.

Cast me not away from thy presence; and take not thy Holy Spirit from me.

Restore unto me the joy of thy salvation: and uphold me with thy free Spirit.

Then will I teach transgressors thy ways; and sinners shall be converted unto thee.

Deliver me from bloodguiltiness, O God, thou God of my salvation:
And my tongue shall sing aloud of thy righteousness.
O Lord, open thou my lips; and my mouth shall shew forth thy praise.
For thou desirest not sacrifice; else would I give it: thou delightest not in burnt offering.
The sacrifices of God are a broken spirit: a broken and a contrite heart, O God, thou wilt not despise.
Do good in thy good pleasure unto Zion: build thou the walls of Jerusalem.
Then shalt thou be pleased with the sacrifices of righteousness, with burnt offering and whole burnt offering: then shall they offer bullocks upon thine altar.

46 PSALM LVII.

Be merciful unto me, O God, be merciful unto me: for my soul trusteth in thee:
Yea, in the shadow of thy wings will I make my refuge, until these calamities be overpast.
I will cry unto God most high; unto God that performeth all things for me.
He shall send from heaven, and save me from the reproach of him that would swallow me up.
God shall send forth his mercy and his truth.
My soul is among lions: and I lie even among them that are set on fire, even the sons of men, whose teeth are spears and arrows, and their tongue a sharp sword.
Be thou exalted, O God, above the heavens; let thy glory be above all the earth.
They have prepared a net for my steps; my soul is bowed down: they have digged a pit before me, into the midst whereof they are fallen themselves.
My heart is fixed, O God, my heart is fixed: I will sing and give praise.
Awake up, my glory; awake, psaltery and harp: I myself will awake early
I will praise thee, O Lord, among the people:
I will sing unto thee among the nations.
For thy mercy is great unto the heavens, and thy truth unto the clouds.
Be thou exalted, O God, above the heavens: let thy glory be above all the earth.

47 PSALM XC.

Lord, thou hast been our dwelling place in all generations.
Before the mountains were brought forth, or ever thou hadst formed the earth and the world, even from everlasting to everlasting, thou art God.
Thou turnest man to destruction; and sayest, Return, ye children of men.
For a thousand years in thy sight are but as yesterday when it is past, and as a watch in the night.

ou carriest them away as with a flood; they are as a sleep: in the
ning they are like grass which groweth up.

*n the morning it flourisheth, and groweth up; in the evening it is cut
n, and withereth.*

or we are consumed by thine anger, and by thy wrath are we troubled.

*Thou hast set our iniquities before thee, our secret sins in the light of thy
tenance.*

or all our days are passed away in thy wrath : we spend our years as a
that is told.

*The days of our years are threescore years and ten; and if by reason of
ngth they be fourscore years, yet is there strength labour and sorrow; for
soon cut off, and we fly away.*

Who knoweth the power of thine anger? even according to thy fear, so
by wrath.

*So teach us to number our days, that we may apply our hearts unto
dom.*

Return, O Lord, how long? and let it repent thee concerning thy
vants.

*O satisfy us early with thy mercy; that we may rejoice and be glad all
r days.*

Make us glad according to the days wherein thou hast afflicted us, and
years wherein we have seen evil.

Let thy work appear unto thy servants, and thy glory unto their children.

And let the beauty of the Lord our God be upon us :

*And establish thou the work of our hands upon us; yea, the work of our
nds establish thou it.*

COMFORT.

---

48   PSALM XVI.

PRESERVE me, O God: for in thee do I put my trust.

O my soul, thou hast said unto the Lord, Thou art my Lord: my goodness extendeth not to thee;

But to the saints that are in the earth, and to the excellent, in whom is all my delight.

Their sorrows shall be multiplied that hasten after another god: their drink offerings of blood will I not offer, nor take up their names unto my lips.

The Lord is the portion of mine inheritance and of my cup: thou maintainest my lot.

The lines are fallen unto me in pleasant places; yea, I have a goodly heritage.

I will bless the Lord, who hath given me counsel: my reins also instruct me in the night seasons.

I have set the Lord always before me: because he is at my right hand, I shall not be moved.

Therefore my heart is glad, and my glory rejoiceth: my flesh also shall rest in hope.

For thou wilt not leave my soul in hell: neither wilt thou suffer thine Holy One to see corruption.

Thou wilt shew me the path of life: in thy presence is fulness of joy.

At thy right hand there are pleasures for evermore.

49   PSALM XX.

THE Lord hear thee in the day of trouble; the name of the God of Jacob defend thee.

Send thee help from the sanctuary, and strengthen thee out of Zion.

Remember all thy offerings, and accept thy burnt sacrifice.

Grant thee according to thine own heart, and fulfill all thy counsel.

We will rejoice in thy salvation, and in the name of our God we will set up our banners: the Lord fulfill all thy petitions.

Now know I that the Lord saveth his anointed;

He will hear from his holy heaven with the saving strength of his right hand.

Some trust in chariots, and some in horses: but we will remember the name of the Lord our God.

They are brought down and fallen; but we are risen, and stand upright.

Save, Lord: let the king hear us when we call.

50

PSALM XXIII.

The Lord is my shepherd; I shall not want.

He maketh me to lie down in green pastures: he leadeth me beside the still waters

He restoreth my soul: he leadeth me in the paths-of righteousness for his name's sake.

Yea, though I walk through the valley of the shadow of death, I will fear no evil: for thou art with me; thy rod and thy staff they comfort me.

Thou preparest a table before me in the presence of mine enemies: thou anointest my head with oil; my cup runneth over.

Surely goodness and mercy shall follow me all the days of my life: and I will dwell in the house of the Lord for ever.

51

PSALM XXVII.

The Lord is my light and my salvation; whom shall I fear? the Lord is the strength of my life; of whom shall I be afraid?

When the wicked, even mine enemies and my foes, came upon me to eat up my flesh, they stumbled and fell.

Though a host should encamp against me, my heart shall not fear: though war should rise against me, in this will I be confident.

One thing have I desired of the Lord, that will I seek after; that I may dwell in the house of the Lord all the days of my life, to behold the beauty of the Lord, and to inquire in his temple.

For in the time of trouble he shall hide me in his pavilion: in the secret of his tabernacle shall he hide me; he shall set me up upon a rock.

And now shall mine head be lifted up above mine enemies round about me: therefore will I offer in his tabernacle sacrifices of joy; I will sing, yea, I will sing praises unto the Lord.

Hear, O Lord, when I cry with my voice: have mercy also upon me, and answer me.

When thou saidst, Seek ye my face; my heart said unto thee, Thy face, Lord, will I seek.

Hide not thy face far from me; put not thy servant away in anger: thou hast been my help; leave me not, neither forsake me, O God of my salvation.

When my father and my mother forsake me, then the Lord will take me up.

Teach me thy way, O Lord, and lead me in a plain path, because of mine enemies.

Deliver me not over unto the will of mine enemies: for false witnesses are risen up against me, and such as breathe out cruelty.

I had fainted, unless I had believed to see the goodness of the Lord in the land of the living.

Wait on the Lord: be of good courage, and he shall strengthen thine heart: wait, I say, on the Lord.

3

52   PSALM XXXII.

BLESSED is he whose transgression is forgiven, whose sin is covered.

Blessed is the man unto whom the Lord imputeth not iniquity, and in whose spirit there is no guile.

When I kept silence, my bones waxed old through my roaring all the day long.

For day and night thy hand was heavy upon me: my moisture is turned into the drought of summer.

I acknowledged my sin unto thee, and mine iniquity have I not hid. I said, I will confess my transgressions unto the Lord; and thou forgavest the iniquity of my sin. Selah.

For this shall every one that is godly pray unto thee in a time when thou mayest be found: surely in the floods of great waters they shall not come nigh unto him.

Thou art my hiding place; thou shalt preserve me from trouble; thou shalt compass me about with songs of deliverance.

I will instruct thee and teach thee in the way which thou shalt go: I will guide thee with mine eye.

Be ye not as the horse, or as the mule, which have no understanding: whose mouth must be held in with bit and bridle, lest they come near unto thee.

Many sorrows shall be to the wicked: but he that trusteth in the Lord, mercy shall compass him about.

Be glad in the Lord, and rejoice, ye righteous:

And shout for joy, all ye that are upright in heart.

53   PSALM XXXIII.

REJOICE in the Lord, O ye righteous: for praise is comely for the upright.

Praise the Lord with harp: sing unto him with the psaltery, and an instrument of ten strings.

Sing unto him a new song; play skillfully with a loud noise.

For the word of the Lord is right; and all his works are done in truth.

He loveth righteousness and judgment: the earth is full of the goodness of the Lord.

By the word of the Lord were the heavens made;

And all the host of them by the breath of his mouth.

He gathereth the waters of the sea together as a heap:

He layeth up the depth in storehouses.

Let all the earth fear the Lord: let all the inhabitants of the world stand in awe of him.

For he spake, and it was done; he commanded, and it stood fast.

The Lord bringeth the counsel of the heathen to naught:

He maketh the devices of the people of none effect.

The counsel of the Lord standeth for ever, the thoughts of his heart to all generations.

Blessed is the nation whose God is the Lord;
And the people whom he hath chosen for his own inheritance.
The Lord looketh from heaven; he beholdeth all the sons of men.
From the place of his habitation he looketh upon all the inhabitants of th. earth.
He fashioneth their hearts alike; he considereth all their works.
There is no king saved by the multitude of an host:
A mighty man is not delivered by much strength.
An horse is a vain thing for safety: neither shall he deliver any by his great strength.
Behold, the eye of the Lord is upon them that fear him, upon them that hope in his mercy;
To deliver their soul from death, and to keep them alive in famine.
Our soul waiteth for the Lord: he is our help and our shield.
For our heart shall rejoice in him, because we have trusted in his holy name.
Let thy mercy, O Lord, be upon us, according as we hope in thee.

54   PSALM XXXVII.

FRET not thyself because of evil doers, neither be thou envious against the workers of iniquity.
For they shall soon be cut down like the grass, and wither as the green herb.
Trust in the Lord, and do good; so shalt thou dwell in the land, and verily thou shalt be fed.
Delight thyself also in the Lord; and he shall give thee the desires of thine heart.
Commit thy way unto the Lord; trust also in him; and he shall bring it to pass.
And he shall bring forth thy righteousness as the light, and thy judgment as the noonday.
Rest in the Lord, and wait patiently for him:
Fret not thyself because of him who prospereth in his way, because of the man who bringeth wicked devices to pass.
A little that a righteous man hath is better than the riches of many wicked.
For the arms of the wicked shall be broken: but the Lord upholdeth the righteous.
The Lord knoweth the days of the upright: and their inheritance shall be for ever.
They shall not be ashamed in the evil time: and in the days of famine they shall be satisfied.
But the wicked shall perish, and the enemies of the Lord shall be as the fat of lambs:

They shall consume; into smoke shall they consume away.

The wicked borroweth, and payeth not again: but the righteous sheweth mercy, and giveth.

For such as be blessed of him shall inherit the earth; and they that be cursed of him shall be cut off.

The steps of a good man are ordered by the Lord: and he delighteth in his way.

Though he fall, he shall not be utterly cast down: for the Lord upholdeth him with his hand.

I have been young, and now am old; yet have I not seen the righteous forsaken, nor his seed begging bread.

Wait on the Lord, and keep his way, and he shall exalt thee to inherit the land: when the wicked are cut off, thou shalt see it.

I have seen the wicked in great power, and spreading himself like a green bay tree.

Yet he passed away, and, lo, he was not: yea, I sought him, but he could not be found.

Mark the perfect man, and behold the upright: for the end of that man is peace.

But the transgressors shall be destroyed together: the end of the wicked shall be cut off.

But the salvation of the righteous is of the Lord: he is their strength in the time of trouble.

And the Lord shall help them, and deliver them: he shall deliver them from the wicked, and save them, because they trust in him.

55   PSALM XLVI.

God is our refuge and strength, a very present help in trouble.

Therefore will not we fear, though the earth be removed, and though the mountains be carried into the midst of the sea;

Though the waters thereof roar and be troubled, though the mountains shake with the swelling thereof.

There is a river, the streams whereof shall make glad the city of God, the holy place of the tabernacles of the Most High.

God is in the midst of her, she shall not be moved; God shall help her, and that right early.

The heathen raged, the kingdoms were moved: he uttered his voice- the earth melted.

The Lord of hosts is with us; the God of Jacob is our refuge.

Come, behold the works of the Lord, what desolations he hath made in the earth.

He maketh wars to cease unto the end of the earth;

He breaketh the bow, and cutteth the spear in sunder: he burneth the chariot in the fire.

Be still, and know that I am God: I will be exalted among the heathen, I will be exalted in the earth.

The Lord of hosts is with us; the God of Jacob is our refuge.

56   PSALM XCI.

HE that dwelleth in the secret place of the Most High shall abide under the shadow of the Almighty.

I will say of the Lord, He is my refuge and my fortress: my God; in him will I trust.

Surely he shall deliver thee from the snare of the fowler, and from the noisome pestilence.

He shall cover thee with his feathers, and under his wings shalt thou trust: his truth shall be thy shield and buckler.

Thou shalt not be afraid for the terror by night; nor for the arrow that flieth by day;

Nor for the pestilence that walketh in darkness; nor for the destruction that wasteth at noonday.

A thousand shall fall at thy side, and ten thousand at thy right hand; but it shall not come nigh thee.

Only with thine eyes shalt thou behold and see the reward of the wicked.

Because thou hast made the Lord, which is my refuge, even the Most High, thy habitation;

There shall no evil befall thee, neither shall any plague come nigh thy dwelling.

For he shall give his angels charge over thee, to keep thee in all thy ways.

They shall bear thee up in their hands, lest thou dash thy foot against a stone.

Thou shalt tread upon the lion and adder: the young lion and the dragon shalt thou trample under feet.

Because he hath set his love upon me, therefore will I deliver him: I will set him on high, because he hath known my name.

He shall call upon me, and I will answer him: I will be with him in trouble; I will deliver him, and honour him.

With long life will I satisfy him, and shew him my salvation.

57   ISAIAH XL. 1-17, 28-31.

COMFORT ye, comfort ye my people, saith your God.

Speak ye comfortably to Jerusalem, and cry unto her, that her warfare is accomplished, that her iniquity is pardoned: for she hath received of the Lord's hand double for all her sins

The voice of him that crieth in the wilderness, Prepare ye the way of the Lord, make straight in the desert a highway for our God.

Every valley shall be exalted, and every mountain and hill shall be made low: and the crooked shall be made straight, and the rough places plain.

And the glory of the Lord shall be revealed, and all flesh shall see it to. gether: for the mouth of the Lord hath spoken it.

The voice said, Cry. And he said, What shall I cry? All flesh is grass, and all the goodliness thereof is as the flower of the field:

The grass withereth, the flower fadeth; because the spirit of the Lord bloweth upon it: surely the people is grass.

The grass withereth, the flower fadeth: but the word of our God shall stand for ever.

O Zion, that bringest good tidings, get thee up into the high mountain; O Jerusalem, that bringest good tidings, lift up thy voice with strength;

Lift it up, be not afraid; say unto the cities of Judah, Behold your God!

Behold, the Lord God will come with strong hand, and his arm shall rule for him: behold, his reward is with him, and his work before him.

He shall feed his flock like a shepherd: he shall gather the lambs with his arm, and carry them in his bosom, and shall gently lead those that are with young.

Who hath measured the waters in the hollow of his hand, and meted out heaven with the span, and comprehended the dust of the earth in a measure, and weighed the mountains in scales, and the hills in a balance?

Who hath directed the Spirit of the Lord, or being his counsellor hath taught him?

With whom took he counsel, and who instructed him, and taught him in the path of judgment, and taught him knowledge, and shewed to him the way of understanding?

Behold, the nations are as a drop of a bucket, and are counted as the small dust of the balance: behold, he taketh up the isles as a very little thing.

And Lebanon is not sufficient to burn, nor the beasts thereof sufficient for a burnt offering.

All nations before him are as nothing; and they are counted to him less than nothing, and vanity.

Hast thou not known? hast thou not heard, that the everlasting God, the Lord, the Creator of the ends of the earth, fainteth not, neither is weary? there is no searching of his understanding.

He giveth power to the faint; and to them that have no might he in-creaseth strength.

Even the youths shall faint and be weary, and the young men shall utterly fall:

But they that wait upon the Lord shall renew their strength; they shall mount up with wings as eagles; they shall run, and not be weary; and they shall walk, and not faint.

58   ISAIAH LII: 1–10.

AWAKE, awake, put on thy strength, O Zion; put on thy beautiful garments, O Jerusalem, the holy city:

For henceforth there shall no more come into thee the uncircumcised and the unclean.

Shake thyself from the dust; arise, and sit down, O Jerusalem:
Loose thyself from the bands of thy neck, O captive daughter of Zion.
For thus saith the Lord, Ye have sold yourselves for nought; and ye shall be redeemed without money.

For thus saith the Lord God, My people went down aforetime into Egypt to sojourn there; and the Assyrian oppressed them without cause.

Now therefore, what have I here, saith the Lord, that my people is taken away for nought? they that rule over them make them to howl, saith the Lord; and my name continually every day is blasphemed.

Therefore my people shall know my name: therefore they shall know in that day that I am he that doth speak: behold, it is I.

How beautiful upon the mountains are the feet of him that bringeth good tidings, that publisheth peace;

That bringeth good tidings of good, that publisheth salvation; that saith unto Zion, Thy God reigneth!

Thy watchmen shall lift up the voice; with the voice together shall they sing:

For they shall see eye to eye, when the Lord shall bring again Zion.

Break forth into joy, sing together, ye waste places of Jerusalem:
For the Lord hath comforted his people, he hath redeemed Jerusalem.
The Lord hath made bare his holy arm in the eyes of all the nations;
And all the ends of the earth shall see the salvation of our God.

59   ISAIAH LV.

Ho, every one that thirsteth, come ye to the waters, and he that hath no money, come ye, buy, and eat; yea, come, buy wine and milk without money and without price.

Wherefore do ye spend money for that which is not bread? and your labour for that which satisfieth not? hearken diligently unto me, and eat ye that which is good, and let your soul delight itself in fatness.

Incline your ear, and come unto me: hear, and your soul shall live; and I will make an everlasting covenant with you, even the sure mercies of David.

Behold, I have given him for a witness to the people, a leader and commander to the people.

Behold, thou shalt call a nation that thou knowest not, and nations that knew not thee shall run unto thee, because of the Lord thy God, and for the Holy One of Israel; for he hath glorified thee.

Seek ye the Lord while he may be found, call ye upon him while he is near:

Let the wicked forsake his way, and the unrighteous man his thoughts:
And let him return unto the Lord, and he will have mercy upon him; and to our God, for he will abundantly pardon.

For my thoughts are not your thoughts, neither are your ways my ways, saith the Lord.

For as the heavens are higher than the earth, so are my ways higher than your ways, and my thoughts than your thoughts.

For as the rain cometh down, and the snow from heaven, and returneth not thither, but watereth the earth, and maketh it bring forth and bud, that it may give seed to the sower, and bread to the eater:

So shall my word be that goeth forth out of my mouth: it shall not return unto me void, but it shall accomplish that which I please, and it shall prosper in the thing whereto I sent it.

For ye shall go out with joy, and be led forth with peace:

The mountains and the hills shall break forth before you into singing, and all the trees of the field shall clap their hands.

Instead of the thorn shall come up the fir tree, and instead of the brier shall come up the myrtle tree:

And it shall be to the Lord for a name, for an everlasting sign that shall not be cut off.

60   MATTHEW V: 1-12.

AND seeing the multitudes, he went up into a mountain: and when he was set, his disciples came unto him:

And he opened his mouth, and taught them, saying,

Blessed are the poor in spirit: for theirs is the kingdom of heaven.

Blessed are they that mourn: for they shall be comforted.

Blessed are the meek: for they shall inherit the earth.

Blessed are they which do hunger and thirst after righteousness: for they shall be filled.

Blessed are the merciful: for they shall obtain mercy.

Blessed are the pure in heart: for they shall see God.

Blessed are the peacemakers: for they shall be called the children of God.

Blessed are they which are persecuted for righteousness' sake: for theirs is the kingdom of heaven.

Blessed are ye, when men shall revile you, and persecute you, and shall say all manner of evil against you falsely, for my sake.

Rejoice, and be exceeding glad: for great is your reward in heaven: for so persecuted they the prophets which were before you.

61   JOHN XIV: 1-20.

LET not your heart be troubled: ye believe in God, believe also in me.

In my Father's house are many mansions: if it were not so, I would have told you. I go to prepare a place for you.

And if I go and prepare a place for you, I will come again, and receive you unto myself; that where I am, there ye may be also.

And whither I go ye know, and the way ye know.

Thomas saith unto him, Lord, we know not whither thou goest; and how can we know the way?

Jesus saith unto him, I am the way, the truth, and the life: no man cometh unto the Father, but by me.

If ye had known me, ye should have known my Father also: and from henceforth ye know him, and have seen him.

Philip saith unto him, Lord, shew us the Father, and it sufficeth us.

Jesus saith unto him, Have I been so long time with you, and yet hast thou not known me, Philip? he that hath seen me hath seen the Father; and how sayest thou then, Shew us the Father?

Believest thou not that I am in the Father, and the Father in me? the words that I speak unto you I speak not of myself: but the Father that dwelleth in me, he doeth the works.

Believe me that I am in the Father, and the Father in me: or else believe me for the very works' sake.

Verily, verily, I say unto you, He that believeth on me, the works that I do shall he do also; and greater works than these shall he do; because I go unto my Father.

And whatsoever ye shall ask in my name, that will I do, that the Father may be glorified in the Son.

If ye shall ask any thing in my name, I will do it.

If ye love me, keep my commandments.

And I will pray the Father, and he shall give you another Comforter, that he may abide with you for ever

Even the Spirit of truth; whom the world cannot receive, because it seeth him not, neither knoweth him: but ye know him; for he dwelleth with you, and shall be in you

I will not leave you comfortless: I will come to you

Yet a little while, and the world seeth me no more; but ye see me: because I live, ye shall live also.

At that day ye shall know that I am in my Father, and ye in me, and I in you.

62   I. CORINTHIANS *XIII.*

THOUGH I speak with the tongues of men and of angels, and have not charity, I am become as sounding brass, or a tinkling cymbal.

And though I have the gift of prophecy, and understand all mysteries, and all knowledge; and though I have all faith, so that I could remove mountains, and have not charity, I am nothing.

And though I bestow all my goods to feed the poor, and though I give my body to be burned, and have not charity, it profiteth me nothing.

Charity suffereth long, and is kind; charity envieth not; charity vaunteth not itself, is not puffed up,

Doth not behave itself unseemly, seeketh not her own, is not easily provoked, thinketh no evil;

Rejoiceth not in iniquity, but rejoiceth in the truth:

Beareth all things, believeth all things, hopeth all things, endureth all things

Charity never faileth: but whether there be prophecies, they shall fail; whether there be tongues, they shall cease; whether there be knowledge, it shall vanish away.

For we know in part, and we prophesy in part.

But when that which is perfect is come, then that which is in part shall be done away.

When I was a child, I spake as a child, I understood as a child, I thought as a child:

But when I became a man, I put away childish things.

For now we see through a glass, darkly; but then face to face: now I know in part; but then shall I know even as also I am known.

And now abideth faith, hope, charity, these three; but the greatest of these is charity.

63 REVELATION XXI: 1–12; 22–27.

AND I saw a new heaven and a new earth: for the first heaven and the first earth were passed away; and there was no more sea.

And I John saw the holy city, new Jerusalem, coming down from God out of heaven, prepared as a bride adorned for her husband.

And I heard a great voice out of heaven saying, Behold, the tabernacle of God is with men, and he will dwell with them, and they shall be his people, and God himself shall be with them, and be their God.

And God shall wipe away all tears from their eyes; and there shall be no more death, neither sorrow, nor crying, neither shall there be any more pain for the former things are passed away.

And he that sat upon the throne said, Behold, I make all things new. And he said unto me, Write: for these words are true and faithful.

And he said unto me, It is done. I am Alpha and Omega, the beginning and the end. I will give unto him that is athirst of the fountain of the water of life freely.

He that overcometh shall inherit all things;

And I will be his God, and he shall be my son.

But the fearful, and unbelieving, and the abominable, and murderers, and whoremongers, and sorcerers, and idolaters, and all liars, shall have their part in the lake which burneth with fire and brimstone:

Which is the second death.

And there came unto me one of the seven angels which had the seven vials full of the seven last plagues, and talked with me, saying, Come hither, I will shew thee the bride, the Lamb's wife.

And he carried me away in the spirit to a great and high mountain, and shewed me that great city, the holy Jerusalem, descending out of heaven from God, having the glory of God:

are the temple of it.

And the city had no need of the sun, neither of the moon, to shine in it

For the glory of God did lighten it, and the Lamb is the light thereof.

And the nations of them which are saved shall walk in the light of it: and the kings of the earth do bring their glory and honour into it.

And the gates of it shall not be shut at all by day: for there shall be no night there.

And they shall bring the glory and honour of the nations into it.

And there shall in no wise enter into it any thing that defileth, neither whatsoever worketh abomination, or maketh a lie: but they which are written in the Lamb's book of life.

64   REVELATION XXII.

AND he shewed me a pure river of water of life, clear as crystal, proceeding out of the throne of God and of the Lamb.

In the midst of the street of it, and on either side of the river, was there the tree of life, which bare twelve manner of fruits, and yielded her fruit every month: and the leaves of the tree were for the healing of the nations.

And there shall be no more curse: but the throne of God and of the Lamb shall be in it; and his servants shall serve him:

And they shall see his face; and his name shall be in their foreheads.

And there shall be no night there; and they need no candle, neither light of the sun;

For the Lord God giveth them light: and they shall reign for ever and ever.

And he said unto me, These sayings are faithful and true: and the Lord God of the holy prophets sent his angel to shew unto his servants the things which must shortly be done.

Behold, I come quickly: blessed is he that keepeth the sayings of the prophecy of this book.

And I John saw these things, and heard them. And when I had heard and seen, I fell down to worship before the feet of the angel which shewed me these things.

Then saith he unto me, See thou do it not: for I am thy fellow servant, and of thy brethren the prophets, and of them which keep the sayings of this book: worship God.

And he saith unto me, Seal not the sayings of the prophecy of this book. for the time is at hand

He that is unjust, let him be unjust still: and he which is filthy, let him be filthy still: and he that is righteous, let him be righteous still: and he that is holy, let him be holy still.

And, behold, I come quickly; and my reward is with me, to give every man according as his work shall be.

I am Alpha and Omega, the beginning and the end, the first and the last.

Blessed are they that do his commandments, that they may have right to the tree of life, and may enter in through the gates into the city.

For without are dogs, and sorcerers, and whoremongers, and murderers, and idolaters, and whosoever loveth and maketh a lie.

I Jesus have sent mine angel to testify unto you these things in the churches. I am the root and the offspring of David, and the bright and morning star.

And the Spirit and the bride say, Come.

And let him that heareth say, Come. And let him that is athirst come.

And whosoever will, let him take the water of life freely.

For I testify unto every man that heareth the words of the prophecy of this book, If any man shall add unto these things, God shall add unto him the plagues that are written in this book:

And if any man shall take away from the words of the book of this prophecy, God shall take away his part out of the book of life, and out of the holy city, and from the things which are written in this book.

He which testifieth these things saith, Surely I come quickly: Amen.

SPECIAL OCCASIONS.

CHRISTMAS

65 ISAIAH IX: 2-7.

THE people that walked in darkness have seen a great light

They that dwell in the land of the shadow of death, upon them hath the light shined.

Thou hast multiplied the nation, and not increased the joy:

They joy before thee according to the joy in harvest, and as men rejoice when they divide the spoil.

For thou hast broken the yoke of his burden, and the staff of his shoulder, the rod of his oppressor, as in the day of Midian.

For every battle of the warrior is with confused noise, and garments rolled in blood; but this shall be with burning and fuel of fire.

For unto us a child is born, unto us a son is given: and the government shall be upon his shoulder:

And his name shall be called Wonderful, Counsellor, The mighty God, The everlasting Father, The Prince of Peace.

Of the increase of his government and peace there shall be no end, upon the throne of David, and upon his kingdom, to order it, and to establish it with judgment and with justice from henceforth even for ever.

The zeal of the Lord of hosts will perform this.

LUKE II: 8-20.

AND there were in the same country shepherds abiding in the field, keeping watch over their flock by night.

And, lo, the angel of the Lord came upon them, and the glory of the Lord shone round about them; and they were sore afraid.

And the angel said unto them, Fear not: for, behold, I bring you good tidings of great joy, which shall be to all people.

For unto you is born this day in the city of David a Saviour, which is Christ the Lord.

And this shall be a sign unto you; Ye shall find the babe wrapped in swaddling clothes, lying in a manger.

And suddenly there was with the angel a multitude of the heavenly host praising God, and saying, Glory to God in the highest, and on earth peace, good will toward men.

And it came to pass, as the angels were gone away from them into heaven, the shepherds said one to another, Let us now go even unto Bethlehem, and see this thing which is come to pass, which the Lord hath made known unto us.

And they came with haste, and found Mary and Joseph, and the babe lying in a manger.

And when they had seen it, they made known abroad the saying which was told them concerning this child.

And all they that heard it wondered at those things which were told them by the shepherds.

But Mary kept all these things, and pondered them in her heart.

And the shepherds returned, glorifying and praising God for all the things that they had heard and seen, as it was told unto them.

EASTER.

66   MATTHEW XXV*III*: 1–10.

In the end of the Sabbath, as it began to dawn toward the first day of the week, came Mary Magdalene and the other Mary to see the sepulchre.

And, behold, there was a great earthquake: for the angel of the Lord descended from heaven, and came and rolled back the stone from the door, and sat upon it.

His countenance was like lightning, and his raiment white as snow.

And for fear of him the keepers did shake, and became as dead men.

And the angel answered and said unto the women, Fear not ye: for I know that ye seek Jesus, which was crucified.

He is not here: for he is risen, as he said. Come, see the place where the Lord lay

And go quickly, and tell his disciples that he is risen from the dead; and, behold, he goeth before you into Galilee; there shall ye see him: lo, I have told you

And they departed quickly from the sepulchre with fear and great joy; and did run to bring his disciples word.

And as they went to tell his disciples, behold, Jesus met them, saying, All hail. And they came and held him by the feet, and worshipped him.

Then said Jesus unto them, Be not afraid: go tell my brethren that they go into Galilee, and there shall they see me

I. CORINTHIANS XV: 20–26, 51–58.

But now is Christ risen from the dead, and become the first fruits of them that slept.

For since by man came death, by man came also the resurrection of the dead.

For as in Adam all die, even so in Christ shall all be made alive.

But every man in his own order: Christ the first fruits; afterward they that are Christ's at his coming.

Then cometh the end, when he shall have delivered up the kingdom to God, even the Father; when he shall have put down all rule, and all authority and power.

For he must reign, till he hath put all enemies under his feet.

The last enemy that shall be destroyed is death.

Behold, I shew you a mystery; We shall not all sleep, but we shall all be changed,

In a moment, in the twinkling of an eye, at the last trump:

For the trumpet shall sound, and the dead shall be raised incorruptible, and we shall be changed.

For this corruptible must put on incorruption, and this mortal must put on immortality.

So when this corruptible shall have put on incorruption, and this mortal shall have put on immortality, then shall be brought to pass the saying that is written, Death is swallowed up in victory.

O death, where is thy sting?

O grave, where is thy victory?

The sting of death is sin; and the strength of sin is the law.

But thanks be to God, which giveth us the victory through our Lord Jesus Christ.

Therefore, my beloved brethren, be ye steadfast, unmoveable, always abounding in the work of the Lord, forasmuch as ye know that your labour is not in vain in the Lord.

MISSIONS.

67 ### SELECTIONS.

THE Lord looked down from heaven upon the children of men to see if there were any that did understand and seek God.

They are all gone aside, they are altogether become filthy: there is none that doeth good, no, not one.

The whole world lieth in wickedness; they are all under sin.

For all have sinned and come short of the glory of God.

The Son of man is come to seek and to save that which is lost.

For whosoever shall call upon the name of the Lord shall be saved.

How then shall they call on him in whom they have not believed? And how shall they believe in him of whom they have not heard?

And how shall they hear without a preacher? And how shall they preach. except they be sent? For it pleased God by the foolishness of preaching to save them that believe.

How beautiful are the feet of them that preach the gospel of peace and bring glad tidings of good things.

Go ye, therefore, and teach all nations, baptizing them in the name of the Father, and of the Son, and of the Holy Ghost, teaching them to observe all things whatsoever I have commanded you.

* * *

Now there were in the church that was at Antioch certain prophets and teachers.

As they ministered to the Lord, and fasted, the Holy Ghost said, Separate me Barnabas and Saul for the work whereunto I have called them.

And when they had fasted and prayed, and laid their hands on them, they sent them away.

So they, being sent forth by the Holy Ghost, departed unto Seleucia.

Now when they had gone throughout Phrygia and the region of Galatia, and were forbidden of the Holy Ghost to preach the word in Asia,

After they were come to Mysia, they assayed to go into Bithynia: but the Spirit suffered them not.

And a vision appeared to Paul in the night; there stood a man of Macedonia, and prayed him, saying, Come over into Macedonia, and help us.

And after he had seen the vision, immediately we endeavored to go into Macedonia, assuredly gathering that the Lord had called us for to preach the gospel unto them.

Therefore seeing we have this ministry, as we have received mercy we faint not;

But have renounced the hidden things of dishonesty, not walking in craftiness, nor handling the word of God deceitfully;

But by manifestation of the truth commending ourselves to every man's conscience in the sight of God.

But if our Gospel be hid, it is hid to them that are lost:

In whom the god of this world hath blinded the minds of them which believe not, lest the light of the glorious gospel of Christ, who is the image of God, should shine unto them.

For God, who commanded the light to shine out of darkness, hath shined in our hearts, to give the light of the knowledge of the glory of God in the face of Jesus Christ.

But we have this treasure in earthen vessels, that the excellency of the power may be of God, and not of us.

We having the same spirit of faith, according as it is written, I believed, and therefore have I spoken; we also believe, and therefore speak.

Knowing that he which raised up the Lord Jesus shall raise up us also by Jesus, and shall present us with you.

For which cause we faint not; but though our outward man perish, yet the inward man is renewed day by day.

For our light affliction, which is but for a moment, worketh for us a far more exceeding and eternal weight of glory.

While we look not at the things which are seen, but at the things which are not seen: for the things which are seen are temporal; but the things which are not seen are eternal.

* * *

ARISE, shine: for thy light is come, and the glory of the Lord is risen upon thee

The Gentiles shall come to thy light, and kings to the brightness of thy rising.

Lift up thine eyes round about, and see: all they gather themselves together, they come to thee; thy sons shall come from far, and thy daughters shall be nursed at thy side.

Awake, awake; put on thy strength, O Zion; put on thy beautiful garments, O Jerusalem, the holy city: for henceforth there shall no more come unto thee the uncircumcised and the unclea.

The Gentiles shall see thy righteousness, and all kings thy glory: and thou shalt be called by a new name, which the mouth of the Lord shall name.

I am sought of them that asked not for me; I am found of them that sought me not: I said, Behold me, behold me, unto a nation that was not called by my name.

The Gentiles shall come unto thee from the ends of the earth, and shall say, Surely our fathers have inherited lies, vanity, and things wherein there is no profit.

It shall come to pass, that from one new moon to another, shall all flesh come to worship before me, saith the Lord.

They shall teach no more every man his neighbor, and every man his brother, saying, Know the Lord: for they shall all know me, from the least of them unto the greatest of them, saith the Lord: for I will forgive their iniquity, and I will remember their sin no more.

In the days of these kings shall the God of heaven set up a kingdom, which shall never be destroyed: and the kingdom shall not be left to other people, but it shall break in pieces and shall consume all these kingdoms and it shall stand forever.

TEMPERANCE.

68

SELECTIONS.

WINE is a mocker, strong drink is raging: and whosoever is deceived thereby is not wise.

Be not among winebibbers: among riotous eaters of flesh:

For the drunkard and the glutton shall come to poverty:

4

And drowsiness shall clothe a man with rags.

Who hath woe? who hath sorrow? who hath contentions? who hath babbling? who hath wounds without cause? who hath redness of eyes?

They that tarry long at the wine; they that go to seek mixed wine.

Look not thou upon the wine when it is red, when it giveth his colour in the cup, when it moveth itself aright.

' *At the last it biteth like a serpent, and stingeth like an adder.*

Yea, thou shalt be as he that lieth down in the midst of the sea, or as he that lieth upon the top of a mast.

They have stricken me, shalt thou say, and I was not sick; they have beaten me, and I felt it not: when shall I awake? I will seek it yet again.

Woe to the crown of pride, to the drunkards of Ephraim, whose glorious beauty is a fading flower, which are on the head of the fat valleys of them that are overcome with wine!

Woe unto them that rise up early in the morning, that they may follow strong drink; that continue until night, till wine inflame them.

And the harp and the viol, the tabret and pipe, and wine, are in their feasts: but they regard not the work of the Lord, neither consider the operation of his hands.

Therefore my people are gone into captivity, because they have no knowledge: and their honourable men are famished, and their multitude dried up with thirst.

Therefore hell hath enlarged herself, and opened her mouth without measure: and their glory, and their multitude, and their pomp, and he that rejoiceth, shall descend into it.

Awake, ye drunkards, and weep; and howl, all ye drinkers of wine.

Woe unto him that giveth his neighbour drink, that puttest thy bottle to him, and makest him drunken also, that thou mayest look on their nakedness!

Woe unto them that call evil good, and good evil;

That put darkness for light, and light for darkness; that put bitter for sweet, and sweet for bitter!

Woe unto them that are wise in their own eyes, and prudent in their own sight!

Woe unto them that are mighty to drink wine, and men of strength to mingle strong drink.

Which justify the wicked for reward, and take away the righteousness of the righteous from him!

* * *

So then every one of us shall give account of himself to God.

Let us not therefore judge one another any more; but judge this rather that no man put a stumbling-block or an occasion to fall in his brother's way.

I know, and am persuaded by the Lord Jesus, that there is nothing unclean of itself:

But to him that esteemeth any thing to be unclean, to him it is unclean.

But if thy brother be grieved with thy meat, now walkest thou not charitably.

Destroy not him with thy meat for whom Christ died.

Let not then your good be evil spoken of: for the kingdom of God is not meat and drink;

But righteousness, and peace, and joy in the Holy Ghost.

Let us therefore follow after the things which make for peace, and things whereby one may edify another.

It is good neither to eat flesh, nor to drink wine, nor anything whereby thy brother stumbleth, or is offended, or is made weak.

We then that are strong ought to bear the infirmities of the weak, and not to please ourselves.

For none of us liveth to himself, and no man dieth to himself.

---

69   THE ANCIENT LITANY.

O God the Father of Heaven, have mercy upon us miserable sinners.

O God the Father of Heaven, have mercy upon us miserable sinners.

O God the Son, Redeemer of the world, have mercy upon us miserable sinners.

O God the Son, Redeemer of the world, have mercy upon us miserable sinners.

O God the Holy Ghost, proceeding from the Father and the Son, have mercy upon us miserable sinners

O God the Holy Ghost, proceeding from the Father and the Son, have mercy upon us miserable sinners.

O holy, blessed, and glorious Trinity, three Persons and one God, have mercy upon us miserable sinners.

O holy, blessed, and glorious Trinity, three Persons and one God, have mercy upon us miserable sinners.

Remember not, Lord, our offenses, nor the offenses of our forefathers; neither take thou vengeance of our sins; spare us, good Lord, spare thy people, whom thou hast redeemed with thy most precious blood, and be not angry with us for ever.

Spare us, good Lord.

From all evil and mischief; from sin; from the crafts and assaults of the devil; from thy wrath, and from everlasting damnation,

Good Lord, deliver us.

From all blindness of heart; from pride, vain-glory, and hypocrisy; from envy, hatred, and malice, and all uncharitableness

Good Lord, deliver us.

From all inordinate and sinful affections; and from all the deceits of the world, the flesh, and the devil,

Good Lord, deliver us.

From lightning and tempest; from plague, pestilence, and famine; from battle and murder, and from sudden death,

Good Lord, deliver us.

From all sedition, privy conspiracy, and rebellion; from all false doctrine, heresy, and schism; from hardness of heart, and contempt of thy Word and commandment,

Good Lord, deliver us.

By the mystery of thy holy incarnation, by thy holy nativity and circumcision; by thy baptism, fasting, and temptation,

Good Lord, deliver us.

By thine agony and bloody sweat; by thy cross and passion; by thy precious death and burial; by thy glorious resurrection and ascension; and by the coming of the Holy Ghost,

Good Lord, deliver us.

In all time of our tribulation; in all time of our prosperity; in the hour of death, and in the day of judgment,

Good Lord, deliver us.

We sinners do beseech thee to hear us, O Lord God; and that it may please thee to rule and govern thy holy Church universal in the right way;

We beseech thee to hear us, good Lord.

That it may please thee to bless and preserve all Christian rulers and magistrates, giving them grace to execute justice, and to maintain truth;

We beseech thee to hear us, good Lord.

That it may please thee to illuminate all pastors and ministers of the Church with true knowledge and understanding of thy Word; and that both by their preaching and living they may set it forth, and show it accordingly;

We beseech thee to hear us, good Lord.

That it may please thee to put an end to all sects and scandals, and to send forth faithful laborers into thy harvest;

We beseech thee to hear us, good Lord.

That it may please thee to bless and keep all thy people;

We beseech thee to hear us, good Lord.

That it may please thee to give to all nations unity, peace, and concord;

We beseech thee to hear us, good Lord.

That it may please thee to give us an heart to love and fear thee, and diligently to live after thy commandments;

We beseech thee to hear us, good Lord.

That it may please thee to give to all thy people increase of grace to hear meekly thy Word, and to receive it with pure affection, and to bring forth the fruits of the Spirit;

We beseech thee to hear us, good Lord.

That it may please thee to bring into the way of truth all such as have erred, and are deceived;

We beseech thee to hear us, good Lord.

That it may please thee to strengthen such as do stand; and to comfort and help the weak-hearted; and to raise up those who fall; and finally to beat down Satan under our feet;

We beseech thee to hear us, good Lord

That it may please thee to succor, help, and comfort all who are in danger, necessity, and tribulation;

We beseech thee to hear us, good Lord.

That it may please thee to preserve all who travel by land or by water, all women in the perils of child-birth, all sick persons, and young children; and to show thy pity upon all prisoners and captives;

We beseech thee to hear us, good Lord.

That it may please thee to defend, and provide for the fatherless children, and widows, and all who are desolate and oppressed;

We beseech thee to hear us, good Lord

That it may please thee to have mercy upon all men;

We beseech thee to hear us, good Lord.

That it may please thee to forgive our enemies, persecutors, and slanderers, and to turn their hearts;

We beseech thee to hear us, good Lord.

That it may please thee to give and preserve to our use the kindly fruits of the earth, so that in due time we may enjoy them;

We beseech thee to hear us, good Lord

That it may please thee to give us true repentance; to forgive us all our sins, negligences and ignorances; and to endue us with the grace of thy Holy Spirit to amend our lives according to thy holy Word:

We beseech thee to hear us, good Lord.

Son of God, we beseech thee to hear us.

Son of God, we beseech thee to hear us

O Lamb of God, who takest away the sins of the world; have mercy upon us.

O Lamb of God, who takest away the sins of the world; grant us thy peace.

INDEX.

Lightning Source UK Ltd.
Milton Keynes UK
UKHW020751211118
332720UK00012B/1063/P